THE HARVARD CLASSICS

The Five-Foot Shelf of Books

Mr. WILLIAM
SHAKESPEARES

COMEDIES,
HISTORIES, &
TRAGEDIES.

Published according to the True Originall Copies.

Martin Droeshout sculpsit London.

LONDON
Printed by Isaac Iaggard, and Ed. Blount. 1623.

THE HARVARD CLASSICS
EDITED BY CHARLES W. ELIOT, LL.D.

English Poetry

IN THREE VOLUMES
VOLUME I

From Chaucer *to* Gray

With Introductions and Notes
Volume 40

P. F. Collier & Son Corporation
NEW YORK

CONTENTS

CONTENTS

8 CONTENTS

CONTENTS

INTRODUCTORY NOTE

THE aim in these three volumes of English Poetry has been to give, as far as the limits of space allowed, a substantial representation of the most distinguished poets of England and America for the last five hundred years. Among previous anthologies an especially wide recognition has been given by the best judges to Francis Turner Palgrave's "Golden Treasury of the Best Songs and Lyrical Poems in the English Language," first published in 1861; and it has been thought best to make that collection the nucleus of the present one. All the poems originally selected by Mr. Palgrave have, accordingly, been retained, with the exception of those by Milton and Burns, which appear in the Harvard Classics in the complete editions of the poetical works of these two authors.

The larger scale of this collection has made it possible to ignore the limitation of most anthologies to lyrical poems, and to include a considerable number of long narrative and didactic poems. Thus we have been able to give the Prologue to Chaucer's "Canterbury Tales," the most vivid series of types of character to be found in any English poem; the "Nun's Priest's Tale," one of the finest specimens of the beast fable; a large group of traditional ballads, including the almost epic "Gest of Robin Hood"; Pope's "Essay on Man"; Byron's "Prisoner of Chillon"; Coleridge's "Ancient Mariner" and "Christabel"; Keats's "Eve of St. Agnes"; Shelley's "Adonais"; Tennyson's "Maud"; Longfellow's "Evangeline"; and many others rarely found in mixed collections. All these poems are given, in accordance with the general practise in this series, in their entirety.

In the case of Chaucer and other older authors, and of poems in the Scottish dialect, the meanings of obsolete and rare words have been given in the foot-notes. The poems of each author will be found together; and the general arrangement is chronological.

GEOFFREY CHAUCER
[*1340(?)–1400*]

I

THE PROLOGUE
TO THE CANTERBURY TALES

WHAN that Aprille with his shoures soote[1]
The droghte[2] of Marche hath perced to the roote,
And bathed every veyne in swich[3] licour,
Of which vertu engendred is the flour;
Whan Zephirus eek with his swete breeth
Inspired hath in every holt[4] and heeth
The tendre croppes,[5] and the yonge sonne
Hath in the Ram his halfe cours y-ronne,[6]
And smale fowles maken melodye,
That slepen al the night with open yë,
(So priketh hem nature in hir corages:[7]
Than longen folk to goon on pilgrimages,
And palmers for to seken straunge strondes,[8]
To ferne halwes,[9] couthe[10] in sondry londes;
And specially, from every shires ende
Of Engelond, to Caunterbury they wende,
The holy blisful martir for to seke,
That hem hath holpen, whan that they were seke.[11]

Bifel that, in that sesoun on a day,
In Southwerk at the Tabard as I lay[12]
Redy to wenden on my pilgrimage
To Caunterbury with ful devout corage,
At night was come in-to that hostelrye
Wel[13] nyne and twenty in a compaignye,
Of sondry folk, by aventure[14] y-falle[15]
In felawshipe, and pilgrims were they alle,

[1] Its sweet showers.   [2] Drought.   [3] Such.   [4] Wood.   [5] Young shoots.
[6] *The sun left the sign of the Ram about the middle of April.*
[7] Hearts.   [8] Foreign strands.   [9] Distant saints.   [10] Known.   [11] Sick.   [12] Lodged.
[13] Full.   [14] Chance.   [15] Fallen.

And carf[57] biforn his fader at the table.
    A YEMAN hadde he,[58] and servaunts namo[59]
At that tyme, for him liste[60] ryde so;
And he was clad in cote and hood of grene;
A sheef [61] of pecok arwes brighte and kene
Under his belt he bar ful thriftily,
(Wel coude he dresse his takel yemanly:
His arwes drouped noght with fetheres lowe),
And in his hand he bar a mighty bowe.
A not-heed[62] hadde he, with a broun visage.
Of wode-craft wel coude[63] he al the usage.
Upon his arm he bar a gay bracer,[64]
And by his syde a swerd and a bokeler,
And on that other syde a gay daggere,
Harneised[65] wel, and sharp as point of spere;
A Cristofre[66] on his brest of silver shene
An horn he bar, the bawdrik[67] was of grene;
A forster was he, soothly, as I gesse.

    Ther was also a Nonne, a PRIORESSE,
That of hir smyling was ful simple and coy;
Hir gretteste ooth was but by sëynt Loy;[68]
And she was cleped[69] madame Eglentyne.
Ful wel she song the service divyne,
Entuned in hir nose ful semely;
And Frensh she spak ful faire and fetisly,[70]
After the scole of Stratford atte Bowe,[71]
For Frensh of Paris was to hir unknowe.
At mete wel y-taught was she with-alle;
She leet no morsel from hir lippes falle,
Ne wette hir fingres in hir sauce depe.
Wel coude she carie a morsel, and wel kepe,
That no drope ne fille up-on hir brest.
In curteisye was set ful moche hir lest.[72]
Hir over lippe[73] wyped she so clene,
That in hir coppe was no ferthing[74] sene
Of grece, whan she dronken hadde hir draughte.

---

[57] Carved.   [58] *The knight.*   [59] No more.   [60] It pleased him.   [61] Twenty-four.
[62] Closely cut hair.   [63] Knew.   [64] Arm-guard of leather.   [65] Mounted.
[66] Image of St. Christopher, his patron saint.   [67] Cord or belt.
[68] *I. e., she did not swear at all, like St. Eligius.*   [69] Called.   [70] Skilfully.
[71] *A convent near London. She spoke Anglo-French.*   [72] Delight.
[73] Upper lip. *Guests drank out of a common cup.*   [74] Smallest particle.

Ful semely after hir mete she raughte,[75]
And sikerly[76] she was of greet disport,[77]
And ful plesaunt, and amiable of port,
And peyned hir to countrefete chere[78]
Of court, and been estatlich[79] of manere,
And to ben holden digne[80] of reverence.
But, for to speken of hir conscience,[81]
She was so charitable and so pitous,
She wolde wepe, if that she sawe a mous
Caught in a trappe, if it were deed or bledde.
Of smale houndes had she, that she fedde
With rosted flesh, or milk and wastel breed.[82]
But sore weep she if oon of hem were deed,
Or if men smoot it with a yerde[83] smerte:
And al was conscience[81] and tendre herte.
Ful semely[84] hir wimpel[85] pinched[86] was;
Hir nose tretys;[87] hir eyen greye as glas;
Hir mouth ful smal, and ther-to softe and reed;
But sikerly she hadde a fair forheed.
It was almost a spanne brood, I trowe;
For, hardily,[88] she was nat undergrowe.
Ful fetis[89] was hir cloke, as I was war.
Of smal coral aboute hir arm she bar
A peire[90] of bedes, gauded[91] al with grene;
And ther-on heng a broche of gold ful shene,
On which ther was first write a crowned A,
And after, *Amor vincit omnia.*[92]

    Another NONNE with hir hadde she,
That was hir chapeleyne, and PREESTES thre.

    A MONK ther was, a fair for the maistrye,[93]
An out-rydere,[94] that lovede venerye;[95]
A manly man, to been an abbot able.
Ful many a deyntee hors hadde he in stable:
And, whan he rood, men mighte his brydel here
Ginglen in a whistling wynd as clere,
And eek as loude as dooth the chapel-belle,

---

[75] Reached.   [76] Certainly.   [77] High spirits.   [78] Took pains to imitate courtly manners.
[79] Dignified.   [80] Worthy.   [81] Sensibility.   [82] Cake.   [83] Stick.   [84] Becomingly.
[85] Kerchief.   [86] Plaited.   [87] Well-formed.   [88] Certainly.   [89] Well-made.   [90] String.
     [91] Having every eleventh bead green.   [92] Love conquers all things.
       [93] In the highest degree.
    [94] *He had charge of the manors attached to his monastery.*   [95] Hunting.

Ther-as[96] this lord was keper of the celle.[97]
The reule of seint Maure or of seint Beneit,
By-cause that it was old and som-del streit,[98]
This ilke monk leet olde thinges pace,
And held after the newe world the space.
He yaf[99] nat of that text a pulled[100] hen,
That seith, that hunters been nat holy men;
Ne that a monk, whan he is cloisterlees[101]
Is likned til a fish that is waterlees;
This is to seyn, a monk out of his cloistre.
But thilke text held he nat worth an oistre.
And I seyde his opinioun was good.
What sholde he studie, and make him-selven wood,[102]
Upon a book in cloistre alwey to poure,
Or swinken[103] with his handes, and laboure,
As Austin bit?[104]   How shal the world be served?
Lat Austin have his swink to him reserved.
Therfor he was a pricasour[105] aright;
Grehoundes he hadde, as swifte as fowel in flight;
Of priking[106] and of hunting for the hare
Was al his lust, for no cost wolde he spare.
I seigh[107] his sleves purfiled[108] at the hond
With grys,[109] and that the fyneste of a lond;
And, for to festne his hood under his chin,
He hadde of gold y-wroght a curious pin:
A love-knot in the gretter ende ther was.
His heed was balled, that shoon as any glas,
And eek his face, as he hadde been anoint.
He was a lord ful fat and in good point;[110]
His eyen stepe,[111] and rollinge in his heed,
That stemed[112] as a forneys of a leed;[113]
His botes souple, his hors in greet estaat.
Now certeinly he was a fair prelat;
He was nat pale as a for-pyned[114] goost.
A fat swan loved he best of any roost.
His palfrey was as broun as is a berye.
    A FRERE ther was, a wantown and a merye,

---

[96] Where.   [97] Branch monastery.   [98] Somewhat strict.   [99] Gave.   [100] Plucked.
[101] Vagabond.   [102] Mad.   [103] Work.   [104] As St. Augustine bids.   [105] Hard rider.
[106] Riding, spurring.   [107] Saw.   [108] Trimmed.   [109] Gray fur.   [110] Plump.
[111] Prominent.   [112] Shone.   [113] Cauldron.   [114] Wasted by torment.

A limitour,[115] a ful solempne[116] man.
In alle the ordres foure[117] is noon that can[118]
So moche of daliaunce and fair langage.
He hadde maad ful many a mariage
Of yonge wommen, at his owne cost.
Un-to his ordre he was a noble post.
Ful wel biloved and famulier was he
With frankeleyns[119] over-al in his contree,
And eek with worthy wommen of the toun:
For he had power of confessioun,
As seyde him-self, more than a curat,
For of his ordre he was licentiat.
Ful swetely herde he confessioun,
And plesaunt was his absolucioun;
He was an esy man to yeve penaunce
Ther as he wiste to han a good pitaunce;[120]
For unto a povre ordre for to yive
Is signe that a man is wel y-shrive.[121]
For if he[122] yaf, he dorste make avaunt,
He wiste that a man was repentaunt.
For many a man so hard is of his herte,
He may nat wepe al-thogh him sore smerte.
Therfore, in stede of weping and preyeres,
Men moot[123] yeve silver to the povre freres.
His tipet was ay farsed[124] ful of knyves
And pinnes, for to yeven faire wyves.
And certeinly he hadde a mery note;
Wel coude he singe and pleyen on a rote.[125]
Of yeddinges[126] he bar utterly the prys.
His nekke whyt was as the flour-de-lys;
Ther-to he strong was as a champioun.
He knew the tavernes wel in every toun,
And everich hostiler and tappestere
Bet[127] than a lazar[128] or a beggestere;[129]
For un-to swich a worthy man as he
Acorded nat, as by his facultee,[130]

---

[115] Holding a license to beg within certain limits. [116] Impressive. [117] *I. e., of friars.*
[118] Knows. [119] Gentlemen farmers. [120] Where he knew he would get a handsome present. [121] Absolved. [122] The penitent. [123] Must. [124] Stuffed.
[125] Fiddle. [126] Proverbs.
[127] Better. [128] Beggar. [129] Female beggar. [130] It was not fitting in a man of his ability.

To have with seke lazars aqueyntaunce.
It is nat honest,[131] it may nat avaunce
For to delen with no swich poraille,[132]
But al with riche and sellers of vitaille.
And over-al,[133] ther-as profit sholde aryse,
Curteys he was, and lowly of servyse.
Ther nas no man nowher so vertuous.[134]
He was the beste beggere in his hous;
For thogh a widwe hadde noght a sho,
So plesaunt was his *"In principio"*,[135]
Yet wolde he have a ferthing, er he wente.
His purchas was wel bettre than his rente.[136]
And rage[137] he coude as it were right a whelpe.
In love-dayes[138] ther coude he mochel helpe.
For ther he was nat lyk a cloisterer,
With a thredbare cope, as is a povre scoler,
But he was lyk a maister or a pope.
Of double worsted was his semi-cope,[139]
That rounded as a belle out of the presse.
Somwhat he lipsed, for his wantownesse,[140]
To make his English swete up-on his tonge;
And in his harping, whan that he had songe,
His eyen twinkled in his heed aright,
As doon the sterres in the frosty night.
This worthy limitour was cleped[141] Huberd.

A MARCHANT was ther with a forked berd,
In mottelee,[142] and hye on horse he sat,
Up-on his heed a Flaundrish bever hat;
His botes clasped faire and fetisly.[143]
His resons[144] he spak ful solempnely,
Sowninge[145] alway thencrees of his winning.
He wolde the see were kept[146] for any thing[147]
Bitwixe Middleburgh and Orewelle.
Wel coude he in eschaunge sheeldes[148] selle.
This worthy man ful wel his wit bisette;[149]
Ther wiste no wight that he was in dette,

---

[131] Proper.   [132] Poor rabble.   [133] Everywhere.   [134] Capable.   [135] *John I, 1; was used as a greeting.*   [136] *This probably means that he made more out of his begging than he paid for the privilege.*
[137] Behave wantonly.   [138] Days for settling differences out of court.   [139] Short cape.
[140] In affectation.   [141] Called.   [142] Motley.   [143] Neatly.   [144] Opinions.   [145] Dealing with.
[146] Guarded.   [147] At any cost.   [148] French crowns.   [149] Used.

So estatly[150] was he of his governaunce,[151]
With his bargaynes, and with his chevisaunce.[152]
For sothe he was a worthy man with-alle,
But sooth to seyn, I noot how men him calle.

A CLERK[153] ther was of Oxenford also,
That un-to logik hadde longe y-go.[154]
As lene was his hors as is a rake,
And he nas nat right fat, I undertake;
But loked holwe, and ther-to soberly.
Ful thredbar was his overest courtepy;[155]
For he had geten him yet no benefice,
Ne was so worldly for to have office.
For him was levere[156] have at his beddes heed
Twenty bokes, clad in blak or reed
Of Aristotle and his philosophye,
Than robes riche, or fithele,[157] or gay sautrye.[158]
But al be that he was a philosophre,
Yet hadde he but litel gold in cofre;
But al that he mighte of his frendes hente,[159]
On bokes and on lerninge he it spente
And bisily gan for the soules preye
Of hem that yaf him wher-with to scoleye.[160]
Of studie took he most cure and most hede.
Noght o word spak he more than was nede,
And that was seyd in forme and reverence,
And short and quik, and ful of hy sentence.[161]
Sowninge in[162] moral vertu was his speche,
And gladly wolde he lerne, and gladly teche.

A SERGEANT OF THE LAWE, war[163] and wys,
That often hadde been at the parvys,[164]
Ther was also, ful riche of excellence.
Discreet he was, and of greet reverence:
He seemed swich, his wordes weren so wyse,
Iustice he was ful often in assyse,
By patente, and by pleyn[165] commissioun;
For his science, and for his heigh renoun
Of fees and robes hadde he many oon.

---

[150] Dignified. [151] Conduct. [152] Borrowings.
[153] Student. [154] Gone, devoted himself. [155] Outer short coat. [156] Rather.
[157] Fiddle. [158] Psaltery. [159] Get. [160] Go to school. [161] Meaning. [162] Tending to.
[163] Wary. [164] *The portico of St. Paul's, where lawyers met.* [165] Full.

So greet a purchasour[166] was nowher noon.
Al was fee simple to him in effect,[167]
His purchasing[168] mighte nat been infect.[169]
Nowher so bisy a man as he ther nas,
And yet he semed bisier than he was.
In termes hadde he caas and domes alle,[170]
That from the tyme of king William were falle.
Therto he oude endyte,[171] and make a thing,
Ther coude no wight pinche[172] at his wryting;
And every statut coude[173] he pleyn by rote.
He rood but hoomly in a medlee[174] cote
Girt with a ceint[175] of silk, with barres smale;
Of his array telle I no lenger tale.

A Frankeleyn was in his compaignye;
Whyt was his berd as is the dayesye.
Of his complexioun he was sangwyn.
Wel loved he by the morwe[176] a sop in wyn.
To liven in delyt was evere his wone,[177]
For he was Epicurus owne sone,
That heeld opinioun that pleyn delyt
Was verraily felicitee parfyt.
An householdere, and that a greet, was he;
Seynt Iulian[178] he was in his contree.
His breed, his ale, was alwey after oon;[179]
A bettre envyned[180] man was no-wher noon.
With-oute bake mete was nevere his hous,
Of fish and flesh, and that so plentevous,
It snewed[181] in his hous of mete and drinke,
Of alle deyntees that men coude thinke.
After the sondry sesons of the yeer,
So chaunged he his mete and his soper.
Ful many a fat partrich hadde he in mewe,[182]
And many a breem[183] and many a luce[183] in stewe.[184]
Wo was his cook, but-if[185] his sauce were
Poynaunt and sharp, and redy al his gere.

---

[166] Conveyancer.
[167] *All forms of land-holding were as easy for him to handle as fee-simple.*
[168] Conveyancing. [169] Invalid. [170] *He had definite knowledge of all cases and decisions.*
[171] Compose. [172] Find fault with. [173] Knew. [174] Motley. [175] Girdle.
[176] In the morning. [177] Custom. [178] *The patron saint of hospitality.*
[179] Of uniform quality. [180] Provided with wine. [181] Snowed.
[182] Coop. [183] A kind of fish. [184] Fish-pond. [185] Unless.

His table dormant[186] in his halle alway
Stood redy covered al the longe day.
At sessiouns ther was he lord and sire.
Ful ofte tyme he was knight of the shire.
An anlas[187] and a gipser[188] al of silk
Heng at his girdel, whyt as morne milk.
A shirreve hadde he been, and a countour;[189]
Was nowher such a worthy vavasour.[190]

    An Haberdassher and a Carpenter,
A Webbe,[191] a Dyere, and a Tapicer,[192]
Were with us eek, clothed in o liveree,[193]
Of a solempne and greet fraternitee.[194]
Ful fresh and newe hir gere apyked[195] was;
Hir knyves were y-chaped[196] noght with bras,
But al with silver, wroght ful clene and weel,
Hir girdles and hir pouches every-deel.
Wel semed ech of hem a fair burgeys,
To sitten in a yeldhalle[197] on a deys.[198]
Everich,[199] for the wisdom that he can,[200]
Was shaply[201] for to been an alderman.
For catel[202] hadde they ynogh and rente,
And eek hir wyves wolde it wel assente;
And elles certein were they to blame.
It is ful fair to been y-clept[203] *"ma dame,"*
And goon to vigilyës[204] al bifore,
And have a mantel roialliche[205] y-bore.[206]

    A Cook they hadde with hem for the nones,[207]
To boille chiknes with the mary-bones,
And poudre-marchant[208] tart, and galingale.[209]
Wel coude he knowe a draughte of London ale.
He coude roste, and sethe,[210] and broille, and frye,
Maken mortreux,[211] and wel bake a pye.
But greet harm was it, as it thoughte me,
That on his shine a mormal[212] hadde he;
For blankmanger,[213] that made he with the beste.

---

[186] Fixed. [187] Knife. [188] Pouch. [189] Treasurer. [190] Squire. [191] Weaver.
[192] Upholsterer. [193] Livery.
[194] Trade guild. [195] Trimmed. [196] Mounted. [197] Guild hall. [198] Dais. [199] Each one.
[200] Knows. [201] Fit. [202] Property. [203] Called. [204] Festival evens. [205] Royally.
[206] Carried before them. [207] For the occasion. [208] A flavoring powder.
[209] Root of sweet cyperus. [210] Boil.
[211] A kind of soup. [212] Gangrene. [213] A delicacy made of minced capon, etc.

A SHIPMAN was ther, woning[214] fer by weste:
For aught I woot, he was of Dertemouthe.
He rood up-on a rouncy,[215] as he couthe,[216]
In a gowne of falding[217] to the knee.
A daggere hanging on a laas hadde he
Aboute his nekke under his arm adoun.
The hote somer had maad his hewe al broun;
And, certeinly, he was a good felawe.
Ful many a draughte of wyn had he y-drawe[218]
From Burdeux-ward, whyl that the chapman[219] sleep.
Of nyce[220] conscience took he no keep.[221]
If that he faught, and hadde the hyer hond,
By water he sente hem hoom[222] to every lond.
But of his craft to rekene wel his tydes,
His stremes[223] and his daungers him bisydes,
His herberwe[224] and his mone, his lodemenage,[225]
Ther nas noon swich from Hulle to Cartage.
Hardy he was, and wys to undertake;[226]
With many a tempest hadde his berd been shake.
He knew wel alle the havenes, as they were,
From Gootlond to the cape of Finistere,
And every cryke in Britayne and in Spayne;
His barge y-cleped was the Maudelayne.

With us ther was a DOCTOUR OF PHISYK,
In al this world ne was ther noon him lyk
To speke of phisik and of surgerye;
For he was grounded in astronomye.
He kepte[227] his pacient a ful greet del
In houres,[228] by his magik naturel.
Wel coude he fortunen the ascendent
Of his images for his pacient.[229]
He knew the cause of everich maladye,
Were it of hoot or cold, or moiste, or drye,
And where engendred, and of what humour;[230]
He was a verrey parfit practisour.

---

[214] Dwelling. [215] Nag. [216] Could. [217] Frieze or serge. [218] Stolen. [219] Merchant.
[220] Scrupulous. [221] Heed. [222] Drowned. [223] Currents. [224] Harbour. [225] Pilotage.
[226] Clever in planning. [227] Watched. [228] Astrological hours favorable for cures.
[229] Choose a fortunate star rising above the horizon, under which to treat images as
a charm to cure the patient.
[230] *Illness was supposed to be due to a humour in excess.*

The cause y-knowe, and of his harm the rote,
Anon he yaf the seke man his bote.[231]
Ful redy hadde he his apothecaries,
To sende him drogges,[232] and his letuaries,[233]
For ech of hem made other for to winne;
Hir frendschipe nas nat newe to biginne.
Wel knew he the olde Esculapius,
And Deiscorides, and eek Rufus;
Old Ypocras, Haly, and Galien;
Serapion, Razis, and Avicen;
Averrois, Damascien, and Constantyn;
Bernard, and Gatesden, and Gilbertyn.[234]
Of his diete mesurable[235] was he,
For it was of no superfluitee,
But of greet norissing and digestible.
His studie was but litel on the Bible.
In sangwin[236] and in pers[237] he clad was al,
Lyned with taffata and with sendal;[238]
And yet he was but esy of dispence;[239]
He kepte that he wan in pestilence.
For gold in phisik is a cordial,
Therfor he lovede gold in special.

A good WYF was ther of bisyde BATHE,
But she was som-del deef, and that was scathe.[240]
Of cloth-making she hadde swiche an haunt,[241]
She passed hem of Ypres and of Gaunt.
In al the parisshe wyf ne was ther noon
That to the offring bifore hir sholde goon;
And if ther dide, certeyn, so wrooth was she,
That she was out of alle charitee.
Hir coverchiefs ful fyne were of ground;[242]
I dorste swere they weyeden ten pound
That on a Sonday were upon hir heed.
Hir hosen weren of fyn scarlet reed,
Ful streite y-teyd,[243] and shoos ful moiste and newe.
Bold was hir face, and fair, and reed of hewe.

---

[231] Remedy.   [232] Drugs.
[233] Medicinal syrups.   [234] *These are the authors of the favorite medical text-books of the Middle Ages.*   [235] Temperate.   [236] Blood-red.   [237] Bluish gray.
[238] A kind of silk.   [239] In spending.   [240] Pity.   [241] Skill.   [242] Texture.
[243] Tied.

She was a worthy womman al hir lyve,
Housbondes at chirche-dore[244] she hadde fyve,
Withouten other compaignye in youthe;
But therof nedeth nat to speke as nouthe.[245]
And thryes hadde she been at Ierusalem;
But hadde passed many a straunge streem;
At Rome she hadde been, and at Boloigne,
In Galice at seint Iame, and at Coloigne.[246]
She coude moche of wandring by the weye.
Gat-tothed[247] was she, soothly for to seye.
Up-on an amblere esily she sat,
Y-wimpled[248] wel, and on hir heed an hat
As brood as is a bokeler or a targe;[249]
A foot-mantel aboute hir hipes large,
And on hir feet a paire[250] of spores sharpe.
In felaweschip wel coude she laughe and carpe.[251]
Of remedies of love she knew per-chaunce,
For she coude of that art the olde daunce.[252]

    A good man was ther of religioun,
And was a povre Persoun[253] of a toun;
But riche he was of holy thoght and werk.
He was also a lerned man, a clerk,
That Cristes gospel trewely wolde preche;
His parisshens devoutly wolde he teche.
Benigne he was, and wonder diligent,
And in adversitee ful pacient;
And swich he was y-preved[254] ofte sythes.[255]
Ful looth were him to cursen[256] for his tythes,
But rather wolde he yeven, out of doute,
Un-to his povre parisshens aboute
Of his offring, and eek of his substaunce.
He coude in litel thing han suffisaunce.
Wyd was his parisshe, and houses fer a-sonder,
But he ne lafte[257] nat, for reyn ne thonder,
In siknes nor in meschief, to visyte
The ferreste in his parisshe, moche and lyte,[258]
Up-on his feet, and in his hand a staf.

---

[244] *Marriages were performed in the church porch.*   [245] At present.
[246] *These were all famous shrines.*   [247] Gap-toothed.   [248] Kerchiefed.   [249] Shield.
[250] *Apparently she rode astride.*   [251] Talk.   [252] The whole game.   [253] Parson.
[254] Proved.   [255] Times.   [256] Excommunicate.   [257] Neglected.   [258] Great and small.

This noble ensample to his sheep he yaf,
That first he wroghte, and afterward he taughte;
Out of the gospel he tho[259] wordes caughte;
And this figure he added eek ther-to,
That if gold ruste, what shal yren do?
For if a preest be foul, on whom we truste,
No wonder is a lewed[260] man to ruste;
And shame it is, if a preest take keep,[261]
A shiten shepherde and a clene sheep.
Wel oghte a preest ensample for to yive,
By his clennesse, how that his sheep shold live.
He sette nat his benefice to hyre,
And leet[262] his sheep encombred in the myre,
And ran to London, un-to sëynt Poules,
To seken him a chaunterie for soules,
Or with a bretherhed to been withholde;
But dwelte at hoom, and kepte wel his folde,
So that the wolf ne made it nat miscarie;
He was a shepherde and no mercenarie.
And though he holy were, and vertuous,
He was to sinful man nat despitous,[263]
Ne of his speche daungerous[264] ne digne,[265]
But in his teching discreet and benigne.
To drawen folk to heven by fairnesse
By good ensample, this was his bisynesse:
But it were any persone obstinat,
What so he were, of heigh or lowe estat,
Him wolde he snibben[266] sharply for the nones.[267]
A bettre preest, I trowe that nowher non is.
He wayted after no pompe and reverence,
Ne maked him a spyced[268] conscience,
But Cristes lore, and his apostles twelve,
He taughte, but first he folwed it him-selve.

    With him ther was a PLOWMAN, was his brother,
That hadde y-lad of dong ful many a fother,[269]
A trewe swinkere[270] and a good was he,
Livinge in pees and parfit charitee.
God loved he best with al his hole herte

---

[259] Those.   [260] Ignorant.   [261] Heed.   [262] Left.
[263] Contemptuous.   [264] Overbearing.   [265] Haughty.   [266] Rebuke.   [267] *This phrase
is often vaguely intensive.*   [268] Suspiciously fastidious.   [269] Cartload.   [270] Laborer.

At alle tymes, thogh him gamed or smerte,[271]
And thanne his neighebour right as him-selve.
He wolde thresshe, and ther-to dyke[272] and delve,
For Cristes sake, for every povre wight,
Withouten hyre, if it lay in his might.
His tythes payed he ful faire and wel,
Bothe of his propre swink[273] and his catel.[274]
In a tabard[275] he rood upon a mere.
   Ther was also a Reve and a Millere,
A Somnour and a Pardoner also,
A Maunciple, and my-self; ther wer namo.[276]
   The MILLER was a stout carl, for the nones,[267]
Ful big he was of braun, and eek of bones;
That proved wel, for over-al ther he cam,
At wrastling he wolde have alwey the ram.[277]
He was short-sholdred, brood, a thikke knarre,[278]
Ther nas no dore that he nolde[279] heve of harre,[280]
Or breke it, at a renning, with his heed.
His berd as any sowe or fox was reed,
And ther-to brood, as though it were a spade.
Up-on the cop[281] right of his nose he hade
A werte, and ther-on stood a tuft of heres,
Reed as the bristles of a sowes eres,
His nose-thirles blake were and wyde.
A swerd and bokeler bar he by his syde;
His mouth as greet was as a greet forneys.
He was a janglere[282] and a goliardeys,[283]
And that was most of sinne and harlotryes.
Wel coude he stelen corn, and tollen[284] thryes;
And yet he hadde a thombe of gold[285] pardee.
A whyt cote and a blew hood wered he.
A baggepype wel coude he blowe and sowne,
And therwithal he broghte us out of towne.
   A gentil MAUNCIPLE[286] was ther of a temple,[287]
Of which achatours[288] mighte take exemple
For to be wyse in bying of vitaille.

---

[271] Pleased or pained him.   [272] Also ditch.   [273] Labor.
[274] Property.   [275] Smock frock.   [276] No more.   [277] *The usual prize.*   [278] Knot.
[279] Would not.   [280] Hinges.   [281] Tip.   [282] Great talker.   [283] Jester.
[284] Take his commission.   [285] *Like all honest millers.*
[286] Steward.   [287] Inn of court, where lawyers lived.   [288] Purchasers.

For whether that he payde, or took by taille,[289]
Algate[290] he wayted so in his achat,[291]
That he was ay biforn[292] and in good stat.
Now is nat that of God a ful fair grace,
That swich a lewed[293] mannes wit shal pace[294]
The wisdom of an heep of lerned men?
Of maistres hadde he mo than thryes ten,
That were of lawe expert and curious;
Of which ther were a doseyn in that hous,
Worthy to been stiwardes of rente and lond
Of any lord that is in Engelond,
To make him live by his propre good,
In honour dettelees, but he were wood,[295]
Or live as scarsly[296] as him list desire;
And able for to helpen al a shire
In any cas that mighte falle or happe;
And yit this maunciple sette hir aller cappe.[297]

The REVE[298] was a sclendre colerik man,
His berd was shave as ny as ever he can.
His heer was by his eres round y-shorn.
His top was dokked lyk a preest biforn.
Ful longe were his legges, and ful lene,
Y-lyk a staf, ther was no calf y-sene.
Wel coude he kepe a gerner[299] and a binne;
Ther was noon auditour coude on him winne.
Wel wiste he, by the droghte, and by the reyn,
The yeldyng of his seed, and of his greyn.
His lordes sheep, his neet, his dayerye,
His swyn, his hors, his stoor,[300] and his pultrye,
Was hoolly in this reves governing,
And by his covenaunt yaf the rekening,
Sin that his lord was twenty yeer of age;
Ther coude no man bringe him in arrerage.[301]
Ther nas baillif, ne herde, ne other hyne,[302]
That he ne knew his sleighte and his covync;[303]
They were adrad of him, as of the deeth.[304]
His woning[305] was ful fair up-on an heeth,

[289] Tally, credit.
[290] Always. [291] Buying. [292] Ahead. [293] Ignorant. [294] Surpass. [295] Mad.
[296] Sparingly. [297] Fooled them all. [298] Bailiff. [299] Garner. [300] Stock.
[301] Arrears. [302] Farm-laborer. [303] Deceit. [304] Pestilence. [305] Dwelling.

With grene treës shadwed was his place.
He coude bettre than his lord purchace.
Ful riche he was astored[306] prively,
His lord wel coude he plesen subtilly,
To yeve and lene him of his owne good,
And have a thank, and yet a cote, and hood.
In youthe he lerned hadde a good mister;[307]
He was a wel good wrighte, a carpenter.
This reve sat up-on a ful good stot,[308]
That was al pomely[309] grey, and highte[310] Scot.
A long surcote[311] of pers[312] up-on he hade,
And by his syde he bar a rusty blade.
Of Northfolk was this reve, of which I telle,
Bisyde a toun men clepen Baldeswelle.
Tukked[313] he was, as is a frere, aboute,
And evere he rood the hindreste of our route.

    A Somnour[314] was ther with us in that place,
That hadde a fyr-reed cherubinnes face,
For sawceflem[315] he was, with eyen narwe.
As hoot he was, and lecherous as a sparwe,
With scalled[316] browes blake, and piled[317] berd;
Of his visage children were aferd.
Ther nas quik-silver, litarge,[318] ne brimstoon,
Boras,[319] ceruce,[320] ne oille of tartre[321] noon,
Ne oynement that wolde clense and byte,
That him mighte helpen of his whelkes[322] whyte,
Ne of the knobbes sitting on his chekes.
Wel loved he garleek, oynons, and eek lekes,
And for to drinken strong wyn, reed as blood.
Thanne wolde he speke, and crye as he were wood.[323]
And whan that he wel dronken hadde the wyn,
Than wolde he speke no word but Latyn.
A fewe termes hadde he, two or thre,
That he had lerned out of som decree;
No wonder is, he herde it al the day;
And eek ye knowen wel, how that a jay

---

[306] Furnished with supplies.   [307] Trade.   [308] Cob.   [309] Dappled.   [310] Was called.
[311] Overcoat.   [312] Bluish gray.   [313] With the skirts of his coat tucked up.
[314] Apparitor, summoner to ecclesiastical courts.   [315] Pimpled.   [316] Scabby.
[317] Thin.   [318] White lead.   [319] Borax.   [320] *A kind of ointment made from white lead.*
[321] Cream of tartar.   [322] Boils.   [323] Mad.

Can clepen 'Watte,' as well as can the pope.
But who-so coude in other thing him grope,[324]
Thanne hadde he spent al his philosophye;
Ay '*Questio quid iuris*' [325] wolde he crye.
He was a gentil harlot[326] and a kynde;
A bettre felawe sholde men noght fynde.
He wolde suffre for a quart of wyn
A good felawe to have his concubyn
A twelf-month, and excuse him atte fulle:
And prively a finch eek coude he pulle.[327]
And if he fond owher a good felawe,
He wolde techen him to have non awe,
In swich cas, of the erchedeknes curs,
But-if[328] a mannes soule were in his purs;
For in his purs he sholde y-punisshed be.
'Purs is the erchedeknes helle,' seyde he.
But wel I woot he lyed right in dede;
Of cursing oghte ech gulty man him drede—
For curs wol slee right as assoilling[329] saveth—
And also war him of a *significavit*[330]
In daunger[331] hadde he at his owne gyse[332]
The yonge girles[333] of the diocyse,
And knew hir counseil, and was al hir reed.[334]
A gerland hadde he set up-on his heed,
As greet as it were for an ale-stake;[335]
A bokeler hadde he maad him of a cake.

    With him ther rood a gentil PARDONER
Of Rouncivale, his frend and his compeer,
That streight was comen fro the court of Rome.
Ful loude he song, 'Com hider, love, to me.'
This somnour bar to him a stiff burdoun,[336]
Was nevere trompe of half so greet a soun.
This pardoner hadde heer as yelow as wex,
But smothe it heng, as doth a strike[337] of flex;
By ounces[338] henge his lokkes that he hadde,

---

[324] Test.   [325] *The question is, What is the law?*   [326] Fellow.
[327] Fleece a greenhorn.   [328] Unless.   [329] Absolution.   [330] *The word which began the writ of excommunication.*
[331] Under his control.   [332] In his own way.   [333] Young people of both sexes.
[334] Adviser.   [335] *As large as the garlands hung on a stake in front of alehouses.*
[336] Bass.   [337] Hank.   [338] Small bunches.

And ther-with he his shuldres overspradde;
But thinne it lay, by colpons[338] oon and oon;
But hood, for jolitee, ne wered he noon,
For it was trussed[339] up in his walet.
Him thoughte, he rood al of the newe jet;[340]
Dischevele, save his cappe, he rood al bare.
Swiche glaringe eyen hadde he as an hare.
A vernicle[341] hadde he sowed on his cappe.
His walet lay biforn him in his lappe,
Bret-ful[342] of pardoun come from Rome al hoot,
A voys he hadde as smal as hath a goot.
No berd hadde he, ne nevere sholde have,
As smothe it was as it were late y-shave;
I trowe he were a gelding or a mare.
But of his craft, fro Berwik into Ware,
Ne was ther swich another pardoner.
For in his male[343] he hadde a pilwe-beer,[344]
Which that, he seyde, was our lady[345] veyl:
He seyde, he hadde a gobet[346] of the seyl
That sëynt Peter hadde, whan that he wente
Up-on the see, til Iesu Crist him hente.
He hadde a croys of latoun,[347] ful of stones,
And in a glas he hadde pigges bones.
But with thise relikes, whan that he fond
A povre person dwelling up-on lond,
Up-on a day he gat him more moneye
Than that the person gat in monthes tweye.
And thus with feyned flaterye and japes,[348]
He made the person and the peple his apes.
But trewely to tellen, atte laste,
He was in chirche a noble ecclesiaste.
Wel coude he rede a lessoun or a storie,
But alderbest[349] he song an offertorie;
For wel he wiste, whan that song was songe,
He moste preche, and wel affyle[350] his tonge,
To winne silver, as he ful wel coude;
Therefore he song so meriely and loude.

---

[339] Packed.   [340] Fashion.
[341] *A small copy of the handkerchief of Veronica with the miraculous portrait of Christ.*
[342] Brimfull.   [343] Bag.   [344] Pillow-case.   [345] Lady's.   [346] Fragment.
[347] A compound of copper and zinc.   [348] Jests.   [349] Best of all.   [350] Make smooth.

Now have I told you shortly, in a clause,
Thestat, tharray, the nombre, and eek the cause
Why that assembled was this compaignye
In Southwerk, at this gentil hostelrye,
That highte[351] the Tabard, faste by the Belle.
But now is tyme to yow for to telle
How that we baren[352] us that ilke[353] night,
Whan we were in that hostelrye alight.
And after wol I telle of our viage[354]
And al the remenaunt of our pilgrimage.
But first I pray yow of your curteisye,
That ye narette[355] it nat my vileinye,[356]
Thogh that I pleynly speke in this matere,
To telle yow hir wordes and hir chere;[357]
Ne thogh I speke hir wordes proprely.
For this ye knowen al-so[358] wel as I,
Who-so shal telle a tale after a man,
He moot reherce, as ny as evere he can,
Everich a word, if it be in his charge,[359]
Al[360] speke he never so rudeliche and large;[361]
Or elles he moot telle his tale untrewe,
Or feyne thing, or fynde wordes newe.
He may nat spare, al-thogh he were his brother;
He moot as wel seye o word as another.
Crist spak him-self ful brode in holy writ,
And wel ye woot, no vileinye[362] is it.
Eek Plato seith, who-so that can him rede,
"The wordes mote[363] be cosin to the dede."
Also I prey yow to foryeve it me,
Al[360] have I nat set folk in hir[364] degree
Here in this tale, as that they sholde stonde;
My wit is short, ye may wel understonde.
  Greet chere made our hoste us everichon,[365]
And to the soper sette he us anon;
And served us with vitaille at the beste.
Strong was the wyn, and wel to drinke us leste.[366]
A semely man our hoste was with-alle

<hr>

351 Was called. 352 Bore, behaved. 353 Same. 354 Journey.
355 Reckon. 356 Ill-breeding. 357 Behavior 358 As.
359 Task. 360 Although. 361 Broad. 362 Vulgarity.
363 Must. 364 Their. 365 Every one. 366 It pleased us.

For to han been a marshal in an halle;
A large man he was with eyen stepe,[367]
A fairer burgeys was ther noon in Chepe:[368]
Bold of his speche, and wys, and wel y-taught,
And of manhod him lakkede right naught.
Eek therto[369] he was right a mery man,
And after soper pleyen he bigan,
And spak of mirthe amonges othere thinges,
Whan that we hadde maad our rekeninges;
And seyde thus: 'Now, lordinges, trewely
Ye ben to me right welcome hertely:
For by my trouthe, if that I shal nat lye,
I ne saugh[370] this yeer so mery a compaignye
At ones in this herberwe[371] as is now.
Fayn wolde I doon yow mirthe, wiste I how.
And of a mirthe I am right now bithoght,
To doon yow ese, and it shall coste noght.

Ye goon to Caunterbury; God yow spede,
The blisful martir quyte yow your mede.[372]
And wel I woot, as ye goon by the weye,
Ye shapen[373] yow to talen[374] and to pleye;
For trewely, confort ne mirthe is noon
To ryde by the weye doumb as a stoon;
And therefore wol I maken yow disport,
As I seyde erst,[375] and doon yow som confort.
And if yow lyketh[376] alle, by oon assent,
Now for to stonden at my jugement,
And for to werken as I shal yow seye,
To-morwe, whan ye ryden by the weye,
Now, by my fader[377] soule, that is deed,
But[378] ye be merye, I wol yeve yow myn heed.
Hold up your hond, withoute more speche.'
Our counseil was nat longe for to seche;
Us thoughte it was noght worth to make it wys,[379]
And graunted him with-outen more avys,[380]
And bad him seye his verdit, as him leste.

'Lordinges,' quod he, 'now herkneth for the beste;
But tak it not, I prey yow, in desdeyn;

---

[367] Prominent.   [368] Cheapside.   [369] Besides.
[370] Saw.   [371] Inn.   [372] Give you your reward.   [373] Prepare.   [374] Tell tales.   [375] Before.
[376] It pleases you.   [377] Father's.   [378] Unless.   [379] To deliberate.   [380] Consideration.

This is the poynt, to speken short and pleyn,
That ech of yow, to shorte with our weye,
In this viage, shal telle tales tweye,
To Caunterbury-ward, I mene it so,
And hom-ward he shal tellen othere two,
Of aventures that whylom[381] han bifalle.
And which of yow that bereth him best of alle,
That is to seyn, that telleth in this cas
Tales of best sentence[382] and most solas,[383]
Shal han a soper at our aller[384] cost
Here in this place, sitting by this post,
Whan that we come agayn fro Caunterbury.
And for to make yow the more mery,
I wol my-selven gladly with yow ryde,
Right at myn owne cost, and be your gyde.
And who-so wol my jugement withseye[385]
Shal paye al that we spenden by the weye.
And if ye vouche-sauf that it be so,
Tel me anon, with-outen wordes mo,
And I wol erly shape[386] me therfore.'

This thing was graunted, and our othes swore
With ful glad herte, and preyden him also
That he wold vouche-sauf for to do so,
And that he wolde been our governour,
And of our tales juge and reportour,
And sette a soper at a certeyn prys;
And we wold reuled been at his devys,[387]
In heigh and lowe; and thus, by oon assent,
We been acorded to his jugement.
And ther-up-on the wyn was fet[388] anoon;
We dronken, and to reste wente echoon,
With-outen any lenger taryinge.
A-morwe, whan that day bigan to springe,
Up roos our host, and was our aller cok,[389]
And gadrede us togidre, alle in a flok,
And forth we riden, a litel more than pas,[390]
Unto the watering[391] of seint Thomas.
And there our host bigan his hors areste,[392]

---

[381] Once upon a time. [382] Meaning.
[383] Pleasure. [384] Of all of us. [385] Gainsay. [386] Prepare. [387] Judgment. [388] Fetched.
[389] Cock of us all; *i. e., waked us.* [390] Walking. [391] Watering-place. [392] To pull up.

And seyde; 'Lordinges, herkneth if yow leste.
Ye woot your forward,[393] and I it yow recorde.[394]
If even-song and morwe-song acorde,
Lat se now who shal telle the firste tale.
As evere mote[395] I drinke wyn or ale,
Who-so be rebel to my jugement
Shal paye for al that by the weye is spent.
Now draweth cut, er that we ferrer twinne;[396]
He which that hath the shortest shal biginne.'
'Sire knight,' quod he, 'my maister and my lord,
Now draweth cut, for that is myn acord.
Cometh neer,' quod he, 'my lady prioresse;
And ye, sir clerk, lat be your shamfastnesse,
Ne studieth noght; ley hond to, every man.'

Anon to drawen every wight bigan,
And shortly for to tellen, as it was,
Were it by aventure, or sort,[397] or cas,[398]
The sothe is this, the cut fil to the knight,
Of which ful blythe and glad was every wight;
And telle he moste his tale, as was resoun,
By forward[399] and by composicioun,[399]
As ye han herd; what nedeth wordes mo?
And whan this goode man saugh[400] it was so,
As he that wys was and obedient
To kepe his forward by his free assent,
He seyde: 'Sin I shal biginne the game,
What, welcome be the cut, a[401] Goddes name!
Now lat us ryde, and herkneth what I seye.'

And with that word we riden forth our weye;
And he bigan with right a mery chere
His tale anon, and seyde in this manere.

2 THE NUN'S PRIEST'S TALE

Here biginneth the Nonne Preestes Tale of the Cok and Hen,
Chauntecleer and Pertelote.

A POVRE widwe somdel stope[1] in age,
Was whylom[2] dwelling in a narwe cotage,
Bisyde a grove, stondyng in a dale.

---

[393] Agreement. [394] Recall. [395] May. [396] Depart further. [397] Fate. [398] Chance.
[399] Agreement. [400] Saw. [401] In. [1] Somewhat advanced. [2] Once upon a time.

This widwe, of which I telle yow my tale,
Sin thilke[3] day that she was last a wyf,
In pacience ladde a ful simple lyf,
For litel was hir catel[4] and hir rente;
By housbondrye, of such as God hir sente,
She fond[5] hir-self, and eek hir doghtren two.
Three large sowes hadde she, and namo,
Three kyn, and eek a sheep that highte[6] Malle.
Ful sooty was hir bour,[7] and eek hir halle
In which she eet ful many a sclendre meel.
Of poynaunt sauce hir neded never a deel.
No deyntee morsel passed thurgh hir throte;
Hir dyete was accordant to hir cote.
Repleccioun ne made hir nevere syk;
Attempree dyete was al hir phisyk,
And exercyse, and hertes suffisaunce.
The goute lette[8] hir no-thing for to daunce,
Ne poplexye[9] shente[10] nat hir heed;
No wyn ne drank she, neither whyt ne reed;
Hir bord was served most with whyt and blak,
Milk and broun breed, in which she fond no lak,
Seynd[11] bacoun, and somtyme an ey[12] or tweye,
For she was as it were a maner deye.[13]

A yerd she hadde, enclosed al aboute
With stikkes, and a drye dich with-oute,
In which she hadde a cok, hight Chauntecleer,
In al the land of crowing nas[14] his peer.
His vois was merier than the merye orgon
On messe-dayes that in the chirche gon;
Wel sikerer[15] was his crowing in his logge,[16]
Than is a clokke, or an abbey orlogge.[17]
By nature knew he ech ascencioun
Of equinoxial in thilke toun;
For whan degrees fiftene were ascended,[18]
Thanne crew he, that it mighte nat ben amended.
His comb was redder than the fyn coral,
And batailed,[19] as it were a castel-wal.

[3] That. [4] Property. [5] Supported. [6] Was called. [7] Inner room. [8] Hindered.
[9] Apoplexy. [10] Harmed. [11] Broiled. [12] Egg. [13] A kind of dairy-woman.
[14] Was not. [15] More certain. [16] Lodge. [17] Clock. [18] *I. e., every hour.*
[19] Indented.

His bile was blak, and as the jeet it shoon;
Lyk asur were his legges, and his toon;[20]
His nayles whytter than the lilie flour,
And lyk the burned[21] gold was his colour.
This gentil cok hadde in his governaunce
Sevene hennes, for to doon al his plesaunce,
Whiche were his sustres and his paramours,
And wonder lyk to him, as of colours.
Of whiche the faireste hewed on hir throte
Was cleped[22] faire damoysele Pertelote.
Curteys she was, discreet, and debonaire,
And compaignable, and bar hir-self so faire,
Sin thilke day that she was seven night old,
That trewely she hath the herte in hold
Of Chauntecleer loken in every lith;[23]
He loved hir so, that wel was him therwith.
But such a joye was it to here hem singe,
Whan that the brighte sonne gan to springe,
In swete accord, 'My lief is faren in londe.'[24]
For thilke[25] tyme, as I have understonde,
Bestes and briddes coude speke and singe.

    And so bifel, that in a dawenynge,
As Chauntecleer among his wyves alle
Sat on his perche, that was in the halle,
And next him sat this faire Pertelote,
This Chauntecleer gan gronen in his throte,
As man that in his dreem is drecched[26] sore.
And whan that Pertelote thus herde him rore,
She was agast, and seyde, 'O herte deere,
What eyleth yow, to grone in this manere?
Ye ben a verray sleper, fy for shame!'
And he answerde and seyde thus, 'Madame,
I pray yow, that ye take it nat a-grief:[27]
By God, me mette[28] I was in swich meschief
Right now, that yet myn herte is sore afright.
Now God,' quod he, 'my swevene[29] rede[30] aright,
And keep my body out of foul prisoun!
Me mette,[28] how that I romed up and doun

[20] Toes.   [21] Burnished.   [22] Called.
[23] Locked in every limb.   [24] 'My dear is gone away'—*a line from a popular song.*
[25] That.   [26] Troubled.   [27] Amiss.   [28] I dreamed.   [29] Dream.   [30] Interpret.

Withinne our yerde, wher-as I saugh a beste,
Was lyk an hound, and wolde han maad areste[31]
Upon my body, and wolde han had me deed.
His colour was bitwixe yelwe and reed;
And tipped was his tail, and bothe his eres
With blak, unlyk the remenant of his heres;
His snowte smal, with glowinge eyen tweye.
Yet of his look for fere almost I deye;
This caused me my groning, douteles.'

'Avoy!' quod she, 'fy on yow, herteles!
Allas!' quod she, 'for, by that God above,
Now han ye lost myn herte and al my love;
I can nat love a coward, by my feith.
For certes, what, so any womman seith,
We alle desyren, if it mighte be,
To han housebondes hardy, wyse, and free,
And secree, and no nigard, ne no fool,
Ne him that is agast of every tool,[32]
Ne noon avauntour,[33] by that God above!
How dorste ye sayn for shame unto youre love,
That any thing mighte make yow aferd?
Have ye no mannes herte, and han a berd?
Allas! and conne ye been agast of swevenis?[34]
No-thing, God wot, but vanitee, in sweven is.
Swevenes engendren of[35] replecciouns,
And ofte of fume,[36] and of complecciouns,[37]
Whan humours been to habundant in a wight.
Certes this dreem, which ye han met to-night,
Cometh of the grete superfluitee
Of youre rede *colera*,[38] pardee,[39]
Which causeth folk to dreden in here dremes
Of arwes, and of fyr with rede lemes,[40]
Of grete bestes, that they wol hem byte,
Of contek,[41] and of whelpes grete and lyte;[42]
Right[43] as the humour of malencolye
Causeth ful many a man, in sleep, to crye,

31 Seized.   32 Weapon.
33 Boaster.   34 Dreams.   35 Are produced by.   36 Vapours rising from the stomach.
37 Particular combinations of humors.   38 *Red choler was one of the four humors, the proportionate amounts of which were supposed to determine the individual temperament or "complexion."*   39 *An oath.*
40 Flames.   41 Strife.   42 Little.   43 Just.

For fere of blake beres, or boles[44] blake,
Or elles, blake develes wole him take.
Of othere humours coude I telle also,
That werken many a man in sleep ful wo;
But I wol passe as lightly as I can.

Lo Catoun, which that was so wys a man,
Seyde he nat thus, ne do no fors of[45] dremes?
Now, sire,' quod she, 'whan we flee fro the bemes,[46]
For Goddes love, as tak som laxatyf;
Up peril of my soule, and of my lyf,
I counseille yow the beste, I wol nat lye,
That both of colere, and of malencolye
Ye purge yow; and for ye shul nat tarie
Though in this toun is noon apotecarie,
I shal my-self to herbes techen[47] yow,
That shul ben for your hele,[48] and for your prow;[49]
And in our yerd tho herbes shal I fynde,
The whiche han of here propretee, by kynde,[50]
To purgen yow binethe, and eek above.
Forget not this, for Goddes owene love!
Ye been ful colerik of compleccioun.
Ware[51] the sonne in his ascencioun
Ne fynde yow nat repleet[52] of humours hote;
And if it do, I dar wel leye[53] a grote,
That ye shul have a fevere terciane,
Or an agu, that may be youre bane.[54]
A day or two ye shul have digestyves
Of wormes, er ye take your laxatyves,
Of lauriol,[55] centaure,[56] and fumetere,[57]
Or elles of ellebor, that groweth there,
Of catapuce,[58] or of gaytres[59] beryis,
Of erbe yve,[60] growing in our yerd, that mery[61] is;
Pekke hem up right as they growe, and ete hem in.
Be mery, housbond, for your fader kyn![62]
Dredeth no dreem; I can say yow na-more.'
'Madame,' quod he, '*graunt mercy*[63] of your lore.
But natheles, as touching daun Catoun,

[44] Bulls.   [45] Pay no attention to.   [46] Perch.   [47] Direct.   [48] Health.   [49] Profit.
[50] Nature.   [51] Beware.   [52] Too full.   [53] Bet.   [54] Death.   [55] Spurge-laurel.
[56] Centaury.   [57] Fumitory.   [58] Caper-spurge.   [59] Buck-thorn.   [60] Herb ivy.
[61] Pleasant.   [62] Father's kin.   [63] Many thanks.

That hath of wisdom such a gret renoun,
Though that he bad no dremes for to drede,
By God, men may in olde bokes rede
Of many a man, more of auctoritee
Than evere Catoun was, so moot I thee,[64]
That al the revers seyn of this sentence,
And han wel founden by experience,
That dremes ben significaciouns,
As wel of joye as tribulaciouns
That folk enduren in this lyf present.
Ther nedeth make of this noon argument;
The verray preve[65] sheweth it in dede.

Oon of the gretteste auctours that men rede[66]
Seith thus, that whylom two felawes wente
On pilgrimage, in a ful good entente;
And happed so, thay come into a toun,
Wher-as ther was swich congregacioun
Of peple, and eek so streit of herbergage,[67]
That they ne founde as muche as o[68] cotage,
In which they bothe mighte y-logged[69] be.
Wherfor thay mosten, of necessitee,
As for that night, departen[70] compaignye;
And ech of hem goth to his hostelrye,
And took his logging as it wolde falle.[71]
That oon of hem was logged in a stalle,
Fer in a yerd, with oxen of the plough;
That other man was logged wel y-nough,
As was his aventure,[72] or his fortune,
That us governeth alle as in commune.

And so bifel, that, longe er it were day,
This man mette[73] in his bed, ther-as[74] he lay,
How that his felawe gan up-on him calle,
And seyde, 'allas! for in an oxes stalle
This night I shal be mordred ther[74] I lye.
Now help me, dere brother, or I dye;
In alle haste com to me,' he sayde.
This man out of his sleep for fere abrayde;[75]
But whan that he was wakned of his sleep,

---

[64] So may I thrive.   [65] True proof.   [66] *Cicero*.   [67] Such crowding in the inns.
[68] One.   [69] Lodged.   [70] Part.   [71] Happen.   [72] Chance.   [73] Dreamed.   [74] Where.
[75] Started.

He turned him, and took of this no keep;[76]
Him thoughte his dreem nas but a vanitee.
Thus twyes in his sleping dremed he.
And atte thridde tyme yet his felawe
Com, as him thoughte, and seide, 'I am now slawe;[77]
Bihold my bloody woundes, depe and wyde!
Arys up erly in the morwe-tyde,
And at the west gate of the toun,' quod he,
'A carte ful of donge ther shaltow see,
In which my body is hid ful prively;
Do thilke carte arresten boldely.
My gold caused my mordre, sooth to sayn;'
And tolde him every poynt how he was slayn,
With a ful pitous face, pale of hewe.
And truste wel, his dreem he fond ful trewe;
For on the morwe, as sone as it was day,
To his felawes in he took the way;
And whan that he cam to this oxes stalle,
After his felawe he bigan to calle.

   The hostiler answerde him anon,
And seyde, 'sire, your felawe is agon,
As sone as day he wente out of the toun.'
This man gan fallen in suspecioun,
Remembring on his dremes that he mette,[78]
And forth he goth, no lenger wolde he lette,[79]
Unto the west gate of the toun, and fond
A dong-carte, as it were to donge lond,
That was arrayed in that same wyse
As ye han herd the dede man devyse;[80]
And with an hardy herte he gan to crye
Vengeaunce and justice of this felonye:—
'My felawe mordred is this same night,
And in this carte he lyth gapinge upright.[81]
I crye out on the ministres,'[82] quod he,
'That sholden kepe and reulen this citee;
Harrow! allas! her lyth my felawe slayn!'
What sholde I more un-to this tale sayn?
The peple out-sterte, and caste the cart to grounde,

[76] Heed.   [77] Slain.   [78] Dreamed.   [79] Delay.   [80] Describe.
[81] On his back.   [82] Magistrates.

And in the middel of the dong they founde
The dede man, that mordred was al newe.

O blisful God, that art so just and trewe!
Lo, how that thou biwreyest mordre alway!
Mordre wol out, that se we day by day.
Mordre is so wlatsom[83] and abhominable
To God, that is so just and resonable,
That he ne wol not suffre it heled[84] be;
Though it abyde a yeer, or two, or three,
Mordre wol out, this[85] my conclusioun.
And right anoon, ministres of that toun
Han hent[86] the carter, and so sore him pyned,[87]
And eek the hostiler so sore engyned,[88]
That thay biknewe[89] hir wikkednesse anoon,
And were an-hanged by the nekke-boon.

Here may men seen that dremes been to drede.[90]
And certes, in the same book I rede,
Right in the nexte chapitre after this,
(I gabbe[91] nat, so have I joye or blis,)
Two men that wolde han passed over see,
For certeyn cause, in-to a fer contree,
If that the wind ne hadde been contrarie,
That made hem in a citee for to tarie,
That stood ful mery upon an haven-syde.
But on a day, agayn[92] the even-tyde,
The wind gan chaunge, and blew right as hem leste.
Jolif and glad they wente un-to hir reste,
And casten[93] hem ful erly for to saille;
But to that oo[94] man fel a greet mervaille.
That oon of hem, in sleping as he lay,
Him mette[95] a wonder dreem, agayn[92] the day;
Him thoughte[96] a man stood by his beddes syde,
And him comaunded, that he sholde abyde,
And seyde him thus, 'If thou to-morwe wende,
Thou shalt be dreynt;[97] my tale is at an ende.'
He wook, and tolde his felawe what he mette,[95]
And preyde him his viage for to lette;[98]
As for that day, he preyde him to abyde.

[83] Heinous.   [84] Concealed.   [85] This is.   [86] Seized.   [87] Tortured.   [88] Racked.
[89] Confessed.   [90] To be dreaded.   [91] Lie.   [92] Towards.   [93] Planned.   [94] The one.
[95] He dreamed.   [96] It seemed to him.   [97] Drowned.   [98] Delay.

His felawe, that lay by his beddes syde,
Gan for to laughe, and scorned him ful faste.
'No dreem,' quod he, 'may so myn herte agaste,[99]
That I wol lette[98] for to do my thinges.
I sette not a straw by thy dreminges,
For swevenes[100] been but vanitees and japes.[101]
Men dreme al-day of owles or of apes,
And eek of many a mase[102] therwithal;
Men dreme of thing that nevere was ne shal.
But sith I see that thou wolt heer abyde,
And thus for-sleuthen[103] wilfully thy tyde,
God wot it reweth[104] me; and have good day.'
And thus he took his leve, and wente his way.
But er that he hadde halfe his cours y-seyled,
Noot[105] I nat why, ne what mischaunce it eyled,
But casuelly[106] the shippes botme rente,
And ship and man under the water wente
In sighte of othere shippes it byside,
That with hem seyled at the same tyde.
And therfor, faire Pertelote so dere,
By swiche ensamples olde maistow lere,[107]
That no man sholde been to recchelees
Of dremes, for I sey thee, doutelees,
That many a dreem ful sore is for to drede.

'Lo, in the lyf of seint Kenelm, I rede,
That was Kenulpus sone, the noble king
Of Mercenrike, how Kenelm mette a thing;
A lyte[108] er he was mordred, on a day.
His mordre in his avisioun he say.[109]
His norice him expouned every del
His sweven,[110] and bad him for to kepe[111] him wel
For[112] traisoun; but he nas but seven yeer old,
And therfore litel tale hath he told[113]
Of any dreem, so holy was his herte.
By God, I hadde levere[114] than my sherte
That ye had rad his legende, as have I.
Dame Pertelote, I sey yow trewely,

---

[99] Frighten. [100] Dreams. [101] Trifles. [102] Bewilderment. [103] Lose through sloth.
[104] Makes me sorry. [105] Know not. [106] By an accident. [107] Mayst thou learn.
[108] Little. [109] Saw. [110] Dream. [111] Guard. [112] Against.
[113] Heed hath he paid. [114] Rather.

Macrobeus, that writ the avisioun
In Affrike of the worthy Cipioun,
Affermeth dremes, and seith that they been
Warning of thinges that men after seen.

And forther-more, I pray yow loketh wel
In the olde testament, of Daniel,
If he held dremes any vanitee.
Reed eek of Joseph, and ther shul ye see
Wher dremes ben somtyme (I sey nat alle)
Warning of thinges that shul after falle.
Loke of Egipt the king, daun Pharao,
His bakere and his boteler also,
Wher they ne felte noon effect in dremes.
Who-so wol seken actes of sondry remes,[115]
May rede of dremes many a wonder thing.

'Lo Cresus, which that was of Lyde king,
Mette he nat that he sat upon a tree,
Which signified he sholde anhanged be?
Lo heer Andromacha, Ectores wyf,
That day that Ector sholde lese[116] his lyf,
She dremed on the same night biforn,
How that the lyf of Ector sholde be lorn,[117]
If thilke day he wente in-to bataille;
She warned him, but it mighte nat availle;
He wente for to fighte natheles,
But he was slayn anoon of Achilles.
But thilke[118] tale is al to long to telle,
And eek it is ny[119] day, I may nat dwelle.
Shortly I seye, as for conclusioun,
That I shal han of this avisioun[120]
Adversitee; and I seye forther-more,
That I ne telle[121] of laxatyves no store,
For they ben venimous, I woot it wel;
I hem defye,[122] I love hem nevere a del.[123]

'Now let us speke of mirthe, and stinte[124] al this;
Madame Pertelote, so have I blis,
Of o[125] thing God hath sent me large grace;
For whan I see the beautee of your face,

---

[115] Realms. [116] Lose. [117] Lost. [118] That. [119] Nigh. [120] Vision.
[121] Count. [122] Despise. [123] Not a bit. [124] Stop. [125] One.

Ye ben so scarlet-reed about youre yën,
It maketh al my drede for to dyen;
For, also siker as *In principio*,[126]
Mulier est hominis confusio; [127]
Madame, the sentence of this Latin is—
Womman is mannes joye and al his blis.
For whan I fele a-night your softe syde,
I am so ful of joye and of solas
That I defyye bothe sweven and dreem.'
And with that word fley doun fro the beem,
For it was day, and eek his hennes alle;
And with a chuk he gan hem for to calle,
For he had founde a corn, lay in the yerd.
Roial he was, he was namore aferd; . . .
He loketh as it were a grim leoun;
And on his toos he rometh up and doun,
Him deyned not to sette his foot to grounde.
He chukketh, whan he hath a corn y-founde,
And to him rennen thanne his wyves alle.
Thus roial, as a prince is in his halle,
Leve I this Chauntecleer in his pasture;
And after wol I telle his aventure.

Whan that the month in which the world bigan,
That highte March, whan God first maked man,
Was complet, and y-passed were also,
Sin March bigan, thritty dayes and two,
Bifel that Chauntecleer, in al his pryde,
His seven wyves walking by his syde,
Caste up his eyen to the brighte sonne,
That in the signe of Taurus hadde y-ronne
Twenty degrees and oon, and somwhat more;
And knew by kynde,[128] and by noon other lore,
That it was pryme, and crew with blisful stevene.[129]
'The sonne,' he sayde, 'is clomben up on hevene
Fourty degrees and oon, and more, y-wis.[130]
Madame Pertelote, my worldes blis,
Herkneth thise blisful briddes how they singe,
And see the fresshe floures how they springe;

---

[126] "In the beginning," *John I. I.*   [127] "Woman is man's confusion."
[128] Nature.   [129] Voice.   [130] Certainly.

Ful is myn hert of revel and solas.' [131]
But sodeinly him fil[132] a sorweful cas;[133]
For evere the latter ende of joye is wo.
Got woot that worldly joye is sone ago;[134]
And if a rethor coude faire endyte,[135]
He in a chronique saufly mighte it write,
As for a sovereyn notabilitee.[136]
Now every wys man, lat him herkne me;
This storie is al-so[137] trewe, I undertake,
As is the book of Launcelot de Lake,
That wommen holde in ful gret reverence.
Now wol I torne agayn to my sentence.[138]

A col-fox,[139] ful of sly iniquitee,
That in the grove hadde woned[140] yeres three,
By heigh imaginacioun forn-cast,[141]
The same night thurgh-out the hegges brast
Into the yerd, ther[142] Chauntecleer the faire
Was wont, and eek his wyves, to repaire;
And in a bed of wortes[143] stille he lay,
Til it was passed undern[144] of the day,
Wayting his tyme on Chauntecleer to falle
As gladly doon thise homicydes alle,
That in awayt liggen to mordre men.
O false mordrer, lurking in thy den!
O newe Scariot, newe Genilon!
False dissimilour, O Greek Sinon,
That broghtest Troye al outrely to sorwe!
O Chauntecleer, acursed be that morwe,
That thou into that yerd flough[145] fro the bemes!
Thou were ful wel y-warned by thy dremes,
That thilke day was perilous to thee.
But what that God forwot[146] mot[147] nedes be,
After the opinioun of certeyn clerkis.
Witnesse on him, that any perfit clerk is,
That in scole is gret altercacioun
In this matere, and greet disputisoun,
And hath ben of an hundred thousand men.

[131] Delight.   [132] Befel.   [133] Accident.   [134] Gone.   [135] Write.   [136] Notorious fact.
[137] As.   [138] Thread of my story.   [139] Fox with black tips.   [140] Dwelt.
[141] Premeditated.   [142] Where.   [143] Herbs.   [144] About 10.30 A. M.   [145] Flew.
[146] Fore-knows.   [147] Must.

But I ne can not bulte it to the bren,[148]
As can the holy doctour Augustyn,
Or Boece, or the bishop Bradwardyn,
Whether that Goddes worthy forwiting[149]
Streyneth[150] me nedely[151] for to doon a thing,
(Nedely clepe[152] I simple necessitee);
Or elles, if free choys be graunted me
To do that same thing, or do it noght,
Though God forwoot it, er that it was wroght;
Or if his writing streyneth[150] nevere a del
But by necessitee condicionel.
I wol not han to do of swich matere;
My tale is of a cok, as ye may here,
That took his counseil of his wyf, with sorwe,
To walken in the yerd upon that morwe
That he had met the dreem, that I yow tolde.
Wommennes counseils been ful ofte colde;[153]
Wommannes counseil broghte us first to wo,
And made Adam fro paradys to go,
Ther as he was ful mery, and wel at ese.
But for I noot, to whom it mighte displese,
If I counseil of wommen wolde blame,
Passe over, for I seyde it in my game.
Rede auctours, wher they trete of swich matere,
And what thay seyn of wommen ye may here.
Thise been the cokkes wordes, and nat myne;
I can noon harme of no womman divyne.

    Faire in the sond, to bathe hire merily,
Lyth Pertelote, and alle hir sustres by,
Agayn[154] the sonne; and Chauntecleer so free
Song merier than the mermayde in the see;
For Phisiologus seith sikerly,
How that they singen wel and merily.
And so bifel, that as he caste his yë,
Among the wortes, on a boterflye,
He was war of this fox that lay ful lowe.
No-thing ne liste him thanne for to crowe,
But cryde anon, 'cok, cok,' and up he sterte,

---

[148] Sift it thoroughly.   [149] Fore-knowledge.
[150] Constraineth.   [151] Of necessity.   [152] Call.   [153] Disastrous.   [154] In.

As man that was affrayed in his herte.
For naturelly a beest desyreth flee
Fro his contrarie, if he may it see,
Though he never erst had seyn it with his yë.
   This Chauntecleer, whan he gan him espye
He wolde han fled, but that the fox anon
Seyde, 'Gentil sire, allas! wher wol ye gon?
Be ye affrayed of me that am your freend?
Now certes, I were worse than a feend,
If I to yow wolde harm or vileinye.
I am nat come your counseil for tespye;
But trewely, the cause of my cominge
Was only for to herkne how that ye singe.
For trewely ye have as mery a stevene,[155]
As eny aungel hath, that is in hevene;
Therwith ye han in musik more felinge
Than hadde Boece, or any that can singe.
My lord your fader (God his soule blesse!)
And eek your moder, of hir gentilesse,
Han in myn hous y-been, to my gret ese;
And certes, sire, ful fayn wolde I yow plese.
But for men speke of singing, I wol saye,
So mote[156] I brouke[157] wel myn eyen tweye,
Save yow, I herde nevere man so singe,
As dide your fader in the morweninge;
Certes, it was of herte, al that he song.
And for to make his voys the more strong,
He wolde so peyne him, that with both his yën
He moste winke, so loude he wolde cryen,
And stonden on his tiptoon ther-with-al,
And strecche forth his nekke long and smal.
And eek he was of swich discrecioun,
That ther nas no man in no regioun
That him in song or wisdom mighte passe.
I have weel rad in daun[158] Burnel the Asse,
Among his vers, how that ther was a cok,
For that a prestes sone yaf him a knok
Upon his leg, whyl he was yong and nyce,[159]
He made him for to lese[160] his benefyce.

[155] Pleasant a voice.   [156] May.   [157] Enjoy.   [158] Sir, Mr.   [159] Foolish.   [160] Lose.

But certeyn, ther nis no comparisoun
Bitwix the wisdom and discrecioun
Of your fader, and of his subtiltee.
Now singeth, sire, for seinte charitee,
Let se, conne ye your fader countrefete?' [161]
This Chauntecleer his winges gan to bete,
As man that coude his tresoun nat espye,
So was he ravisshed with his flaterye.

   Allas! ye lordes, many a fals flatour
Is in your courtes, and many a losengeour,[162]
That plesen yow wel more, by my feith,
Than he that soothfastnesse unto yow seith.
Redeth Ecclesiaste of flaterye;
Beth war, ye lordes, of hir trecherye.

   This Chauntecleer stood hye up-on his toos,
Strecching his nekke, and held his eyen cloos,
And gan to crowe loude for the nones;[163]
And daun[158] Russel the fox sterte up at ones,
And by the gargat[164] hente[165] Chauntecleer,
And on his bak toward the wode him beer,
For yet ne was ther no man that him sewed.[166]
O destinee, that mayst nat ben eschewed!
Allas, that Chauntecleer fleigh[167] fro the bemes!
Allas, his wyf ne roghte[168] nat of dremes!
And on a Friday fil al this meschaunce.
O Venus, that art goddesse of plesaunce,
Sin that thy servant was this Chauntecleer,
And in thy service dide al his poweer,
More for delyt, than world to multiplye,
Why woldestow suffre him on thy day to dye?
O Gaufred, dere mayster soverayn,
That, whan thy worthy king Richard was slayn
With shot, compleynedest his deth so sore,
Why ne hadde I now thy sentence and thy lore,
The Friday for to chide, as diden ye?
(For on a Friday soothly slayn was he.)
Than wolde I shewe yow how that I coude pleyne
For Chauntecleres drede, and for his peyne.

[161] Imitate.   [162] Flatterer.   [163] Extremely.   [164] Throat.   [165] Seized.   [166] Pursued.
[167] Flew.   [168] Recked.

Certes, swich cry ne lamentacioun
Was nevere of ladies maad, whan Ilioun
Was wonne, and Pirrus with his streite[169] swerd,
Whan he hadde hent[165] king Priam by the berd,
And slayn him (as saith us *Eneydos*),
As maden alle the hennes in the clos,[170]
Whan they had seyn of Chauntecleer the sighte.
But sovereynly[171] dame Pertelote shrighte,[172]
Ful louder than dide Hasdrubales wyf,
Whan that hir housbond hadde lost his lyf,
And that the Romayns hadde brend Cartage,
She was so ful of torment and of rage,
That wilfully into the fyr she sterte,
And brende hir-selven with a stedfast herte.
O woful hennes, right so cryden ye,
As, whan that Nero brende the citee
Of Rome, cryden senatoures wyves,
For that hir housbondes losten alle hir lyves;
Withouten gilt this Nero hath hem slayn.
Now wol I torne to my tale agayn:
    This sely[173] widwe, and eek hir doghtres two,
Herden thise hennes crye and maken wo,
And out at dores sterten thay anoon,
And syen[174] the fox toward the grove goon,
And bar upon his bak the cok away;
And cryden, 'Out! harrow! and weylaway!
Ha, ha, the fox!' and after him they ran,
And eek with staves many another man;
Ran Colle our dogge, and Talbot, and Gerland,
And Malkin, with a distaf in hir hand;
Ran cow and calf, and eek the verray hogges
So were they fered for berking of the dogges
And shouting of the men and wimmen eke,
They ronne so, hem thoughte hir herte breke.
They yelleden as feendes doon in helle;
The dokes cryden as men wolde hem quelle;[175]
The gees for fere flowen over the trees;
Out of the hyve cam the swarm of bees;
So hidous was the noyse, a! *benedicite!*

<hr>

[169] Naked.   [170] Yard.   [171] Especially.   [172] Shrieked.   [173] Harmless.   [174] Saw.   [175] Kill.

Certes, he Jakke Straw, and his meynee,[176]
Ne maden nevere shoutes half so shrille,
Whan that they wolden any Fleming kille,
As thilke day was maad upon the fox.
Of bras thay broghten bemes,[177] and of box,
Of horn, of boon, in whiche they blewe and pouped,[178]
And therwithal thay shryked and they houped;
It semed as that hevene sholde falle.
Now, gode men, I pray yow herkneth alle!
    Lo, how fortune turneth sodeinly
The hope and pryde eek of hir enemy!
This cok, that lay upon the foxes bak,
In al his drede, un-to the fox he spak,
And seyde, 'sire, if that I were as ye,
Yet sholde I seyn (as wis[179] God helpe me),
Turneth agayn, ye proude cherles alle!
A verray pestilence up-on yow falle!
Now am I come un-to this wodes syde,
Maugree[180] your heed, the cok shal heer abyde;
I wol him ete in feith, and that anon.'—
The fox answerde, 'In feith, it shal be don,'—
And as he spak that word, al sodeinly
This cok brak from his mouth deliverly,[181]
And heighe up-on a tree he fleigh anon.
And whan the fox saugh that he was y-gon,
'Allas!' quod he, 'O Chauntecleer, allas!
I have to yow,' quod he, 'y-doon trespas,
In-as-muche as I maked yow aferd,
Whan I yow hente,[182] and broghte out of the yerd;
But, sire, I dide it in no wikke entente;
Com doun, and I shal telle yow what I mente.
I shal seye sooth to yow, God help me so.'
'Nay than,' quod he, 'I shrewe[183] us bothe two,
And first I shrewe my-self, bothe blood and bones,
If thou bigyle me ofter than ones.
Thou shalt namore, thurgh thy flaterye
Do me to singe and winke with myn yë.
For he that winketh, whan he sholde see,

---

[176] Followers.   [177] Trumpets.   [178] Puffed.   [179] Surely.   [180] In spite of.
[181] Nimbly.   [182] Seized.   [183] Curse.

Al wilfully, God lat him never thee!' [184]
'Nay,' quod the fox, 'but God yeve him meschaunce,
That is so undiscreet of governaunce,
That iangleth whan he sholde holde his pees.'
    Lo, swich it is for to be recchelees,
And necligent, and truste on flaterye.
But ye that holden this tale a folye,
As of a fox, or of a cok and hen,
Taketh the moralitee, good men.
For seint Paul seith, that al that writen is,
To our doctryne it is y-write, y-wis.[185]
Taketh the fruyt, and lat the chaf be stille.
    Now, gode God, if that it be thy wille,
As seith my lord, so make us alle good men;
And bringe us to his heighe blisse. Amen.
            Here is ended the Nonne Preestes Tale.

Epilogue to the Nun's Priest's Tale

'Sir Nonne Preest,' our hoste seyde anoon,
'Y-blessed be thy breche, and every stoon!
This was a mery tale of Chauntecleer.
But by my trouthe, if thou were seculer,
Thy woldest been a trede-foul a-right.
For, if thou have corage as thou hast might,
Thee were nede of hennes, as I wene,
Ya, mo than seven tymes seventene.
See, whiche braunes hath this gentil Preest,
So greet a nekke, and swich a large breest!
He loketh as a sperhauk with his yën;
Him nedeth not his colour for to dyen
With brasil, ne with greyn of Portingale.
Now sire, faire falle yow for youre tale!'

3   ### The Douglas Tragedy[1]

"Rise up, rise up, now, Lord Douglas," she says,
    "And put on your armour so bright,

---

[184] Thrive.   [185] Certainly.
[1] This and the following ballads are of unknown authorship and of uncertain date.

Let it never be said that a daughter of thine
   Was married to a lord under night.

"Rise up, rise up, my seven bold sons,
   And put on your armour so bright,
And take better care of your youngest sister.
   For your eldest's awa[2] the last night."

He's mounted her on a milk-white steed,
   And himself on a dapple grey,
With a bugelet horn hung down by his side,
   And lightly they rode away.

Lord William lookit oer his left shoulder,
   To see what he could see,
And there he spy'd her seven brethren bold,
   Come riding over the lee.

"Light down, light down, Lady Margret," he said,
   "And hold my steed in your hand,
Until that against your seven brethren bold,
   And your father I mak a stand."

She held his steed in her milk-white hand,
   And never shed one tear,
Until that she saw her seven brethren fa,
   And her father hard fighting, who lovd her so dear.

"O hold your hand, Lord William!" she said,
   "For your strokes they are wondrous sair;
True lovers I can get many a ane,
   But a father I can never get mair."

O she's taen out her handkerchief,
   It was o the holland sae fine,
And aye she dighted[3] her father's bloody wounds,
   That were redder than the wine.

"O chuse, O chuse, Lady Margret," he said,
   "O whether will ye gang or bide?"

           [2] Away.   [3] Wiped.

"I'll gang, I'll gang, Lord William," she said,
"For ye have left me no other guide."

He's lifted her on a milk-white steed,
And himself on a dapple grey,
With a bugelet horn hung down by his side,
And slowly they baith rade away.

O they rade on, and on they rade,
And a' by the light of the moon,
Until they came to yon wan water,
And there they lighted down.

They lighted down to tak a drink
Of the spring that ran sae clear,
And down the stream ran his gude heart's blood,
And sair she gan to fear.

"Hold up, hold up, Lord William," she says,
"For I fear that you are slain;"
" 'Tis naething but the shadow of my scarlet cloak,
That shines in the water sae plain."

O they rade on, and on they rade,
And a' by the light of the moon,
Until they cam to his mother's ha door,
And there they lighted down.

"Get up, get up, lady mother," he says,
"Get up, and let me in!
Get up, get up, lady mother," he says,
"For this night my fair lady I've win.

"O mak my bed, lady mother," he says,
"O make it braid and deep,
And lay lady Margret close at my back,
And the sounder I will sleep."

Lord William was dead lang ere midnight,
Lady Margret lang ere day,
And all true lovers that go thegither,
May they have mair luck than they!

Lord William was buried in St. Mary's kirk,
  Lady Margret in Mary's quire;
Out o the lady's grave grew a bonny red rose,
  And out o the knight's a brier.

And they twa met, and they twa plat,[4]
  And fain they wad be near;
And a' the warld might ken right weel
  They were twa lovers dear.

But bye and rade the Black Douglas,
  And wow but he was rough!
For he pulld up the bonny brier,
  And flang't in St. Mary's Loch.

4 THE TWA SISTERS

THERE was twa sisters in a bowr,
  Binnorie, O Binnorie
There was twa sisters in a bowr,
  Binnorie, O Binnorie
There was twa sisters in a bowr,
There came a knight to be their wooer,
  By the bonny mill-dams of Binnorie.

He courted the eldest wi glove an ring,
But he lovd the youngest above a' thing.

He courted the eldest wi brotch an knife,
But lovd the youngest as his life.

The eldest she was vexed sair,
An much envi'd her sister fair.

Into her bowr she could not rest,
Wi grief an spite she almos brast.

Upon a morning fair an clear,
She cried upon her sister dear:

"O sister, come to yon sea stran,
An see our father's ships come to lan."

[4] Intertwined.

She's taen her by the milk-white han,
And led her down to yon sea stran.

The younges[t] stood upon a stane,
The eldest came an threw her in.

She tooke her by the middle sma,
And dashd her bonny back to the jaw.[1]

"O sister, sister, tak my han,
An Ise[2] mack you heir to a' my lan.

"O sister, sister, tak my middle,
An yes[3] get my goud[4] and my gouden girdle.

"O sister, sister, save my life,
An I swear Ise never be nae man's wife."

"Foul fa the han that I should tacke,
It twin'd[5] me an my wardles make.[6]

"Your cherry cheeks an yellow hair
Gars[7] me gae maiden for evermair."

Sometimes she sank, an sometimes she swam,
Till she came down yon bonny mill-dam.

O out it came the miller's son,
An saw the fair maid swimmin in.

"O father, father, draw your dam,
Here's either a mermaid or a swan."

The miller quickly drew the dam,
An there he found a drownd woman.

You coudna see her yellow hair
For gold and pearle that were so rare.

You coudna see her middle sma
For gouden girdle that was sae braw.

[1] Current. [2] I will. [3] Ye shall. [4] Gold. [5] Separated. [6] World's mate. [7] Causes.

You coudna see her fingers white,
For gouden rings that was sae gryte.[8]

An by there came a harper fine,
That harped to the king at dine.

When he did look that lady upon,
He sighd and made a heavy moan.

He's taen three locks o her yellow hair,
An wi them strung his harp sae fair.

The first tune he did play and sing,
Was, "Farewell to my father the king."

The nextin tune that he playd syne,[9]
Was, "Farewell to my mother the queen."

The lasten tune that he playd then,
Was, "Wae to my sister, fair Ellen."

EDWARD

"WHY dois your brand sae drap wi bluid,
      Edward, Edward,
Why dois your brand sae drap wi bluid,
 And why sae sad gang[1] yee O?"
"O I hae killed my hauke sae guid,[2]
      Mither, mither,
O I hae killed my hauke sae guid,
 And I had nae mair bot hee O."

"Your haukis bluid was nevir sae reid,
      Edward, Edward,
Your haukis bluid was nevir sae reid,
 My deir son I tell thee O."
"O I hae killed my reid-roan steid,
      Mither, mither,

[8] Great. [9] Then. [1] Go. [2] So good.

O I hae killed my reid-roan steid,
  That erst was sae fair and frie O."

"Your steid was auld, and ye hae gat mair,
                    Edward, **Edward,**
Your steid was auld, and ye hae gat mair,
  Sum other dule[3] ye drie[4] O."
"O I hae killed my fadir deir,
                Mither, mither,
O I hae killed my fadir deir,
  Alas, and wae is mee O!"

"And whatten[5] penance wul ye drie for that,
                Edward, Edward,
And whatten penance will ye drie for that?
  My deir son, now tell me O."
"Ile set my feit in yonder boat,
                Mither, mither,
Ile set my feit in yonder boat,
  And Ile fare ovir the sea O."

"And what wul ye doe wi your towirs and your ha,
                Edward, Edward?
And what wul you doe wi your towirs and your ha,
  That were sae fair to see O?"
"Ile let thame stand tul they doun fa,
                Mither, mither,
Ile let thame stand till they down fa,
  For here nevir mair maun I bee O."

"And what wul ye leive to your bairns and your wife,
                Edward, Edward?
And what wul ye leive to your bairns and your wife,
  Whan ye gang ovir the sea O?"
"The warldis room, late them beg thrae life,
                Mither, **mither,**
The warldis room, late them beg thrae life,
  For thame nevir mair wul I see O."

"And what wul ye leive to your ain mither deir,
                Edward, **Edward?**

[3] Sorrow.   [4] Suffer.   [5] What kind of.

And what wul ye leive to your ain mither deir?
　My deir son, now tell me O."
"The curse of hell frae me sall ye beir,
　　　　　　　　　　　　Mither, mither,
The curse of hell frae me sall ye beir,
　Sic counseils ye gave to me O."

6   BABYLON; OR, THE BONNIE BANKS O FORDIE

　　THERE were three ladies lived in a bower,
　　　Eh vow bonnie
　　And they went out to pull a flower,
　　　On the bonnie banks o Fordie

　　They hadna pu'ed a flower but ane,
　　When up started to them a banisht man.

　　He's taen the first sister by her hand,
　　And he's turned her round and made her stand.

　　"It's whether will ye be a rank robber's wife,
　　Or will ye die by my wee pen-knife?"

　　"It's I'll not be a rank robber's wife,
　　But I'll rather die by your wee pen-knife."

　　He's killed this may, and he's laid her by,
　　For to bear the red rose company.

　　He's taken the second ane by the hand,
　　And he's turned her round and made her stand.

　　"It's whether will ye be a rank robber's wife,
　　Or will ye die by my wee pen-knife?"

　　"I'll not be a rank robber's wife,
　　But I'll rather die by your wee pen-knife."

　　He's killed this may, and he's laid her by,
　　For to bear the red rose company.

He's taken the youngest ane by the hand,
And he's turned her round and made her stand.

Says, "Will ye be a rank robber's wife,
Or will ye die by my wee pen-knife?"

"I'll not be a rank robber's wife,
Nor will I die by your wee pen-knife.

"For I hae a brother in this wood,
And gin ye kill me, it's he'll kill thee."

"What's thy brother's name? come tell to me."
"My brother's name is Baby Lon."

"O sister, sister, what have I done!
O have I done this ill to thee!

"O since I've done this evil deed,
Good sall[1] never be seen o me."

He's taken out his wee pen-knife,
And he's twyned[2] himsel o his ain sweet life.

Hind Horn

In Scotland there was a babie born,
And his name it was called young Hind Horn.
    Lilie lal, etc. With a fal lal, etc.

He sent a letter to our king
That he was in love with his daughter Jean.

He's gien to her a silver wand,
With seven living lavrocks[3] sitting thereon.

She's gien[4] to him a diamond ring,
With seven bright diamonds set therein.

"When this ring grows pale and wan,
You may know by it my love is gane."

[1] Shall.   [2] Deprived.   [3] Larks.   [4] Given.

One day as he looked his ring upon,
He saw the diamonds pale and wan.

He left the sea and came to land,
And the first that he met was an old beggar man.

"What news, what news?" said young Hind Horn;
"No news, no news," said the old beggar man.

"No news," said the beggar, "no news at a',
But there's a wedding in the king's ha.

"But there is a wedding in the king's ha,
That has halden[5] these forty days and twa."

"Will ye lend me your begging coat?
And I'll lend you my scarlet cloak.

"Will you lend me your beggar's rung?[6]
And I'll gie you my steed to ride upon.

"Will you lend me your wig o hair,
To cover mine, because it is fair?"

The auld beggar man was bound for the mill,
But young Hind Horn for the king's hall.

The auld beggar man was bound for to ride,
But young Hind Horn was bound for the bride.

When he came to the king's gate,
He sought a drink for Hind Horn's sake.

The bride came down with a glass of wine,
When he drank out of the glass, and dropt in the ring.

"O got ye this by sea or land?
Or got ye it off a dead man's hand?"

"I got not it by sea, I got it by land,
And I got it, madam, out of your own hand."

[5] Been held.   [6] Staff.

"O I'll cast off my gowns of brown,
And beg wi you frae town to town.

"O I'll cast off my gowns of red,
And I'll beg wi you to win my bread."

"Ye needna cast off your gowns of brown,
For I'll make you lady o many a town.

"Ye needna cast off your gowns of red,
It's only a sham, the begging o my bread."

The bridegroom he had wedded the bride,
But young Hind Horn he took her to bed.

8   Lord Thomas and Fair Annet

Lord Thomas and Fair Annet
   Sate a' day on a hill;
Whan night was cum, and sun was sett,
   They had not talkt their fill.

Lord Thomas said a word in jest,
   Fair Annet took it ill:
"A, I will nevir wed a wife
   Against my ain friends' will."

"Gif ye wull nevir wed a wife,
   A wife wull neir wed yee:"
Sae he is hame to tell his mither,
   And knelt upon his knee.

"O rede,[1] O rede, mither," he says,
   "A gude rede gie[2] to mee;
O sall I tak the nut-browne bride,
   And let Faire Annet bee?"

"The nut-browne bride haes gowd[3] and gear,[4]
   Fair Annet she has gat nane;
And the little beauty Fair Annet haes
   O it wull soon be gane."

[1] Advice.　　[2] Give.　　[3] Gold.　　[4] Goods.

And he has till his brother gane:
  "Now, brother, rede[5] ye mee;
A, sall I marrie the nut-browne bride,
  And let Fair Annet bee?"

"The nut-browne bride has oxen, brother,
  The nut-browne bride has kye;[6]
I wad hae ye marrie the nut-browne bride,
  And cast Fair Annet bye."

"Her oxen may dye i the house, billie,
  And her kye into the byre,[7]
And I sall hae nothing to mysell
  Bot a fat fadge[8] by the fyre."

And he has till his sister gane:
  "Now, sister, rede ye mee;
O sall I marrie the nut-browne bride,
  And set Fair Annet free?"

"Ise rede ye tak Fair Annet, Thomas,
  And let the browne bride alane;
Lest ye sould sigh, and say, Alace,
  What is this we brought hame!"

"No, I will tak my mither's counsel,
  And marrie me owt o hand;[9]
And I will tak the nut-browne bride,
  Fair Annet may leive the land."

Up then rose Fair Annet's father,
  Twa hours or it wer day,
And he is gane into the bower
  Wherein Fair Annet lay.

"Rise up, rise up, Fair Annet," he says,
  "Put on your silken sheene;
Let us gae to St. Marie's kirke,
  And see that rich weddeen."

[5] Advise.   [6] Cattle.   [7] Cow-stable.   [8] Clumsy woman.   [9] At once.

"My maides, gae to my dressing-roome,
    And dress to me my hair;
Whaireir yee laid a plait before,
    See yee lay ten times mair.

"My maids, gae to my dressing-room,
    And dress to me my smock;
The one half is o the holland fine,
    The other o needle-work."

The horse Fair Annet rade upon,
    He amblit like the wind;
Wi siller[10] he was shod before,
    Wi burning gowd behind.

Four and twenty siller bells
    Wer a' tyed till his mane,
And yae tift o the norland wind,
    They tinkled ane by ane.

Four and twenty gay gude knichts
    Rade by Fair Annet's side,
And four and twenty fair ladies,
    As gin she had bin a bride.

And whan she cam to Marie's kirk,
    She sat on Marie's stean:
The cleading[11] that Fair Annet had on
    It skinkled[12] in their een.

And whan she cam into the kirk,
    She shimmerd like the sun;
The belt that was about her waist
    Was a' wi pearles bedone.[13]

She sat her by the nut-browne bride,
    And her een they wer sae clear,
Lord Thomas he clean forgat the bride,
    Whan Fair Annet drew near.

[10] Silver.   [11] Clothing.   [12] Sparkled.   [13] Ornamented.

He had a rose into his hand,
   He gae it kisses three,
And reaching by the nut-browne bride,
   Laid it on Fair Annet's knee.

Up then spak the nut-browne bride,
   She spak wi meikle spite:
"And whair gat ye that rose-water,
   That does mak yee sae white?"

"O I did get the rose-water
   Whair ye wull neir get nane,
For I did get that very rose-water
   Into my mither's wame." [14]

The bride she drew a long bodkin[15]
   Frae out her gay head-gear,
And strake Fair Annet unto the heart,
   That word spak nevir mair.

Lord Thomas he saw Fair Annet wex pale,
   And marvelit what mote[16] bee;
But whan he saw her dear heart's blude,
   A' wood-wroth[17] wexed hee.

He drew his dagger, that was sae sharp,
   That was sae sharp and meet,
And drave it into the nut-browne bride,
   That fell deid at his feit.

"Now stay for me, dear Annet," he sed,
   "Now stay, my dear," he cry'd;
Then strake the dagger untill his heart,
   And fell deid by her side.

Lord Thomas was buried without kirkwa,
   Fair Annet within the quiere,
And o the tane thair grew a birk,
   The other a bonny briere.

[14] Womb.   [15] Dagger.   [16] Might.   [17] Mad with anger.

And ay they grew, and ay they threw,
  As they wad faine be neare;
And by this ye may ken right weil
  They were twa luvers deare.

9 ## LOVE GREGOR

"O WHA will shoe my fu fair foot?
  And wha will glove my hand?
And wha will lace my middle jimp,[1]
  Wi the new made London band?

"And wha will kaim[2] my yellow hair,
  Wi the new made silver kaim?
And wha will father my young son,
  Till Love Gregor come hame?"

"Your father will shoe your fu fair foot,
  Your mother will glove your hand;
Your sister will lace your middle jimp
  Wi the new made London band.

"Your brother will kaim your yellow hair,
  Wi the new made silver kaim;
And the king of heaven will father your bairn,
  Till Love Gregor come haim."

"But I will get a bonny boat,
  And I will sail the sea,
For I maun gang[3] to Love Gregor,
  Since he canno come hame to me."

O she has gotten a bonny boat,
  And sailld the sa't sea fame;[4]
She langd to see her ain true-love,
  Since he could no come hame.

"O row your boat, my mariners,
  And bring me to the land,
For yonder I see my love's castle,
  Closs by the sa't sea strand."

[1] Slim. [2] Comb. [3] Must go. [4] Foam.

She has taen her young son in her arms,
  And to the door she 's gone,
And lang she's knocked and sair she ca'd,
  But answer got she none.

"O open the door, Love Gregor," she says,
  "O open, and let me in;
For the win blaws thro my yellow hair,
  And the rain draps oer my chin."

"Awa, awa, ye ill woman,
  You'r nae come here for good;
You'r but some witch, or wile warlock,[5]
  Or mer-maid of the flood."

"I am neither a witch nor a wile warlock,
  Nor mer-maid of the sea,
I am Fair Annie of Rough Royal;
  O open the door to me."

"Gin ye be Annie of Rough Royal—
  And I trust ye are not she—
Now tell me some of the love-tokens
  That past between you and me."

"O dinna you mind now, Love Gregor,
  When we sat at the wine,
How we changed the rings frae our fingers?
  And I can show thee thine.

"O yours was good, and good enneugh,
  But ay the best was mine;
For yours was o the good red goud,
  But mine o the dimonds fine.

"But open the door now, Love Gregor,
  O open the door I pray,
For your young son that is in my arms
  Will be dead ere it be day."

[5] Wizard.

"Awa, awa, ye ill woman,
    For here ye shanno win[6] in;
Gae drown ye in the raging sea,
    Or hang on the gallows-pin."

When the cock had crawn, and day did dawn,
    And the sun began to peep,
Then it raise him Love Gregor,
    And sair, sair did he weep.

"O I dreamd a dream, my mother dear,
    The thoughts o it gars[7] me greet,[8]
That Fair Annie of Rough Royal
    Lay cauld dead at my feet."

"Gin it be for Annie of Rough Royal
    That ye make a' this din,
She stood a' last night at this door,
    But I trow she wan[9] no in."

"O wae betide[10] ye, ill woman,
    An ill dead[10] may ye die!
That ye woudno open the door to her,
    Nor yet woud waken me."

O he has gone down to yon shore-side,
    As fast as he could fare;
He saw Fair Annie in her boat,
    But the wind it tossed her sair.

And "Hey, Annie!" and "How, Annie!
    O Annie, winna ye bide?"
But ay the mair that he cried Annie,
    The braider grew the tide.

And "Hey, Annie!" and "How, Annie!
    Dear Annie, speak to me!"
But ay the louder he cried Annie,
    The louder roard the sea.

[6] Shall not get.   [7] Makes.   [8] Weep.   [9] Got.   [10] Death.

The wind blew loud, the sea grew rough,
  And dashd the boat on shore;
Fair Annie floats on the raging sea,
  But her young son raise no more.

Love Gregor tare his yellow hair,
  And made a heavy moan;
Fair Annie's corpse lay at his feet,
  But his bonny young son was gone.

O cherry, cherry was her cheek,
  And gowden was her hair,
But clay cold were her rosy lips,
  Nae spark of life was there.

And first he's kissd her cherry cheek,
  And neist he's kissed her chin;
And saftly pressed her rosey lips,
  But there was nae breath within.

"O wae betide my cruel mother,
  And an ill dead may she die!
For she turnd my true-love frae my door,
  When she came sae far to me."

10

Bonny Barbara Allan

It was in and about the Martinmas time,
  When the green leaves were a falling,
That Sir John Græme, in the West Country,
  Fell in love with Barbara Allan.

He sent his man down through the town,
  To the place where she was dwelling:
"O haste and come to my master dear,
  Gin ye be Barbara Allan."

O hooly,[1] hooly rose she up,
  To the place where he was lying,
And when she drew the curtain by,
  "Young man, I think you're dying."

[1] Softly.

"O it's I'm sick, and very, very sick,
　And 'tis a' for Barbara Allan:"
"O the better for me ye's never be,
　Tho your heart's blood were a spilling.

"O dinna ye mind, young man," said she,
　"When ye was in the tavern a drinking,
That ye made the healths gae round and round,
　And slighted Barbara Allan?"

He turned his face unto the wall,
　And death was with him dealing:
"Adieu, adieu, my dear friends all,
　And be kind to Barbara Allan."

And slowly, slowly raise she up,
　And slowly, slowly left him,
And sighing said, she coud not stay,
　Since death of life had reft him.

She had not gane a mile but twa,
　When she heard the dead-bell ringing,
And every jow that the dead-bell gied,
　It cry'd, Woe to Barbara Allan!

"O mother, mother, make my bed!
　O make it saft and narrow!
Since my love died for me to-day,
　I'll die for him to-morrow."

11   The Gay Goss-Hawk

"O well 's me o my gay goss-hawk,
　That he can speak and flee;
He'll carry a letter to my love,
　Bring back another to me."

"O how can I your true-love ken,[1]
　Or how can I her know?
Whan frae her mouth I never heard couth,[2]
　Nor wi my eyes her saw."

　　　　[1] Know.　[2] Sound.

"O well sal ye my true-love ken,
   As soon as you her see;
For, of a' the flowrs in fair Englan,
   The fairest flowr is she.

"At even at my love's bowr-door
   There grows a bowing birk,[3]
An sit ye down and sing thereon,
   As she gangs to the kirk.

"An four-and-twenty ladies fair
   Will wash and go to kirk,
But well shall ye my true-love ken,
   For she wears goud on her skirt.

"An four and twenty gay ladies
   Will to the mass repair,
But well sal ye my true-love ken,
   For she wears goud on her hair."

O even at that lady's bowr-door
   There grows a bowin birk,
An he set down and sang thereon,
   As she ged to the kirk.

"O eet and drink, my marys[4] a',
   The wine flows you among,
Till I gang to my shot-window,
   An hear yon bonny bird's song.

"Sing on, sing on, my bonny bird,
   The song ye sang the streen,[5]
For I ken by your sweet singin
   You're frae my true-love sen."[6]

O first he sang a merry song,
   An then he sang a grave,
An then he peckd his feathers gray,
   To her the letter gave.

[3] Birch.   [4] Maids.   [5] Last night.   [6] Sent.

Ha, there's a letter frae your love,
  He says he sent you three;
He canno wait your love langer,
  But for your sake he'll die.

"He bids you write a letter to him;
  He says he's sent you five;
He canno wait your love langer,
  Tho you're the fairest woman alive."

"Ye bid him bake his bridal-bread,
  And brew his bridal-ale,
An I'll meet him in fair Scotlan
  Lang, lang or it be stale."

She's doen[7] her to her father dear,
  Fa'n low down on her knee:
"A boon, a boon, my father dear,
  I pray you, grant it me."

"Ask on, ask on, my daughter,
  An granted it sal be;
Except ae squire in fair Scotlan,
  An him you sall never see."

"The only boon, my father dear,
  That I do crave of thee,
Is, gin[8] I die in southin[9] lands,
  In Scotlan to bury me.

"An the firstin[10] kirk that ye come till,
  Ye gar the bells be rung,
An the nextin kirk that ye come till,
  Ye gar the mess be sung.

"An the thirdin kirk that ye come till,
  You deal gold for my sake,
An the fourthin kirk that ye come till,
  You tarry there till night."

[7] Gone.   [8] If.   [9] Southern.   [10] First.

She is doen her to her bigly bowr,[11]
　　As fast as she coud fare,
An she has tane a sleepy draught,
　　That she had mixed wi care.

She's laid her down upon her bed,
　　An soon she's fa'n asleep,
And soon oer every tender limb
　　Cauld death began to creep.

Whan night was flown, an day was come,
　　Nae ane that did her see
But thought she was as surely dead
　　As ony lady coud be.

Her father an her brothers dear
　　Gard[12] make to her a bier;
The tae[13] half was o guid red gold,
　　The tither[14] o silver clear.

Her mither an her sisters fair
　　Gard work for her a sark;
The tae half was o cambrick fine,
　　The tither o needle wark.

The firstin kirk that they came till,
　　They gard the bells be rung,
An the nextin kirk that they came till,
　　They gard the mess be sung.

The thirdin kirk that they came till,
　　They dealt gold for her sake,
An the fourthin kirk that they came till,
　　Lo, there they met her make!

"Lay down, lay down the bigly bier.
　　Lat me the dead look on;"
Wi cheery cheeks and ruby lips
　　She lay an smil'd on him.

[11] Handsome chamber.　　[12] Caused.　　[13] One.　　[14] Other.

"O ae sheave[15] o your bread, true-love,
  An ae glass o your wine,
For I hae fasted for your sake
  These fully days is nine.

"Gang hame, gang hame, my seven bold brothers,
  Gang hame and sound your horn;
An ye may boast in southin lans
  Your sister's playd you scorn."

12   THE THREE RAVENS

THERE were three rauens sat on a tree,
  Downe a downe, hay down, hay downe
There were three rauens sat on a tree,
  With a downe
There were three rauens sat on a tree,
They were as blacke as they might be.
  With a downe derrie, derrie, derrie, downe, downe.

The one of them said to his mate,
"Where shall we our breakefast take?"

"Downe in yonder greene field,
There lies a knight slain vnder his shield.

"His hounds they lie downe at his feete,
So well they can their master keepe.

"His haukes they flie so eagerly,
There's no fowle dare him come nie." [1]

Downe there comes a fallow doe,
As great with yong as she might goe.

She lift vp his bloudy hed,
And kist his wounds that were so red.

She got him vp vpon her backe,
And carried him to earthen lake.[2]

                 [15] Slice.   [1] Nigh.   [2] Pit.

She buried him before the prime,
She was dead herselfe ere euen-song time.

God send euery gentleman,
Such haukes, such hounds, and such a leman.[3]

13   THE TWA CORBIES[1]

As I was walking all alane,
I heard two corbies making a mane;
The tane unto the t' other say,
"Where sall we gang and dine to-day?"

"In behint yon auld fail[2] dyke,
I wot[3] there lies a new slain knight;
And naebody kens[4] that he lies there,
But his hawk, his hound, and lady fair.

"His hound is to the hunting gane,
His hawk to fetch the wild-fowl hame,
His lady's ta'en another mate,
So we may mak our dinner sweet.

"Ye'll sit on his white hause-bane,[5]
And I'll pike out his bonny blue een;
Wi ae lock o his gowden hair
We'll theek[6] our nest when it grows bare.

"Mony a one for him makes mane,[7]
But nane sall ken where he is gane;
Oer his white banes when they are bare,
The wind sall blaw for evermair."

14   SIR PATRICK SPENCE

THE king sits in Dumferling toune,
    Drinking the blude-reid wine:
"O whar will I get guid sailor,
    To sail this schip of mine?"

---

[3] Sweetheart.   [1] Crows.   [2] Turf.   [3] Know.   [4] Knows.   [5] Neck-bone.
[6] Thatch.   [7] Moan.

Up and spak an eldern[1] knicht,
  Sat at the kings richt kne:
"Sir Patrick Spence is the best sailor
  That sails upon the se."

The king has written a braid letter,
  And signd it wi his hand,
And sent it to Sir Patrick Spence,
  Was walking on the sand.

The first line that Sir Patrick red,
  A loud lauch lauched he;
The next line that Sir Patrick red,
  The teir blinded his ee.

"O wha is this has don this deid,
  This ill deid don to me,
To send me out this time o' the yeir,
  To sail upon the se!

"Mak haste, mak haste, my mirry men all,
  Our guid schip sails the morne:"
"O say na sae, my master deir,
  For I feir a deadlie storme.

"Late late yestreen I saw the new moone,
  Wi the auld moone in her arme,
And I feir, I feir, my deir master,
  That we will cum to harme."

O our Scots nobles wer richt laith
  To weet their cork-heild schoone;
Bot lang owre a' the play wer play'd,
  Thair hats they swam aboone.

O lang, lang may their ladies sit,
  Wi thair fans into their hand,
Or eir they se Sir Patrick Spence
  Cum sailing to the land.

[1] Old.

O lang, lang may the ladies stand,
  Wi thair gold kems in their hair,
Waiting for thair ain deir lords,
  For they'll se thame na mair.

Haf owre,[2] half owre to Aberdour,
  It's fiftie fadom deip,
And thair lies guid Sir Patrick Spence,
  Wi the Scots lords at his feit.

15   THOMAS RYMER AND THE QUEEN OF ELFLAND

TRUE THOMAS lay oer yond grassy bank,
  And he beheld a ladie gay,
A ladie that was brisk and bold,
  Come riding oer the fernie brae.[1]

Her skirt was of the grass-green silk,
  Her mantel of the velvet fine,
At ilka tett[2] of her horse's mane
  Hung fifty silver bells and nine.

True Thomas he took off his hat,
  And bowed him low down till his knee:
"All hail, thou mighty Queen of Heaven!
  For your peer on earth I never did see."

"O no, O no, True Thomas," she says,
  "That name does not belong to me;
I am but the queen of fair Elfland,
  And I'm come here for to visit thee.

"But ye maun go wi me now, Thomas,
  True Thomas, ye maun go wi me,
For ye maun[3] serve me seven years,
  Thro weel or wae as may chance to be."

She turned about her milk-white steed,
  And took True Thomas up behind,
And aye wheneer her bridle rang,
  The steed flew swifter than the wind.

[2] Over.   [1] Brow (of a hill).   [2] Lock.   [3] Must.

For forty days and forty nights
 He wade thro red blude to the knee,
And he saw neither sun nor moon,
 But heard the roaring of the sea.

O they rade on, and further on,
 Until they came to a garden green:
"Light down, light down, ye ladie free,
 Some of that fruit let me pull to thee."

"O no, O no, True Thomas," she says,
 "That fruit maun not be touched by thee,
For a' the plagues that are in hell
 Light on the fruit of this countrie.

"But I have a loaf here in my lap,
 Likewise a bottle of claret wine,
And now ere we go farther on,
 We 'll rest a while, and ye may dine."

When he had eaten and drunk his fill,
 "Lay down your head upon my knee,"
The lady sayd, "ere we climb yon hill,
 And I will show you fairlies[4] three.

"O see not ye yon narrow road,
 So thick beset wi thorns and briers?
That is the path of righteousness,
 Tho after it but few enquires.

"And see not ye that braid braid road,
 That lies across yon lillie leven[5]?
That is the path of wickedness,
 Tho some call it the road to heaven.

"And see not ye that bonnie road,
 Which winds about the fernie brae?
That is the road to fair Elfland,
 Whe[re] you and I this night maun gae.

   [4] Wonders. [5] Meadow.

"But Thomas, ye maun hold your tongue,
    Whatever you may hear or see,
For gin ae word you should chance to speak,
    You will neer get back to your ain countrie."

He has gotten a coat of the even cloth,
    And a pair of shoes of velvet green,
And till seven years were past and gone
    True Thomas on earth was never seen.

16   SWEET WILLIAM'S GHOST

WHAN bells war rung, an mass was sung,
    A wat a' man to bed were gone,
Clark Sanders came to Margret's window,
    With mony a sad sigh and groan.

"Are ye sleeping, Margret," he says,
    "Or are ye waking, presentlie?
Give me my faith and trouthe again,
    A wat,[1] trew-love, I gied[2] to thee."

"Your faith and trouth ye's[3] never get,
    Nor our trew love shall never twain,[4]
Till ye come with me in my bower,
    And kiss me both cheek and chin."

"My mouth it is full cold, Margret,
    It has the smell now of the ground;
And if I kiss thy comely mouth,
    Thy life-days will not be long.

"Cocks are crowing a merry mid-larf,[5]
    I wat the wild fule[6] boded day;
Gie me my faith and trouthe again,
    And let me fare me on my way."

"Thy faith and trouth thou shall na get,
    Nor our trew love shall never twin,[4]
Till ye tell me what comes of women
    A wat[1] that dy's in strong travelling."

[1] I know.   [2] Gave.   [3] Ye shall.   [4] Part.   [5] *Unintelligible.*   [6] Fowl.

"Their beds are made in the heavens high,
   Down at the foot of our good Lord's knee,
Well set about wi gilly-flowers,
   A wat sweet company for to see.

"O cocks are crowing a merry midd-larf,
   A wat the wilde foule boded day;
The salms of Heaven will be sung,
   And ere now I'le be misst away."

Up she has tain a bright long wand,
   And she has straked[7] her trouth thereon;
She has given (it) him out at the shot-window,[8]
   Wi many a sad sigh and heavy groan.

"I thank you, Margret, I thank you, Margret,
   And I thank you hartilie;
Gine[9] ever the dead come for the quick,
   Be sure, Margret, I'll come again for thee."

It's hose an shoon and gound[10] alane
   She clame the wall and followed him,
Until she came to a green forest,
   On this she lost the sight of him.

"Is there any room at your head, Sanders?
   Is there any room at your feet?
Or any room at your twa sides?
   Whare fain, fain woud I sleep."

"Their is na room at my head, Margret,
   Their is na room at my feet;
There is room at my twa sides,
   For ladys for to sleep.

"Cold meal[11] is my covering owre,
   But an my winding sheet;
My bed it is full low, I say,
   Down among the hongerey worms I sleep.

[7] Stroked.   [8] A window opening out on a hinge; or a bow-window.   [9] If.
[10] Stockings and shoes and gown.   [11] Mould.

"Cold meal is my covering owre,
    But an my winding sheet;
The dew it falls na sooner down
    Then ay it is full weet."

17   THE WIFE OF USHER'S WELL

THERE lived a wife at Usher's Well,
    And a wealthy wife was she;
She had three stout and stalwart sons,
    And sent them oer the sea.

They hadna been a week from her,
    A week but barely ane,
Whan word came to the carline[1] wife
    That her three sons were gane.

They hadna been a week from her,
    A week but barely three,
Whan word came to the carlin wife
    That her sons she'd never see.

"I wish the wind may never cease,
    Nor fashes[2] in the flood,
Till my three sons come hame to me,
    In earthly flesh and blood."

It fell about the Martinmass,
    When nights are lang and mirk.[3]
The carlin wife's three sons came hame,
    And their hats were o the birk.[4]

It neither grew in syke[5] nor ditch,
    Nor yet in ony sheugh;[6]
But at the gates o Paradise,
    That birk grew fair eneugh.

"Blow up the fire, my maidens,
    Bring water from the well;
For a' my house shall feast this night,
    Since my three sons are well."

[1] Old woman.   [2] Storms(?).   [3] Dark.   [4] Birch.   [5] Trench.   [6] Furrow.

And she has made to them a bed,
  She's made it large and wide,
And she's taen her mantle her about,
  Sat down at the bed-side.

  .   .   .   .   .   .

Up then crew the red, red cock,
  And up and crew the gray;
The eldest to the youngest said,
  " 'Tis time we were away."

The cock he hadna crawd but once,
  And clappd his wings at a',
When the youngest to the eldest said,
  "Brother, we must awa."

"The cock doth craw, the day doth daw,
  The channerin[7] worm doth chide;
Gin we be mist out o our place,
  A sair pain we maun bide.

"Lie still, lie still but a little wee while,
  Lie still but if we may;
Gin my mother should miss us when she wakes,
  She'll go mad ere it be day."

"Faer ye weel, my mother dear!
  Fareweel to barn and byre!
And fare ye weel, the bonny lass
  That kindles my mother's fire!"

18   HUGH OF LINCOLN

Four and twenty bonny boys
  Were playing at the ba,[1]
And by it came him sweet Sir Hugh,
  And he playd oer them a'.

He kicked the ba with his right foot,
  And catchd it wi his knee,

[7] Fretting.   [1] Ball.

And throuch-and-thro the Jew's window
  He gard the bonny ba flee.

He's doen him to the Jew's castell,
  And walkd it round about;
And there he saw the Jew's daughter,
  At the window looking out.

"Throw down the ba, ye Jew's daughter,
  Throw down the ba to me!"
"Never a bit," says the Jew's daughter,
  "Till up to me come ye."

"How will I come up? How can I come up?
  How can I come to thee?
For as ye did to my auld father,
  The same ye'll do me."

She's gane till her father's garden,
  And pu'd an apple red and green;
'Twas a' to wyle[2] him sweet Sir Hugh,
  And to entice him in.

She's led him in through ae dark door,
  And sae has she thro nine;
She's laid him on a dressing-table,
  And stickit him like a swine.

And first came out the thick, thick blood,
  And syne came out the thin,
And syne came out the bonny heart's blood;
  There was nae mair within.

She's rowd[3] him in a cake o lead,
  Bade him lie still and sleep;
She's thrown him in Our Lady's draw-well,
  Was fifty fathom deep.

When bells were rung, and mass was sung,
  And a' the bairns came hame,

<hr />

² Entice.   ³ Rolled.

When every lady gat hame her son,
  The Lady Maisry gat nane.

She's taen her mantle her about,
  Her coffer by the hand,
And she's gane out to seek her son,
  And wanderd oer the land.

She's doen her to the Jew's castell,
  Where a' were fast asleep:
"Gin ye be there, my sweet Sir Hugh,
  I pray you to me speak."

She's doen[4] her to the Jew's garden,
  Thought he had been gathering fruit:
"Gin[5] ye be there, my sweet Sir Hugh,
  I pray you to me speak."

She heard Our Lady's deep draw-well,
  Was fifty fathom deep:
"Whareer ye be, my sweet Sir Hugh,
  I pray you to me speak."

"Gae hame, gae hame, my mither dear,
  Prepare my winding sheet,
And at the back o merry Lincoln
  The morn I will you meet."

Now Lady Maisry is gane hame,
  Made him a winding sheet,
And at the back o merry Lincoln
  The dead corpse did her meet.

And a' the bells o merry Lincoln
  Without men's hands were rung,
And a' the books o merry Lincoln
  Were read without man's tongue,
And neer was such a burial
  Sin Adam's days begun.

[4] Gone.   [5] If.

Young Bicham

In London city was Bicham born,
   He longd strange countries for to see,
But he was taen by a savage Moor,
   Who handld him right cruely.

For thro his shoulder he put a bore,[1]
   An thro the bore has pitten[2] a tree,[3]
An he's gard[4] him draw the carts o wine,
   Where horse and oxen had wont to be.

He's casten [him] in a dungeon deep,
   Where he coud neither hear nor see;
He's shut him up in a prison strong,
   And he's handld him right cruely.

O this Moor he had but ae daughter,
   I wot her name was Shusy Pye;
She's doen her to the prison-house,
   And she's calld Young Bicham one word by.

"O hae ye ony lands or rents,
   Or citys in your ain country,
Coud free you out of prison strong,
   An coud mantain a lady free?"

"O London city is my own,
   An other citys twa or three
Coud loose me out o prison strong,
   An coud mantain a lady free."

O she has bribed her father's men
   Wi meikle goud and white money,
She's gotten the key o the prison doors,
   An she has set Young Bicham free.

She's gi'n him a loaf o good white bread,
   But an a flask o Spanish wine,

[1] Hole.   [2] Put.   [3] Piece of wood.   [4] Made.

And she bad him mind on[5] the ladie's love
   That sae kindly freed him out o pine.[6]

"Go set your foot on good ship-board,
   An haste you back to your ain country,
An before that seven years has an end,
   Come back again, love, and marry me."

It was lang or seven years had an end
   She longd fu sair her love to see;
She's set her foot on good ship-board,
   An turnd her back on her ain country.

She's saild up, so has she doun,
   Till she came to the other side;
She's landed at Young Bicham's gates,
   An I hop this day she sal be his bride.

"Is this Young Bicham's gates?" says she,
   "Or is that noble prince within?"
"He's up the stairs wi his bonny bride,
   An monny a lord and lady wi him."

"O has he taen a bonny bride,
   An has he clean forgotten me!"
An sighing said that gay lady,
   "I wish I were in my ain country!"

But she's pitten[7] her han in her pocket,
   An gin the porter guineas three;
Says, "Take ye that, ye proud porter,
   An bid the bridegroom speak to me."

O whan the porter came up the stair,
   He's fa'n[8] low down upon his knee:
"Won[9] up, won up, ye proud porter,
   An what makes a' this courtesy?"

"O I've been porter at your gates
   This mair nor seven years an three,

[5] Recall.   [6] Suffering.   [7] Put.   [8] Fallen.   [9] Get.

But there is a lady at them now
    The like of whom I never did see.

"For on every finger she has a ring,
    An on the mid-finger she has three,
An there's as meikle goud aboon her brow
    As woud buy an earldome o lan to me."

Then up it started Young Bicham,
    An sware so loud by Our Lady,
"It can be nane but Shusy Pye,
    That has come oer the sea to me."

O quickly ran he down the stair,
    O fifteen steps he has made but three;
He's tane[10] his bonny love in his arms,
    An a wot[11] he kissed her tenderly.

"O hae[12] you taen a bonny bride?
    An hae you quite forsaken me?
An hae ye quite forgotten her
    That gae[13] you life an liberty?"

She's lookit oer her left shoulder
    To hide the tears stood in her ee;
"Now fare thee well, Young Bicham," she says,
    "I'll strive to think nae mair on thee."

"Take back your daughter, madam," he says,
    "An a double dowry I'll gi her wi;
For I maun[14] marry my first true love,
    That's done and suffered so much for me."

He's take his bonny love by the han,
    And led her to yon fountain stane;
He's changd her name frae Shusy Pye,
    An he's cald her his bonny love, Lady Jane.

[10] Taken.   [11] I know.   [12] Have.   [13] Gave.   [14] Must.

20   ## GET UP AND BAR THE DOOR

It fell about the Martinmas time,
  And a gay time it was then,
When our good wife got puddings to make,
  And she's boild them in the pan.

The wind sae cauld blew south and north,
  And blew into the floor;
Quoth our goodman to our goodwife,
  "Gae[1] out and bar the door."

"My hand is in my hussyfskap,[2]
  Goodman, as ye may see;
An it shoud nae be barrd this hundred year,
  It's no be barrd for me."

They made a paction tween them twa,
  They made it firm and sure,
That the first word whaeer shoud speak,
  Shoud rise and bar the door.

Then by there came two gentlemen,
  At twelve o'clock at night,
And they could neither see house nor hall,
  Nor coal nor candle-light.

"Now whether is this a rich man's house,
  Or whether is it a poor?"
But neer a word wad ane o them speak,
  For barring of the door.

And first they ate the white puddings,
  And then they ate the black;
Tho muckle thought the goodwife to hersel,
  Yet neer a word she spake.

Then said the one unto the other,
  "Here, man, tak ye my knife;
Do ye tak aff the auld man's beard,
  And I'll kiss the goodwife."

          [1] Go.   [2] Housewifery.

"But there's nae water in the house,
    And what shall we do than?"
"What ails thee at the pudding-broo,[3]
    That boils into the pan?"

O up then started our goodman,
    An angry man was he:
"Will ye kiss my wife before my een,
    And scad[4] me wi pudding-bree?"

Then up and started our goodwife,
    Gied three skips on the floor:
"Goodman, you've spoken the foremost **word**,
    Get up and bar the door."

21   THE BATTLE OF OTTERBURN

IT fell about the Lammus time,
    When the muir-men won[1] their hay,
That the doughty Earl Douglas went
    Into England to catch a prey.

He chose the Gordons and the Graemes,
    With the Lindsays light and gay;
But the Jardines wadna wi him ride,
    And they rued it to this day.

And he has burnt the dales o Tine
    And part of Almonshire.
And three good towers on Roxburgh fells
    He left them all on fire.

Then he marched up to Newcastle,
    And rode it round about:
"O whae's the lord of this castle,
    Or whae's the lady o't?"

But up spake proud Lord Piercy then,
    And O but he spake hie![2]

---

[3] Water in which the puddings were boiled.   [4] Scald.
[1] Dry, make.   [2] High.

"I am the lord of this castle,
    And my wife's the lady gaye."

"If you are lord of this castle,
    Sae weel it pleases me;
For ere I cross the borden again
    The ane of us shall die."

He took a lang speir in his hand,
    Was made of the metal free,
And for to meet the Douglas then
    He rode most furiously.

But O how pale his lady lookd,
    Frae off the castle wa,
When down before the Scottish spear
    She saw brave Piercy fa!

How pale and wan his lady lookd,
    Frae off the castle hieght,
When she beheld her Piercy yield
    To Doughty Douglas' might!

"Had we twa been upon the green,
    And never an eye to see,
I should have had ye flesh and fell;
    But your sword shall gae wi me."

"But gae[3] you up to Otterburn,
    And there wait dayes three,
And if I come not ere three days' end
    A fause[4] lord ca ye me."

"The Otterburn's a bonny burn,
    'Tis pleasant there to be,
But there is naught at Otterburn
    To feed my men and me.

"The deer rins wild owr hill and dale,
    The birds fly wild frae tree to tree,

3 Go.   4 False.

And there is neither bread nor kale[5]
  To fend[6] my men and me.

"But I will stay at Otterburn,
  Where you shall welcome be;
And if ye come not at three days' end
  A coward I'll ca thee."

"Then gae your ways to Otterburn,
  And there wait dayes three;
And if I come not ere three days' end
  A coward ye's ca me."

They lighted high on Otterburn,
  Upon the bent[7] so brown,
They lighted high on Otterburn,
  And threw their pallions[8] down.

And he that had a bonny boy
  Sent his horses to grass,
And he that had not a bonny boy,
  His ain[9] servant he was.

But up then spak a little page,
  Before the peep of the dawn;
"O waken ye, waken ye, my good lord,
  For Piercy's hard at hand!"

"Ye lie, ye lie, ye loud liar,
  Sae loud I hear ye lie!
The Piercy hadna men yestreen[10]
  To dight[11] my men and me.

"But I have seen a dreary dream;
  Beyond the isle o Sky;
I saw a dead man won the fight,
  And I think that man was I."

He belted on his good broad-sword
  And to the field he ran,

5 Broth.   6 Support.   7 Grassy field.   8 Pavilions.   9 Own.   10 Last night.
11 Dress; attack.

Where he met wi the proud Piercy,
   And a' his goodly train.

When Piercy wi the Douglas met,
   I wat he was right keen;
They swakked[12] their swords till sair they swat,
   And the blood ran them between.

But Piercy wi his good broad-sword,
   Was made o the metal free,
Has wounded Douglas on the brow
   Till backward he did flee.

Then he calld on his little page,
   And said, Run speedily,
And bring my ain dear sister's son,
   Sir Hugh Montgomery.

[Who, when he saw the Douglas bleed,
   His heart was wonder wae:
"Now, by my sword, that haughty lord
   Shall rue before he gae."

"My nephew bauld," the Douglas said,
   "What boots the death of ane?[13]
Last night I dreamed a dreary dream,
   And I ken the day's thy ain.[14]

"I dreamd I saw a battle fought
   Beyond the isle o Sky,
When lo! a dead man wan the field,
   And I thought that man was I.

"My wound is deep, I fain wad sleep,
   Nae mair I'll fighting see;
Gae lay me in the breaken[15] bush
   That grows on yonder lee.[16]

"But tell na ane of my brave men
   That I lye bleeding wan,

[12] Smote.   [13] One.   [14] Own.   [15] Fern.   [16] Meadow.

But let the name of Douglas still
  Be shouted in the van.

"And bury me here on this lee,
  Beneath the blooming briar,
And never let a mortal ken
  A kindly Scot lyes here."

He liftit up that noble lord,
  Wi the saut tear in his ee,
And hid him in the breaken bush,
  On yonder lily lee.

The moon was clear, the day drew near,
  The spears in flinters flew,
But mony gallant Englishman
  Ere day the Scotsman slew.

Sir Hugh Montgomery he rode
  Thro all the field in sight,
And loud the name of Douglas still
  He urgd wi a' his might.

The Gordons good, in English blood
  They steeped their hose and shoon,
The Lindsays flew like fire about,
  Till a' the fray was doon.]

When stout Sir Hugh wi Piercy met,
  I wat he was right fain;
They swakked their swords till sair they swat,
  And the blood ran down like rain.

"O yield thee, Piercy," said Sir Hugh,
  "O yield, or ye shall die!"
"Fain wad I yield," proud Piercy said,
  "But neer to loun[17] like thee."

"Thou shalt not yield to knave nor loun,
  Nor shalt thou yield to me;
  _____
  [17] Fellow.

But yield thee to the breaken bush
   That grows on yonder lee."

"I will not yield to bush or brier,
   Nor will I yield to thee;
But I will yield to Lord Douglas,
   Or Sir Hugh Montgomery."

[When Piercy knew it was Sir Hugh,
   He fell low on his knee,
But soon he raisd him up again,
   Wi mickle courtesy.]

He left not an Englishman on the field

.   .   .   .

That he hadna either killd or taen
   Ere his heart's blood was cauld.

22   CHEVY CHASE

God prosper long our noble k*ing,*
   our liffes[1] and saftyes all!
A woefull hunting once there did
   in Cheuy Chase befall.

To dr*i*ue the deere w*i*th hound and horne
   Erle Pearcy took the way:
The child may rue *tha*t is vnborne
   the hunting of *tha*t day!

The stout Erle of Northumberland
   a vow to God did make
His pleasure in the Scottish woods
   three som*m*ers days to take,

The cheefest harts in Cheuy C[h]ase
   to kill and beare away:
These tydings to Erle Douglas came
   in Scottland, where he lay.

[1] Lives.

Who sent Erle Pearcy present word
  he would prevent his sport;
The English erle, not fearing that,
  did to the woods resort,

With fifteen hundred bowmen bold,
  All chosen men of might,
Who knew ffull well in time of neede
  to ayme their shafts arright.

The gallant greyhound[s] swiftly ran
  to chase the fallow deere;
On Munday they began to hunt,
  ere daylight did appeare.

And long before high noone the had
  a hundred fat buckes slaine;
Then hauing dined, the drouyers went
  to rouze the deare againe.

The bowmen mustered on the hills,
  well able to endure;
Theire backsids all with speciall care
  *tha*t day were guarded sure.

The hounds ran swiftly through the woods
  the nimble deere to take,
*Tha*t with their cryes the hills and dales
  an eccho shrill did make.

Lord Pearcy to the querry[2] went
  to view the tender deere;
Quoth he, "Erle Douglas promised once
  this day to meete me heere;

"But if I thought he wold not come,
  noe longer wold I stay."
With *tha*t a braue younge gentlman
  thus to the erle did say:

2 Slaughtered game.

"Loe, yonder doth Erle Douglas come,
   hys men in armour bright;
Full twenty hundred Scottish speres
   all marching in our sight.

"All men of pleasant Tiuydale,
   fast by the riuer Tweede:"
"O ceaze your sportts!" Erle Pearcy said,
   "and take your bowes with speede.

"And now with me, my countrymen,
   your courage forth advance!
For there was neuer champion yett,
   in Scottland nor in Ffrance,

"*That* euer did on horsbacke come,
   [but], and if my hap it were,
I durst encounter man for man,
   with him to break a spere."

Erle Douglas on his milke-white steede,
   most like a baron bold,
Rode formost of his company,
   whose armor shone like gold.

"Shew me," sayd hee, "whose men you bee
   that hunt soe boldly heere,
That without my consent doe chase
   and kill my fallow deere."

The first man *that* did answer make
   was noble Pearcy hee,
Who sayd, "Wee list not to declare
   nor shew whose men wee bee;

"Yett wee will spend our deerest blood
   thy cheefest harts to slay."
Then Douglas swore a solempne oathe,
   and thus in rage did say:

"Ere thus I will outbraued bee,
    one of vs tow shall dye;
I know thee well, an erle thou art;
    Lord Pearcy, soe am I.

"But trust me, Pearcye, pittye it were,
    and great offence, to kill
Then any of these our guiltlesse men,
    for they haue done none ill.

"Let thou and I the battell trye,
    and set our men aside:"
"Accurst bee [he!]" Erle Pearcye sayd,
    "by whome it is denyed."

Then stept a gallant squire forth—
    Witherington was his name—
Who said, "I wold not haue it told
    To Henery our *king,* for shame,

"*That* ere my captaine fought on foote,
    and I stand looking on.
You bee two Erles," q*uo*th Witherington,
    "and I a squier alone;

"I'le doe the best *that* doe I may,
    while I haue power to stand;
While I haue power to weeld my sword,
    I'lt fight w*i*th hart and hand."

Our English archers bent their bowes;
    their harts were good and trew;
Att the first flight of arrowes sent,
    full foure score Scotts the slew.

To driue the deere w*i*th hound and horne,
    Douglas bade[3] on the bent;
Two captaines moued w*i*th mickle[4] might,
    their speres to shiuers went.

         [3] Abode.   [4] Great.

They closed full fast on eue*r*ye side
  noe slackness there was found,
But many a gallant gentleman
  lay gasping on the ground.

O Christ! it was great greeue[5] to see
  how eche man chose his spere,
And how the blood out of their brests
  did gush like water cleare.

At last these two stout erles did meet,
  like captaines of great might;
Like lyons woode[6] they layd on lode;
  the made a cruell fight.

The fought vntil they both did sweat,
  w*i*th swords of tempered steele,
Till blood downe their cheekes like raine
  the trickling downe did feele.

"O yeeld thee, Pearcye!" Douglas sayd,
  "And in faith I will thee bringe
Where thou shall high advanced bee
  by Iames our Scottish k*i*ng.

"Thy ransome I will freely giue,
  and this report of thee,
Thou art the most couragious k*nigh*t
  [that ever I did see.]"

"Noe, Douglas!" q*u*oth Erle Percy then,
  "thy p*r*ofer I doe scorne;
I will not yeelde to any Scott
  *tha*t eu*er* yett was borne!"

W*i*th *th*at there came an arrow keene,
  out of an English bow,
Which stroke Erle Douglas on the brest
  a deepe and deadlye blow.

  [5] Grief.   [6] Mad.

Who neu*er* sayd more words than these;
  "Fight on, my merry men all!
For why, my life is att [an] end,
  lo*rd* Pearcy sees my fall."

Then leauing liffe, Erle Pearcy tooke
  the dead man by the hand;
Who said, "Erle Dowglas, for thy life,
  Wold I had lost my land!

"O Christ! my verry hart doth bleed
  for sorrow for thy sake,
For sure, a more redoubted k*nigh*t
  mischance cold neu*er* take."

A k*nigh*t amongst the Scotts there was
  w*h*i*c*h saw Erle Douglas dye,
Who streight in hart did vow revenge
  vpon the Lord Pearcye.

Si*r* Hugh Mountgomerye was he called,
  who, w*i*th a spere full bright,
Well mounted on a gallant steed,
  ran feircly through the fight,

And past the English archers all,
  w*i*thout all dread or feare,
And through Erle Percyes body then
  he thrust his hatfull spere.

W*i*th such a vehement force and might
  his body he did gore,
The staff ran through the other side
  a large cioth-yard and more.

Thus did both those nobles dye,
  whose courage none cold staine;
An English archer then p*er*ceiued
  the noble erle was slaine.

He had [a] good bow in his hand,
    made of a trusty tree;
An arrow of a cloth-yard long
    to the hard head haled hee.

Against Sir Hugh Mountgomerye
    his shaft full right he sett;
The grey-goose-winge *that* was there-on
    in his harts bloode was wett.

This fight from breake of day did last
    till setting of the sun,
For when the rung the euening-bell
    the battele scarse was done.

With stout Erle Percy there was slaine
    Sir Iohn of Egerton,
Sir Robert Harcliffe and Sir William,
    Sir Iames, that bold barron.

And with Sir George and Sir Iames,
    both k*nigh*ts of good account,
Good Sir Raphe Rebbye there was slaine,
    whose prowesse did surmount.

For Witherington needs must I wayle
    as one in dolefull dumpes,
For when his leggs were smitten of,
    he fought vpon his stumpes.

And with Erle Dowglas there was slaine
    Sir Hugh Mountgomerye,
And Sir Charles Morrell, *tha*t from feelde
    one foote wold neu*er* flee;

Sir Roger Heuer of Harcliffe tow,
    his sisters sonne was hee;
Sir David Lambwell, well esteemed,
    but saved he cold not bee.

And the Lord Maxwell, in like case,
  with Douglas he did dye;
Of twenty hundred Scottish speeres,
  scarce fifty-fiue did flye.

Of fifteen hundred Englishmen
  went home but fifty-three;
The rest in Cheuy Chase were slaine,
  vnder the greenwoode tree.

Next day did many widdowes come
  their husbands to bewayle;
They washt their wounds in brinish teares,
  but all wold not prevayle.

Theyr bodyes, bathed in purple blood,
  the bore with them away;
They kist them dead a thousand times
  ere the were cladd in clay.

The newes was brought to Eddenborrow,
  where Scottlands king did rayne,
That braue Erle Douglas soddainlye
  was with an arrow slaine.

"O heauy newes!" King Iames can say;
  "Scotland may wittenesse bee
I haue not any captaine more
  of such account as hee."

Like tydings to King Henery came,
  within as short a space,
That Pearcy of Northumberland
  was slaine in Cheuy Chase.

"Now God be with him!" said our king,
  "sith it will noe better bee;
I trust I haue within my realme
  fiue hundred as good as hee.

"Yett shall not Scotts nor Scottland say
    but I will vengeance take,
And be revenged on them all
    for braue Erle Percyes sake."

This vow the king did well performe
    after on Humble-downe;
In one day fifty knights were slayne,
    with lords of great renowne.

And of the rest, of small account,
    did many hundreds dye:
Thus endeth the hunting in Cheuy Chase,
    made by the Erle Pearcye.

God saue our king, and blesse this land
    with plentye, ioy, and peace,
And grant hencforth that foule debate
    twixt noble men may ceaze!

23   JOHNIE ARMSTRONG

There dwelt a man in faire Westmerland,
    Ionnë Armestrong men did him call,
He had nither lands nor rents coming in,
    Yet he kept eight score men in his hall.

He had horse and harness for them all,
    Goodly steeds were all milke-white;
O the golden bands an about their necks,
    And their weapons, they were all alike.

Newes then was brought unto the king
    That there was sicke a won[1] as hee,
That livëd lyke a bold out-law,
    And robbëd all the north country.

The king he writt an letter then,
    A letter which was large and long;
He signëd it with his owne hand,
    And he promised to doe him no wrong.

[1] Such a one.

When this letter came Ionnë untill,
　His heart it was as blythe as birds on the tree:
"Never was I sent for before any king,
　My father, my grandfather, nor none but mee.

"And if wee goe the king before,
　I would we went most orderly;
Every man of you shall have his scarlet cloak,
　Laced with silver laces three.

"Every won of you shall have his velvett coat,
　Laced with sillver lace so white;
O the golden bands an about your necks,
　Black hatts, white feathers, all alyke."

By the morrow morninge at ten of the clock,
　Towards Edenburough gon was hee,
And with him all his eight score men;
　Good lord, it was a goodly sight for to see!

When Ionnë came befower the king,
　He fell downe on his knee;
"O pardon, my soveraine leige," he said,
　"O pardon my eight score men and mee!"

"Thou shalt have no pardon, thou traytor strong,
　For thy eight score men nor thee;
For to-morrow morning by ten of the clock,
　Both thou and them shall hang on the gallow-tree."

But Ionnë look'd over his left shoulder,
　Good Lord, what a grevious look looked hee!
Saying, "Asking grace of a graceles face—
　Why there is none for you nor me."

But Ionnë had a bright sword by his side,
　And it was made of the mettle so free,
That had not the king stept his foot aside,
　He had smitten his head from his faire boddë.

Saying, "Fight on, my merry men all,
   And see that none of you be taine;
For rather then men shall say we were hange'd,
   Let them report how we were slaine."

Then, God wott, faire Eddenburrough rose,
   And so besett poore Ionnë rounde,
That fowerscore and tenn of Ionnes best men
   Lay gasping all upon the ground.

Then like a mad man Ionne laide about,
   And like a mad man then fought hee,
Untill a falce Scot came Ionne behinde,
   And runn him through the faire boddee.

Saying, "Fight on, my merry men all,
   And see that none of you be taine;
For I will stand by and bleed but awhile,
   And then will I come and fight againe."

Newes then was brought to young Ionne Armestrong,
   As he stood by his nurses knee,
Who vowed if ere he live'd for to be a man,
   O the treacherous Scots revengd hee'd be.

24   CAPTAIN CAR

It befell at Martynmas,
   When wether waxed colde,
Captaine Care said to his men,
   We must go take a holde.

      Syck, sike, and to-towe sike,
         And sike and like to die;
      The sikest nighte that euer I abode,
         God lord haue mercy on me![1]

"Haille, master, and wether you will,
   And wether ye like it best";
"To the castle of Crecrynbroghe,
   And there we will take our reste."

[1] The refrain here, as often, has no significance for the story.

"I knowe wher is a gay castle,
 Is builded of lyme and stone;
Within their is a gay ladie,
 Her lord is riden and gone."

The ladie she lend[2] on her castle-walle,
 She loked vpp and downe;
There was she ware of an host of men,
 Come riding to the towne.

"Se yow, my meri men all,
 And se yow what I see?
Yonder I see a host of men,
 I muse who they bee."

She thought he had ben her wed lord,
 As he comd riding home;
Then was it traitur Captaine Care,
 The lord of Ester-towne.

They wer no soner at supper sett,
 Then after said the grace,
Or Captaine Care and all his men
 Wer lighte aboute the place.

"Gyue ouer thi howsse, thou lady gay,
 And I will make the a bande;[3]
To-nighte thou shall ly within my armes,
 To-morrowe thou shall ere my lande."

Then bespacke the eldest sonne,
 That was both whitt and redde:
"O mother dere, geue ouer your howsse,
 Or elles we shalbe deade."

"I will not geue ouer my hous," she saithe,
 "Not for feare of my lyffe;
It shalbe talked throughout the land,
 The slaughter of a wyffe."

   [2] Leaned. [3] Agreement.

"Fetch me my pestilett,[4]
  And charge me my gonne,
That I may shott at yonder bloddy butcher,
  The lord of Easter-towne."

Styfly vpon her wall she stode,
  And lett the pellettes flee;
But then she myst the blody bucher,
  And she slew other three.

"[I will] not geue ouer my hous," she saithe,
  "Netheir for lord nor lowne;
Nor yet for traitour Captaine Care,
  The lord of Easter-towne.

"I desire of Captaine Care,
  And all his bloddye band,
That he would saue my eldest sonne,
  The eare[5] of all my lande."

"Lap him in a shete," he sayth,
  "And let him downe to me,
And I shall take him in my armes,
  His waran[6] shall I be."

The captayne sayd unto him selfe:
  Wyth sped, before the rest,
He cut his tonge out of his head,
  His hart out of his brest.

He lapt them in a handkerchef,
  And knet it of knotes three,
And cast them ouer the castell-wall,
  At that gay ladye.

"Fye vpon the, Captayne Care,
  And all thy bloddy band!
For thou hast slayne my eldest sonne,
  The ayre[5] of all my land."

[4] Pistolet.   [5] Heir.   [6] Warrant.

Then bespake the yongest sonne,
That sat on the nurses knee,
Sayth, "Mother gay, geue ouer your house;
It smoldereth me."

"I wold geue my gold," she saith,
"And so I wolde my ffee,[7]
For a blaste of the westryn wind,
To dryue the smoke from thee.

"Fy vpon the, John Hamleton,
That euer I paid the hyre!
For thou hast broken my castle-wall,
And kyndled in the ffyre."

The lady gate[8] to her close parler,
The fire fell aboute her head;
She toke vp her children thre,
Set, "Babes, we are all dead."

Then bespake the hye steward,
That is of hye degree;
Saith, "Ladie gay, you are in close,
Wether ye fighte or flee."

Lord Hamleton dremd in his dream,
In Caruall where he laye,
His halle were all of fyre,
His ladie slayne or daye.

"Busk[9] and bowne,[10] my mery men all,
Even and go ye with me;
For I dremd that my haal was on fyre,
My lady slayne or[11] day."

He buskt him and bownd hym,
And like a worthi knighte;
And when he saw his hall burning,
His harte was no dele lighte.

[7] Property.   [8] Went.   [9] Prepare.   [10] Make ready.   [11] Ere.

He sett a trumpett till his mouth,
  He blew as it plesd his grace;
Twenty score of Hamlentons
  Was light aboute the place.

"Had I knowne as much yesternighte
  As I do to-daye,
Captaine Care and all his men
  Should not haue gone so quite.

"Fye vpon the, Captaine Care,
  And all thy blody bande!
Thou haste slayne my lady gay,
  More wurth then all thy lande.

"If thou had ought eny ill will," he saith,
  "Thou shoulde haue taken my lyffe,
And haue saved my children, thre,
  All and my louesome wyffe."

25   The Bonny Earl of Murray

Ye Highlands, and ye Lawlands,
  Oh where have you been?
They have slain the Earl of Murray,
  And they layd him on the green.

"Now wae[1] be to thee, Huntly!
  And wherefore did you sae?
I bade you bring him wi you,
  But forbade you him to slay."

He was a braw gallant,
  And he rid at the ring;
And the bonny Earl of Murray,
  Oh he might have been a king!

He was a braw gallant,
  And he playd at the ba;

[1] Woe.

And the bonny Earl of Murray
   Was the flower amang them a'.

He was a braw gallant,
   And he played at the glove;
And the bonny Earl of Murray,
   Oh he was the Queen's love!

Oh lang will his lady
   Look oer the castle Down,
Eer she see the Earl of Murray
   Come sounding thro the town!
Eer she, etc.

26   KINMONT WILLIE

O HAVE ye na heard o the fause Sakelde?
   O have ye na heard o the keen Lord Scroop?
How they hae taen bauld Kinmont Willie,
   On Hairibee to hang him up?

Had Willie had but twenty men,
   But twenty men as stout as he,
Fause Sakelde had never the Kinmont taen,
   Wi eight score in his companie.

They band his legs beneath the steed,
   They tied his hands behind his back;
They guarded him, fivesome on each side,
   And they brought him ower the Liddel-rack.

They led him thro the Liddel-rack,
   And also thro the Carlisle sands;
They brought him to Carlisle castell,
   To be at my Lord Scroope's commands.

"My hands are tied, but my tongue is free,
   And whae will dare this deed avow?
Or answer by the border law?
   Or answer to the bauld Buccleuch?"

"Now haud thy tongue, thou rank reiver![1]
   There's never a Scot shall set ye free;
Before ye cross my castle-yate,[2]
   I trow ye shall take farewell o me."

"Fear na ye that, my lord," quo Willie;
   "By the faith o my bodie, Lord Scroop," he said,
"I never yet lodged in a hostelrie
   But I paid my lawing[3] before I gaed."

Now word is gane to the bauld Keeper,
   In Branksome Ha where that he lay,
That Lord Scroope has taen the Kinmont Willie
   Between the hours of night and day.

He has taen the table wi his hand,
   He garrd[4] the red wine spring on hie;
"Now Christ's curse on my head," he said,
   "But avenged of Lord Scroop I'll be!

"O is my basnet[5] a widow's curch?
   Or my lance a wand of the willow-tree?
Or my arm a ladye's lilye hand?
   That an English lord should lightly[6] me.

"And have they taen him Kinmont Willie,
   Against the truce of Border tide,
And forgotten that the bauld Bacleuch
   Is keeper here on the Scottish side?

"And have they een taen him Kinmont Willie,
   Withouten either dread or fear,
And forgotten that the bauld Bacleuch
   Can back a steed, or shake a spear?

"O were there war between the lands,
   As well I wot that there is none,
I would slight[7] Carlisle castell high,
   Tho it were builded of marble-stone.

---

[1] Robber.   [2] Gate.   [3] Bill.   [4] Made.
[5] Helmet.   [6] Treat scornfully.   [7] Demolish.

"I would set that castell in a low,[8]
  And sloken[9] it with English blood;
There's nevir a man in Cumberland
  Should ken where Carlisle castell stood.

"But since nae war's between the lands,
  And there is peace, and peace should be,
I'll neither harm English lad or lass,
  And yet the Kinmont freed shall be!"

He has calld him forty marchmen bauld,
  I trow they were of his ain name,
Except Sir Gilbert Elliot, calld
  The Laird of Stobs, I mean the same.

He has calld him forty marchmen bauld,
  Were kinsmen to the bauld Buccleuch,
With spur on heel, and splent on spauld,[10]
  And gleuves of green, and feathers blue.

There were five and five before them a',
  Wi hunting-horns and bugles bright;
And five and five came wi Buccleuch,
  Like Warden's men, arrayed for fight.

And five and five like a mason-gang,
  That carried the ladders lang and hie;
And five and five like broken men;
  And so they reached the Woodhouselee.

And as we crossed the Bateable Land,
  When to the English side we held,
The first o men that we met wi,
  Whae sould it be but fause Sakelde!

"Where be ye gaun, ye hunters keen?"
  Quo fause Sakelde; "come tell to me!"
"We go to hunt an English stag,
  Has trespassed on the Scots countrie."

---

[8] Flame.   [9] Slake.   [10] Armor-plates on shoulder.

"Where be ye gaun, ye marshal-men?"
    Quo fause Sakelde; "come tell to me true!"
"We go to catch a rank reiver,
    Has broken faith wi the bauld Buccleuch."

"Where are ye gaun, ye mason-lads,
    Wi a' your ladders lang and hie?"
"We gang to herry[11] a corbie's[12] nest,
    That wons not far frae Woodhouselee."

"Where be ye gaun, ye broken men?"
    Quo fause Sakelde; "come tell to me!"
Now Dickie of Dryhope led that band,
    And the never a word o lear[13] had he.

"Why trespass ye on the English side
    Row-footed[14] outlaws, stand!" quo he;
The neer a word had Dickie to say,
    Sae he thrust the lance thro his fause bodie.

Then on we held for Carlisle toun,
    And at Staneshaw-bank the Eden we crossd;
The water was great, and meikle of spait,[15]
    But the nevir a horse nor man we lost.

And when we reached the Stanshaw-bank,
    The wind was rising loud and hie;[16]
And there the laird garrd[17] leave our steeds,
    For fear that they should stamp and nie.[18]

And when we left the Staneshaw-bank,
    The wind began full loud to blaw;
But 'twas wind and weet, and fire and sleet
    When we came beneath the castel-wa.

We crept on knees, and held our breath,
    Till we placed the ladders against the wa;
And sae ready was Buccleuch himsell
    To mount the first before us a'.

[11] Rob.   [12] Crow's.   [13] Learning.   [14] Rough-footed.   [15] In high flood.   [16] High.
[17] Caused.   [18] Neigh.

He has taen the watchman by the throat,
   He flung him down upon the lead:
"Had there not been peace between our lands,
   Upon the other side thou hadst gaed.

"Now sound out, trumpets!" quo Buccleuch;
   "Let's waken Lord Scroope right merrilie!"
Then loud the Warden's trumpets blew
   "O whae dare meddle wi me?"

Then speedilie to wark we gaed,
   And raised the slogan[19] ane and a',
And cut a hole thro a sheet of lead,
   And so we wan to the castel-ha.

They thought King James and a' his men
   Had won the house wi bow and speir:
It was but twenty Scots and ten
   That put a thousand in sic a stear![20]

Wi coulters and wi forehammers,
   We garrd the bars bang merrilie,
Untill we came to the inner prison,
   Where Willie o Kinmont he did lie.

And when we cam to the lower prison,
   Where Willie o Kinmont he did lie,
"O sleep ye, wake ye, Kinmont Willie,
   Upon the morn that thou's to die?"

"O I sleep saft, and I wake aft,
   It's lang since sleeping was fleyd[21] frae me;
Gie my service back to my wyfe and bairns,
   And a' gude fellows that speer[22] for me."

Then Red Rowan has hente[23] him up,
   The starkest men in Teviotdale:
"Abide, abide now, Red Rowan,
   Till of my Lord Scroope I take farewell.

[19] War-cry. [20] Stir. [21] Scared. [22] Ask. [23] Taken.

"Farewell, farewell, my gude Lord Scroope!
  My gude Lord Scroope, farewell!" he cried;
"I'll pay you for my lodging-maill[24]
  When first we meet on the border-side."

Then shoulder high, with shout and cry,
  We bore him down the ladder lang;
At every stride Red Rowan made,
  I wot the Kinmont's airns playd clang.

"O mony a time," quo Kinmont Willie,
  "I have ridden horse baith wild and wood;
But a rougher beast than Red Rowan
  I ween my legs have neer bestrode.

"And mony a time," quo Kinmont Willie,
  "I've pricked a horse out oure the furs;[25]
But since the day I backed a steed
  I nevir wore sic cumbrous spurs."

We scarce had won the Staneshaw-bank,
  When a' the Carlisle bells were rung,
And a thousand men, in horse and foot,
  Cam wi the keen Lord Scroope along.

Buccleuch has turned to Eden Water,
  Even where it flowd frae bank to brim,
And he has plunged in wi a' his band,
  And safely swam them thro the stream.

He turned him on the other side,
  And at Lord Scroope his glove flung he:
"If ye like na my visit in merry England,
  In fair Scotland come visit me!"

All sore astonished stood Lord Scroope,
  He stood as still as rock of stane;
He scarcely dared to trew his eyes
  When thro the water they had gane.

[24] Rent. [25] Furrows.

"He is either himsell a devil frae hell,
　　Or else his mother a witch maun be;
I wad na have ridden that wan water
　　For a' the gowd in Christentie."

27　　　　BONNIE GEORGE CAMPBELL

HIE upon Hielands,
　　and laigh upon Tay,
Bonnie George Campbell
　　rode out on a day.

He saddled, he bridled,
　　and gallant rode he,
And hame cam his guid horse,
　　but never cam he.

Out cam his mother dear,
　　greeting fu sair,
And out cam his bonnie bryde,
　　riving[1] her hair.

"The meadow lies green,
　　the corn is unshorn,
But bonnie George Campbell
　　will never return,"

Saddled and bridled
　　and booted rode he,
A plume in his helmet,
　　A sword at his knee.

But toom[2] cam his saddle,
　　all bloody to see,
Oh, hame cam his guid horse,
　　but never cam he!

　　　　[1] Tearing.　　[2] Empty.

28   THE DOWY HOUMS O YARROW

Late at een, drinkin the wine,
  Or early in a mornin,
The set a combat them between,
  To fight it in the dawnin.

"O stay at hame, my noble lord!
  O stay at hame, my marrow!
My cruel brother will you betray,
  On the dowy[1] houms[2] o Yarrow."

"O fare ye weel, my lady gaye!
  O fare ye weel, my Sarah!
For I maun gae, tho I neer return
  Frae the dowy banks o Yarrow."

She kissed his cheek, she kaimd[3] his hair,
  As she had done before, O;
She belted on his noble brand,
  An he's awa to Yarrow.

O he's gane up yon high, high hill—
  I wat he gaed wi sorrow—
And in a den spied nine armd men,
  I the dowy houms o Yarrow.

"O ir[4] ye come to drink the wine,
  As ye hae doon before, O?
Or ir ye come to wield the brand,
  On the bonny banks o Yarrow?"

"I im no come to drink the wine,
  As I hae don before, O,
But I im come to wield the brand,
  On the dowy houms o Yarrow."

Four he hurt, and five he slew,
  On the dowy houms o Yarrow,

[1] Sad.   [2] Flat land by a river.   [3] Combed.   [4] Are.

Till that stubborn knight came him behind.
An ran his body thorrow.

"Gae hame, gae hame, good-brother John,
And tell your sister Sarah
To come and lift her noble lord,
Who's sleepin sound on Yarrow."

"Yestreen[5] I dreamed a dolefu dream;
I kend[6] there wad be sorrow;
I dreamd I pu'd the heather green,
On the dowy banks o Yarrow."

She gaed up yon high, high hill—
I wat she gaed wi sorrow—
An in a den spy'd nine dead men,
On the dowy houms o Yarrow.

She kissed his cheek, she kaimd his hair,
As oft she did before, O;
She drank the red blood frae him ran,
On the dowy houms o Yarrow.

"O haud your tongue, my douchter dear,
For what needs a' this sorrow?
I'll wed you on a better lord
Than him you lost on Yarrow."

"O haud your tongue, my father dear,
An dinna grieve your Sarah;
A better lord was never born
Than him I lost on Yarrow.

"Tak hame your ousen,[7] tak hame your kye,[8]
For they hae bred our sorrow;
I wiss that they had a' gane mad
Whan they cam first to Yarrow."

[5] Last night.   [6] Knew.   [7] Oxen.   [8] Cows.

29

Mary Hamilton

Word's gane to the kitchen,
  And word's gane to the ha,
That Marie Hamilton has born a bairn
  To the hichest Stewart of a'.

She's tyed it in her apron
  And she's thrown it in the sea;
Says, 'Sink ye, swim ye, bonny wee babe,
  You'll ne'er get mair o me.'

Down then cam the auld Queen,
  Goud[1] tassels tying her hair:
'O Marie, where's the bonny wee babe
  That I heard greet[2] sae sair?'[3]

'There was never a babe intill[4] my room,
  As little designs to be;
It was but a touch o my sair side,
  Came o'er my fair bodie.'

'O Marie, put on your robes o black,
  Or else your robes o brown,
For ye maun gang[5] wi me the night,
  To see fair Edinbro town.'

'I winna put on my robes o black,
  Nor yet my robes o brown;
But I'll put on my robes o white,
  To shine through Edinbro town.'

When she gaed up the Cannogate,
  She laughd loud laughters three;
But when she cam down the Cannogate
  The tear blinded her ee.

When she gaed up the Parliament stair,
  The heel cam aff her shee;[6]

1 Gold.   2 Weep.   3 Sore.   4 Into, in.   5 Must go.   6 Shoe.

And lang or she cam down again
  She was condemnd to dee.

When she came down the Cannogate,
  The Cannogate sae free,
Many a ladie lookd o'er her window,
  Weeping for this ladie.

'Make never meen[7] for me,' she says,
  'Make never meen for me;
Seek never grace frae a graceless face,
  For that ye'll never see.

'Bring me a bottle of wine,' she says,
  'The best that eer ye hae,'[8]
That I may drink to my weil-wishers,
  And they may drink to me.

'And here's to the jolly sailor lad
  That sails upon the faem;
And let not my father nor mother get wit
  But that I shall come again.

'And here's to the jolly sailor lad
  That sails upon the sea;
But let not my father nor mother get wit[9]
  O the death that I maun dee.

'O little did my mother think,
  The day she cradled me,
What lands I was to travel through,
  What death I was to dee.

'O little did my father think,
  The day he held up me,
What lands I was to travel through,
  What death I was to dee.

'Last nicht I washd the Queen's feet,
  And gently laid her down;

[7] Moan.   [8] Ever you have.   [9] Knowledge.

And a' the thanks I've gotten the nicht
To be hangd in Edinbro town!

'Last nicht there was four Maries,
    The nicht there'll be but three;
There was Marie Seton, and Marie Beton,
    And Marie Carmichael, and me.'

30   THE BARON OF BRACKLEY

INVEREY cam doun Deeside, whistlin and playin,
He was at brave Braikley's yett[1] ere it was dawin.[2]

He rappit fu loudly an wi a great roar,
Cried, 'Cum doun, cum doun, Braikley, and open the door.

'Are ye sleepin, Baronne, or are ye wakin?
Ther's sharpe swords at your yett, will gar[3] your blood spin.

'Open the yett, Braikley, and lat us within,
Till we on the green turf gar your bluid rin.'

Up spak his ladie, at his bak where she lay,
'Get up, get up, Braikley, an be not afraid;
The'r but young hir'd widifus[4] wi belted plaids.'

'Cum kiss me, mi Peggy, I'le nae langer stay,
For I will go out and meet Inverey.

'But haud your tongue, Peggy, and mak nae sic din,
For yon same hir'd widifus will prove themselves men.'

She called on her marys,[5] they cam to her hand;
Cries, 'Bring me your rocks,[6] lassies, we will them command.

'Get up, get up, Braikley, and turn bak your ky,[7]
Or me an mi women will them defy.

'Cum forth then, mi maidens, and show them some play;
We'll ficht them, and shortly the cowards will fly.

[1] Gate. [2] Dawning. [3] Make. [4] Gallows-birds. [5] Maidens. [6] Distaffs. [7] Cattle.

'Gin I had a husband, whereas I hae nane,
He woud nae ly i his bed and see his ky taen.[8]

'Ther's four-and-twenty milk-whit calves, twal o them ky,[9]
In the woods o Glentanner, it's ther thei a' ly.

'Ther's goat i the Etnach, and sheep o the brae,
An a' will be plundered by young Inverey.'

'Now haud your tongue, Peggy, and gie me a gun,
Ye'll see me gae furth, but I'll never cum in.

'Call mi brother William, mi unkl also,
Mi cousin James Gordon; we'll mount and we'll go.'

When Braikley was ready and stood i the closs,
He was the bravest baronne that eer mounted horse.

Whan all wer assembled o the castell green,
No man like brave Braikley was ther to be seen.

. . . .

'Turn bak, brother William, ye are a bridegroom;

'Wi bonnie Jean Gordon, the maid o the mill;
O sichin and sobbin she'll soon get her fill.'

'I'm no coward, brother, 'tis kend I'm a man;
'I'll ficht, my dear brother, wi heart and gudewill,

'I'll ficht i your quarral as lang's I can stand.
And so will young Harry that lives at the mill.

'But turn, mi dear brother, and nae langer stay:
What'll cum o your ladie, gin Braikley thei slay?

'What'll cum o your ladie and bonnie young son?
O what'll cum o them when Braikley is gone?'

'I never will turn: do you think I will fly?
But here I will ficht, and here I will die.'

[8] Taken.   [9] Cows.

'Strik dogs,' crys Inverey, 'and ficht till ye're slayn,
For we are four hundred, ye are but four men.

'Strik, strik, ye proud boaster, your honour is gone,
Your lands we will plunder, your castell we'll burn.'

At the head o the Etnach the battel began,
At Little Auchoilzie thei killd the first man.

First thei killd ane, and soon they killd twa,
Thei killd gallant Braikley, the flour o them a',

Thei killd William Gordon, and James o the Knox,
And brave Alexander, the flour o Glenmuick.

What sichin and moaning was heard i the glen,
For the Baronne o Braikley, who basely was slayn!

'Cam ye bi the castell, and was ye in there?
Saw ye pretty Peggy tearing her hair?'

'Yes, I cam by Braikley, and I gaed in there,
And there saw his ladie braiding her hair.

'She was rantin, and dancin, and singin for joy,
And vowin that nicht she woud feest Inverey.

'She eat wi him, drank wi him, welcomd him in,
Was kind to the man that had slain her baronne.'

Up spake the son on the nourice's knee,
'Gin I live to be a man, revenged I'll be.'

Ther's dool[10] i the kitchin, and mirth i the ha,
The Baronne o Braikley is dead and awa.

31   BEWICK AND GRAHAME

Old Grahame he is to Carlisle gone,
    Where Sir Robert Bewick there met he;
In arms to the wine they are gone,
    And drank till they were both merry.

[10] Grief.

Old Grahame he took up the cup,
  And said, 'Brother Bewick, here's to thee,
And here's to our two sons at home,
  For they live best in our country.'

'Nay, were thy son as good as mine,
  And of some books he could but read,
With sword and buckler by his side,
  To see how he could save his head,

'They might have been calld two bold brethren
  Where ever they did go or ride;
They might have been calld two bold brethren,
  They might have crackd[1] the Border-side.

'Thy son is bad, and is but a lad,
  And bully[2] to my son cannot be;
For my son Bewick can both write and read,
  And sure I am that cannot he.'

'I put him to school, but he would not learn,
  I bought him books, but he would not read;
But my blessing he's never have
  Till I see how his hand can save his head.'

Old Grahame called for an account,
  And he askd what was for to pay;
There he paid a crown, so it went round,
  Which was all for good wine and hay.

Old Grahame is into the stable gone,
  Where stood thirty good steeds and three;
He's taken his own steed by the head,
  And home rode he right wantonly.

When he came home, there did he espy
  A loving sight to spy or see,
There did he espy his own three sons,
  Young Christy Grahame, the foremost was he.

[1] Defied.   [2] Mate, chum, sworn brother.

There did he espy his own three sons,
  Young Christy Grahame, the foremost was he:
'Where have you been all day, father,
  That no counsel you would take by me?'

'Nay, I have been in Carlisle town,
  Where Sir Robert Bewick there met me;
He said thou was bad, and calld thee a lad,
  And a baffled man by thou I be.

'He said thou was bad, and calld thee a lad,
  And bully to his son cannot be;
For his son Bewick can both write and read,
  And sure I am that cannot thee.

'I put thee to school, but thou would not learn,
  I bought thee books, but thou would not read;
But my blessing thou's never have
  Till I see with Bewick thou can save thy head.'

'O, pray forbear, my father dear;
  That ever such a thing should be!
Shall I venture my body in field to fight
  With a man that's faith and troth to me?'

'What's that thou sayst, thou limmer loon?[3]
  Or how dare thou stand to speak to me?
If thou do not end this quarrel soon,
  Here is my glove thou shalt fight me.'

Christy stoopd low unto the ground,
  Unto the ground, as you'll understand:
'O father, put on your glove again,
  The wind hath blown it from your hand.'

'What's that thou sayst, thou limmer loon?
  Or how dare thou stand to speak to me?
If thou do not end this quarrel soon,
  Here is my hand thou shalt fight me.'

[3] Rascally fellow.

Christy Grahame is to his chamber gone,
   And for to study, as well might be,
Whether to fight with his father dear,
   Or with his bully Bewick he.

'If it be my fortune my bully to kill,
   As you shall boldly understand,
In every town that I ride through,
   They'll say, There rides a brotherless man!

'Nay, for to kill my bully dear,
   I think it will be a deadly sin;
And for to kill my father dear,
   The blessing of heaven I ne'er shall win.

'O give me my blessing, father,' he said,
   'And pray well for me for to thrive;
If it be my fortune my bully to kill,
   I swear I'll neer come home alive.'

He put on his back a good plate-jack,
   And on his head a cap of steel,
With sword and buckler by his side;
   O gin[4] he did not become them weel!

'O fare thee well, my father dear!
   And fare thee well, thou Carlisle town!
If it be my fortune my bully to kill,
   I swear I'll neer eat bread again.'

Now we'll leave talking of Christy Grahame,
   And talk of him again belive;[5]
But we will talk of bonny Bewick,
   Where he was teaching his scholars five.

Now when he had learnd them well to fence,
   To handle their swords without any doubt,
He's taken his own sword under his arm,
   And walkd his father's close about.

[4] If.   [5] Soon.

He lookd between him and the sun,
  To see what farleys[6] he could see;
There he spy'd a man with armour on,
  As he came riding over the lee.

'I wonder much what man yon be
  That so boldly this way does come;
I think it is my nighest friend,
  I think it is my bully Grahame.

'O welcome, O welcome, bully Grahame!
  O man, thou art my dear, welcome!
O man, thou art my dear, welcome!
  For I love thee best in Christendom.'

'Away, away, O bully Bewick,
  And of thy bullyship let me be!
The day is come I never thought on;
  Bully, I'm come here to fight with thee.'

'O no! not so, O bully Grahame!
  That eer such a word should spoken be!
I was thy master, thou was my scholar:
  So well as I have learned thee.'

'My father he was in Carlisle town,
  Where thy father Bewick there met he;
He said I was bad, and he calld me a lad,
  And a baffled man by thou I be.'

'Away, away, O bully Grahame,
  And of all that talk, man, let us be!
We'll take three men of either side
  To see if we can our fathers agree.'

'Away, away, O bully Bewick,
  And of thy bullyship let me be!
But if thou be a man, as I trow thou art,
  Come over this ditch and fight with me.'

[6] Wonders.

'O no, not so, my bully Grahame!
  That eer such a word should spoken be!
Shall I venture my body in field to fight
  With a man that's faith and troth to me?'

'Away, away, O bully Bewick,
  And of all that care, man, let us be!
If thou be a man, as I trow thou art,
  Come over this ditch and fight with me.'

'Now, if it be my fortune thee, Grahame, to kill,
  As God's will, man, it all must be;
But if it be my fortune thee, Grahame, to kill,
  'Tis home again I'll never gae.'

'Thou art of my mind, then, bully Bewick,
  And sworn-brethren will we be:
If thou be a man, as I trow thou art,
  Come over this ditch and fight with me.'

He flang his cloak from off his shoulders,
  His psalm-book out of his hand flung he,
He clapd his hand upon the hedge,
  And oer lap[7] he right wantonly.

When Grahame did see his bully come,
  The salt tear stood long in his eye:
'Now needs must I say that thou art a man,
  That dare venture thy body to fight with me.

'Now I have a harness on my back;
  I know that thou hath none on thine;
But as little as thou hath on thy back,
  Sure as little shall there be on mine.'

He flang his jack from off his back,
  His steel cap from his head flang he;
He's taken his sword into his hand,
  He's tyed his horse unto a tree.

             [7] Leapt.

Now they fell to it with two broad swords,
  For two long hours fought Bewick and he;
Much sweat was to be seen on them both,
  But never a drop of blood to see.

Now Grahame gave Bewick an ackward stroke,
  An ackward stroke surely struck he;
He struck him now under the left breast,
  Then down to the ground as dead fell he.

'Arise, arise, O bully Bewick,
  Arise, and speak three words to me!
Whether this be thy deadly wound,
  Or God and good surgeons will mend thee.'

'O horse, O horse, O bully Grahame,
  And pray do get thee far from me!
Thy sword is sharp, it hath wounded my heart,
  And so no further can I gae.

'O horse, O horse, O bully Grahame,
  And get thee far from me with speed!
And get thee out of this country quite!
  That none may know who's done the deed.'

'O if this be true, my bully dear,
  The words that thou dost tell to me,
The vow I made, and the vow I'll keep,
  I swear I'll be the first to die.'

Then he stuck his sword in a moudie-hill,[8]
  Where he lap thirty good foot and three;
First he bequeathed his soul to God,
  And upon his own sword-point lap he.

Now Grahame he was the first that died,
  And then came Robin Bewick to see;
'Arise, arise, O son,' he said,
  'For I see thou's won the victory.

[8] Mole-hill.

'Arise, arise, O son,' he said,
    'For I see thou's won the victory;'
'Father, could ye not drunk your wine at home,
    And letten me and my brother be?

'Nay, dig a grave both low and wide,
    And in it us two pray bury;
But bury my bully Grahame on the sun-side,
    For I'm sure he's won the victory.'

Now we'll leave talking of these two brethren,
    In Carlisle town where they lie slain,
And talk of these two good old men,
    Where they were making a pitiful moan.

With that bespoke now Robin Bewick:
    'O man was I not much to blame?
I have lost one of the liveliest lads
    That ever was bred unto my name.'

With that bespoke my good lord Grahame:
    'O man, I have lost the better block;
I have lost my comfort and my joy,
    I have lost my key, I have lost my lock.

'Had I gone through all Ladderdale,
    And forty horse had set on me,
Had Christy Grahame been at my back,
    So well as he would guarded me.'

I have no more of my song to sing,
    But two or three words to you I'll name;
But 'twill be talked in Carlisle town
    That these two old men were all the blame.

A GEST OF ROBYN HODE

c. 15th century

Lythe[1] and listin, gentilmen,
    That be of frebore[2] blode;

[1] Listen.   [2] Freeborn.

I shall you tel of a gode yeman,
  His name was Robyn Hode.

Robyn was a prude[3] outlaw,
  Whyles he walked on grounde;
So curteyse an outlaw as he was one
  Was never non yfounde.[4]

Robyn stode in Bernesdale,
  And lenyd hym to a tre;
And bi him stode Litell Johnn
  A gode yeman was he.

And alsoo dyd gode Scarlok,
  And Much, the miller's son;
There was none ynch of his bodi
  But it was worth a grome.[5]

Than bespake Lytell Johnn
  All untoo Robyn Hode:
Maister, and[6] ye wolde dyne betyme
  It wolde doo you moche gode.

Than bespake hym gode Robyn:
  To dyne have I noo lust,
Till that I have som bolde baron
  Or som unkouth[7] gest.

. . . .

That may pay for the best,
Or some knyght or som squyer
  That dwelleth here bi west.

A gode maner than had Robyn;
  In londe where that he were,
Every day or he wold dyne
  Thre messis wolde he here.

The one in the worship of the Fader,
  And another of the Holy Gost,

[3] Proud.   [4] Found.   [5] Worthy of a man.   [6] If.   [7] Strange.

The thirde was of Our dere Lady
   That he loved allther[8] moste.

Robyn loved Oure dere Lady;
   For dout[9] of dydly synne,
Wolde he never do compani harme
   That any woman was in.

'Maistar,' than sayde Lytil Johnn,
   'And we our borde shal sprede,
Tell us wheder that we shall go
   And what life that we shall lede.

'Where we shall take, where we shall leve,
   Where we shall abide behynde;
Where we shall robbe, where we shall reve,
   Where we shall bete and bynde.'

'Thereof no force,' [10] than sayde Robyn;
   'We shall do well inowe;[11]
But loke ye do no husbonde harme
   That tilleth with his ploughe.

'No more ye shall no gode yeman
   That walketh by grene-wode shawe;
Ne no knyght ne no squyer
   That wol be a gode felawe.

'These bisshoppes and these archebishoppes,
   Ye shall them bete and bynde;
The hye sherif of Notyngham,
   Hym holde ye in your mynde.'

'This worde shalbe holde,' sayde Lytell Johnn,
   'And this lesson we shall lere;
It is fer dayes;[12] God sende us a gest,
   That we were at our dynere.'

'Take thy gode bowe in thy honde,' sayde Robyn;
   'Late[13] Much wende with the;

[8] Of all.   [9] Fear.   [10] No matter.   [11] Enough.   [12] Late in the day.   [13] Let.

And so shal Willyam Scarlok,
    And no man abyde with me.

'And walke up to the Saylis
    And so to Watlinge Strete,
And wayte after some unkuth gest,
    Up chaunce ye may them mete.

'Be he erle, or ani baron,
    Abbot, or ani knyght,
Bringhe hym to lodge to me;
    His dyner shall be dight.' [14]

They wente up to the Saylis,
    These yemen all three;
They loked est, they loked weest,
    They myght no man see.

But as they loked in to Bernysdale,
    Bi a dernë[15] strete,
Than came a knyght ridinghe;
    Full sone they gan hym mete.

All dreri was his semblaunce,
    And lytell was his pryde;
His one fote in the styrop stode,
    That othere wavyd beside.

His hode hanged in his iyn[16] two;
    He rode in symple aray;
A soriar man than he was one
    Rode never in somer day.

Litell Johnn was full curteyes,
    And sette hym on his kne:
'Welcom be ye, gentyll knyght,
    Welcom ar ye to me.

'Welcom be thou to grenë wode,
    Hendë[17] knyght and fre;

[14] Prepared.   [15] Secret.   [16] Eyes.   [17] Gentle.

My maister hath abiden you fastinge,
    Syr, al these oures thre.'

'Who is thy maister?' sayde the knyght;
    Johnn sayde, 'Robyn Hode';
'He is a gode yoman,' sayde the knyght,
    'Of hym I have herde moche gode.

'I graunte,' he sayde, 'with you to wende,
    My bretherne, all in fere;[18]
My purpos was to have dyned to day
    At Blith or Dancastere.'

Furth than went this gentyl knight,
    With a carefull chere;
The teris oute of his iyen ran,
    And fell downe by his lere.[19]

They brought him to the lodgë-dore;
    Whan Robyn gan hym see,
Full curtesly dyd of his hode
    And sette hym on his knee.

'Welcome, sir knight,' than sayde Robyn,
    'Welcome art thou to me;
I have abyden you fastinge, sir,
    All these ouris thre.'

Than answered the gentyll knight,
    With wordes fayre and fre:
'God the save, goode Robyn,
    And all thy fayre meyne.' [20]

They wasshed togeder and wyped bothe,
    And sette to theyr dynere;
Brede and wyne they had right ynoughe,
    And noumbles[21] of the dere.

Swannes and fessauntes[22] they had full gode,
    And foules of the ryvere;

[18] Together.   [19] Cheek.   [20] Retinue.   [21] Entrails.   [22] Pheasants.

There fayled none so litell a birde
    That ever was bred on bryre.

'Do gladly, sir knight,' sayde Robyn;
    'Gramarcy, sir,' sayde he;
'Suche a dinere had I nat
    Of all these wekys thre.

'If I come ageyne, Robyn,
    Here by thys contrë,
As gode a dyner I shall the make
    As thou haest made to me.'

'Gramarcy, knyght,' sayde Robyn;
    'My dyner whan I have,
I was never so gredy, by dere worthi God,
    My dyner for to crave.

'But pay or ye wende,' sayde Robyn;
    'Me thynketh it is gode ryght;
It was never the maner, by dere worthi God,
    A yoman to pay for a knyght.'

'I have nought in my coffers,' saide the knyght,
    'That I may profer for shame':
'Litell John, go loke,' sayde Robyn,
    'Ne lat not for no blame.

'Tel me truth,' than saide Robyn,
    'So God have parte of the':
'I have no more but ten shelynges,' sayde the
      knyght,
    'So God have parte of me.'

'If thou have no more,' sayde Robyn,
    'I woll nat one peny;
And yf thou have nede of any more,
    More shall I lend the.

'Go nowe furth, Litell Johnn,
    The truth tell thou me;

If there be no more but ten shelinges,
  No peny that I se.'

Lyttell Johnn sprede downe hys mantell
  Full fayre upon the grounde,
And there he fonde in the knyghtes cofer
  But even halfe a pounde.

Littell Johnn let it lye full styll,
  And went to hys maysteer full lowe;
'What tydynges, Johnn?' sayde Robyn;
  'Sir, the knyght is true inowe.'

'Fyll of the best wine,' sayde Robyn,
  'The knyght shall begynne;
Moche wonder thinketh me
  Thy clothynge is so thinne.

'Tell me one worde,' sayde Robyn,
  'And counsel shal it be;
I trowe thou wert made a knyght of force,
  Or ellys of yemanry.

'Or ellys thou hast been a sori husbande,[23]
  And lyved in stroke and strife;
An okerer,[24] or ellis a lechoure,' sayde Robyn,
  'Wyth wronge hast led thy lyfe.'

'I am none of those,' sayde the knyght,
  'By God that madë me;
An hundred wynter here before
  Myn auncetres knyghtes have be.

'But oft it hath befal, Robyn,
  A man hath be disgrate;[25]
But God that sitteth in heven above
  May amende his state.

'Withyn this two yere, Robyne,' he sayde,
  'My neghbours well it knowe,

[23] Manager.   [24] Usurer.   [25] Fallen in fortune.

Foure hundred pounde of gode money
  Ful well than myght I spende.

'Nowe have I no gode,' saide the knyght,
  'God hath shapen such an ende,
But my chyldren and my wyfe,
  Tyll God yt may amende.'

'In what maner,' than sayde Robyn,
  'Hast thou lorne[26] thy rychesse?'
'For my greate foly,' he sayde,
  'And for my kyndenesse.

'I had a sone, forsoth, Robyn,
  That shulde have ben myn ayre,
Whanne he was twenty wynter olde,
  In felde wolde just full fayre.

'He slewe a knyght of Lancashire,
  And a squyer bolde;
For to save him in his ryght
  My godes beth sette and solde.

'My londes beth sette to wedde,[27] Robyn,
  Untyll a certayn day,
To a ryche abbot here besyde
  Of Seynt Mari Abbey.'

'What is the som?' sayde Robyn;
  'Trouth than tell thou me';
'Sir,' he sayde, 'foure hundred pounde;
  The abbot told it to me.'

'Nowe and thou lese[28] thy lond,' sayde Robyn,
  'What shall fall of the?'
'Hastely I wol me buske[29] [sayd the knyght]
  Over the saltë see,

'And se where Criste was quyke and dede,
  On the mount of Calverë;

[26] Lost.   [27] Pledge.   [28] Lose.   [29] Get ready to go.

Fare wel, frende, and have gode day;
   It may not better be.'

Teris fell out of hys eyen two;
   He wolde have gone hys way;
'Farewel, frendes, and have gode day,
   I have no more to pay.'

'Where be thy frendes?' sayde Robyn:
   'Syr, never one wol me knowe;
While I was ryche ynowe at home
   Great boste than wolde they blowe.

'And nowe they renne away fro me,
   As bestis on a rowe;
They take no more hede of me
   Thanne they me never sawe.'

For ruthe thanne wept Litell Johnn,
   Scarlok and Much in fere;
'Fyl of the best wyne,' sayde Robyn,
   'For here is a symple chere.[30]

'Hast thou any frends,' sayde Robyn,
   'Thy borowes[31] that wyll be?'
'I have none,' than sayde the knyght,
   'But God that dyed on tree.'

'Do away thy japis,'[32] sayde Robyn,
   'Thereof wol I right none;
Wenest thou I wolde have God to borowe,
   Peter, Poule, or Johnn?

'Nay, by hym that made me,
   And shope[33] both sonne and mone,
Fynde me a better borowe,' sayde Robyn,
   'Or money getest thou none.'

'I have none other,' sayde the knyght,
   'The sothe for to say,

[30] Entertainment.   [31] Securities.   [32] Jests.   [33] Created.

But yf yt be Our dere Lady;
   She fayled me never or thys day.'

'By dere worthy God,' sayde Robyn,
   'To seche all Englonde thorowe,
Yet fonde I never to my pay[34]
   A moche better borowe.

'Come nowe furth, Litell Johnn,
   And go to my tresourë,
And bringe me foure hundered pound,
   And loke well tolde it be.'

Furth than went Litell Johnn,
   And Scarlok went before;
He told oute four hundred pounde
   By eight and twenty score.

'Is thys well tolde?' sayde litell Much;
   Johnn sayde: 'What greveth the?
It is almus[35] to helpe a gentyll knyght
   That is fal in povertë.

'Master,' than sayde Lityll John,
   'His clothinge is full thynne;
Ye must gyve the knight a lyveray,
   To lappe his body therein.

'For ye have scarlet and grene, mayster,
   And many a riche aray;
Ther is no marchaunt in mery Englond
   So ryche, I dare well say.'

'Take hym thre yerdes of every colour,
   And loke well mete[36] that it be';
Lytell Johnn toke none other mesure
   But his bowë-tree.

And at every handfull that he met
   He lept over fotes three;

[34] Satisfaction.   [35] Alms.   [36] Measured.

'What devylles drapar,' sayd litell Much,
  'Thynkest thou for to be?'

Scarlok stode full stil and loughe,
  And sayd, 'By God Almyght,
Johnn may gyve hym gode mesure,
  For it costeth hym but lyght.'

'Mayster,' than said Litell Johnn
  All unto Robyn Hode,
'Ye must give the knight a hors
  To lede home al this gode.'

'Take him a gray coursar,' sayde Robyn,
  'And a saydle newe;
He is Oure Ladye's messangere;
  God graunt that he be true.'

'And a gode palfray,' sayde lytell Much,
  'To mayntene hym in his right';
'And a peyre of botes,' sayde Scarlok,
  'For he is a gentyll knight.'

'What shalt thou gyve hym, Litell John?' [said
    Robyn;]
  'Sir, a peyre of gilt sporis clene,
To pray for all this company;
  God bringe hym oute of tene.' [37]

'Whan shal mi day be,' said the knight,
  'Sir, and your wyll be?'
'This day twelve moneth,' saide Robyn,
  'Under this grene-wode tre.

'It were greate shame,' sayde Robyn,
  'A knight alone to ryde,
Withoutë squyre, yoman, or page,
  To walkë by his syde.

[37] Sorrow.

'I shal the lende Litell Johnn, my man,
  For he shalbe thy knave;[38]
In a yeman's stede he may the stande,
  If thou greate nedë have.'

THE SECOND FYTTE

Now is the knight gone on his way;
  This game hym thought full gode;
Whanne he loked on Bernesdale
  He blessyd Robyn Hode.

And whanne he thought on Bernysdale,
  On Scarlok, Much and Johnn,
He blessyd them for the best company
  That ever he in come.

Than spake that gentyll knyght,
  To Lytel Johan gan he saye,
'To-morrowe I must to Yorke toune
  To Saynt Mary abbay.

'And to the abbot of that place
  Foure hundred pounde I must pay;
And but I be there upon this nyght
  My londe is lost for ay.'

The abbot sayd to his covent,
  There he stode on grounde,
'This day twelfe moneth came a knyght
  And borowed foure hondred pounde.

['He borowed four hondred pounde]
  Upon his londe and fee;
But he come this ylkë[1] day
  Disherited[2] shall he be.'

'It is full erely,' sayd the pryoure,
  The day is not yet ferre gone;
[38] Servant.   [1] Same.   [2] Dispossessed.

I had lever³ to pay an hondred pounde,
  And lay it downe anone.

'The knyght is ferre beyonde the see,
  In Englonde is his ryght,
And suffreth honger and colde
  And many a sory nyght.

'It were grete pytë,' said the pryoure,
  'So to have his londe;
And ye be so lyght of your consyence,
  Ye do to hym moch wronge.'

'Thou arte ever in my berde,' ⁴ sayd the abbot,
  'By God and Saynt Rycharde';
With that cam in a fat-heded monke,
  The heygh selerer.⁵

'He is dede or hanged,' sayd the monke,
  'By God that bought me dere,
And we shall have to spende in this place
  Foure hondred pounde by yere.'

The abbot and the hy selerer
  Stertë forthe full bolde,
The highe justyce of Englonde
  The abbot there dyde holde.

The hye justyce and many mo
  Had taken into theyr honde
Holy⁶ all the knyghtes det,
  To put that knyght to wronge.

They demed the knyght wonder sore,
  The abbot and his meynë
'But⁷ he come this ylkë day
  Disherited shall he be.'

---

³ Rather.   ⁴ You are always in open opposition to me.   ⁵ Cellarer, purveyor.
          ⁶ Wholly.   ⁷ Unless.

'He wyll not come yet,' sayd the justyce,
   'I dare well undertake';
But in sorowe tymë for them all
   The knyght came to the gate.

Than bespake that gentyll knyght
   Untyll his meynë:
'Now put on your symple wedes[8]
   That ye brought fro the see.'

[They put on their symple wedes,]
   They came to the gates anone;
The porter was redy hymselfe
   And welcomed them everychone.

'Welcome, syr knyght,' sayd the porter,
   'My lorde to mete is he,
And so is many a gentyll man,
   For the love of the.'

The porter swore a full grete othe:
   'By God that madë me,
Here be the best coresed[9] hors
   That ever yet sawe I me.

'Lede them in to the stable,' he sayd,
   'That eased myght they be';
'They shall not come therin,' sayd the knyght,
   'By God that dyed on a tre.'

Lordës were to mete isette[10]
   In that abbotes hall;
The knyght went forth and kneled downe,
   And salued them grete and small.

'Do gladly, syr abbot,' sayd the knyght,
   'I am come to holde my day':
The fyrst word that the abbot spake,
   'Hast thou brought my pay?'

[8] Plain clothes.   [9] Harnessed (?), or conditioned (?).   [10] Set at meat.

'Not one peny,' sayd the knyght,
  'By God that maked me';
'Thou art a shrewed[11] dettour,' sayd the abbot;
  'Syr justyce, drynke to me.

'What doost thou here,' sayd the abbot,
  'But thou haddest brought thy pay?'
'For God,' than sayed the knyght,
  'To pray of a lenger daye.'

'Thy daye is broke,' sayd the justyce,
  'Londe gettest thou none':
'Now, good syr justyce, be my frende
  And fende me of my fone!'[12]

'I am holde with the abbot,' sayd the justyce,
  'Both with cloth and fee':
'Now, good syr sheryf, be my frende!'
  'Nay, for God,' sayd he.

'Now, good syr abbot, be my frende,
  For thy curteysë,
And holde my londës in thy honde
  Tyll I have made the gree!'[13]

'And I wyll be thy true servaunte,
  And trewely serve the,
Tyll ye have foure hondred pounde
  Of money good and free.'

The abbot sware a full grete othe,
  'By God that dyed on a tree,
Get thy londe where thou may,
  For thou getest none of me.'

'By dere worthy God,' then sayd the knyght,
  'That all this worldë wrought,
But I have my londe agayne,
  Full dere it shall be bought.

[11] Cursed.   [12] Defend me from my foes.   [13] Satisfaction.

'God, that was of a mayden borne,
  Leve us well to spede!
For it is good to assay a frende
  Or[14] that a man have nede.'

The abbot lothely on hym gan loke,
  And vylaynesly hym gan call;
'Out,' he sayd, 'thou false knyght,
  Spede the out of my hall!'

'Thou lyest,' then sayd the gentyll knyght,
  'Abbot, in thy hal;
False knyght was I never,
  By God that made us all.'

Up then stode that gentyll knyght,
  To the abbot sayd he,
'To suffre a knyght to knele so longe,
  Thou canst no curteysye.

'In joustes and in tournaments
  Full ferre than have I be,
And put myself as ferre in prees[15]
  As ony that ever I see.'

'What wyll ye gyve more,' sayd the justyce,
  'And the knyght shall make a releyse?
And elles dare I safly swere
  Ye holde never your londe in pees.'

'An hondred pounde,' sayd the abbot;
  The justice sayd, 'Gyve hym two';
'Nay, be God,' sayd the knyght,
  'Ye get not my land so.

'Though ye wolde gyve a thousand more,
  Yet were ye never the nere;
Shal there never be myn heyre
  Abbot, justice ne frere.'

[14] Before.   [15] The thick of the fight.

He stert[16] hym to a borde anone,
  Tyll a table rounde,
And there he shoke oute of a bagge
  Even four hundred pound.

'Have here thi golde, sir abbot,' saide the knight,
  'Which that thou lentest me;
Had thou ben curtes at my comynge,
  I would have rewarded thee.'

The abbot sat styll, and ete no more,
  For all his ryall fare;
He cast his hede on his shulder,
  And fast began to stare.

'Take[17] me my golde agayne,' saide the abbot,
  'Sir justice, that I toke the.'
'Not a peni,' said the justice,
  'Bi God, that dyed on tree.'

'Sir abbot, and ye men of lawe,
  Now have I holde my daye;
Now shall I have my londe agayne,
  For ought that you can saye.'

The knyght stert out of the dore,
  Awaye was all his care,
And on he put his good clothynge
  The other he lefte there.

He wente hym forth full mery syngynge,
  As men have told in tale;
His lady met hym at the gate,
  At home in Verysdale.

'Welcome, my lorde,' sayd his lady;
  'Syr, lost is all your good?'
'Be mery, dame,' sayd the knyght,
  'And pray for Robyn Hode,

[16] Turned quickly.   [17] Give.

'That ever his soule be in blysse:
  He holpe me out of tene;
Ne had be[18] his kyndënesse,
  Beggers had we bene.

'The abbot and I accorded ben,
  He is served of his pay;
The god yoman lent it me
  As I cam by the way.'

This knight than dwelled fayre at home,
  The sothe for to saye,
Tyll he had got four hundred pound,
  Al redy for to pay.

He purveyed him an hundred bowes,
  The strynges well ydyght,
An hundred shefe of arowes gode,
  The hedys burneshed full bryght;

And every arowe an ellë longe,
  With pecok well idyght,
Inocked[19] all with whyte silver;
  It was a semely syght.

He purveyed him an hondreth men,
  Well harnessed in that stede,
And hym selfe in that same suite,
  And clothed in whyte and rede.

He bare a launsgay[20] in his honde,
  And a man ledde his male,[21]
And reden with a lyght songe
  Unto Bernysdale.

[But at Wentbrydge] there was a wrastelyng,
  And there taryed was he,
And there was all the best yemen
  Of all the west countree.

[18] If it had not been.   [19] Notched.   [20] Spear.   [21] Pack, baggage.

A full fayre game there was up set,
  A whyte bulle up i-pyght,[22]
A grete courser, with sadle and brydil,
  With golde burnyssht full bryght.

A payre of gloves, a rede golde rynge,
  A pype of wyne, in fay;[23]
What man that bereth hym best i-wys[24]
  The pryce shall bere away.

There was a yoman in that place,
  And best worthy was he,
And for he was ferre and frembde bested,[25]
  Slayne he shulde have be.

The knight had ruthe of this yoman,
  In place where that he stode;
He sayde that yoman shulde have no harme,
  For love of Robyn Hode.

The knyght pressed in to the place,
  An hundreth folowed hym free,
With bowes bent and arowes sharpe,
  For to shende[26] that companye.

They shulderd all and made hym rome,
  To wete[27] what he wolde say;
He toke the yeman bi the hande,
  And gave hym al the play.

He gave hym five marke for his wyne,
  There it lay on the molde,[28]
And bad it shulde be set a broche,[29]
  Drynkë who so wolde.

Thus longe taried this gentyll knyght,
  Tyll that play was done;
So longe abode Robyn fastinge
  Thre houres after the none.

[22] Pitched, set up as a prize.   [23] In faith.   [24] Certainly.   [25] Because he was far from home and situated as a stranger.   [26] Punish.   [27] Know.   [28] Ground.   [29] Tapped and left running.

The Thirde Fytte

Lyth and lystyn, gentilmen,
　All that nowe be here;
Of Litell Johnn, that was the knightes man,
　Goode myrth ye shall here.

It was upon a mery day
　That yonge men wolde go shete;
Lytell Johnn fet his bowe anone,
　And sayde he wolde them mete.

Thre tymes Litell Johnn shet aboute,
　And alway cleft the wande;
The proude sherif of Notingham
　By the markes gan stande.

The sherif swore a full greate othe:
　By hym that dyede on a tre,
This man is the best arschere
　That ever I dyd see.

'Say me nowe, wight yonge man,
　What is nowe thy name?
In what countre were thou borne,
　And where is thy wonynge wane?' [1]

'In Holdernes, sir, I was borne,
　I-wys al of my dame;
Men cal me Reynolde Grenelef
　Whan I am at home.'

'Sey me, Reynolde Grenelefe,
　Wolde thou dwell with me?
And every yere I woll the gyve
　Twenty marke to thy fee.'

'I have a maister,' sayde Litell Johnn,
　'A curteys knight is he;
　　　[1] Dwelling place.

May ye levë gete of hym,
　The better may it be.'

The sherif gate Litell John
　Twelve moneths of the knight;
Therefore he gave him right anone
　A gode hors and a wight.[2]

Nowe is Litell John the sherifes man,
　God lende us well to spede!
But alwey thought Lytell John
　To quyte hym wele his mede.[3]

'Nowe so God me helpe,' sayde Litell John,
　'And by my true leutye,[4]
I shall be the worst servaunt to hym
　That ever yet had he.'

It fell upon a Wednesday
　The sherif on huntynge was gone,
And Litel John lay in his bed,
　And was foriete[5] at home.

Therfore he was fastinge
　Til it was past the none;
'Gode sir stuarde, I pray to the,
　Gyve me my dynere,' saide Litell John.

'It is to longe for Grenelefe
　Fastinge thus for to be;
Therfor I pray the, sir stuarde,
　Mi dyner gif thou me.'

'Shalt thou never ete ne drynke,' saide the stuarde,
　'Tyll my lorde be come to towne':
'I make myn avowe to God,' saide Litell John,
　'I had lever to crake thy crowne.'

The boteler was full uncurteys,
　There he stode on flore;

<hr/>

[2] Strong.　　[3] To reward him well.　　[4] Loyalty.　　[5] Forgotten.

He start to the botery
And shet fast the dore.

Lytell Johnn gave the boteler suche a tap
  His backe went nere in two;
Though he liveth an hundred wynter,
  The wors he still shall goe.

He sporned the dore with his fote;
  It went open wel and fyne;
And there he made large lyveray,[6]
  Bothe of ale and of wyne.

'Sith ye wol nat dyne,' sayde Litell John,
  'I shall gyve you to drinke;
And though ye lyve an hundred wynter,
  On Lytel Johnn ye shall thinke.'

Litell John ete, and Litel John drank,
  The whilë that he wolde;
The sherife had in his kechyn a coke,
  A stoute man and a bolde.

'I make myn avowe to God,' saide the coke,
  'Thou arte a shrewde hyne[7]
In ani householde for to dwel,
  For to aske thus to dyne.'

And there he lent Litell John
  Godë strokis thre;
'I make myn avowe,' sayde Lytell John,
  'These strokis lyked well me.

'Thou arte a bolde man and a hardy,
  And so thinketh me;
And or I pas fro this place
  Assayed better shalt thou be.'

Lytell Johnn drew a ful gode sworde,
  The coke toke another in hande;

---

[6] Delivery of rations.   [7] Cursed fellow.

They thought no thynge for to fle,
But stifly for to stande.

There they faught sore togedere
Two mylë way[8] and more;
Myght neyther other harme done,
The mountnaunce of an owre.[9]

'I make myn avowe to God,' sayde Litell Johnn,
'And by my true lewtë;
Thou art one of the best sworde-men
That ever yit sawe I me.

'Cowdest thou shote as well in a bowe,
To grene wode thou shuldest with me,
And two times in the yere thy clothinge
Chaunged shuldë be;

'And every yere of Robyn Hode
Twenty merke to thy fe;'
'Put up thy swerde,' saide the coke
'And felowes woll we be.'

Thanne he fet to Lytell Johnn
The nowmbles of a do,
Gode brede and full gode wyne;
They ete and drank theretoo.

And when they had dronkyn well,
Theyre trouthes togeder they plight
That they wolde by with Robyn
That ylkë samë[10] nyght.

They dyd them[11] to the tresoure-hows,
As fast as they myght gone;
The lokkes, that were of full gode stele,
They brake them everichone.

---

[8] As long as it would take to go two miles.   [9] The length of an hour.   [10] Very same.   [11] Went.

They toke away the silver vessell,
  And all that thei might get;
Pecis,[12] masars,[13] ne sponis,
  Wolde thei not forget.

Also they toke the gode pens,
  Thre hundred pounde and more,
And did them streyte to Robyn Hode,
  Under the grene wode hore.

'God the save, my dere mayster,
  And Criste the save and se!'
And thanne sayde Robyn to Litell Johnn
  'Welcome myght thou be.

'Also be that fayre yeman
  Thou bryngest there with the;
What tydynges fro Notyngham?
  Lytill Johnn, tell thou me.'

'Well the gretith the proude sheryf.
  And sendeth the here by me
His cok and his silver vessell,
  And thre hundred pounde and thre.'

'I make myne avowe to God,' sayde Robyn,
  'And to the Trenytë,
It was never by his gode wyll
  This gode is come to me.'

Lytyll Johnn there hym bethought
  On a shrewde wyle;[14]
Fyve myle in the forest he ran,
  Hym happed all his wyll.[15]

Than he met the proude sheref,
  Huntynge with houndes and horne;
Lytell Johnn coude[16] of curtesye,
  And knelyd hym beforne.

[12] Cups.   [13] Bowls.   [14] Wicked trick.   [15] What he wished happened to him.
[16] Knew.

'God the save, my dere mayster,
   And Criste the save and se!'
'Reynolde Grenelefe,' sayde the shyref,
   'Where hast thou nowe be?'

'I have be in this forest;
   A fayre syght can I se;
It was one of the fayrest syghtes
   That ever yet sawe I me.

'Yonder I sawe a ryght fayre harte,
   His coloure is of grene;
Seven score of dere upon a herde
   Be with hym all bydene.[17]

'Their tyndes[18] are so sharp, maister,
   Of sexty, and well mo,
That I durst not shote for drede,
   Lest they wolde me slo.[19]

'I make myn avowe to God,' sayde the shyref,
   'That syght wolde I fayne se':
'Buske you thyderwarde, mi dere mayster,
   Anone, and wende with me.'

The sherif rode, and Litell Johnn
   Of fote he was full smerte,
And whane they came before Robyn,
   'Lo, here is the mayster-herte.'

Still stode the proude sherief,
   A sory man was he;
'Wo the worthe, Raynolde Grenelefe,
   Thou hast betrayed me.'

'I make myn avowe to God,' sayde Litell Johnn,
   'Mayster, ye be to blame;
I was mysserved of my dynere
   When I was with you at home.'

[17] At once.   [18] Tines.   [19] Slay.

Sone he was to souper sette,
  And served with silver white,
And when the sherif sawe his vessell,
  For sorowe he myght nat ete.

'Make glad chere,' sayde Robyn Hode,
  'Sherif, for charitë,
And for the love of Litill Johnn
  Thy lyfe I graunt to the.'

Whan they had souped well,
  The day was al gone;
Robyn commaunded Litell Johnn
  To drawe of his hose and shone;

His kirtell, and his cote a pye,[20]
  That was fured well and fine
And toke hym a grene mantel,
  To lap his body therein.

Robyn commaundyd his wight yonge men,
  Under the grene wode tree,
  They shulde lye in that same sute
  That the sherif myght them see.

All nyght lay the proude sherif
  In his breche and in his schert;
No wonder it was, in grene wode;
  Though his sydes gan to smerte.

'Make glad chere,' sayde Robyn Hode,
  'Sheref, for charitë;
For this is our ordre i-wys
  Under the grene-wode tree.

'This is harder order,' sayde the sherief,
  'Than any ankir[21] or frere;
For all the golde in mery Englonde
  I wolde nat longe dwell her.'

[20] Short coat.   [21] Anchorite, hermit.

'All this twelve monthes,' sayde Robin,
  'Thou shalt dwell with me;
I shall the teche, proude sherif,
  An outlawe for to be.'

'Or I here another nyght lye,' sayde the sherif,
  'Robyn, nowe pray I the,
Smyte of mijn hede rather to-morowe,
  And I forgyve it the.

'Lat me go,' than sayde the sherif,
  'For saynte charite,
And I woll be the best frende
  That ever yet had ye.'

'Thou shalt swere me an othe,' sayde Robyn,
  'On my bright bronde;
Shalt thou never awayte me scathe[22]
  By water ne by lande.

'And if thou fynde any of my men,
  By nyght or by day,
Upon thyn othe thou shalt swere
  To helpe them that thou may.'

Nowe hathe the sherif sworne his othe,
  And home he began to gone;
He was as full of grene wode
  As ever was hepe[23] of stone.

The Fourth Fytte

The sherif dwelled in Notingham;
  He was fayne he was agone;
And Robyn and his mery men
  Went to wode anone.

'Go we to dyner,' sayde Littell Johnn;
  Robyn Hode sayde, 'Nay;

[22] Lie in wait to harm me.   [23] Hip.

For I drede Our Lady be wroth with me,
 For she sent me nat my pay.'

'Have no doute, maister,' sayde Litell Johnn;
 'Yet is not the sonne at rest;
For I dare say, and savely swere,
 The knight is true and truste.'

'Take thy bowe in thy hande,' sayde Robyn,
 'Late Much wende with the,
And so shal Wyllyam Scarlok,
 And no man abyde with me.

'And walke up under the Sayles,
 And to Watlynge-strete,
And wayte after some unketh gest;
 Up-chaunce ye may them mete.

'Whether he be messengere,
 Or a man that myrthës can,
Of my good he shall have some,
 Yf he be a pore man.'

Forth then stert Lytel Johan,
 Half in tray and tene,[1]
And gyrde hym with a full good swerde,
 Under a mantel of grene.

They went up to the Sayles,
 These yemen all thre;
They loked est, they loked west,
 They myght no man se.

But as they loked in Bernysdale,
 By the hyë waye,
Than were they ware of two blacke monkes,
 Eche on a good palferay.

Then bespake Lytell Johan,
 To Much he gan say,
   [1] Grief and sorrow.

'I dare lay my lyfe to wedde,[2]
These monkes have brought our pay.

'Make glad chere,' sayd Lytell Johan,
    'And frese[3] our bowes of ewe,
And loke your hertes be seker[4] and sad,[5]
    Your strynges trusty and trewe.

'The monke hath two and fifty men,
    And seven somers[6] full stronge;
There rydeth no bysshop in this londe
    So ryally, I understond.

'Brethren,' sayd Lytell Johan,
    'Here are no more but we thre;
But we brynge them to dyner,
    Our mayster dare we not se.

'Bende your bowes,' sayd Lytell Johan,
    'Make all yon prese[7] to stonde;
The formost monke, his lyfe and his deth
    Is closed in my honde.

'Abyde, chorle[8] monke,' sayd Lytell Johan,
    'No ferther that thou gone;
Yf thou doost, by dere worthy God,
    Thy deth is in my honde.

'And evyll thryfte[9] on thy hede,' sayd Lytell Johan,
    'Ryght under thy hattes bonde,
For thou hast made our mayster wroth,
    He is fastynge so longe.'

'Who is your mayster?' sayd the monke;
    Lytell Johan sayd, Robyn Hode;
'He is a stronge thefe,' sayd the monke,
    'Of hym herd I never good.'

---

[2] Pledge.   [3] *Apparently,* prepare.   [4] Firm.   [5] Steadfast.   [6] Pack-horses.   [7] Throng.
[8] Churl.   [9] Ill luck.

'Thou lyest,' than sayd Lytell Johan,
  'And that shall rewë the;
He is a yeman of the forest,
  To dyne he hath bodë[10] the.'

Much was redy with a bolte,
  Redly and anone,
He set[11] the monke to-fore the brest,
  To the grounde that he can gone.

Of two and fyfty wyght yonge yemen
  There abode not one,
Saf a lytell page and a grome,
  To lede the somers with Lytel Johan.

They brought the monke to the lodge-dore,
  Whether he were loth or lefe,[12]
For to speke with Robyn Hode,
  Maugre in[13] theyr tethe.

Robyn dyde a downe his hode,
  The monke whan that he se;
The monke was not so curteyse,
  His hode then let he be.

'He is a chorle, mayster, by dere worthy God,'
  Than sayd Lytell Johan:
'Thereof no force,' sayd Robyn,
  'For curteysy can he none.

'How many men,' sayd Robyn,
  'Had this monke, Johan?'
'Fyfty and two whan that we met,
  But many of them be gone.'

'Let blowe a horne,' sayd Robyn,
  'That felaushyp may us knowe';
Seven score of wyght yemen,
  Came pryckynge on a rowe.[14]

[10] Invited.   [11] Shot.   [12] Unwilling or willing.   [13] In spite of.   [14] Spurring
one behind another.

And everych of them a good mantell
　Of scarlet and of raye;[15]
All they came to good Robyn,
　To wyte[16] what he wolde say.

They made the monke to wasshe and wype,
　And syt at his denere,
Robyn Hode and Lytell Johan
　They served him both in-fere.[17]

'Do gladly, monke,' sayd Robyn.
　'Gramercy, syr,' sayd he.
'Where is your abbay, whan ye are at home,
　And who is your avowë?'[18]

'Saynt Mary abbay,' sayd the monke,
　'Though I be symple here.'
'In what offyce?' said Robyn:
　'Syr, the hye selerer.'

'Ye be the more welcome,' sayd Robyn,
　'So ever mote I the:[19]
Fyll of the best wyne,' sayd Robyn,
　'This monke shall drynke to me.

'But I have grete mervayle,' sayd Robyn,
　'Of all this longë day;
I drede Our Lady be wroth with me,
　She sent me not my pay.'

'Have no doute, mayster,' sayd Lytell Johan,
　'Ye have no nede, I saye;
This monke hath brought it, I dare well swere,
　For he is of her abbay.'

'And she was a borowe,'[20] sayd Robyn,
　'Betwene a knyght and me,
Of a lytell money that I hym lent,
　Under the grene-wode tree.

---

[15] Striped cloth.　[16] Know.　[17] Together.　[18] Patron.　[19] May I thrive.　[20] Security.

'And yf thou hast that sylver ibrought,
    I pray the let me se;
And I shall helpë the eftsones,[21]
    Yf thou have nede to me.'

The monke swore a full grete othe,
    With a sory chere,
'Of the borowehode thou spekest to me,
    Herde I never ere.'

'I make myn avowe to God,' sayd Robyn,
    'Monke, thou art to blame;
For God is holde a ryghtwys man,
    And so is his dame.

'Thou toldest with thyn owne tonge,
    Thou may not say nay,
How thou arte her servaunt,
    And servest her every day.

'And thou art made her messengere.
    My money for to pay;
Therefore I cun the morë thanke
    Thou arte come at thy day.

'What is in your cofers?' sayd Robyn,
    'Trewe than tell thou me':
'Syr,' he sayd, 'twenty marke,
    Al so mote I the.'

'Yf there be no more,' sayd Robyn,
    'I wyll not one peny;
Yf thou hast myster[22] of ony more,
    Syr, more I shall lende to the.'

'And yf I fynde more,' sayd Robyn,
    'I-wys[23] thou shalte it for gone;[24]
For of thy spendynge-sylver, monke,
    Thereof wyll I ryght none.

[21] Again.   [22] Need.   [23] Certainly.   [24] Give up.

'Go nowe forthe, Lytell Johan,
    And the trouth tell thou me;
If there be no more but twenty marke,
    No peny that I se.'

Lytell Johan spred his mantell downe,
    As he had done before,
And he tolde out of the monkes male[25]
    Eyght hondred pounde and more.

Lytell Johan let it lye full styll,
    And went to his mayster in hast;
'Syr,' he sayd, 'the monke is trewe ynowe,
    Our Lady hath doubled your cast.' [26]

'I make myn avowe to God,' sayd Robyn—
    'Monke, what tolde I the?—
Our Lady is the trewest woman
    That ever yet founde I me.

'By dere worthy God,' sayd Robyn,
    'To seche all Englond thorowe,
Yet founde I never to my pay[27]
    A moche better borowe.

'Fyll of the best wyne, and do hym drynke,' sayd
        Robyn,
    'And grete well thy lady hende,[28]
And yf she have nede to Robyn Hode,
    A frende she shall hym fynde.

'And yf she nedeth ony more sylver,
    Come thou agayne to me,
And, by this token she hath me sent,
    She shall have such thre.'

The monke was goynge to London ward,
    There to hold grete mote,[29]
The knyght that rode so hye on hors,
    To brynge hym under fote.

[25] Wallet.   [26] Venture.   [27] Satisfaction.   [28] Gentle.   [29] Meeting.

'Whether be ye away?' sayd Robyn:
  'Syr, to maners in this londe,
Too reken with our reves,
  That have done moch wronge.'

'Come now forth, Lytell Johan,
  And harken to my tale;
A better yemen I knowe none,
  To seke[30] a monkës male.'

'How moch is in yonder other corser?'[31] sayd Robyn,
  'The soth must we see';
By Our Lady,' than sayd the monke,
  'That were no curteysye,

'To bydde a man to dyner,
  And syth[32] hym bete and bynde.'
'It is our olde maner,' sayd Robyn,
  'To leve but lytell behynde.'

The monke toke the hors with spore,
  No lenger wolde he abyde:
'Aske to drynke,' than sayd Robyn,
  'Or that ye forther ryde.'

'Nay, for God,' than sayd the monke,
  'Me reweth[33] I cam so nere;
For better chepe I myght have dyned
  In Blythe or in Dankestere.'

'Grete well your abbot,' sayd Robyn,
  'And your pryour, I you pray,
And byd hym send me such a monke
  To dyner every day.'

Now lete we that monke be styll,
  And speke we of that knyght:
Yet he came to holde his day,
  Whyle that it was lyght.

[30] Search.   [31] Perhaps a mistake for *forcer* = coffer.   [32] Afterwards.
[33] It repents me.

He dyde him streyt to Bernysdale,
  Under the grene-wode tre,
And he founde there Robyn Hode,
  And all his mery meynë.

The knyght lyght doune of his good palfray;
  Robyn whan he gan see,
So curteysly he dyde adoune his hode,
  And set hym on his knee.

'God the save, Robyn Hode,
  And all this company':
'Welcome be thou, gentyll knyght,
  And ryght welcome to me.'

Than bespake hym Robyn Hode,
  To that knyght so fre:
What nede dryveth the to grene-wode?
  I praye the, syr knyght, tell me.

'And welcome be thou, gentyll knyght,
  Why hast thou be so longe?'
'For the abbot and the hye iustyce
  Wolde have had my londe.'

'Hast thou thy londe agayne?' sayd Robyn;
  'Treuth than tell thou me':
'Ye, for God,' sayd the knyght,
  'And that thanke I God and the.

'But take no grefe, that I have be so longe;
  I came by a wrastelynge,
And there I holpe a pore yeman,
  With wronge was put behynde.'

'Nay, for God,' sayd Robyn,
  'Syr knyght, that thanke I the;
What man that helpeth a good yeman,
  His frende than wyll I be.'

'Have here foure hondred pounde,' sayd the knyght,
    'The whiche ye lent to me;
And here is also twenty marke
    For your curteysy.'

'Nay, for God,' sayd Robyn,
    'Thou broke[34] it well for ay;
For Our Lady, by her hye selerer,
    Hath sent to me my pay.

'And yf I toke it i-twyse,
    A shame it were to me;
But trewely, gentyll knyght,
    Welcome arte thou to me.'

Whan Robyn had tolde his tale,
    He leugh and made good chere:
'By my trouthe,' then sayd the knyght,
    'Your money is redy here.'

'Broke it well,' said Robyn,
    'Thou gentyll knyght so fre;
And welcome be thou, gentyll knyght,
    Under my trystell-tre.[35]

'But what shall these bowes do?' sayd Robyn,
    'And these arowes ifedred[36] fre?'
'By God,' than sayd the knyght,
    'A pore present to the.'

'Come now forth, Lytell Johan,
    And go to my treasurë,
And brynge me there foure hondred pounde;
    The monke over-tolde it me.

'Have here foure hondred pounde,
    Thou gentyll knyght and trewe,
And bye thee hors and harnes good,
    And gylte thy spores all newe.

34 Enjoy.   **35** Tree appointed for meetings.   **36** Feathered.

'And yf thou fayle ony spendynge,
   Com to Robyn Hode,
And by my trouth thou shalt none fayle,
   The whyles I have any good.

'And broke well thy foure hondred pound,
   Whiche I lent to the,
And make thy selfe no more so bare,
   By the counsell of me.'

Thus than holpe hym good Robyn,
   The knyght all of his care:
God, that syt[37] in heven hye,
   Graunte us well to fare!

The Fyfth Fytte

Now hath the knyght his leve i-take,
   And wente hym on his way;
Robyn Hode and his mery men
   Dwelled styll full many a day.

Lyth and lysten, gentil men,
   And herken what I shall say,
How the proud sheryfe of Notyngham
   Dyde crye[1] a full fayre play;

That all the best archers of the north
   Sholde come upon a day,
And he that shoteth allther[2] best
   The game shall bere away.

He that shoteth allther best,
   Furthest fayre and lowe,
At a payre of fynly[3] buttes,
   Under the grene wode shawe,

A ryght good arowe he shall have,
   The shaft of sylver whyte,
The hede and feders of ryche rede golde,
   In Englond is none iyke.

---

[37] Sitteth.   [1] Caused to be announced.   [2] Of all.   [3] Goodly.

This than herde good Robyn,
Under his trystell-tre:
'Make you redy, ye wyght yonge men;
That shotynge wyll I se.

'Buske⁴ you, my mery yonge men;
Ye shall go with me;
And I wyll wete⁵ the shryvës fayth,
Trewe and yf he be.'

Whan they had theyr bowes i-bent,
Theyr takles fedred fre,
Seven score of wyght yonge men
Stode by Robyns kne.

Whan they cam to Notyngham,
The buttes were fayre and longe;
Many was the bolde archere
That shot with bowës stronge.

'There shall but syx shote with me;
The other shal kepe my he[ve]de,⁶
And stande with good bowes bent,
That I be not desceyved.'

The fourth outlawe his bowe gan bende,
And that was Robyn Hode,
And that behelde the proud sheryfe,
All by the but he stode.

Thryës Robyn shot about,
And alway he slist the wand,
And so dyde good Gylberte
With the whytë hande.

Lytell Johan and good Scatheloke
Were archers good and fre;
Lytell Much and good Reynolde,
The worste wolde they not be.

⁴ Prepare.   ⁵ Know.   ⁶ Head, safety.

Whan they had shot aboute,
   These archours fayre and good,
Evermore was the best,
   For soth, Robyn Hode.

Hym was delyvered the good arowe,
   For best worthy was he;
He toke the yeft[7] so curteysly,
   To grene-wode wolde he.

They cryed out on Robyn Hode,
   And grete hornes gan they blowe:
'Wo worth the,[8] treason!' sayd Robyn
   'Full evyl thou art to knowe.

'An wo be thou! thou proude sheryf,
   Thus gladdynge thy gest;
Other wyse thou behote[9] me
   In yonder wylde forest.

'But had I the in grene-wode,
   Under my trystell-tre,
Thou sholdest leve me a better wedde
   Than thy trewe lewtë.

Full many a bowë there was bent,
   And arowes let they glyde;
Many a kyrtell there was rent,
   And hurt many a syde.

The outlawes shot was so stronge
   That no man myght them dryve,
And the proud sheryfes men,
   They fled away full blyve.[10]

Robyn sawe the busshement[11] to-broke,
   In grene wode he wolde have be;
Many an arowe there was shot
   Amonge that company.

[7] Gift.   [8] Woe be to thee.   [9] Promised.   [10] Quickly.   [11] Ambuscade.

Lytell Johan was hurte full sore,
  With an arowe in his kne,
That he myght neyther go[12] nor ryde;
  It was full grete pytë.

'Mayster,' then sayd Lytell Johan,
  'If ever thou lovedst me,
And for that ylkë lordës love
  That dyed upon a tre,

'And for the medes of my servyce,
  That I have served the,
Lete never the proud sheryf
  Alyve now fyndë me.

'But take out thy browne swerde,
  And smyte all of my hede,
And gyve me woundës depe and wyde;
  No lyfe on me be lefte.'

'I wolde not that,' sayd Robyn,
  'Johan, that thou were slawe,[13]
For all the golde in merry Englonde,
  Though it lay now on a rawe.'

'God forbede,' sayd Lytell Much,
  'That dyed on a tre,
That thou sholdest, Lytell Johan,
  Parte our company.'

Up he toke hym on his backe,
  And bare hym well a myle;
Many a tyme he layd him downe,
  And shot another whyle.

Then was there a fayre castell,
  A lytell within the wode;
Double-dyched it was about,
  And walled, by the rode.

  ¹² Walk.   ¹³ Slain.

And there dwelled that gentyll knyght,
   Syr Rychard at the Lee,
That Robyn had lent his good,
   Under the grene-wode tree.

In he toke good Robyn,
   And all his company:
'Welcome be thou, Robyn Hode,
   Welcome art thou to me;

'And moche I thanke the of thy comfort,
   And of thy curteysye,
And of thy grete kyndnesse,
   Under the grene-wode tre.

'I love no man in all this worlde
   So much as I do the;
For all the proud sheryf of Notyngham,
   Ryght here shalt thou be.

'Shutte the gates, and drawe the brydge,
   And let no man come in,
And arme you well, and make you redy,
   And to the walles ye wynne.[14]

'For one thynge, Robyn, I the behote;
   I swere by Saynt Quyntyne,
These forty dayes thou wonnest[15] with me,
   To soupe, ete, and dyne.'

Bordes were layde, and clothes were spredde,
   Redely[16] and anone;
Robyn Hode and his merry men
   To metë can they gone.[17]

The Sixth Fytte

Lythe and lysten, gentylmen,
   And herkyn to your songe;
Howe the proude shyref of Notyngham,
   And men of armys stronge,

[14] Go.   [15] Dwellest.   [16] Quickly.   [17] Did they go.

Full fast cam to the hye shyref,
  The contrë up to route,
And they besette the knyghtes castell,
  The wallës all aboute.

The proude shyref loude gan crye,
  And sayde, 'Thou traytour knight,
Thou kepest here the kynges enemys,
  Agaynst the lawe and right.'

'Sir, I wyll avow that I have done,
  The dedys that here be dyght,[1]
Upon all the landës that I have,
  As I am a trewe knyght.

'Wende furth, sirs, on your way,
  And do no more to me
Tyll ye wyt oure kyngës wille,
  What he wyll say to the.'

The shyref thus had his answere,
  Without any lesynge;[2]
Forth he yede[3] to London towne,
  All for to tel our kinge.

Ther he telde him of that knight,
  And eke of Robyn Hode,
And also of the bolde archars,
  That were soo noble and gode.

'He wyll avowe that he hath done,
  To mayntene the outlawes stronge;
He wyll be lorde, and set you at nought,
  In all the northe londe.'

'I wil be at Notyngham,' saide our kynge,
  'Within this fourteenyght,
And take I wyll Robyn Hode
  And so I wyll that knight.

[1] Prepared.   [2] Falsehood.   [3] Went.

'Go nowe home, shyref,' sayde our kynge,
  'And do as I byd the;
And ordeyn gode archers ynowe,
  Of all the wyde contrë.'

The shyref had his leve i-take,
  And went hym on his way,
And Robyn Hode to grene wode,
  Upon a certen day.

And Lytel John was hole of the arowe
  That shot was in his kne,
And dyd hym streyght to Robyn Hode,
  Under the grene wode tree.

Robyn Hode walked in the forest,
  Under the levys grene;
The proude shyref of Notyngham
  Thereof he had grete tene.[4]

The shyref there fayled of Robyn Hode,
  He myght not have his pray;
Than he awayted[5] this gentyll knyght,
  Bothe by nyght and day.

Ever he wayted[5] the gentyll knyght,
  Syr Richarde at the Lee,
As he went on haukynge by the ryver-syde,
  And lete his haukës flee.

Toke he there this gentyll knight,
  With men of armys stronge,
And led hym to Notynghamwarde,
  Bound bothe fote and hande.

The shyref sware a full grete othe,
  Bi him that dyed on rode,
He had lever than an hundred pound
  That he had Robyn Hode.

  [4] Annoyance.   [5] Lay in wait for.

This harde the knyghtës wyfe,
  A fayr lady and a free;
She set hir on a gode palfrey,
  To grene wode anone rode she.

Whanne she cam in the forest,
  Under the grene wode tree,
Fonde she there Robyn Hode,
  And al his fayre menë.[6]

'God the save, gode Robyn,
  And all thy company;
For Our dere Ladyes sake,
  A bone graunte thou me.

'Late never my wedded lorde
  Shamefully slayne be;
He is fast bound to Notinghamwarde,
  For the love of the.'

Anone than saide goode Robyn
  To that lady so fre,
'What man hath your lorde ytake?'
  'The proude shirife,' than sayd she.

. . . .
  'For soth as I the say;
He is nat yet thre mylës
  Passed on his way.'

Up than sterte gode Robyn,
  As man that had ben wode:
'Buske you, my mery men,
  For hym that dyed on rode.

'And he that this sorowe forsaketh,
  By hym that dyed on tre,
Shall he never in grene wode
  No lenger dwel with me.'

[6] Retinue.

Sone there were gode bowës bent,
    Mo than seven score;
Hedge ne dyche spared they none
    That was them before.

'I make myn avowe to God,' sayde Robyn
    'The sherif wolde I fayne see;
And if I may him take,
    I-quyt[7] then shall he be.'

And when they came to Notingham,
    They walked in the strete;
And with the proude sherif i-wys
    Sonë can they mete.

'Abyde, thou proude sherif,' he sayde,
    'Abyde, and speke with me;
Of some tidinges of oure kinge
    I wolde fayne here of the.

'This seven yere, by dere worthy God,
    Ne yede[8] I this fast on fote;
I make myn avowe to God, thou proude sherif,
    It is not for thy gode.'

Robyn bent a full goode bowe,
    An arrowe he drowe at wyll;
He hit so the proude sherife
    Upon the grounde he lay full still.

And or he myght up aryse,
    On his fete to stonde,
He smote of the sherifs hede
    With his bright bronde.

'Lye thou there, thou proude sherife;
    Evyll mote[9] thou thryve:
There myght no man to the truste
    The whyles thou were a lyve.'

[7] Requited.   [8] Went.   [9] May.

His men drewe out theyr bryght swerdes,
  That were so sharpe and kene,
And layde on the sheryves men,
  And dryved them downe bydene.[10]

Robyn stert to that knyght,
  And cut a two his bonde,
And toke hym in his hand a bowe,
  And bad hym by hym stonde.

'Leve thy hors the behynde,
  And lerne for to renne;
Thou shalt with me to grene wode,
  Through myre, mosse, and fenne.

'Thou shalt with me to grene wode,
  Without ony leasynge,
Tyll that I have gete us grace
  Of Edwarde, our comly kynge.'

THE SEVENTH FYTTE

The kynge came to Notynghame,
  With knyghtes in grete araye,
For to take that gentyll knyght
  And Robyn Hode, and yf he may.

He asked men of that countrë,
  After Robyn Hode,
And after that gentyll knyght,
  That was so bolde and stout.

Whan they had tolde hym the case
  Our kynge understode ther tale,
And seased in his honde
  The knyghtës londës all.

All the passe[1] of Lancasshyre
  He went both ferre and nere,

---

[10] Quickly.   [1] Extent (?).

Tyll he came to Plomton Parke;
He faylyd[2] many of his dere.

There[3] our kynge was wont to se
Herdës many one,
He coud unneth fynde one dere,
That bare ony good horne.

The kynge was wonder wroth with all,
And swore by the Trynytë,
'I wolde I had Robyn Hode,
With eyen I myght hym se.

'And he that wolde smyte of the knyghtës hede,
And brynge it to me,
He shall have the knyghtës londes,
Syr Rycharde at the Le.

'I gyve it hym with my charter,
And sele it with my honde,
To have and holde for ever more,
In all mery Englonde.'

Than bespake a fayre olde knyght,
That was treue in his fay:
'A, my leegë lorde the kynge,
One worde I shall you say.

'There is no man in this countrë
May have the knyghtës londes,
Whyle Robyn Hode may ryde or gone,
And bere a bowe in his hondes.

'That he ne shall lese[4] his hede,
That is the best ball in his hode:
Give it no man, my lorde the kynge,
That ye wyll any good.'

Half a yere dwelled our comly kynge
In Notyngham, and well more;

---

[2] Missed.   [3] Where.   [4] Lose.

Coude he not here of Robyn Hode,
    In what countrë that he were.

But alway went good Robyn
    By halke[5] and eke by hyll,
And alway slewe the kyngës dere,
    And welt[6] them at his wyll.

Than bespake a proude fostere,
    That stode by our kyngës kne:
'Yf ye wyll see good Robyn,
    Ye must do after me.

'Take fyve of the best knyghtes
    That be in your lede,[7]
And walke downe by yon abbay,
    And gete you monkës wede.[8]

And I wyll be your ledes-man,[9]
    And lede you the way,
And or ye come to Notyngham,
    Myn hede then dare I lay,

That ye shall mete with good Robyn,
    On lyve[10] yf that he be;
Or ye come to Notyngham,
    With eyen ye shall hym se.

Full hastely our kynge was dyght,[11]
    So were his knyghtës fyve,
Everych of them in monkës wede,
    And hasted them thyder blyve.[12]

Our kynge was grete above his cole,[13]
    A brode hat on his crowne,
Ryght as he were abbot-lyke,
    They rode up into the towne.

---

[5] Hiding place.   [6] Controlled.   [7] Company.   [8] Garments.   [9] Guide.   [10] Alive.
[11] Prepared.   [12] Quickly.   [13] Cowl.

Styf botes our kynge had on,
  Forsoth as I you say;
He rode syngynge to grene wode,
  The covent[14] was clothed in graye.

His male-hors[15] and his grete somers[16]
  Folowed our kynge behynde,
Tyll they came to grene wode,
  A myle under the lynde.[17]

There they met with good Robyn,
  Stondynge on the waye,
And so dyde many a bolde archere,
  For soth as I you say.

Robyn toke the kyngës hors,
  Hastely in that stede,
And sayd, Syr abbot, by your leve,
  A whyle ye must abyde.

'We be yemen of this foreste,
  Under the grene-wode tre;
We lyve by our kyngës dere,
  Other shift have not wee.

'And ye have chyrches and rentës both,
  And gold full grete plentë;
Gyve us some of your spendynge,
  For saynt charytë.'

Than bespake our cumly kynge,
  Anone than sayd he;
'I brought no more to grene-wode
  But forty pounde with me.

'I have layne at Notyngham,
  This fourtynyght with our kynge,
And spent I have full moche good
  On many a grete lordynge.

14 The knights dressed as members of a convent.   15 Pack-horse.   16 Sumpter-horse.
17 Linden.

'And I have but forty pounde,
　　No more than have I me:
But if I had an hondred pounde,
　　I would give it to thee.'

Robyn toke the forty pounde,
　　And departed it in two partye;
Halfendell[18] he gave his mery men,
　　And bad them mery to be.

Full curteysly Robyn gan say;
　　'Syr, have this for your spendyng;
We shall mete another day;'
　　'Gramercy,' than sayd our kynge.

'But well the greteth Edwarde, our kynge,
　　And sent to the his seale,
And byddeth the com to Notyngham,
　　Both to mete and mele.'

He toke out the brode targe,[19]
　　And sone he lete hym se;
Robyn coud his courteysy,
　　And set hym on his kne.

'I love no man in all the worlde
　　So well as I do my kynge;
Welcome is my lordës seale;
　　And, monke, for thy tydynge,

'Syr abbot, for thy tydynges,
　　To day thou shalt dyne with me,
For the love of my kynge,
　　Under my trystell-tre.'

Forth he lad our comly kynge,
　　Full fayre by the honde;
Many a dere there was slayne,
　　And full fast dyghtande.[20]

[18] Half.　　[19] Charter.　　[20] Preparing.

Robyn toke a full grete horne,
  And loude he gan blowe;
Seven score of wyght yonge men
  Came redy on a rowe.

All they kneled on theyr kne,
  Full fayre before Robyn:
The kynge sayd hym selfe untyll,
  And swore by Saynt Austyn,

'Here is a wonder semely sight;
  Me thynketh, by Goddës pyne,[21]
His men are more at his byddynge
  Then my men be at myn.'

Full hastely was theyr dyner idyght,[22]
  And therto gan they gone;
They served our kynge with all theyr myght,
  Both Robyn and Lytell Johan.

Anone before our kynge was set
  The fattë venyson,
The good whyte brede, the good rede wyne,
  And therto the fyne ale and browne.

'Make good chere,' said Robyn,
  'Abbot, for charytë;
And for this ylkë[23] tydynge,
  Blyssed mote thou be.

'Now shalte thou se what lyfe we lede,
  Or[24] thou hens wende;
Than thou may enfourme our kynge,
  Whan ye togyder lende.'[25]

Up they sterte all in hast,
  Theyr bowes were smartly bent;
Our kynge was never so sore agast,
  He wende[26] to have be shente.[27]

[21] Passion.   [22] Got ready.   [23] Same.   [24] Before.   [25] Dwell.   [26] Thought.   [27] Injured.

Two yerdes there were up set,
 Thereto gan they gange;
By fyfty pase, our kynge sayd,
 The merkës were to longe.

On every syde a rose-garlonde,
 They shot under the lyne:[28]
'Who so fayleth of the rose-garlonde,' sayd Robyn,
 'His takyll he shall tyne.'[29]

'And yelde it to his mayster,
 Be it never so fyne;
For no man wyll I spare,
 So drynke I ale or wyne;

'And bere a buffet on his hede,
 I-wys ryght all bare':
And all that fell in Robyns lote,
 He smote them wonder sare.

Twyse Robyn shot aboute,
 And ever he cleved the wande,
And so dyde good Gylberte
 With the whytë hande.

Lytell Johan and good Scathelocke,
 For nothynge wolde they spare;
When they fayled of the garlonde,
 Robyn smote them full sore.

At the last shot that Robyn shot,
 For all his frendës fare,[30]
Yet he fayled of the garlonde
 Thre fyngers and mare.

Than bespake good Gylberte,
 And thus he gan say;
'Mayster,' he sayd, 'your takyll is lost,
 Stande forth and take your pay.'

[28] Linden-tree.   [29] Lose.   [30] In spite of what his friends had done.

'If it be so,' sayd Robyn,
   'That may no better be,
Syr abbot, I delyver the myn arowe,
   I pray the, syr, serve thou me.'

'It falleth not for myn ordre,' sayd our kynge,
   'Robyn, by thy leve,
For to smyte no good yeman,
   For doute I sholde hym greve.'

'Smyte on boldely,' sayd Robyn,
   'I give the largë leve':
Anone our kynge, with that worde,
   He folde up his sleve.

And sych a buffet he gave Robyn,
   To grounde he yede[31] full nere:
'I make myn avowe to God,' sayd Robyn,
   'Thou arte a stalworthe frere.

'There is pith in thyn arme,' sayd Robyn,
   'I trowe thou canst well shete';
Thus our kynge and Robyn Hode
   Togeder gan they mete.

Robyn behelde our comly kynge
   Wystly[32] in the face,
So dyde Syr Rycharde at the Le,
   And kneled downe in that place.

And so dyde all the wylde outlawes,
   Whan they se them knele:
'My lorde the kynge of Englonde,
   Now I knowe you well.'

'Mercy then, Robyn,' sayd our kynge,
   'Under your trystyll-tre,
Of thy goodnesse and thy grace,
   For my men and me!'

[31] Went.   [32] Thoughtfully.

'Yes, for God,' sayd Robyn,
'And also God me save,
I aske mercy, my lorde the kynge,
And for my men I crave.'

'Yes, for God,' than sayd our kynge,
'And therto sent I me,
With that thou leve the grene-wode,
And all thy company;

'And come home, syr, to my courte,
And there dwell with me.'
'I make myn avowe to God,' sayd Robyn,
'And ryght so shall it be.

'I wyll come to your courte,
Your servyse for to se,
And brynge with me of my men
Seven score and thre.

'But me lyke[33] well your servyse,
I wyll come agayne full soone,
And shote at the donnë[34] dere,
As I am wonte to done.'

THE EIGHTH FYTTE

'Haste thou ony grene cloth,' sayd our kynge,
'That thou wylte sell nowe to me?'
'Ye, for God,' sayd Robyn,
'Thyrty yerdes and thre.'

'Robyn,' sayd our kynge,
'Now pray I the,
Sell me some of that cloth,
To me and my meynë.'

'Yes, for God,' then sayd Robyn,
'Or elles I were a fole;
Another day ye wyll me clothe,
I trowe, ayenst the Yole.'[1]

[33] Unless I like.   [34] Dun.   [1] In preparation for Christmas.

The kynge kest of his cole then,
  A grene garment he dyde on,
And every knyght also, iwys,
  Another had full sone.

Whan they were clothed in Lyncolne grene,
  They keste away theyr graye;
'Now we shall to Notyngham,'
  All thus our kynge gan say.

They bente theyr bowes and forth they went,
  Shotynge all in-fere,[2]
Towarde the towne of Notyngham,
  Outlawes as they were.

Our kynge and Robyn rode togyder,
  For soth as I you say,
And they shote plucke-buffet,
  As they went by the way.

And many a buffet our kynge wan
  Of Robyn Hode that day,
And nothynge spared good Robyn
  Our kynge when he did pay.

'So God me helpë,' sayd our kynge,
  'Thy game is nought to lere[3];
I sholde not get a shote of the,
  Though I shote all this yere.'

All the people of Notyngham
  They stode and behelde;
They sawe nothynge but mantels of grene
  That covered all the felde.

Than every man to other gan say,
  'I drede our kynge be slone[4];
Come Robyn Hode to the towne, i-wys
  On lyve he lefte never one.'

Full hastely they began to fle,
  Both yemen and knaves,
And olde wyves that myght evyll goo,
  They hypped on theyr staves.

The kynge loughe full fast,
  And commaunded theym agayne;
When they se our comly kynge,
  I-wys they were full fayne.

They ete and dranke, and made them glad,
  And sange with notës hye;
Than bespake our comly kynge
  To Syr Richarde at the Lee.

He gave hym there his londe agayne,
  A good man he bad hym be;
Robyn thanked our comly kynge,
  And set hym on his kne.

Had Robyn dwelled in the kynges courte
  But twelve monethes and thre,
That he had spent an hondred pounde,
  And all his mennes fe.

In every place where Robyn came
  Ever more he layde downe,[5]
Both for knyghtës and for squyres,
  To gete hym grete renowne.

By than the yere was all agone
  He had no man but twayne,
Lytell Johan and good Scathelocke,
  With hym all for to gone.

Robyn sawe yonge men shote
  Full faire upon a day;
'Alas!' than sayd good Robyn,
  'My welthe is went away.

[5] Paid liberally.

'Somtyme I was an archere good,
 A styffe and eke a stronge;
I was compted the best archere
 That was in mery Englonde.

'Alas!' then sayd good Robyn,
 'Alas and well a woo!
Yf I dwele lenger with the kynge,
 Sorowe wyll me sloo.'

Forth than went Robyn Hode
 Tyll he came to our kynge:
'My lorde the kynge of Englonde,
 Graunte me myn askynge.

'I made a chapell in Bernysdale,
 That semely is to se,
It is of Mary Magdaleyne,
 And thereto wolde I be.

'I myght never in this seven nyght
 No tyme to slepe ne wynke,
Nother all these seven dayes
 Nother ete ne drynke.

'Me longeth sore to Bernysdale,
 I may not be therfro;
Barefote and wolwarde[6] I have hyght[7]
 Thyder for to go.'

'Yf it be so,' than sayd our kynge,
 'It may no better be;
Seven nyght I gyve the leve,
 No lengre, to dwell fro me.'

'Gramercy, lorde,' then sayd Robyn,
 And set hym on his kne;
He toke his leve full courteysly,
 To grene wode then went he.

[6] Doing penance by wearing wool next the skin.   [7] Promised.

Whan he came to grene wode,
  In a mery mornynge,
There he herde the notës small
  Of byrdës mery syngynge.

'It is ferre gone,' sayd Robyn,
  'That I was last here;
Me lyste[8] a lytell for to shote
  At the donnë dere.'

Robyn slewe a full grete harte;
  His horne than gan he blow,
That all the outlawes of that forest
  That horne coud they knowe,

And gadred them togyder,
  In a lytell throwe.
Seven score of wyght yonge men
  Came redy on a rowe,

And fayre dyde of theyr hodes,
  And set them on theyr kne:
'Welcome,' they sayd, 'our mayster,
  Under this grene-wode tre.'

Robyn dwelled in grene wode
  Twenty yere and two;
For all drede of Edwarde our kynge,
  Agayne wolde he not goo.

Yet he was begyled, i-wys,
  Through a wycked woman,
The pryoresse of Kyrkësly,
  That nye was of hys kynne:

For the love of a knyght,
  Syr Roger of Donkesly,
That was her ownë speciall;
  Full evyll mote they the![9]

[8] It pleases me.   [9] May they thrive!

They toke togyder theyr counsell
　Robyn Hode for to sle,
And how they myght best do that dede,
　His banis[10] for to be.

Than bespake good Robyn,
　In place where as he stode,
'To morow I muste to Kyrke[s]ly,
　Craftely[11] to be leten blode.'

Syr Roger of Donkestere,
　By the pryoresse he lay,
And there they betrayed good Robyn Hode,
　Through theyr falsë playe.

Cryst have mercy on his soule,
　That dyed on the rode!
For he was a good outlawe,
　And dyde pore men moch god.

ANONYMOUS

[16th Century]

33　　　　BALOW

BALOW, my babe, lie still and sleep!
It grieves me sore to see thee weep.
Wouldst thou be quiet I'se be glad,
Thy mourning makes my sorrow sad:
Balow my boy, thy mother's joy,
Thy father breeds me great annoy—
　　　　　Balow, la-low!

When he began to court my love,
And with his sugred words me move,
His faynings false and flattering cheer
To me that time did not appear:
But now I see most cruellye.
He cares ne for my babe nor me—
　　　　　Balow, la-low!

[10] Murderer.　[11] Skillfully.

Lie still, my darling, sleep awhile,
And when thou wak'st thou'le sweetly smile:
But smile not as thy father did,
To cozen maids: nay, God forbid!
But yet I fear thou wilt go near
Thy father's heart and face to bear—
Balow, la-low!

I cannot choose but ever will
Be loving to thy father still;
Where'er he go, where'er he ride,
My love with him doth still abide;
In weal or woe, where'er he go,
My heart shall ne'er depart him fro—
Balow, la-low!

But do not, do not, pretty mine,
To faynings false thy heart incline!
Be loyal to thy lover true,
And never change her for a new:
If good or fair, of her have care
For women's banning's wondrous sare-
Balow, la-low!

Bairn, by thy face I will beware;
Like Sirens' words, I'll come not near;
My babe and I together will live;
He'll comfort me when cares do grieve.
My babe and I right soft will lie,
And ne'er respect man's crueltye—
Balow, la-low!

Farewell, farewell, the falsest youth
That ever kist a woman's mouth!
I wish all maids be warn'd by me
Never to trust man's curtesye;
For if we do but chance to bow,
They'll use us then they care not how—
Balow, la-low!

34   THE OLD CLOAK

                          [*16th Century* (?)]

THIS winter's weather it waxeth cold,
  And frost it freezeth on every hill,
And Boreas blows his blast so bold
  That all our cattle are like to spill.
Bell, my wife, she loves no strife;
  She said unto me quietlye,
Rise up, and save cow Crumbock's life!
  Man, put thine old cloak about thee!

He.

O Bell my wife, why dost thou flyte?
  Thou kens my cloak is very thin:
It is so bare and over worn,
  A crickè thereon cannot renn.
Then I'll no longer borrow nor lend;
  For once I'll new apparell'd be;
To-morrow I'll to town and spend;
  For I'll have a new cloak about me.

She.

Cow Crumbock is a very good cow:
  She has been always true to the pail;
She has helped us to butter and cheese, I trow,
  And other things she will not fail.
I would be loth to see her pine.
  Good husband, counsel take of me:
It is not for us to go so fine—
  Man, take thine old cloak about thee!

He.

My cloak it was a very good cloak,
  It hath been always true to the wear;
But now it is not worth a groat:
  I have had it four and forty year'.
Sometime it was of cloth in grain:
  'Tis now but a sigh clout, as you may see:
It will neither hold out wind nor rain;
  And I'll have a new cloak about me.

She.

It is four and forty years ago
  Sine the one of us the other did ken;
And we have had, betwixt us two,
  Of children either nine or ten:
We have brought them up to women and men:
  In the fear of God I trow they be.
And why wilt thou thyself misken?
  Man, take thine old cloak about thee!

He.

O Bell my wife, why dost thou flyte?
  Now is now, and then was then:
Seek now all the world throughout,
  Thou kens not clowns from gentlemen:
They are clad in black, green, yellow and blue,
  So far above their own degree.
Once in my life I'll take a view;
  For I'll have a new cloak about me.

She.

King Stephen was a worthy peer;
  His breeches cost him but a crown;
He held them sixpence all too dear,
  Therefore he called the tailor 'lown.'
He was a king and wore the crown,
  And thou'se but of a low degree:
It's pride that puts this country down:
  Man, take thy old cloak about thee!

He.

Bell my wife, she loves not strife,
  Yet she will lead me, if she can;
And to maintain an easy life
  I oft must yield, though I'm good-man.
It's not for a man with a woman to threap,
  Unless he first give o'er the plea:
As we began, so will we keep,
  And I'll take my old cloak about me.

35   JOLLY GOOD ALE AND OLD
          [*16th Century*]

Back and side go bare, go bare,
Both hand and foot go cold;
But, belly, God send thee good ale enough
Whether it be new or old.

But if[1] that I may have truly
    Good ale my belly full,
I shall look like one, by sweet Saint John,
    Were shorn against the wool.
Though I go bare, take ye no care,
    I am nothing a-cold;
I stuff my skin so full within
    Of jolly good ale and old.

I cannot eat but little meat,
    My stomach is not good;
But sure I think that I could drink
    With him that weareth an hood.
Drink is my life; although my wife
    Some time do chide and scold,
Yet spare I not to ply the pot
    Of jolly good ale and old.

I love no roast but a brown toast,
    Or a crab in the fire;
A little bread shall do me stead,
    Much bread I never desire.
Nor frost, nor snow, nor wind, I trow,
    Can hurt me if it wolde;
I am so wrapped within, and lapped
    With jolly good ale and old.

I care right nought, I take no thought
    For clothes to keep me warm;
Have I good drink, I surely think
    Nothing can do me harm.

         [1] Unless.

For truly than I fear no man,
  Be he never so bold,
When I am armed and throughly warmed
  With jolly good ale and old.

But now and than I curse and ban,
  They make their ale so small!
God give them care, and evil to fare!
  They strye[2] the malt and all.
Such peevish pew,[3] I tell you true,
  Not for a crown of gold
There cometh one sip within my lip,
  Whether it be new or old.

Good ale and strong maketh me among
  Full jocund and full light,
That oft I sleep, and take no keep
  From morning until night.
Then start I up and flee to the cup,
  The right way on I hold;
My thirst to stanch I fill my paunch
  With jolly good ale and old.

And Kit, my wife, that as her life
  Loveth well good ale to seek,
Full oft drinketh she that ye may see
  The tears run down her cheek.
Then doth she troll to me the bowl
  As a good malt-worm should,
And say, "Sweetheart, I take my part
  Of jolly good ale and old."

They that do drink till they nod and wink,
  Even as good fellows should do,
They shall not miss to have the bliss
  That good ale hath brought them to.
And all poor souls that scour black bowls,
  And hath them lustily troll'd,

[2] Destroy.   [3] Wretched stuff.

God save the lives of them and their wives,
   Whether they be young or old!
   Back and side, etc.

SIR THOMAS WYATT
[1503(?)–1542]

36   A SUPPLICATION

FORGET not yet the tried intent
Of such a truth as I have meant;
My great travail so gladly spent,
            Forget not yet!

Forget not yet when first began
The weary life ye know, since whan
The suit, the service none tell can;
            Forget not yet!

Forget not yet the great assays,
The cruel wrong, the scornful ways,
The painful patience in delays,
            Forget not yet!

Forget not! O, forget not this,
How long ago hath been, and is
The mind that never meant amiss—
            Forget not yet!

Forget not then thine own approved
The which so long hath thee so loved,
Whose steadfast faith yet never moved—
            Forget not this!

37   THE LOVER'S APPEAL

AND wilt thou leave me thus!
Say nay! say nay! for shame!
To save thee from the blame
Of all my grief and grame.
And wilt thou leave me thus?
Say nay! say nay!

And wilt thou leave me thus,
That hath loved thee so long
In wealth and woe among:
And is thy heart so strong
As for to leave me thus?
Say nay! say nay!

And wilt thou leave me thus,
That hath given thee my heart
Never for to depart
Neither for pain nor smart:
And wilt thou leave me thus?
Say nay! say nay!

And wilt thou leave me thus,
And have no more pity
Of him that loveth thee?
Alas! thy cruelty!
And wilt thou leave me thus?
Say nay! say nay!

HENRY HOWARD, EARL OF SURREY
[1517(?)−1547]

38   COMPLAINT OF THE ABSENCE OF HER LOVER
BEING UPON THE SEA

O HAPPY dames! that may embrace
The fruit of your delight,
Help to bewail the woful case
And eke the heavy plight
Of me, that wonted to rejoice
The fortune of my pleasant choice:
Good ladies, help to fill my mourning voice.

In ship, freight with remembrance
Of thoughts and pleasures past,
He sails that hath in governance
My life while it will last:
With scalding sighs, for lack of gale,
Furthering his hope, that is his sail,
Toward me, the swete port of his avail.

Alas! how oft in dreams I see
  Those eyes that were my food;
Which sometime so delighted me,
  That yet they do me good:
Wherewith I wake with his return
Whose absent flame did make me burn:
But when I find the lack, Lord! how I mourn!

When other lovers in arms across
  Rejoice their chief delight,
Drownèd in tears, to mourn my loss
  I stand the bitter night
In my window where I may see
Before the winds how the clouds flee:
Lo! what a mariner love hath made me!

And in green waves when the salt flood
  Doth rise by rage of wind,
A thousand fancies in that mood
  Assail my restless mind.
Alas! now drencheth my sweet foe,
That with the spoil of my heart did go,
And left me; but alas! why did he so?

And when the seas wax calm again
  To chase fro me annoy,
My doubtful hope doth cause me pain;
  So dread cuts off my joy.
Thus in my wealth mingled with woe
And of each thought a doubt doth grow;
—Now he comes! Will he come? Alas! no, no.

39   THE MEANS TO ATTAIN HAPPY LIFE

MARTIAL, the things that do attain
  The happy life be these, I find:—
The richesse left, not got with pain;
  The fruitful ground, the quiet mind;

The equal friend; no grudge, no strife;
  No charge of rule, nor governance;

Without disease, the healthful life;
The household of continuance;

The mean diet, no delicate fare;
True wisdom join'd with simpleness;
The night dischargèd of all care,
Where wine the wit may not oppress.

The faithful wife, without debate;
Such sleeps as may beguile the night:
Contented with thine own estate
Ne wish for death, ne fear his might.

GEORGE GASCOIGNE
[*1525(?)–1577*]

40

A Lover's Lullaby

Sing lullaby, as women do,
Wherewith they bring their babes to rest;
And lullaby can I sing too,
As womanly as can the best.
With lullaby they still the child;
And if I be not much beguiled,
Full many a wanton babe have I,
Which must be still'd with lullaby.

First lullaby my youthful years,
It is now time to go to bed:
For crookèd age and hoary hairs
Have won the haven within my head.
With lullaby, then, youth be still;
With lullaby content thy will;
Since courage quails and comes behind,
Go sleep, and so beguile thy mind!

Next lullaby my gazing eyes,
Which wonted were to glance apace;
For every glass may now suffice
To show the furrows in thy face.

With lullaby then wink awhile;
With lullaby your looks beguile;
Let no fair face, nor beauty bright,
Entice you eft with vain delight.

And lullaby my wanton will;
    Let reason's rule now reign thy thought;
Since all too late I find by skill
    How dear I have thy fancies bought;
With lullaby now take thine ease,
With lullaby thy doubts appease;
For trust to this, if thou be still,
My body shall obey thy will.

Thus lullaby my youth, mine eyes,
    My will, my ware, and all that was:
I can no more delays devise;
    But welcome pain, let pleasure pass.
With lullaby now take your leave;
With lullaby your dreams deceive;
And when you rise with waking eye,
Remember then this lullaby.

NICHOLAS BRETON
[*1545(?)-1626(?)*]

41   PHILLIDA AND CORIDON

IN the merry month of May,
In a morn by break of day,
Forth I walk'd by the wood-side
When as May was in his pride:
There I spièd all alone
Phillida and Coridon.
Much ado there was, God wot!
He would love and she would not.
She said, Never man was true;
He said, None was false to you.
He said, He had loved her long;
She said, Love should have no wrong.

Coridon would kiss her then;
She said, Maids must kiss no men
Till they did for good and all;
Then she made the shepherd call
All the heavens to witness truth
Never loved a truer youth.
Thus with many a pretty oath,
Yea and nay, and faith and troth,
Such as silly shepherds use
When they will not Love abuse,
Love, which had been long deluded,
Was with kisses sweet concluded;
And Phillida, with garlands gay,
Was made the Lady of the May.

ANONYMOUS

42

A Sweet Lullaby

From The Arbor of Amorous Devices

Come little babe, come silly soul,
    Thy father's shame, thy mother's grief,
Born as I doubt to all our dole,
And to thyself unhappy chief:
    Sing lullaby, and lap it warm,
    Poor soul that thinks no creature harm.

Thou little think'st and less dost know
The cause of this thy mother's moan;
Thou want'st the wit to wail her woe,
And I myself am all alone:
    Why dost thou weep? why dost thou wail?
    And know'st not yet what thou dost ail.

Come, little wretch—ah, silly heart!
Mine only joy, what can I more?
If there be any wrong thy smart,
That may the destinies implore:
    'Twas I, I say, against my will,
    I wail the time, but be thou still.

And dost thou smile? Oh, thy sweet face!
Would God Himself He might thee see!—
No doubt thou wouldst soon purchase grace,
I know right well, for thee and me:
    But come to mother, babe, and play,
    For father false is fled away.

Sweet boy, if it by fortune chance
Thy father home again to send,
If death do strike me with his lance,
Yet mayst thou me to him commend:
    If any ask thy mother's name,
    Tell how by love she purchased blame.

Then will his gentle heart soon yield:
I know him of a noble mind:
Although a lion in the field,
A lamb in town thou shalt him find:
    Ask blessing, babe, be not afraid,
    His sugar'd words hath me betray'd.

Then mayst thou joy and be right glad;
Although in woe I seem to moan,
Thy father is no rascal lad,
A noble youth of blood and bone:
    His glancing looks, if he once smile,
    Right honest women may beguile.

Come, little boy, and rock asleep;
Sing lullaby and be thou still;
I, that can do naught else but weep,
Will sit by thee and wail my fill:
    God bless my babe, and lullaby
    From this thy father's quality.

43   PREPARATIONS

From a Christ Church MS.

YET if His Majesty, our sovereign lord,
Should of his own accord

Friendly himself invite,
And say 'I'll be your guest to-morrow night,'
How should we stir ourselves, call and command
All hands to work! 'Let no man idle stand!'

'Set me fine Spanish tables in the hall;
See they are fitted all;
Let there be room to eat
And order taken that there want no meat.
See every sconce and candlestick made bright,
That without tapers they may give a light.

'Look to the presence: are the carpets spread,
The dazie o'er the head,
The cushions in the chairs,
And all the candles lighted on the stairs?
Perfume the chambers, and in any case
Let each man give attendance in his place!'
Thus, if a king were coming, would we do;
And 'twere good reason too;
For 'tis a duteous thing
To show all honour to an earthly king,
And after all our travail and our cost,
So he be pleased, to think no labour lost.

But at the coming of the King of Heaven
All's set at six and seven;
We wallow in our sin,
Christ cannot find a chamber in the inn.
We entertain Him always like a stranger,
And, as at first, still lodge Him in the manger.

44   THE UNFAITHFUL SHEPHERDESS

[*From Byrd's Songs of Sundry Natures, 1589*]

WHICH that the sun with his beams hot
Scorchéd the fruits in vale and mountain,
Philon the shepherd, late forgot,
Sitting beside a crystal fountain,

In shadow of a green oak tree
Upon his pipe this song play'd he:
Adieu Love, adieu Love, untrue Love;
Untrue Love, untrue Love, adieu Love;
Your mind is light, soon lost for new love.

So long as I was in your sight
I was your heart, your soul, and treasure;
And evermore you sobb'd and sigh'd
Burning in flames beyond all measure:
    —Three days endured your love to me,
    And it was lost in other three!
Adieu Love, adieu Love, untrue Love,
Untrue Love, untrue Love, adieu Love;
Your mind is light, soon lost for new love.

Another Shepherd you did see
To whom your heart was soon enchainéd;
Full soon your love was leapt from me,
Full soon my place he had obtainéd.
    Soon came a third, your love to win,
    And we were out and he was in.
Adieu Love, adieu Love, untrue Love,
Untrue Love, untrue Love, adieu Love;
Your mind is light, soon lost for new love.

Sure you have made me passing glad
That you your mind so soon removéd,
Before that I the leisure had
To choose you for my best belovéd:
    For all your love was past and done
    Two days before it was begun:—
Adieu Love, adieu Love, untrue Love,
Untrue Love, untrue Love, adieu Love;
Your mind is light, soon lost for new love.

ANTHONY MUNDAY
[*1553-1663*]

45   BEAUTY BATHING

BEAUTY sat bathing by a spring
    Where fairest shades did hide her;
The winds blew calm, the birds did sing,
    The cool streams ran beside her.
My wanton thoughts enticed mine eye
    To see what was forbidden:
But better memory said, fie!
    So vain desire was chidden:—
        Hey nonny nonny O!
        Hey nonny nonny!

Into a slumber then I fell,
    When fond imagination
Seeméd to see, but could not tell
    Her feature or her fashion.
But, ev'n as babes in dreams do smile,
    And sometimes fall a-weeping,
So I awaked, as wise this while
    As when I fell a-sleeping:—
        Hey nonny nonny O!
        Hey nonny nonny!

RICHARD EDWARDES
[*1523-1566*]

46   AMANTIUM IRAE

IN going to my naked bed as one that would have slept,
I heard a wife sing to her child, that long before had wept;
She sighèd sore and sang full sweet, to bring the babe to rest,
That would not cease but crièd still, in sucking at her breast.
She was full weary of her watch, and grievèd with her child,
She rockèd it and rated it, till that on her it smiled.
Then did she say, Now have I found this proverb true to prove,
The falling out of faithful friends renewing is of love.

Then took I paper, pen, and ink, this proverb for to write,
In register for to remain of such a worthy wight:
As she proceeded thus in song unto her little brat,
Much matter utter'd she of weight, in place whereas she sat:
And provèd plain there was no beast, nor creature bearing life,
Could well be known to live in love without discord and strife:
Then kissèd she her little babe, and sware by God above,
The falling out of faithful friends renewing is of love.

She said that neither king nor prince nor lord could live aright,
Until their puissance they did prove, their manhood and their might.
When manhood shall be matched so that fear can take no place,
Then weary works make warriors each other to embrace,
And left their force that failèd them, which did consume the rout,
That might before have lived their time, their strength and nature out:
Then did she sing as one that thought no man could her reprove,
The falling out of faithful friends renewing is of love.

She said she saw no fish nor fowl, nor beast within her haunt,
That met a stranger in their kind, but could give it a taunt:
Since flesh might not endure, but rest must wrath succeed,
And force the fight to fall to play in pasture where they feed,
So noble nature can well end the work she hath begun,
And bridle well that will not cease her tragedy in some:
Thus in song she oft rehearsed, as did her well behove.
The falling out of faithful friends renewing is of love.

I marvel much pardy (quoth she) for to behold the rout,
To see man, woman, boy and beast, to toss the world about:
Some kneel, some crouch, some beck, some check, and some can
    smoothly smile
And some embrace others in arm, and there think many a wile,
Some stand aloof at cap and knee, some humble and some stout,
Yet are they never friends in deed until they once fall out:
Thus ended she her song and said, before she did remove,
The falling out of faithful friends renewing is of love.

SIR WALTER RALEIGH
[1552(?)–1618]

47

HIS PILGRIMAGE

GIVE me my scallop-shell of quiet,
  My staff of faith to walk upon,
My scrip of joy, immortal diet,
  My bottle of salvation,
My gown of glory, hope's true gage;
And thus I'll take my pilgrimage.

Blood must be my body's balmer;
  No other balm will there be given;
Whilst my soul, like quiet palmer,
  Travelleth towards the land of heaven;
Over the silver mountains,
Where spring the nectar fountains:
    There will I kiss
    The bowls of bliss;
And drink mine everlasting fill
Upon every milken hill.
My soul will be a-dry before;
But, after, it will thirst no more.

Then by that happy blissful day,
  More peaceful pilgrims I shall see,
That have cast off their rags of clay,
  And walk apparelled fresh like me.
    I'll take them first
    To quench their thirst
And taste of nectar suckets,
    At those clear wells
    Where sweetness dwells,
  Drawn up by saints in crystal buckets.

And when our bottles and all we
Are filled with immortality,
Then the blessed paths we'll travel,
Strowed with rubies thick as gravel;

Ceilings of diamonds, sapphire floors,
High walls of coral and pearly bowers.
From thence to heaven's bribeless hall,
Where no corrupted voices brawl;
No conscience molten into gold,
No forged accuser bought or sold,
No cause deferred, no vain-spent journey,
For there Christ is the king's Attorney,
Who pleads for all without degrees,
And He hath angels, but no fees.
And when the grand twelve-million jury
Of our sins, with direful fury,
Against our souls black verdicts give,
Christ pleads His death, and then we live.

Be Thou my speaker, taintless pleader,
Unblotted lawyer, true proceeder!
Thou givest salvation even for alms;
Not with a bribed lawyer's palms.
And this is mine eternal plea
To Him that made heaven, earth, and sea,
That, since my flesh must die so soon,
And want a head to dine at noon,
Just at the stroke, when my veins start and spread,
Set on my soul an everlasting head!
Then am I ready, like a palmer fit,
To tread those blest paths which before I writ.
　　Of death and judgment, heaven and hell,
　　Who oft doth think, must needs die well.

THE LIE

48

Go, Soul, the body's guest,
　　Upon a thankless arrant:
Fear not to touch the best;
　　The truth shall be thy warrant:
Go, since I needs must die,
And give the world the lie.

Say to the court, it glows
　　And shines like rotten wood;

Say to the church, it shows
  What's good, and doth no good:
If church and court reply,
Then give them both the lie.

Tell potentates, they live
  Acting by others' action;
Not loved unless they give,
  Not strong, but by a faction:
If potentates reply,
Give potentates the lie.

Tell men of high condition,
  That manage the estate,
Their purpose is ambition,
  Their practice only hate:
And if they once reply,
Then give them all the lie.

Tell them that brave it most,
  They beg for more by spending,
Who, in their greatest cost,
  Seek nothing but commending:
And if they make reply,
Then give them all the lie.

Tell zeal it wants devotion;
  Tell love it is but lust;
Tell time it is but motion;
  Tell flesh it is but dust:
And wish them not reply,
For thou must give the lie.

Tell age it daily wasteth;
  Tell honour how it alters;
Tell beauty how she blasteth;
  Tell favour how it falters:
And as they shall reply,
Give every one the lie.

Tell wit how much it wrangles
  In tickle points of niceness;

Tell wisdom she entangles
   Herself in over-wiseness:
And when they do reply,
Straight give them both the lie.

Tell physic of her boldness;
   Tell skill it is pretension;
Tell charity of coldness;
   Tell law it is contention:
And as they do reply,
So give them still the lie.

Tell fortune of her blindness;
   Tell nature of decay;
Tell friendship of unkindness;
   Tell justice of delay;
And if they will reply,
Then give them all the lie.

Tell arts they have no soundness,
   But vary by esteeming;
Tell schools they want profoundness,
   And stand too much on seeming:
If arts and schools reply,
Give arts and schools the lie.

Tell faith it's fled the city;
   Tell how the country erreth;
Tell, manhood shakes off pity;
   Tell, virtue least preferreth:
And if they do reply,
Spare not to give the lie.

So when thou hast, as I
   Commanded thee, done blabbing,—
Although to give the lie
   Deserves no less than stabbing,—
Stab at thee he that will,
No stab the soul can kill.

49 VERSES

FOUND IN HIS BIBLE IN THE GATE-HOUSE AT WESTMINSTER. SAID TO HAVE
BEEN WRITTEN THE NIGHT BEFORE HIS DEATH

EVEN such is time, that takes in trust
 Our youth, our joys, our all we have,
And pays us but with earth and dust;
 Who, in the dark and silent grave,
When we have wandered all our ways,
Shuts up the story of our days;
But from this earth, this grave, this dust,
My God shall raise me up, I trust.

50   WHAT IS OUR LIFE

WHAT is our life? The play of passion.
Our mirth? The music of division:
Our mothers' wombs the tiring-houses be,
Where we are dressed for life's short comedy.
The earth the stage; Heaven the spectator is,
Who sits and views whosoe'er doth act amiss.
The graves which hide us from the scorching sun
Are like drawn curtains when the play is done.
Thus playing post we to our latest rest,
And then we die in earnest, not in jest.

SIR EDWARD DYER
[D. 1607]

51   MY MIND TO ME A KINGDOM IS

My mind to me a kingdom is;
 Such present joys therein I find,
That it excels all other bliss
 That earth affords or grows by kind:
Though much I want that most would have,
Yet still my mind forbids to crave.

No princely pomp, no wealthy store,
 No force to win the victory,
No wily wit to salve a sore,

No shape to feed a loving eye;
To none of these I yield as thrall;
For why? my mind doth serve for all.

I see how plenty surfeits oft,
   And hasty climbers soon do fall;
I see that those which are aloft
   Mishap doth threaten most of all:
They get with toil, they keep with fear:
Such cares my mind could never bear.

Content I live, this is my stay;
   I seek no more than may suffice;
I press to bear no haughty sway;
   Look, what I lack my mind supplies.
Lo, thus I triumph like a king,
Content with that my mind doth bring.

Some have too much, yet still do crave;
   I little have, and seek no more.
They are but poor, though much they have,
   And I am rich with little store;
They poor, I rich; they beg, I give;
They lack, I leave; they pine, I live.

I laugh not at another's loss,
   I grudge not at another's gain;
No worldly waves my mind can toss;
   My state at one doth still remain:
I fear no foe, I fawn no friend;
I loathe not life, nor dread my end.

Some weigh their pleasure by their lust,
   Their wisdom by their rage of will;
Their treasure is their only trust,
   A cloakèd craft their store of skill;
But all the pleasure that I find
Is to maintain a quiet mind.

My wealth is health and perfect ease,
   My conscience clear my chief defence;
I neither seek by bribes to please,

Nor by deceit to breed offence:
Thus do I live; thus will I die;
Would all did so as well as I!

JOHN LYLY

[*1553–1606*]

52   CUPID AND CAMPASPE

CUPID and my Campaspe play'd
At cards for kisses—Cupid paid:
He stakes his quiver, bow, and arrows,
His mother's doves, and team of sparrows;
Loses them too; then down he throws
The coral of his lip, the rose
Growing on's cheek (but none knows how);
With these, the crystal of his brow,
And then the dimple of his chin:
All these did my Campaspe win.
At last he set her both his eyes—
She won, and Cupid blind did rise.
     O Love! has she done this for thee?
     What shall, alas! become of me?

53   SPRING'S WELCOME

WHAT bird so sings, yet so does wail?
O 'tis the ravish'd nightingale.
'Jug, jug, jug, jug, tereu!' she cries!
And still her woes at midnight rise,
Brave prick-song! Who is't now we hear?
None but the lark so shrill and clear;
Now at heaven's gate she claps her wings,
The morn not waking till she sings.
Hark, hark, with what a pretty throat
Poor robin redbreast tunes his note!
Hark how the jolly cuckoos sing
Cuckoo! to welcome in the spring!
Cuckoo! to welcome in the spring!

SIR PHILIP SIDNEY
[*1554–1586*]

54   SONG

Doubt you to whom my Muse these notes intendeth;
Which now my breast o'ercharged to music lendeth!
To you! to you! all song of praise is due:
Only in you, my song begins and endeth.

Who hath the eyes which marry State with Pleasure?
Who keeps the key of Nature's chiefest treasure?
To you! to you! all song of praise is due:
Only for you, the heaven forgat all measure.

Who hath the lips, where Wit in fairness reigneth?
Who mankind at once both decks and staineth?
To you! to you! all song of praise is due:
Only by you, Cupid his crown maintaineth.

Who hath the feet, whose step all sweetness planteth?
Who else, for whom Fame worthy trumpets wanteth?
To you! to you! all song of praise is due:
Only to you, her sceptre Venus granteth.

Who hath the breast, whose milk doth passions nourish?
Whose grace is such, that when it chides doth cherish?
To you! to you! all song of praise is due:
Only through you, the tree of life doth flourish.

Who hath the hand, which without stroke subdueth?
Who long-dead beauty with increase reneweth?
To you! to you! all song of praise is due:
Only at you, all envy hopeless rueth.

Who hath the hair, which loosest fastest tieth?
Who makes a man live, then glad when he dieth?
To you! to you! all song of praise is due:
Only of you, the flatterer never lieth.

Who hath the voice, which soul from senses sunders?
Whose force but yours the bolts of beauty thunders?
To you! to you! all song of praise is due:
Only with you, not miracles are wonders.

Doubt you to whom my Muse these notes intendeth,
Which now my breast o'ercharged to music lendeth?
To you! to you! all song of praise is due:
Only in you, my song begins and endeth.

55.   A DIRGE

RING out your bells, let mourning shews be spread;
        For Love is dead.
    All Love is dead, infected
With plague of deep disdain;
    Worth, as nought worth, rejected,
And Faith, fair scorn doth gain.
    From so ungrateful fancy,
    From such a female franzy,
    From them that use men thus,
    Good Lord, deliver us!

Weep, neighbours, weep; do you not hear it said
        That Love is dead?
    His death-bed, peacock's folly;
His winding-sheet is shame;
    His will, false-seeming holy;
His sole exec'tor, blame.
    From so ungrateful fancy,
    From such a female franzy,
    From them that use men thus,
    Good Lord, deliver us!

Let dirge be sung, and trentals rightly read,
        For Love is dead.
    Sir Wrong his tomb ordaineth,
My mistress' marble heart;
    Which epitaph containeth,
"Her eyes were once his dart."

From so ungrateful fancy,
From such a female franzy,
From them that use men thus,
Good Lord, deliver us!

Alas, I lie: rage hath this error bred;
   Love is not dead.
Love is not dead, but sleepeth
In her unmatchèd mind,
   Where she his counsel keepeth,
Till due deserts she find.
   Therefore from so vile fancy,
   To call such wit a franzy,
   Who Love can temper thus,
   Good Lord, deliver us!

56   A DITTY

My true-love hath my heart, and I have his,
By just exchange one for another given:
I hold his dear, and mine he cannot miss,
There never was a better bargain driven:
   My true-love hath my heart, and I have his.

His heart in me keeps him and me in one,
My heart in him his thoughts and senses guides:
He loves my heart, for once it was his own,
I cherish his because in me it bides:
   My true-love hath my heart, and I have his.

57   LOVING IN TRUTH

Loving in truth, and fain in verse my love to show,
That She, dear She, might take some pleasure of my pain;
Pleasure might cause her read, reading might make her know,
Knowledge might pity win, and pity grace obtain;
I sought fit words to paint the blackest face of woe,
Studying inventions fine, her wits to entertain;
Oft turning others' leaves, to see if thence would flow
Some fresh and fruitful showers upon my sunburned brain.
But words came halting forth, wanting Invention's stay;

Invention, Nature's child, fled step-dame Study's blows;
And others' feet still seemed but strangers in my way.
Thus, great with child to speak, and helpless in my throes,
Biting my truant pen, beating myself for spite.
"Fool," said my Muse to me, "look in thy heart, and write!"

58   BE YOUR WORDS MADE, GOOD SIR, OF INDIAN WARE

BE your words made, good Sir, of Indian ware,
That you allow me them by so small rate?
Or do you cutted Spartans imitate?
Or do you mean my tender ears to spare
That to my questions you so total are?
When I demand of Phœnix-Stella's state,
You say, forsooth, you left her well of late:
O God, think you that satisfies my care?

I would know whether she did sit or walk;
How clothed; how waited on; sighed she, or smiled;
Whereof, with whom, how often did she talk;
With what pastime Time's journey she beguiled;
If her lips deigned to sweeten my poor name:
Say all; and, all well said, still say the same.

59   TO SLEEP

COME, Sleep; O Sleep! the certain knot of peace,
The baiting-place of wit, the balm of woe,
The poor man's wealth, the prisoner's release,
Th' indifferent judge between the high and low;
With shield of proof, shield me from out the prease
Of those fierce darts Despair at me doth throw:
O make in me those civil wars to cease;
I will good tribute pay, if thou do so.
Take thou of me smooth pillows, sweetest bed,
A chamber deaf to noise and blind to light,
A rosy garland and a weary head:
And if these things, as being thine by right,
    Move not thy heavy grace, thou shalt in me,
    Livelier than elsewhere, Stella's image see.

60

To the Moon

With how sad steps, O moon, thou climb'st the skies!
How silently, and with how wan a face!
What! may it be that even in heavenly place
That busy archer his sharp arrows tries?
Sure, if that long-with-love-acquainted eyes
Can judge of love, thou feel'st a lover's case:
I read it in thy looks; thy languish'd grace
To me, that feel the like, thy state descries.
Then, even of fellowship, O Moon, tell me,
Is constant love deem'd there but want of wit?
Are beauties there as proud as here they be?
Do they above love to be loved, and yet
    Those lovers scorn whom that love doth possess?
    Do they call 'virtue' there—ungratefulness?

THOMAS LODGE
[1558–1625]

61

Rosalind's Madrigal

Love in my bosom like a bee
    Doth suck his sweet:
Now with his wings he plays with me,
    Now with his feet.
Within mine eyes he makes his nest,
His bed amidst my tender breast;
My kisses are his daily feast
And yet he robs me of my rest:
    Ah! wanton, will ye?

And if I sleep, then percheth he
    With pretty flight,
And makes his pillow of my knee
    The livelong night.

Strike I my lute, he tunes the string;
He music plays if so I sing,
He lends me every lovely thing,
Yet cruel he my heart doth sting:
    Whist, wanton, still ye!

Else I with roses every day
    Will whip you hence,
And bind you, when you long to play,
    For your offence.
I'll shut mine eyes to keep you in;
I'll make you fast it for your sin;
I'll count your power not worth a pin.
—Alas! what hereby shall I win
    If he gainsay me?

What if I beat the wanton boy
    With many a rod?
He will repay me with annoy,
    Because a god.
Then sit thou safely on my knee;
Then let thy bower my bosom be;
Lurk in mine eyes, I like of thee;
O Cupid, so thou pity me,
    Spare not, but play thee!

62

ROSALINE

LIKE to the clear in highest sphere
Where all imperial glory shines,
Of selfsame colour is her hair
Whether unfolded, or in twines:
    Heigh ho, fair Rosaline!
Her eyes are sapphires set in snow
Resembling heaven by every wink;
The Gods do fear whenas they glow,
And I do tremble when I think
    Heigh ho, would she were mine!

Her cheeks are like the blushing cloud
That beautifies Aurora's face,
Or like the silver crimson shroud
That Phoebus' smiling looks doth grace;
    Heigh ho, fair Rosaline!
Her lips are like two budded roses
Whom ranks of lilies neighbour nigh,
Within which bounds she balm encloses

Apt to entice a deity:
    Heigh ho, would she were mine!

Her neck is like a stately tower
Where Love himself imprison'd lies,
To watch for glances every hour
From her divine and sacred eyes:
    Heigh ho, fair Rosaline!
Her paps are centres of delight,
Her breasts are orbs of heavenly frame,
Where Nature moulds the dew of light
To feed perfection with the same:
    Heigh ho, would she were mine!

With orient pearl, with ruby red,
With marble white, with sapphire blue
Her body every way is fed,
Yet soft in touch and sweet in view:
    Heigh ho, fair Rosaline!
Nature herself her shape admires;
The Gods are wounded in her sight;
And Love forsakes his heavenly fires
And at her eyes his brand doth light:
    Heigh ho, would she were mine!

Then muse not, Nymphs, though I bemoan
The absence of fair Rosaline,
Since for a fair there's fairer none,
Nor for her virtues so divine:
    Heigh ho, fair Rosaline!
Heigh ho, my heart! would God that she were mine!

63   PHILLIS

Love guards the roses of thy lips
    And flies about them like a bee;
If I approach he forward skips,
    And if I kiss he stingeth me.

Love in thine eyes doth build his bower,
    And sleeps within their pretty shine;

And if I look the boy will lower,
    And from their orbs shoot shafts divine.

Love works thy heart within his fire,
    And in my tears doth firm the same;
And if I tempt it will retire,
    And of my plaints doth make a game.

Love, let me cull her choicest flowers;
    And pity me, and calm her eye;
Make soft her heart, dissolve her lowers;
    Then will I praise thy deity.

But if thou do not, Love, I'll truly serve her
In spite of thee, and by firm faith deserve her.

GEORGE PEELE

[*1558–1597*]

PARIS AND ŒNONE

64
Œnone.

    FAIR and fair, and twice so fair,
      As fair as any may be;
    The fairest shepherd on our green,
      A love for any lady.

Paris.

    Fair and fair, and twice so fair,
      As fair as any may be;
    Thy love is fair for thee alone,
      And for no other lady.

Œnone.

    My love is fair, my love is gay,
    As fresh as bin the flowers in May,
    And of my love my roundelay,
    My merry, merry, merry roundelay.
      Concludes with Cupid's curse,—
    'They that do change old love for new
      Pray gods they change for worse!'

Ambo Simul.

    They that do change old love for new,
      Pray gods they change for worse!

Œnone.

    Fair and fair, etc.

Paris.

    Fair and fair, etc.
    Thy love is fair, etc.

Œnone.

    My love can pipe, my love can sing,
    My love can many a pretty thing,
    And of his lovely praises ring
    My merry, merry, merry roundelays
      Amen to Cupid's curse,—
    'They that do change,' etc.

Paris.

    They that do change, etc.

Ambo.

    Fair and fair, etc.

ROBERT SOUTHWELL

[*1561(?)–1595*]

65   THE BURNING BABE

    As I in hoary winter's night
      Stood shivering in the snow,
    Surprised I was with sudden heat
      Which made my heart to glow;
    And lifting up a fearful eye
      To view what fire was near,
    A pretty babe all burning bright
      Did in the air appear;
    Who, scorchèd with excessive heat,
      Such floods of tears did shed,
    As though His floods should quench His flames,
      Which with His tears were bred:
    'Alas!' quoth He, 'but newly born
      In fiery heats I fry,

Yet none approach to warm their hearts
  Or feel my fire but I!

'My faultless breast the furnace is;
  The fuel, wounding thorns;
Love is the fire, and sighs the smoke;
  The ashes, shames and scorns;
The fuel Justice layeth on,
  And Mercy blows the coals,
The metal in this furnace wrought
  Are men's defilèd souls:
For which, as now on fire I am
  To work them to their good,
So will I melt into a bath,
  To wash them in my blood.'
With this He vanish'd out of sight
  And swiftly shrunk away,
And straight I callèd unto mind
  That it was Christmas Day.

SAMUEL DANIEL
[1562–1619]

Beauty, Time, and Love
Sonnets

I

Fair is my Love and cruel as she's fair;
Her brow-shades frown, although her eyes are sunny,
Her smiles are lightning, though her pride despair,
And her disdains are gall, her favours honey:
A modest maid, deck'd with a blush of honour,
Whose feet do tread green paths of youth and love;
The wonder of all eyes that look upon her,
Sacred on earth, design'd a Saint above.
Chastity and Beauty, which were deadly foes,
Live reconcilèd friends within her brow;
And had she Pity to conjoin with those,
Then who had heard the plaints I utter now?
  For had she not been fair, and thus unkind,
  My Muse had slept, and none had known my mind.

II

My spotless love hovers with purest wings,
About the temple of the proudest frame,
Where blaze those lights, fairest of earthly things,
Which clear our clouded world with brightest flame.
My ambitious thoughts, confinèd in her face
Affect no honour but what she can give;
My hopes do rest in limits of her grace;
I weigh no comforts unless she relieve.
For she, that can my heart imparadise,
Holds in her fairest hand what dearest is;
My Fortune's wheel's the circle of her eyes,
Whose rolling grace deign once a turn of bliss.
    All my life's sweet consists in her alone;
    So much I love the most Unloving one.

III

And yet I cannot reprehend the flight
Or blame th' attempt presuming so to soar;
The mounting venture for a high delight
Did make the honour of the fall the more.
For who gets wealth, that puts not from the shore?
Danger hath honour, great designs their fame;
Glory doth follow, courage goes before;
And though th' event oft answers not the same—
Suffice that high attempts have never shame.
The mean observer, whom base safety keeps,
Lives without honour, dies without a name,
And in eternal darkness ever sleeps.—
    And therefore, *Delia,* 'tis to me no blot
    To have attempted, tho' attain'd thee not.

IV

When men shall find thy flow'r, thy glory, pass,
And thou with careful brow, sitting alone,
Receivèd hast this message from thy glass,
That tells the truth and says that *All is gone;*
Fresh shalt thou see in me the wounds thou mad'st,
Though spent thy flame, in me the heat remaining:

I that have loved thee thus before thou fad'st—
My faith shall wax, when thou art in thy waning.
The world shall find this miracle in me,
That fire can burn when all the matter's spent:
Then what my faith hath been thyself shalt see,
And that thou wast unkind thou may'st repent.—
    Thou may'st repent that thou hast scorn'd my tears,
    When Winter snows upon thy sable hairs.

V

Beauty, sweet Love, is like the morning dew,
Whose short refresh upon the tender green
Cheers for a time, but till the sun doth show,
And straight 'tis gone as it had never been.
Soon doth it fade that makes the fairest flourish,
Short is the glory of the blushing rose;
The hue which thou so carefully dost nourish,
Yet which at length thou must be forced to lose.
When thou, surcharged with burthen of thy years,
Shalt bend thy wrinkles homeward to the earth;
And that, in Beauty's Lease expired, appears
The Date of Age, the Calends of our Death—
    But ah, no more!—this must not be foretold,
    For women grieve to think they must be old.

VI

I must not grieve my Love, whose eyes would read
Lines of delight, whereon her youth might smile;
Flowers have time before they come to seed,
And she is young, and now must sport the while.
And sport, Sweet Maid, in season of these years,
And learn to gather flowers before they wither;
And where the sweetest blossom first appears,
Let Love and Youth conduct thy pleasures thither.
Lighten forth smiles to clear the clouded air,
And calm the tempest which my sighs do raise;
Pity and smiles do best become the fair;
Pity and smiles must only yield thee praise.
    Make me to say when all my griefs are gone,
    Happy the heart that sighed for such a one!

VII

Let others sing of Knights and Paladines
In agèd accents and untimely words,
Paint shadows in imaginary lines,
Which well the reach of their high wit records:
But I must sing of thee, and those fair eyes
Authentic shall my verse in time to come;
When yet th' unborn shall say, *Lo, where she lies!*
Whose beauty made him speak, that else was dumb!
These are the arcs, the trophies I erect,
That fortify thy name against old age;
And these thy sacred virtues must protect
Against the Dark, and Time's consuming rage.
    Though th' error of my youth in them appear,
    Suffice, they show I lived, and loved thee dear.

67   To Sleep

Care-charmer Sleep, son of the sable Night,
Brother to Death, in silent darkness born,
Relieve my languish, and restore the light;
With dark forgetting of my care return.
And let the day be time enough to mourn
The shipwreck of my illadventured youth:
Let waking eyes suffice to wail their scorn,
Without the torment of the night's untruth.
Cease, dreams, the images of day-desires,
To model forth the passions of the morrow;
Never let rising Sun approve you liars,
To add more grief to aggravate my sorrow:
    Still let me sleep, embracing clouds in vain,
    And never wake to feel the day's disdain.

MICHAEL DRAYTON
[*1563-1631*]

68   Agincourt

Fair stood the wind for France
When we our sails advance,
Nor now to prove our chance
    Longer will tarry;

But putting to the main,
At Caux, the mouth of Seine,
With all his martial train
 Landed King Harry.

And taking many a fort,
Furnish'd in warlike sort,
Marcheth tow'rds Agincourt
 In happy hour;
Skirmishing day by day
With those that stopp'd his way,
Where the French gen'ral lay
 With all his power.

Which, in his height of pride,
King Henry to deride,
His ransom to provide
 Unto him sending;
Which he neglects the while
As from a nation vile,
Yet with an angry smile
 Their fall portending.

And turning to his men,
Quoth our brave Henry then,
'Though they to one be ten
 Be not amazèd:
Yet have we well begun;
Battles so bravely won
Have ever to the sun
 By fame been raisèd.

'And for myself (quoth he)
This my full rest shall be:
England ne'er mourn for me
 Nor more esteem me:
Victor I will remain
Or on this earth lie slain,
Never shall she sustain
 Loss to redeem me.

'Poitiers and Cressy tell,
When most their pride did swell,
Under our swords they fell:
    No less our skill is
Than when our grandsire great,
Claiming the regal seat,
By many a warlike feat
    Lopp'd the French lilies.'

The Duke of York so dread
The eager vaward led;
With the main Henry sped
    Among his henchmen.
Excester had the rear,
A braver man not there;
O Lord, how hot they were
    On the false Frenchmen!

They now to fight are gone,
Armour on armour shone,
Drum now to drum did groan,
    To hear was wonder.
That with the cries they make
The very earth did shake:
Trumpet to trumpet spake,
    Thunder to thunder.

Well it thine age became,
O noble Erpingham,
Which didst the signal aim
    To our hid forces!
When from a meadow by,
Like a storm suddenly
The English archery
    Stuck the French horses.

With Spanish yew so strong,
Arrows a cloth-yard long
That like to serpents stung,
    Piercing the weather;

None from his fellow starts,
But playing manly parts,
And like true English hearts
    Stuck close together.

When down their bows they threw,
And forth their bilbos drew,
And on the French they flew,
    Not one was tardy;
Arms were from shoulders sent,
Scalps to the teeth were rent,
Down the French peasants went—
    Our men were hardy.

This while our noble king,
His broadsword brandishing,
Down the French host did ding
    As to o'erwhelm it;
And many a deep wound lent,
His arms with blood besprent,
And many a cruel dent
    Bruisèd his helmet.

Gloster, that duke so good,
Next of the royal blood,
For famous England stood
    With his brave brother;
Clarence, in steel so bright,
Though but a maiden knight,
Yet in that furious fight
    Scarce such another.

Warwick in blood did wade,
Oxford the foe invade,
And cruel slaughter made
    Still as they ran up;
Suffolk his axe did ply,
Beaumont and Willoughby
Bare them right doughtily,
    Ferrers and Fanhope.

Upon Saint Crispin's Day
Fought was this noble fray,
Which fame did not delay
    To England to carry;
O when shall English men
With such acts fill a pen?
Or England breed again
    Such a King Harry?

69   To the Virginian Voyage

You brave heroic minds
    Worthy your country's name,
      That honour still pursue;
      Go and subdue!
Whilst loitering hinds
    Lurk here at home with shame.

Britons, you stay too long:
    Quickly aboard bestow you,
      And with a merry gale
      Swell your stretch'd sail
With vows as strong
    As the winds that blow you.

Your course securely steer,
    West and by south forth keep!
      Rocks, lee-shores, nor shoals
      When Eolus scowls
You need not fear;
    So absolute the deep.

And cheerfully at sea
    Success you still entice
      To get the pearl and gold,
      And ours to hold
Virginia,
    Earth's only paradise.

Where nature hath in store
    Fowl, venison, and fish,

And the fruitfull'st soil
Without your toil
Three harvests more,
All greater than your wish.

And the ambitious vine
Crowns with his purple mass
The cedar reaching high
To kiss the sky,
The cypress, pine,
And useful sassafras.

To whom the Golden Age
Still nature's laws doth give,
No other cares attend,
But them to defend
From winter's rage,
That long there doth not live.

When as the luscious smell
Of that delicious land
Above the seas that flows
The clear wind throws,
Your hearts to swell
Approaching the dear strand;

In kenning of the shore
(Thanks to God first given)
O you the happiest men,
Be frolic then!
Let cannons roar,
Frighting the wide heaven.

And in regions far,
Such heroes bring ye forth
As those from whom we came;
And plant our name
Under that star
Not known unto our North.

And as there plenty grows
  Of laurel everywhere—
      Apollo's sacred tree—
      You it may see
  A poet's brows
      To crown, that may sing there.

  Thy *Voyages* attend,
    Industrious Hakluyt,
        Whose reading shall inflame
        Men to seek fame,
    And much commend
        To after times thy wit.

70   LOVE'S FAREWELL

SINCE there's no help, come let us kiss and part,—
Nay I have done, you get no more of me;
And I am glad, yea, glad with all my heart,
That thus so cleanly I myself can free;
Shake hands for ever, cancel all our vows,
And when we meet at any time again,
Be it not seen in either of our brows
That we one jot of former love retain.
Now at the last gasp of love's latest breath,
When his pulse failing, passion speechless lies,
When faith is kneeling by his bed of death,
And innocence is closing up his eyes,
    —Now if thou would'st, when all have given him over,
From death to life thou might'st him yet decover!

71   HENRY CONSTABLE
                  [*1562–1613*]

                DIAPHENIA

DIAPHENIA like the daffadowndilly,
White as the sun, fair as the lily,
Heigh ho, how I do love thee!
I do love thee as my lambs
Are belovéd of their dams;
How blest were I if thou would'st prove me.

Diaphenia like the spreading roses,
That in thy sweets all sweets encloses,
Fair sweet, how I do love thee!
I do love thee as each flower
Loves the sun's life-giving power;
For dead, thy breath to life might move me.

Diaphenia like to all things blessèd,
When all thy praises are expressèd,
Dear joy, how I do love thee!
As the birds do love the spring,
Or the bees their careful king:
Then in requite, sweet virgin, love me!

72
EDMUND SPENSER
[1552–1599]

PROTHALAMION

CALME was the day, and through the trembling ayre
Sweete-breathing Zephyrus did softly play
A gentle spirit, that lightly did delay
Hot Titans beames, which then did glyster fayre;
When I, (whom sullein care,
Through discontent of my long fruitlesse stay
In Princes Court, and expectation vayne
Of idle hopes, which still doe fly away,
Like empty shaddowes, did afflict my brayne,)
Walkt forth to ease my payne
Along the shoare of silver streaming Themmes;
Whose rutty Bancke, the which his River hemmes,
Was paynted all with variable flowers,
And all the meades adornd with daintie gemmes
Fit to decke maydens bowres,
And crowne their Paramours
Against the Brydale dale, which is not long:
   Sweete Themmes! runne softly, till I end my Song.

There, in a Meadow, by the Rivers side,
A Flocke of Nymphes I chauncèd to espy,
All lovely Daughters of the Flood thereby,

With goodly greenish locks, all loose untyde,
As each had bene a Bryde;
And each one had a little wicker basket,
Made of fine twigs, entraylèd curiously,
In which they gathered flowers to fill their flasket,
And with fine Fingers cropt full featously
The tender stalkes on hye.
Of every sort, which in that Meadow grew,
They gathered some; the Violet, pallid blew,
The little Dazie, that at evening closes,
The virgin Lillie, and the Primrose trew,
With store of vermeil Roses,
To decke their Bridegromes posies
Against the Brydale day, which was not long:
  Sweete Themmes! runne softly, till I end my Song.

With that I saw two Swannes of goodly hewe
Come softly swimming downe along the Lee;
Two fairer Birds I yet did never see;
The snow, which doth the top of Pindus strew,
Did never whiter shew;
Nor Jove himselfe, when he a Swan would be,
For love of Leda, whiter did appeare;
Yet Leda was (they say) as white as he,
Yet not so white as these, nor nothing neare;
So purely white they were,
That even the gentle streame, the which them bare,
Seem'd foule to them, and bad his billowes spare
To wet their silken feathers, least they might
Soyle their fayre plumes with water not so fayre,
And marre their beauties bright,
That shone as heavens light,
Against their Brydale day, which was not long:
  Sweete Themmes! runne softly, till I end my Song.

Eftsoones the Nymphes, which now had Flowers their fill,
Ran all in haste to see that silver brood,
As they came floating on the Cristal Flood;
Whom when they sawe, they stood amazèd still,
Their wondring eyes to fill;

Them seem'd they never saw a sight so fayre,
Of Fowles, so lovely, that they sure did deeme
Them heavenly borne, or to be that same payre
Which through the Skie draw Venus silver Teeme:
For sure they did not seeme
To be begot of any earthly Seede,
But rather Angels, or of Angels breede;
Yet were they bred of Somers-heat, they say,
In sweetest Season, when each Flower and weede
The earth did fresh aray;
So fresh they seem'd as day,
Even as their Brydale day, which was not long:
   Sweete Themmes! runne softly, till I end my Song.

Then forth they all out of their baskets drew
Great store of Flowers, the honour of the field,
That to the sense did fragrant odours yield,
All which upon those goodly Birds they threw
And all the Waves did strew,
That like old Peneus Waters they did seeme,
When downe along by pleasant Tempes shore,
Scattred with Flowres, through Thessaly they streeme,
That they appeare, through Lillies plenteous store,
Like a Brydes Chamber flore.
Two of those Nymphes, meane while, two Garlands bound
Of freshest Flowres which in that Mead they found,
The which presenting all in trim Array,
Their snowie Foreheads therewithall they crownd,
Whil'st one did Sing this Lay,
Prepar'd against that Day,
Against their Brydale day, which was not long:
   Sweete Themmes! runne softly, till I end my Song.

'Ye gentle Birdes! the worlds faire ornament,
And heavens glorie, whom this happie hower
Doth leade unto your lovers blisfull bower,
Joy may you have, and gentle hearts content
Of your loves couplement;
And let faire Venus, that is Queene of love,
With her heart-quelling Sonne upon you smile,

Whose smile, they say, hath vertue to remove
All Loves dislike, and friendships faultie guile
For ever to assoile.
Let endlesse Peace your steadfast hearts accord,
And blessed Plentie wait upon your bord;
And let your bed with pleasures chast abound,
That fruitfull issue may to you afford,
Which may your foes confound,
And make your joyes redound
Upon your Brydale day, which is not long:
   Sweete Themmes! runne softlie, till I end my Song.'

So ended she; and all the rest around
To her redoubled that her undersong,
Which said their brydale daye should not be long:
And gentle Eccho from the neighbor ground
Their accents did resound.
So forth those joyous Birdes did passe along,
Adowne the Lee, that to them murmurde low,
As he would speake, but that he lackt a tong,
Yet did by signes his glad affection show,
Making his streame run slow.
And all the foule which in his flood did dwell
Gan flock about these twaine, that did excell
The rest, so far as Cynthia doth shend
The lesser starres. So they, enrangèd well,
Did on those two attend,
And their best service lend
Against their wedding day, which was not long:
   Sweete Themmes! runne softly, till I end my Song.

At length they all to mery London came,
To mery London, my most kyndly Nurse,
That to me gave this Lifes first native sourse,
Though from another place I take my name,
An house of auncient fame:
There when they came, whereas those bricky towres
The which on Themmes brode agèd backe doe ryde,
Where now the studious Lawyers have their bowers,
There whylome wont the Templar Knights to byde,

Till they decayd through pride:
Next whereunto there standes a stately place,
Where oft I gayned giftes and goodly grace
Of that great Lord, which therein wont to dwell,
Whose want too well now feeles my freendles case;
But ah! here fits not well
Olde woes, but joyes, to tell
Against the Brydale daye, which is not long:
　　Sweete Themmes! runne softly, till I end my Song.

Yet therein now doth lodge a noble Peer,
Great Englands glory, and the Worlds wide wonder,
Whose dreadfull name late through all Spaine did thunder,
And Hercules two pillors standing neere
Did make to quake and feare:
Faire branch of Honor, flower of Chevalrie!
That fillest England with thy triumphes fame,
Joy have thou of thy noble victorie,
And endlesse happinesse of thine owne name
That promiseth the same;
That through thy prowesse, and victorious armes,
Thy country may be freed from forraine harmes;
And great Elisaes glorious name may ring
Through al the world, fil'd with thy wide Alarmes,
Which some brave muse may sing
To ages following,
Upon the Brydale day, which is not long:
　　Sweete Themmes! runne softly, till I end my Song.

From those high Towers this noble Lord issuing,
Like Radiant Hesper, when his golden hayre
In th' Ocean billowes he hath bathèd fayre,
Descended to the Rivers open vewing,
With a great train ensuing.
Above the rest were goodly to bee seene
Two gentle Knights of lovely face and feature,
Beseeming well the bower of anie Queene,
With gifts of wit, and ornaments of nature,
Fit for so goodly stature,
That like the twins of Jove they seem'd in sight,

Which decke the Bauldricke of the Heavens bright;
They two, forth pacing to the Rivers side,
Received those two faire Brides, their Loves delight;
Which, at th' appointed tyde,
Each one did make his Bryde
Against their Brydale day, which is not long:
  Sweete Themmes! runne softly, till I end my Song.

73   EPITHALAMION

Ye learnèd sisters, which have oftentimes
Beene to me ayding, others to adorne,
Whom ye thought worthy of your gracefull rymes,
That even the greatest did not greatly scorne
To heare theyr names sung in your simple layes,
But joyed in theyr praise;
And when ye list your owne mishaps to mourne,
Which death, or love, or fortunes wreck did rayse,
Your string could soone to sadder tenor turne,
And teach the woods and waters to lament
Your doleful dreriment:
Now lay those sorrowfull complaints aside;
And, having all your heads with girlands crownd,
Helpe me mine owne loves prayses to resound;
Ne let the same of any be envide:
So Orpheus did for his owne bride!
So I unto my selfe alone will sing;
The woods shall to me answer, and my Eccho ring.

Early, before the worlds light-giving lampe
His golden beame upon the hils doth spred,
Having disperst the nights unchearefull dampe,
Doe ye awake; and, with fresh lusty-hed,
Go to the bowre of my belovèd love,
My truest turtle dove;
Bid her awake; for Hymen is awake,
And long since ready forth his maske to move,
With his bright Tead that flames with many a flake,
And many a bachelor to waite on him,
In theyr fresh garments trim.
Bid her awake therefore, and soone her dight,

For lo! the wishèd day is come at last,
That shall, for all the paynes and sorrowes past,
Pay to her usury of long delight:
And, whylest she doth her dight,
Doe ye to her of joy and solace sing,
That all the woods may answer, and your eccho ring.

Bring with you all the Nymphes that you can heare
Both of the rivers and the forrests greene,
And of the sea that neighbours to her neare:
Al with gay girlands goodly wel beseene.
And let them also with them bring in hand
Another gay girland
For my fayre love, of lillyes and of roses,
Bound truelove wize, with a blew silke riband.
And let them make great store of bridale poses,
And let them eeke bring store of other flowers,
To deck the bridale bowers.
And let the ground whereas her foot shall tread,
For feare the stones her tender foot should wrong,
Be strewed with fragrant flowers all along,
And diapred lyke the discolored mead.
Which done, doe at her chamber dore awayt,
For she will waken strayt;
The whiles doe ye this song unto her sing,
The woods shall to you answer, and your Eccho ring.

Ye Nymphes of Mulla, which with carefull heed
The silver scaly trouts doe tend full well,
And greedy pikes which use therein to feed:
(Those trouts and pikes all others doo excell;)
And ye likewise, which keep the rushy lake,
Where none doo fishes take;
Bynd up the locks the which hang scattered light,
And in his waters, which your mirror make,
Behold your faces as the christall bright,
That when you come whereas my love doth lie,
No blemish she may spie.
And eke, ye lightfoot mayds, which keep the deere,
That on the hoary mountayne used to towre;

And the wylde wolves, which seeke them to devoure,
With your steel darts doo chace from coming neer,
Be also present heere,
To helpe to decke her, and to help to sing,
That all the woods may answer, and your eccho ring.

Wake now, my love, awake! for it is time;
The Rosy Morne long since left Tithones bed,
All ready to her silver coche to clyme;
And Phœbus gins to shew his glorious hed.
Hark! how the cheereful birds do chaunt theyr laies
And carrol of Loves praise.
The merry Larke hir mattins sings aloft;
The Thrush replyes; the Mavis descant playes;
The Ouzell shrills; the Ruddock warbles soft;
So goodly all agree, with sweet consent,
To this dayes merriment.
Ah! my deere love, why doe ye sleepe thus long?
When meeter were that ye should now awake,
T' awayt the comming of your joyous make,
And hearken to the birds love-learnèd song,
The deawy leaves among!
For they of joy and pleasance to you sing,
That all the woods them answer, and theyr eccho ring.

My love is now awake out of her dreames,
And her fayre eyes, like stars that dimmèd were
With darksome cloud, now shew theyr goodly beams
More bright then Hesperus his head doth rere.
Come now, ye damzels, daughters of delight,
Helpe quickly her to dight:
But first come ye fayre houres, which were begot
In Joves sweet paradice of Day and Night;
Which doe the seasons of the yeare allot,
And al, that ever in this world is fayre,
Doe make and still repayre:
And ye three handmayds of the Cyprian Queene,
The which doe still adorne her beauties pride,
Helpe to addorne my beautifullest bride:
And, as ye her array, still throw betweene

Some graces to be seene;
And, as ye use to Venus, to her sing,
The whiles the woods shal answer, and your eccho ring.

Now is my love all ready forth to come:
Let all the virgins therefore well awayt:
And ye fresh boyes, that tend upon her groome,
Prepare yourselves; for he is comming strayt.
Set all your things in seemely good array,
Fit for so joyfull day:
The joyfulst day that ever sunne did see.
Faire Sun! shew forth thy favourable ray,
And let thy lifull heat not fervent be,
For feare of burning her sunshyny face,
Her beauty to disgrace.
O fayrest Phœbus! father of the Muse!
If ever I did honour thee aright,
Or sing the thing that mote thy mind delight,
Doe not thy servants simple boone refuse;
But let this day, let this one day, be myne;
Let all the rest be thine.
Then I thy soverayne prayses loud wil sing,
That all the woods shal answer, and theyr eccho ring.

Harke! how the Minstrils gin to shrill aloud
Their merry Musick that resounds from far,
The pipe, the tabor, and the trembling Croud,
That well agree withouten breach or jar.
But, most of all, the Damzels doe delite
When they their tymbrels smyte,
And thereunto doe daunce and carrol sweet,
That all the sences they doe ravish quite;
The whyles the boyes run up and downe the street,
Crying aloud with strong confusèd noyce,
As if it were one voyce,
Hymen, iö Hymen, Hymen, they do shout;
That even to the heavens theyr shouting shrill
Doth reach, and all the firmament doth fill;
To which the people standing all about,
As in approvance, doe thereto applaud,

And loud advaunce her laud;
And evermore they Hymen, Hymen sing,
That al the woods them answer, and theyr eccho ring.

Loe! where she comes along with portly pace,
Lyke Phoebe, from her chamber of the East,
Arysing forth to run her mighty race,
Clad all in white, that seemes a virgin best.
So well it her beseemes, that ye would weene
Some angell she had beene.
Her long loose yellow locks lyke golden wyre,
Sprinckled with perle, and perling flowres atweene,
Doe lyke a golden mantle her attyre;
And, being crownèd with a girland greene,
Seeme lyke some mayden Queene.
Her modest eyes, abashèd to behold
So many gazers as on her do stare,
Upon the lowly ground affixèd are;
Ne dare lift up her countenance too bold,
But blush to heare her prayses sung so loud,
So farre from being proud.
Nathless doe ye still loud her prayses sing,
That all the woods may answer, and your eccho ring.

Tell me, ye merchants daughters, did ye see
So fayre a creature in your towne before;
So sweet, so lovely, and so mild as she,
Adorned with beautyes grace and vertues store?
Her goodly eyes lyke Saphyres shining bright,
Her forehead yvory white,
Her cheeks lyke apples which the sun hath rudded,
Her lips like cherryes charming men to byte,
Her brest like to a bowle of creame uncrudded,
Her paps lyke lyllies budded,
Her snowie neck lyke to a marble towre;
And all her body like a pallace fayre,
Ascending up, with many a stately stayre,
To honours seat and chastities sweet bowre.
Why stand ye still ye virgins in amaze,
Upon her so to gaze,

Whiles ye forget your former lay to sing,
To which the woods did answer, and your eccho ring?

But if ye saw that which no eyes can see,
The inward beauty of her lively spright,
Garnisht with heavenly guifts of high degree,
Much more then would ye wonder at that sight,
And stand astonisht lyke to those which red
Medusaes mazeful hed.
There dwels sweet love, and constant chastity,
Unspotted fayth, and comely womanhood,
Regard of honour, and mild modesty;
There vertue raynes as Queene in royal throne,
And giveth lawes alone,
The which the base affections doe obay,
And yeeld theyr services unto her will;
Ne thought of thing uncomely ever may
Thereto approch to tempt her mind to ill.
Had ye once seene these her celestial threasures,
And unrevealèd pleasures,
Then would ye wonder, and her prayses sing,
That al the woods should answer, and your eccho ring.

Open the temple gates unto my love,
Open them wide that she may enter in,
And all the postes adorne as doth behove,
And all the pillours deck with girlands trim,
For to receyve this Saynt with honour dew,
That commeth in to you.
With trembling steps, and humble reverence,
She commeth in, before th' Almighties view;
Of her ye virgins learne obedience,
When so ye come into those holy places,
To humble your proud faces:
Bring her up to th' high altar, that she may
The sacred ceremonies there partake,
The which do endlesse matrimony make;
And let the roring Organs loudly play
The praises of the Lord in lively notes;
The whiles, with hollow throates,

The Choristers the joyous Antheme sing,
That al the woods may answere, and their eccho ring.

Behold, whiles she before the altar stands,
Hearing the holy priest that to her speakes,
And blesseth her with his two happy hands,
How the red roses flush up in her cheekes,
And the pure snow, with goodly vermill stayne
Like crimsin dyde in grayne:
That even th' Angels, which continually
About the sacred Altare doe remaine,
Forget their service and about her fly,
Ofte peeping in her face, that seems more fayre,
The more they on it stare.
But her sad eyes, still fastened on the ground,
Are governèd with goodly modesty,
That suffers not one looke to glaunce awry,
Which may let in one little thought unsownd.
Why blush ye, love, to give to me your hand,
The pledge of all our band!
Sing, ye sweet Angels, Alleluya sing,
That all the woods may answere, and your eccho ring.

Now al is done: bring home the bride againe;
Bring home the triumph of our victory:
Bring home with you the glory of her gaine
With joyance bring her and with jollity.
Never had man more joyfull day then this,
Whom heaven would heape with blis,
Make feast therefore now all this live-long day;
This day for ever to me holy is.
Poure out the wine without restraint or stay,
Poure not by cups, but by the belly full,
Poure out to all that wull,
And sprinkle all the postes and wals with wine,
That they may sweat, and drunken be withall.
Crowne ye God Bacchus with a coronall,
And Hymen also crowne with wreathes of vine;
And let the Graces daunce unto the rest,

For they can doo it best:
The whiles the maydens doe theyr carroll sing,
To which the woods shall answer, and theyr eccho ring.

Ring ye the bels, ye yong men of the towne,
And leave your wonted labors for this day:
This day is holy; doe ye write it downe,
That ye for ever it remember may.
This day the sunne is in his chiefest hight,
With Barnaby the bright,
From whence declining daily by degrees,
He somewhat loseth of his heat and light,
When once the Crab behind his back he sees.
But for this time it ill ordainèd was,
To chose the longest day in all the yeare,
The shortest night, when longest fitter weare:
Yet never day so long, but late would passe.
Ring ye the bels, to make it weare away,
And bonefiers make all day;
And daunce about them, and about them sing,
That all the woods may answer, and your eccho ring.

Ah! when will this long weary day have end,
And lende me leave to come unto my love?
How slowly do the houres theyr numbers spend?
How slowly does sad Time his feathers move?
Hast thee, O fayrest Planet, to thy home,
Within the Westerne fome:
Thy tyrèd steedes long since have need of rest.
Long though it be, at last I see it gloome,
And the bright evening-star with golden creast
Appeare out of the East.
Fayre childe of beauty! glorious lampe of love!
That all the host of heaven in rankes doost lead,
And guydest lovers through the nights sad dread,
How chearefully thou lookest from above,
And seemst to laugh atweene thy twinkling light,
As joying in the sight
Of these glad many, which for joy doe sing,
That all the woods them answer, and their eccho ring.

Now ceasse, ye damsels, your delights fore-past;
Enough it is that all the day was youres:
Now day is doen, and night is nighing fast,
Now bring the Bryde into the brydall boures.
The night is come, now soon her disaray,
And in her bed her lay;
Lay her in lillies and in violets,
And silken courteins over her display,
And odourd sheetes, and Arras coverlets,
Behold how goodly my faire love does ly,
In proud humility!
Like unto Maia, when as Jove her took
In Tempe, lying on the flowry gras,
Twixt sleepe and wake, after she weary was,
With bathing in the Acidalian brooke.
Now it is night, ye damsels may be gon,
And leave my love alone,
And leave likewise your former lay to sing:
The woods no more shall answere, nor your eccho ring.

Now welcome, night! thou night so long expected,
That long daies labour doest at last defray,
And all my cares, which cruell Love collected,
Hast sumd in one, and cancellèd for aye:
Spread thy broad wing over my love and me,
That no man may us see;
And in thy sable mantle us enwrap,
From feare of perrill and foule horror free.
Let no false treason seeke us to entrap,
Nor any dread disquiet once annoy
The safety of our joy;
But let the night be calme, and quietsome,
Without tempestuous storms or sad afray:
Lyke as when Jove with fayre Alcmena lay,
When he begot the great Tirynthian groome:
Or lyke as when he with thy selfe did lie
And begot Majesty.
And let the mayds and yong men cease to sing;
Ne let the woods them answer nor theyr eccho ring.

Let no lamenting cryes, nor dolefull teares
Be heard all night within, nor yet without:
Ne let false whispers, breeding hidden feares,
Breake gentle sleepe with misconceivèd dout.
Let no deluding dreames, nor dreadfull sights,
Make sudden sad affrights;
Ne let house-fyres, nor lightnings helpelesse harmes,
Ne let the Pouke, nor other evill sprights,
Ne let mischivous witches with theyr charmes,
Ne let hob Goblins, names whose sence we see not,
Fray us with things that be not;
Let not the shriech Oule nor the Storke be heard,
Nor the night Raven, that still deadly yels:
Nor dammèd ghosts, cald up with mighty spels,
Nor griesly vultures, make us once affeard:
Ne let th' unpleasant Quyre of Frogs still croking
Make us to wish theyr choking.
Let none of these theyr drery accents sing;
Ne let the woods them answer, nor theyr eccho ring.

But still let Silence trew night-watches keepe,
That sacred Peace may in assurance rayne,
And tymely Sleep, when it is tyme to sleepe,
May poure his limbs forth on your pleasant playne;
The whiles an hundred little wingèd loves,
Like divers-fethered doves,
Shall fly and flutter round about your bed,
And in the secret darke, that none reproves,
Their prety stealthes shal worke, and snares shal spread
To filch away sweet snatches of delight,
Conceald through covert night.
Ye sonnes of Venus, play your sports at will!
For greedy pleasure, carelesse of your toyes,
Thinks more upon her paradise of joyes,
Then what ye do, albe it good or ill.
All night therefore attend your merry play,
For it will soone be day:
Now none doth hinder you, that say or sing;
Ne will the woods now answer, nor your Eccho ring.

Who is the same, which at my window peepes?
Or whose is that faire face that shines so bright?
Is it not Cinthia, she that never sleepes,
But walkes about high heaven al the night?
O! fayrest goddesse, do thou not envy
My love with me to spy:
For thou likewise didst love, though now unthought
And for a fleece of wooll, which privily
The Latmian shepherd once unto thee brought,
His pleasures with thee wrought.
Therefore to us be favourable now;
And sith of wemens labours thou hast charge,
And generation goodly dost enlarge,
Encline thy will t'effect our wishfull vow,
And the chaste wombe informe with timely seed,
That may our comfort breed:
Till which we cease our hopefull hap to sing;
Ne let the woods us answere, nor our Eccho ring.

And thou, great Juno! which with awful might
The lawes of wedlock still dost patronize;
And the religion of the faith first plight
With sacred rites hast taught to solemnize;
And eeke for comfort often callèd art
Of women in their smart;
Eternally bind thou this lovely band,
And all thy blessings unto us impart.
And thou, glad Genius! in whose gentle hand
The bridale bowre and geniall bed remaine,
Without blemish or staine;
And the sweet pleasures of theyr loves delight
With secret ayde doest succor and supply,
Till they bring forth the fruitfull progeny;
Send us the timely fruit of this same night.
And thou, fayre Hebe! and thou, Hymen free!
Grant that it may so be.
Till which we cease your further prayse to sing;
Ne any woods shall answer, nor your Eccho ring.

And ye high heavens, the temple of the gods,
In which a thousand torches flaming bright

Doe burne, that to us wretched earthly clods
In dreadful darknesse lend desirèd light;
And all ye powers which in the same remayne,
More then we men can fayne!
Poure out your blessing on us plentiously,
And happy influence upon us raine,
That we may raise a large posterity,
Which from the earth, which they may long possesse
With lasting happinesse,
Up to your haughty pallaces may mount;
And for the guerdon of theyr glorious merit,
May heavenly tabernacles there inherit,
Of blessèd Saints for to increase the count.
So let us rest, sweet love, in hope of this,
And cease till then our tymely joyes to sing:
The woods no more us answer, nor our eccho ring!

Song! made in lieu of many ornaments,
With which my love should duly have been dect,
Which cutting off through hasty accidents,
Ye would not stay your dew time to expect,
But promist both to recompens;
Be unto her a goodly ornament,
And for short time an endlesse moniment.

74   A DITTY

In praise of Eliza, Queen of the Shepherds

SEE where she sits upon the grassie greene,
          (O seemely sight!)
Yclad in Scarlot, like a mayden Queene,
          And ermines white:
Upon her head a Cremosin coronet
With Damaske roses and Daffadillies set:
          Bay leaves betweene,
          And primroses greene,
Embellish the sweete Violet.

Tell me, have ye seene her angelick face
          Like Phœbe fayre?

Her heavenly haveour, her princely grace,
       Can you well compare?
The Redde rose medled with the White yfere,
In either cheeke depeincten lively chere:
       Her modest eye,
       Her Majestie,
Where have you seene the like but there?

I see Calliope speede her to the place,
       Where my Goddesse shines;
And after her the other Muses trace
       With their Violines.
Bene they not Bay braunches which they do beare,
All for Elisa in her hand to weare?
       So sweetely they play,
       And sing all the way,
That it a heaven is to heare.

Lo, how finely the Graces can it foote
       To the Instrument:
They dauncen deffly, and singen soote,
       In their meriment.
Wants not a fourth Grace to make the daunce even?
Let that rowme to my Lady be yeven.
       She shal be a Grace,
       To fyll the fourth place,
And reigne with the rest in heaven.

Bring hether the Pincke and purple Cullambine,
       With Gelliflowres;
Bring Coronations, and Sops-in-wine
       Worne of Paramoures:
Strowe me the ground with Daffadowndillies,
And Cowslips, and Kingcups, and lovèd Lillies:
       The pretie Pawnce,
       And the Chevisaunce,
Shall match with the fayre flowre Delice.

Now ryse up, Elisa, deckèd as thou art
       In royall aray;

And now ye daintie Damsells may depart
    Eche one her way.
I feare I have troubled your troupes to longe:
Let dame Elisa thanke you for her song:
    And if you come hether
    When Damsines I gether,
I will part them all you among.

75   PERIGOT AND WILLIE'S ROUNDELAY

    IT fell upon a holly eve,
      Hey ho, hollidaye!
    When holly fathers wont to shrieve,
      Now gynneth this roundelay.
    Sitting upon a hill so hye,
      Hey ho, the high hyll!
    The while my flocke did feede thereby,
      The while the shepheard selfe did spill:

    I saw the bouncing Bellibone,
      Hey ho, Bonibell!
    Tripping over the dale alone:
      She can trippe it very well;
    Well decked in a frocke of gray,
      Hey ho, gray is greete!
    And in a kirtle of greene saye,
      The greene is for maydens meete.

    A chapelet on her head she wore,
      Hey ho, chapelet!
    Of sweete violets therein was store,
      —She sweeter then the violet.
    My sheepe did leave theyr wonted foode,
      Hey ho, seely sheepe!
    And gazd on her, as they were wood,
      —Woode as he, that did them keepe.

    As the bonnilasse passed bye,
      Hey ho, bonilasse!
    She rovde at me with glauncing eye,
      As cleare as the christall glasse:

All as the sunnye beame so bright,
  Hey ho, the sunne beame!
Glaunceth from Phœbus face forthright,
  So love into my hart did streame:

Or as the thonder cleaves the cloudes,
  Hey ho, the thonder!
Wherein the lightsome levin shroudes,
  So cleaves thy soule asonder:
Or as Dame Cynthias silver raye
  Hey ho, the moonelight!
Upon the glyttering wave doth playe:
  Such play is a pitteous plight!

The glaunce into my heart did glide,
  Hey ho, the glyder!
Therewith my soule was sharply gryde;
  Such woundes soone wexen wider.
Hasting to raunch the arrow out,
  Hey ho, Perigot!
I left the head in my hart roote:
  It was a desperate shot.

There itranckleth ay more and more,
  Hey ho, the arrowe!
Ne can I find salve for my sore:
  Love is a cureless sorrowe.
And though my bale with death I brought,
  Hey ho, heavie cheere!
Yet should thilk lasse not from my thought:
  So you may buye gold to deare.

But whether in paynefull love I pyne,
  Hey ho, pinching payne!
Or thrive in welth, she shalbe mine.
  But if thou can her obteine.
And if for gracelesse griefe I dye,
  Hey ho, graceless griefe!
Witnesse, shee slewe me with her eye:
  Let thy follye be the priefe.

And you that sawe it, simple shepe,
 Hey ho, the fayre flocke!
For priefe thereof my death shall weepe,
 And mone with many a mocke.
So learnd I love on a hollye eve,—
 Hey ho, holidaye!
That ever since my hart did greve:
 Now endeth our roundelay.

76   EASTER

MOST glorious Lord of Lyfe! that, on this day,
Didst make Thy triumph over death and sin;
And, having harrowd hell, didst bring away
Captivity thence captive, us to win:
This joyous day, deare Lord, with joy begin;
And grant that we, for whom thou diddest dye,
Being with Thy deare blood clene washt from sin,
May live for ever in felicity!
And that Thy love we weighing worthily,
May likewise love Thee for the same againe;
And for Thy sake, that all lyke deare didst buy,
With love may one another entertayne!
 So let us love, deare Love, lyke as we ought,
 —Love is the lesson which the Lord us taught.

77   WHAT GUILE IS THIS?

WHAT guile is this, that those her golden tresses
She doth attire under a net of gold;
And with sly skill so cunningly them dresses,
That which is gold or hair may scarce be told?
Is it that men's frail eyes, which gaze too bold,
She may entangle in that golden snare;
And, being caught, may craftily enfold
Their weaker hearts, which are not well aware?
Take heed, therefore, mine eyes, how ye do stare
Henceforth too rashly on that guileful net,
In which, if ever ye entrappèd are,
Out of her bands ye by no means shall get.
 Fondness it were for any, being free,
 To cover fetters, though they golden be.

78

Fair Is My Love

Fair is my love, when her fair golden hairs
With the loose wind ye waving chance to mark;
Fair, when the rose in her red cheeks appears;
Or in her eyes the fire of love does spark.
Fair, when her breast, like a rich-laden bark,
With precious merchandise she forth doth lay;
Fair, when that cloud of pride, which oft doth dark
Her goodly light, with smiles she drives away.
But fairest she, when so she doth display
The gate with pearls and rubies richly dight;
Through which her words so wise do make their way
To bear the message of her gentle sprite.
    The rest be works of nature's wonderment:
    But this the work of heart's astonishment.

79

So Oft as I Her Beauty do Behold

So oft as I her beauty do behold,
And therewith do her cruelty compare,
I marvel of what substance was the mould,
The which her made at once so cruel fair,
Not earth, for her high thoughts more heavenly are;
Not water, for her love doth burn like fire;
Not air, for she is not so light or rare;
Not fire, for she doth freeze with faint desire.
Then needs another element inquire
Whereof she mote be made—that is, the sky;
For to the heaven her haughty looks aspire,
And eke her mind is pure immortal high.
    Then, sith to heaven ye likened are the best,
    Be like in mercy as in all the rest.

80

Rudely Thou Wrongest My Dear
Heart's Desire

Rudely thou wrongest my dear heart's desire,
In finding fault with her too portly pride:
The thing which I do most in her admire,
Is of the world unworthy most envied;

For in those lofty looks is close implied
Scorn of base things, and 'sdain of foul dishonour,
Threatening rash eyes which gaze on her so wide,
That loosely they ne dare to look upon her.
Such pride is praise, such portliness is honour,
That boldened innocence bears in her eyes;
And her fair countenance, like a goodly banner,
Spreads in defiance of all enemies.
  Was never in this world aught worthy tried,
  Without some spark of such self-pleasing pride.

81   ONE DAY I WROTE HER NAME UPON
                    THE STRAND

ONE day I wrote her name upon the strand,
But came the waves and washèd it away:
Again I wrote it with a second hand,
But came the tide and made my pains his prey.
Vain man (said she) that dost in vain assay
A mortal thing so to immortalise;
For I myself shall like to this decay,
And eke my name be wipèd out likewise.
Not so (quod I); let baser things devise
To die in dust, but you shall live by fame;
My verse your virtues rare shall eternise,
And in the heavens write your glorious name:
  Where, when as Death shall all the world subdue,
  Our love shall live, and later life renew.

82   LIKE AS THE CULVER, ON THE BARED BOUGH

LIKE as the culver, on the barèd bough,
Sits mourning for the absence of her mate;
And, in her songs, sends many a wishful vow
For his return that seems to linger late:
So I alone, now left disconsolate,
Mourn to myself the absence of my love;
And, wandering here and there all desolate,
Seek with my plaints to match that mournful dove
Ne joy of aught that under heaven doth hove,
Can comfort me, but her own joyous sight

Whose sweet aspect both God and man can move,
In her unspotted pleasance to delight.
Dark is my day, whiles her fair light I miss,
And dead my life that wants such lively bliss.

WILLIAM HABINGTON
[1605-1654]

83   To Roses in the Bosom of Castara

Ye blushing virgins happy are
    In the chaste nunnery of her breasts—
For he'd profane so chaste a fair,
    Whoe'er should call them Cupid's nests.

Transplanted thus how bright ye grow!
    How rich a perfume do ye yield!
In some close garden cowslips so
    Are sweeter than i' th' open field.

In those white cloisters live secure
    From the rude blasts of wanton breath!—
Each hour more innocent and pure,
    Till you shall wither into death.

Then that which living gave you room,
    Your glorious sepulchre shall be.
There wants no marble for a tomb
    Whose breast hath marble been to me.

84   Nox Nocti Indicat Scientiam

When I survey the bright
    Celestial sphere;
So rich with jewels hung, that Night
    Doth like an Ethiop bride appear:

My soul her wings doth spread
    And heavenward flies,
Th' Almighty's mysteries to read
    In the large volume of the skies.

For the bright firmament
 Shoots forth no flame
So silent, but is eloquent
 In speaking the Creator's name.

No unregarded star
 Contracts its light
Into so small a character,
 Removed far from our human sight,

But if we steadfast look
 We shall discern
In it, as in some holy book,
 How man may heavenly knowledge learn.

It tells the conqueror
 That far-stretch'd power,
Which his proud dangers traffic for,
 Is but the triumph of an hour:

That from the farthest North,
 Some nation may,
Yet undiscover'd, issue forth,
 And o'er his new-got conquest sway:

Some nation yet shut in
 With hills of ice
May be let out to scourge his sin,
 Till they shall equal him in vice.

And then they likewise shall
 Their ruin have;
For as yourselves your empires fall,
 And every kingdom hath a grave.

Thus those celestial fires,
 Though seeming mute,
The fallacy of our desires
 And all the pride of life confute:—

For they have watch'd since first
The World had birth:
And found sin in itself accurst,
And nothing permanent on Earth.

CHRISTOPHER MARLOWE
[1564-1593]

85   THE PASSIONATE SHEPHERD TO HIS LOVE

COME live with me and be my Love,
And we will all the pleasures prove
That hills and valleys, dales and field,
Or woods or steepy mountain yields.

And we will sit upon the rocks
And see the shepherds feed their flocks,
By shallow rivers, to whose falls
Melodious birds sing madrigals.

And I will make thee beds of roses
And a thousand fragrant posies,
A cap of flowers, and a kirtle
Embroider'd all with leaves of myrtle.

A gown made of the finest wool,
Which from our pretty lambs we pull,
Fair linèd slippers for the cold,
With buckles of the purest gold.

A belt of straw and ivy buds
With coral clasps and amber studs:
And if these pleasures may thee move,
Come live with me and be my Love.

Thy silver dishes for thy meat
As precious as the gods do eat,
Shall on an ivory table be
Prepared each day for thee and me.

The shepherd swains shall dance and sing
For thy delight each May-morning:
If these delights thy mind may move,
Then live with me and be my Love.

86   HER REPLY

(*Written by Sir Walter Raleigh*)

IF all the world and love were young,
And truth in every shepherd's tongue,
These pretty pleasures might me move
To live with thee and be thy Love.

But Time drives flocks from field to fold;
When rivers rage and rocks grow cold;
And Philomel becometh dumb;
The rest complains of cares to come.

The flowers do fade, and wanton fields
To wayward Winter reckoning yields:
A honey tongue, a heart of gall,
Is fancy's spring, but sorrow's fall.

Thy gowns, thy shoes, thy beds of roses,
Thy cap, thy kirtle, and thy posies,
Soon break, soon wither—soon forgotten,
In folly ripe, in reason rotten.

Thy belt of straw and ivy-buds,
Thy coral clasps and amber studs,—
All these in me no means can move
To come to thee and be thy Love.

But could youth last, and love still breed,
Had joys no date, nor age no need,
Then these delights my mind might move
To live with thee and be thy Love.

RICHARD ROWLANDS
[1565–1620]

87   OUR BLESSED LADY'S LULLABY

UPON my lap, my Sovereign sits,
   And sucks upon my breast;
Meanwhile his love sustains my life,
   And gives my body rest.
     Sing, lullaby, my little boy,
     Sing, lullaby, my livës joy.

When thou hast taken thy repast,
   Repose, my babe, on me.
So may thy mother and thy nurse,
   Thy cradle also be.
     Sing, lullaby, my little boy,
     Sing, lullaby, my livës joy.

I grieve that duty doth not work
   All that my wishing would,
Because I would not be to thee
   But in the best I should.
     Sing, lullaby, my little boy,
     Sing, lullaby, my livës joy.

Yet as I am and as I may,
   I must and will be thine,
Though all too little for thyself
   Vouchsafing to be mine.
     Sing, lullaby, my little boy,
     Sing, lullaby, my livës joy.

My wits, my words, my deeds, my thoughts,
   And else what is in me,
I rather will not wish to use,
   If not in serving thee.
     Sing, lullaby, my little boy,
     Sing, lullaby, my livës joy.

My babe, my bliss, my child, my choice,
　My fruit, my flower, and bud,
My Jesus, and my only joy,
　The sum of all my good.
　　Sing, lullaby, my little boy,
　　Sing, lullaby, my livës joy.

My sweetness, and the sweetest most
　That heaven could earth deliver,
Soul of my love, spirit of my life,
　Abide with me for ever.
　　Sing, lullaby, my little boy,
　　Sing, lullaby, my livës joy.

Live still with me, and be my love,
　And death will me refrain,
Unless thou let me die with thee,
　To live with thee again.
　　Sing, lullaby, my little boy,
　　Sing, lullaby, my livës joy.

Leave now to wail, thou luckless wight
　That wrought'st thy race's woe,
Redress is found, and foilèd is
　Thy fruit-alluring foe.
　　Sing, lullaby, my little boy,
　　Sing, lullaby, my livës joy.

The fruit of death from Paradise
　Made the exiled mourn;
My fruit of life to Paradise
　Makes joyful thy return.
　　Sing, lullaby, my little boy,
　　Sing, lullaby, my livës joy.

Grow up, good fruit be nourished by
　These fountains two of me,
That only flow with maiden's milk,
　The only meat for thee.
　　Sing, lullaby, my little boy,
　　Sing, lullaby, my livës joy.

The earth has now a heaven become,
   And this base bower of mine,
A princely palace unto me,
   My son doth make to shine.
     Sing, lullaby, my little boy,
     Sing, lullaby, my livës joy.

His sight gives clearness to my sight,
   When waking I him see,
And sleeping, his mild countenance
   Gives favour unto me.
     Sing, lullaby, my little boy,
     Sing, lullaby, my livës joy.

When I him in mine arms embrace,
   I feel my heart embraced,
Even by the inward grace of his.
   Which he in me hath placed.
     Sing, lullaby, my little boy,
     Sing, lullaby, my livës joy.

And when I kiss his loving lips,
   Then his sweet-smelling breath
Doth yield a savour to my soul,
   That feeds love, hope, and faith.
     Sing, lullaby, my little boy,
     Sing, lullaby, my livës joy.

The shepherds left their keeping sheep,
   For joy to see my lamb;
How may I more rejoice to see
   Myself to be the dam.
     Sing, lullaby, my little boy,
     Sing, lullaby, my livës joy.

Three kings their treasures hither brought
   Of incense, myrrh, and gold;
The heaven's treasure, and the king
   That here they might behold.
     Sing, lullaby, my little boy,
     Sing, lullaby, my livës joy.

One sort an angel did direct,
  A star did guide the other,
And all the fairest son to see
  That ever had a mother.
    Sing, lullaby, my little boy,
    Sing, lullaby, my livës joy.

This sight I see, this child I have,
  This infant I embrace,
O endless comfort of the earth,
  And heaven's eternal grace.
    Sing, lullaby, my little boy,
    Sing, lullaby, my livës joy.

Thee sanctity herself doth serve,
  Thee goodness doth attend,
Thee blessedness doth wait upon,
  And virtues all commend.
    Sing, lullaby, my little boy,
    Sing, lullaby, my livës joy.

Great kings and prophets wishèd have
  To see that I possess,
Yet wish I never thee to see,
  If not in thankfulness.
    Sing, lullaby, my little boy,
    Sing, lullaby, my livës joy.

Let heaven and earth, and saints and men,
  Assistance give to me,
That all their most concurring aid
  Augment my thanks to thee.
    Sing, lullaby, my little boy,
    Sing, lullaby, my livës joy.

And let the ensuing blessèd race,
  Thou wilt succeeding raise,
Join all their praises unto mine,
  To multiply thy praise.
    Sing, lullaby, my little boy,
    Sing, lullaby, my livës joy.

And take my service well in worth,
    And Joseph's here with me,
Who of my husband bears the **name,**
    Thy servant for to be.
    Sing, lullaby, my little boy,
    Sing, lullaby, my livës joy.

THOMAS NASHE

[*1567–1601*]

88   IN TIME OF PESTILENCE

ADIEU, farewell earth's bliss!
This world uncertain is:
Fond are life's lustful joys,
Death proves them all but toys.
None from his darts can fly;
I am sick, I must die—
       Lord, have mercy on us!

Rich men, trust not in wealth,
Gold cannot buy you health;
Physic himself must fade;
All things to end are made;
The plague full swift goes by;
I am sick, I must die—
       Lord, have mercy on us!

Beauty is but a flower
Which wrinkles will devour;
Brightness falls from the air;
Queens have died young and fair;
Dust hath closed Helen's eye;
I am sick, I must die—
       Lord, have mercy on us!

Strength stoops unto the grave,
Worms feed on Hector brave;
Swords may not fight with fate;
Earth still holds ope her gate;

Come, come! the bells do cry;
I am sick, I must die—
    Lord, have mercy on us!

Wit with his wantonness
Tasteth death's bitterness;
Hell's executioner
Hath no ears for to hear
What vain art can reply:
I am sick, I must die—
    Lord, have mercy on us!

Haste therefore each degree
To welcome destiny;
Heaven is our heritage,
Earth but a player's stage.
Mount we unto the sky;
I am sick, I must die—
    Lord, have mercy on us!

89   SPRING

SPRING, the sweet Spring, is the year's pleasant king;
Then blooms each thing, then maids dance in a ring
Cold doth not sting, the pretty birds do sing,
    Cuckoo, jug-jug, pu-we, to-witta-woo!

The palm and may make country houses gay,
Lambs frisk and play, the shepherds pipe all day,
And we hear aye birds tune this merry lay,
    Cuckoo, jug-jug, pu-we, to-witta-woo!

The fields breathe sweet, the daisies kiss our feet,
Young lovers meet, old wives a-sunning sit,
In every street these tunes our ears do greet,
    Cuckoo, jug-jug, pu-we, to-witta-woo!
        Spring! the sweet Spring!

WILLIAM SHAKESPEARE
[1564–1616]

90　WINTER

WHEN icicles hang by the wall
　And Dick the shepherd blows his nail,
And Tom bears logs into the hall,
　And milk comes frozen home in pail;
When blood is nipt, and ways be foul,
Then nightly sings the staring owl
　　　　Tu-whoo!
To-whit, Tu-whoo! A merry note!
While greasy Joan doth keel the pot.

When all about the wind doth blow,
　And coughing drowns the parson's saw,
And birds sit brooding in the snow,
　And Marian's nose looks red and raw;
When roasted crabs hiss in the bowl—
Then nightly sings the staring owl
　　　　Tu-whoo!
To-whit, Tu-whoo! A merry note!
While greasy Joan doth keel the pot.

91　O MISTRESS MINE

O MISTRESS mine, where are you roaming?
O stay and hear! your true-love's coming
　That can sing both high and low;
Trip no further, pretty sweeting,
Journeys end in lovers' meeting—
　Every wise man's son doth know.

What is love? 'tis not hereafter;
Present mirth hath present laughter;
　What's to come is still unsure:
In delay there lies no plenty,—
Then come kiss me, Sweet-and-twenty,
　Youth's a stuff will not endure.

92   ### FANCY

TELL me where is Fancy bred,
Or in the heart, or in the head?
How begot, how nourishèd?
        Reply, reply.

It is engender'd in the eyes;
With gazing fed; and Fancy dies
In the cradle where it lies:
Let us all ring Fancy's knell;
I'll begin it,—Ding, dong, bell.
        —Ding, dong, bell.

93   ### UNDER THE GREENWOOD TREE

        UNDER the greenwood tree
        Who loves to lie with me,
        And tune his merry note
        Unto the sweet bird's throat—
Come hither, come hither, come hither!
        Here shall he see
        No enemy
But winter and rough weather.

        Who doth ambition shun
        And loves to live i' the sun,
        Seeking the food he eats
        And pleased with what he gets—
Come hither, come hither, come hither!
        Here shall he see
        No enemy
But winter and rough weather.

94   ### A LOVER AND HIS LASS

IT was a lover and his lass
        With a hey and a ho, and a hey-nonino!
That o'er the green corn-field did pass
In the spring time, the only pretty ring time,
When birds do sing hey ding a ding:
        Sweet lovers love the Spring.

Between the acres of the rye
These pretty country folks would lie:
This carol they began that hour,
How that life was but a flower:

And therefore take the present time
    With a hey and a ho, and a hey-nonino!
For love is crownéd with the prime
In the spring time, the only pretty ring time,
When birds do sing hey ding a ding:
    Sweet lovers love the Spring.

95   SILVIA

WHO is Silvia? What is she?
    That all our swains commend her?
Holy, fair, and wise is she:
    The heaven such grace did lend her,
That she might admiréd be.

Is she kind as she is fair?
    For beauty lives with kindness:
Love doth to her eyes repair,
    To help him of his blindness;
And, being help'd, inhabits there.

Then to Silvia let us sing,
    That Silvia is excelling;
She excels each mortal thing
    Upon the dull earth dwelling:
To her let us garlands bring.

96   SPRING

WHEN daisies pied and violets blue,
    And lady-smocks all silver-white,
And cuckoo-buds of yellow hue
    Do paint the meadows with delight,
The cuckoo then, on every tree,
Mocks married men; for thus sings he,
                    Cuckoo!

Cuckoo, cuckoo!—O word of fear,
Unpleasing to a married ear!

When shepherds pipe on oaten straws,
  And merry larks are ploughmen's clocks,
When turtles tread, and rooks, and daws,
  And maidens bleach their summer smocks,
The cuckoo then, on every tree,
Mocks married men; for thus sings he,
            Cuckoo!
Cuckoo, cuckoo!—O word of fear,
Unpleasing to a married ear!

97   LULLABY

You spotted snakes with double tongue,
  Thorny hedgehogs, be not seen;
Newts and blind-worms, do no wrong;
  Come not near our fairy queen.

      Philomel, with melody,
        Sing in our sweet lullaby;
Lulla, lulla, lullaby; lulla, lulla, lullaby!
        Never harm,
        Nor spell nor charm,
      Come our lovely lady nigh;
      So, good night, with lullaby.

Weaving spiders, come not here;
  Hence, you long-legg'd spinners, hence!
Beetles black, approach not near;
  Worm nor snail, do no offence.

      Philomel, with melody,
        Sing in our sweet lullaby;
Lulla, lulla, lullaby; lulla, lulla, lullaby!
        Never harm,
        Nor spell nor charm,
      Come our lovely lady nigh;
      So, good night, with lullaby.

98   OPHELIA'S SONG

How should I your true love know
    From another one?
By his cockle hat and staff,
    And his sandal shoon.

He is dead and gone, lady,
    He is dead and gone;
At his head a grass-green turf,
    At his heels a stone.

White his shroud as the mountain snow,
    Larded with sweet flowers,
Which bewept to the grave did go
    With true-love showers.

99   WHERE THE BEE SUCKS

WHERE the bee sucks, there suck I:
    In a cowslip's bell I lie;
There I couch when owls do cry.
On the bat's back I do fly.
After summer merrily:
    Merrily, merrily, shall I live now
    Under the blossom that hangs on the bough.

100   LOVE'S PERJURIES

ON a day, alack the day!
Love, whose month is ever May,
Spied a blossom passing fair
Playing in the wanton air;
Through the velvet leaves the wind,
All unseen, 'gan passage find;
That the lover, sick to death,
Wish'd himself the heaven's breath.
Air, quoth he, thy cheeks may blow;
Air, would I might triumph so!
But, alack, my hand is sworn
Ne'er to pluck thee from thy thorn:

Vow, alack, for youth unmeet;
Youth so apt to pluck a sweet.
Do not call it sin in me
That I am forsworn for thee:
Thou for whom e'en Jove would swear
Juno but an Ethiope were,
And deny himself for Jove,
Turning mortal for thy love.

101   TAKE, O TAKE

TAKE, O take those lips away
That so sweetly were forsworn,
And those eyes, the break of day,
Lights that do mislead the morn:
But my kisses bring again,
              Bring again—
Seals of love, but seal'd in vain,
              Seal'd in vain!

102   A MADRIGAL

CRABBED Age and Youth
Cannot live together:
Youth is full of pleasance,
Age is full of care;
Youth like summer morn,
Age like winter weather,
Youth like summer brave,
Age like winter bare:
Youth is full of sport,
Age's breath is short,
Youth is nimble, Age is lame:
Youth is hot and bold,
Age is weak and cold,
Youth is wild, and Age is tame:—
Age, I do abhor thee,
Youth, I do adore thee;
O! my Love, my Love is young!
Age, I do defy thee—
O sweet shepherd, hie thee,
For methinks thou stay'st too long.

103

Amiens' Song

Blow, blow, thou winter wind,
Thou art not so unkind
As man's ingratitude;
Thy tooth is not so keen
Because thou art not seen,
Although thy breath be rude.
Heigh ho! sing heigh ho! unto the green holly:
Most friendship is feigning, most loving mere folly:
Then, heigh ho! the holly!
This life is most jolly.

Freeze, freeze, thou bitter sky,
Thou dost not bite so nigh
As benefits forgot:
Though thou the waters warp,
Thy sting is not so sharp
As friend remember'd not.
Heigh ho! sing heigh ho! unto the green holly:
Most friendship is feigning, most loving mere folly:
Then, heigh ho! the holly!
This life is most jolly.

104

Dawn Song

Hark! hark! the lark at heaven's gate sings,
And Phœbus 'gins arise,
His steeds to water at those springs
On chaliced flowers that lies;
And winking Mary-buds begin
To ope their golden eyes:
With everything that pretty bin,
My lady sweet, arise!
Arise, arise!

105

Dirge of Love

Come away, come away, Death,
And in sad cypres let me be laid;
Fly away, fly away, breath;
I am slain by a fair cruel maid.

My shroud of white, stuck all with yew,
 O prepare it!
My part of death no one so true
 Did share it.

 Not a flower, not a flower sweet
On my black coffin let there be strown;
 Not a friend, not a friend greet
My poor corpse, where my bones shall be thrown;
A thousand thousand sighs to save,
 Lay me, O where
Sad true lover never find my grave,
 To weep there.

106   FIDELE'S DIRGE

FEAR no more the heat o' the sun
 Nor the furious winter's rages;
Thou thy worldly task hast done,
 Home art gone and ta'en thy wages:
Golden lads and girls all must,
As chimney-sweepers, come to dust.

Fear no more the frown o' the great,
 Thou art past the tyrant's stroke;
Care no more to clothe and eat;
 To thee the reed is as the oak:
The sceptre, learning, physic, must
All follow this, and come to dust.

Fear no more the lightning-flash
 Nor the all-dreaded thunder-stone;
Fear not slander, censure rash;
 Thou hast finish'd joy and moan:
All lovers young, all lovers must
Consign to thee, and come to dust.

No exorciser harm thee!
 Nor no witchcraft charm thee!
Ghost unlaid forbear thee!
 Nothing ill come near thee!
Quiet consummation have;
And renowned be thy grave!

107

A Sea Dirge

FULL fathom five thy father lies:
    Of his bones are coral made;
Those are pearls that were his eyes:
    Nothing of him that doth fade,
But doth suffer a sea-change
Into something rich and strange.
Sea-nymphs hourly ring his knell:
    Hark! now I hear them,—
        Ding, dong, bell.

108

Eighteenth Sonnet

SHALL I compare thee to a summer's day?
Thou art more lovely and more temperate;
Rough winds do shake the darling buds of May,
And summer's lease hath all too short a date:
Sometime too hot the eye of heaven shines,
And often is his gold complexion dimm'd:
And every fair from fair sometime declines,
By chance, or nature's changing course, untrimm'd.
But thy eternal summer shall not fade,
Nor lose possession of that fair thou owest;
Nor shall Death brag thou wanderest in his shade
When in eternal lines to time thou growest.
    So long as men can breathe, or eyes can see
    So long lives this, and this gives life to thee.

109

Twenty-ninth Sonnet

WHEN in disgrace with fortune and men's eyes
I all alone beweep my outcast state,
And trouble deaf heaven with my bootless cries,
And look upon myself, and curse my fate;
Wishing me like to one more rich in hope,
Featured like him, like him with friends possest,
Desiring this man's art, and that man's scope,
With what I most enjoy contented least;
Yet in these thoughts myself almost despising,
Haply I think on thee—and then my state,
Like to the lark at break of day arising

From sullen earth, sings hymns at heaven's gate;
For thy sweet love remember'd, such wealth brings
That then I scorn to change my state with kings.

110 THIRTIETH SONNET

WHEN to the sessions of sweet silent thought
I summon up remembrance of things past,
I sigh the lack of many a thing I sought,
And with old woes new wail my dear time's waste;
Then can I drown an eye, unused to flow,
For precious friends hid in death's dateless night,
And weep afresh love's long-since cancell'd woe,
And moan the expense of many a vanish'd sight.
Then can I grieve at grievances foregone,
And heavily from woe to woe tell o'er
The sad account of fore-bemoanèd moan,
Which I new pay as if not paid before:
But if the while I think on thee, dear friend,
All losses are restored, and sorrows end.

111 THIRTY-FIRST SONNET

THY bosom is endearèd with all hearts
Which I, by lacking, have supposèd dead:
And there reigns Love, and all Love's loving parts,
And all those friends which I thought burièd.
How many a holy and obsequious tear
Hath dear religious love stol'n from mine eye,
As interest of the dead!—which now appear
But things removed that hidden in thee lie.
Thou art the grave where buried love doth live,
Hung with the trophies of my lovers gone,
Who all their parts of me to thee did give;
That due of many now is thine alone:
Their images I loved I view in thee,
And thou, all they, hast all the all of me.

112 THIRTY-SECOND SONNET

IF thou survive my well-contented day
When that churl Death my bones with dust shall cover,
And shalt by fortune once more re-survey

These poor rude lines of thy deceaséd lover;
Compare them with the bettering of the time,
And though they be outstripp'd by every pen,
Reserve them for my love, not for their rhyme
Exceeded by the height of happier men.
O then vouchsafe me but this loving thought—
'Had my friend's muse grown with this growing age,
A dearer birth than this his love had brought,
To march in ranks of better equipage:
 But since he died, and poets better prove,
 Theirs for their style I'll read, his for his love.'

113   Thirty-third Sonnet

Full many a glorious morning have I seen
Flatter the mountain tops with sovereign eye,
Kissing with golden face the meadows green,
Gilding pale streams with heavenly alchemy;
Anon permit the basest clouds to ride
With ugly rack on his celestial face,
And from the forlorn world his visage hide,
Stealing unseen to west with this disgrace:
Even so my sun one early morn did shine
With all-triumphant splendour on my brow;
But out, alack! he was but one hour mine;
The region-cloud hath mask'd him from me now.
 Yet him for this my love no whit disdaineth;
 Suns of the world may stain when heaven's sun
  staineth.

114   Fifty-fourth Sonnet

O how much more doth beauty beauteous seem
By that sweet ornament which truth doth give!
The Rose looks fair, but fairer we it deem
For that sweet odour which doth in it live.
The Canker-blooms have full as deep a dye
As the perfuméd tincture of the Roses,
Hang on such thorns, and play as wantonly
When summer's breath their maskéd buds discloses;
But—for their virtue only is their show—

They live unwoo'd and unrespected fade,
Die to themselves. Sweet Roses do not so;
Of their sweet deaths are sweetest odours made.
    And so of you, beauteous and lovely youth,
    When that shall fade, my verse distils your truth.

115

FIFTY-FIFTH SONNET

Not marble, nor the gilded monuments
Of princes, shall outlive this powerful rhyme;
But you shall shine more bright in these contents
Than unswept stone, besmear'd with sluttish time.
When wasteful war shall statues overturn,
And broils root out the work of masonry,
Nor Mars his sword nor war's quick fire shall burn
The living record of your memory.
'Gainst death and all-oblivious enmity
Shall you pace forth; your praise shall still find room
Even in the eyes of all posterity
That wear this world out to the ending doom.
    So, till the judgment that yourself arise,
    You live in this, and dwell in lovers' eyes.

116

FIFTY-SEVENTH SONNET

Being your slave, what should I do but tend
Upon the hours and times of your desire?
I have no precious time at all to spend
Nor services to do, till you require:
Nor dare I chide the world-without-end hour
Whilst I, my sovereign, watch the clock for you,
Nor think the bitterness of absence sour
When you have bid your servant once adieu:
Nor dare I question with my jealous thought
Where you may be, or your affairs suppose,
But like a sad slave, stay and think of nought
Save, where you are, how happy you make those.
    So true a fool is love, that in your will,
    Though you do anything, he thinks no ill.

117

SIXTIETH SONNET

LIKE as the waves make towards the pebbled shore
So do our minutes hasten to their end;
Each changing place with that which goes before,
In sequent toil all forwards do contend.
Nativity once in the main of light,
Crawls to maturity, wherewith being crown'd,
Crooked eclipses 'gainst his glory fight,
And Time, that gave, doth now his gift confound.
Time doth transfix the flourish set on youth,
And delves the parallels in beauty's brow;
Feeds on the rarities of nature's truth,
And nothing stands but for his scythe to mow:
   And yet, to times in hope, my verse shall stand
   Praising thy worth, despite his cruel hand.

118

SIXTY-FOURTH SONNET

WHEN I have seen by Time's fell hand defaced
The rich-proud cost of outworn buried age;
When sometime lofty towers I see down-razed,
And brass eternal, slave to mortal rage;
When I have seen the hungry ocean gain
Advantage on the kingdom of the shore,
And the firm soil win of the watery main,
Increasing store with loss, and loss with store;
When I have seen such interchange of state,
Or state itself confounded to decay,
Ruin hath taught me thus to ruminate—
That Time will come and take my Love away:
   This thought is as a death, which cannot choose
   But weep to have that which it fears to lose.

119

SIXTY-FIFTH SONNET

SINCE brass, nor stone, nor earth, nor boundless sea,
But sad mortality o'ersways their power,
How with this rage shall beauty hold a plea,
Whose action is no stronger than a flower?
O how shall summer's honey breath hold out
Against the wreckful siege of battering days,

When rocks impregnable are not so stout
Nor gates of steel so strong, but time decays?
O fearful meditation! where, alack!
Shall Time's best jewel from Time's chest lie hid?
Or what strong hand can hold his swift foot back,
Or who his spoil of beauty can forbid?
   O none, unless this miracle have might,
   That in black ink my love may still shine bright.

120

Sixty-sixth Sonnet

Tired with all these, for restful death I cry,—
As, to behold desert a beggar born,
And needy nothing trimm'd in jollity,
And purest faith unhappily forsworn,
And gilded honour shamefully misplaced,
And maiden virtue rudely strumpeted,
And right perfection wrongfully disgraced,
And strength by limping sway disabled,
And art made tongue-tied by authority,
And folly, doctor-like, controlling skill,
And simple truth miscall'd simplicity,
And captive Good attending captain Ill:
   Tired with all these, from these would I be gone,
   Save that, to die, I leave my Love alone.

121

Seventy-first Sonnet

No longer mourn for me when I am dead
Than you shall hear the surly sullen bell
Give warning to the world, that I am fled
From this vile world, with vilest worms to dwell;
Nay, if you read this line, remember not
The hand that writ it; for I love you so,
That I in your sweet thoughts would be forgot
If thinking on me then should make you woe.
O, if, I say, you look upon this verse
When I perhaps compounded am with clay,
Do not so much as my poor name rehearse,
But let your love even with my life decay,
   Lest the wise world should look into your moan,
   And mock you with me after I am gone.

122

SEVENTY-THIRD SONNET

THAT time of year thou may'st in me behold
When yellow leaves, or none, or few, do hang
Upon those boughs which shake against the cold,
Bare ruin'd choirs, where late the sweet birds sang:
In me thou see'st the twilight of such day
As after sunset fadeth in the west,
Which by and by black night doth take away,
Death's second self, that seals up all in rest:
In me thou seest the glowing of such fire,
That on the ashes of his youth doth lie
As the deathbed whereon it must expire,
Consumed with that which it was nourish'd by:
　　This thou perceiv'st, which makes thy love more
　　　　strong,
　　To love that well which thou must leave ere long.

123

EIGHTY-SEVENTH SONNET

FAREWELL! thou art too dear for my possessing,
And like enough thou know'st thy estimate:
The charter of thy worth gives thee releasing;
My bonds in thee are all determinate.
For how do I hold thee but by thy granting?
And for that riches where is my deserving?
The cause of this fair gift in me is wanting,
And so my patent back again is swerving.
Thyself thou gav'st, thy own worth then not knowing,
Or me, to whom thou gav'st it, else mistaking;
So thy great gift, upon misprision growing,
Comes home again, on better judgment making.
　　Thus have I had thee as a dream doth flatter;
　　In sleep, a king; but waking, no such matter.

124

NINETIETH SONNET

THEN hate me when thou wilt; if ever, now;
Now, while the world is bent my deeds to cross,
Join with the spite of fortune, make me bow,
And do not drop in for an after-loss:

Ah! do not, when my heart hath 'scaped this sorrow,
Come in the rearward of a conquer'd woe;
Give not a windy night a rainy morrow,
To linger out a purposed overthrow.
If thou wilt leave me, do not leave me last,
When other petty griefs have done their spite,
But in the onset come: so shall I taste
At first the very worst of fortune's might;
   And other strains of woe, which now seem woe,
   Compared with loss of thee will not seem so.

125
NINETY-FOURTH SONNET

THEY that have power to hurt, and will do none,
That do not do the thing they most do show,
Who, moving others, are themselves as stone,
Unmovèd, cold, and to temptation slow,—
They rightly do inherit Heaven's graces,
And husband nature's riches from expense;
They are the lords and owners of their faces,
Others, but stewards of their excellence.
The summer's flower is to the summer sweet,
Though to itself it only live and die;
But if that flower with base infection meet,
The basest weed outbraves his dignity:
   For sweetest things turn sourest by their deeds;
   Lilies that fester smell far worse than weeds.

126
NINETY-SEVENTH SONNET

How like a winter hath my absence been
From thee, the pleasure of the fleeting year!
What freezings have I felt, what dark days seen,
What old December's bareness everywhere!
And yet this time removed was summer's time;
The teeming autumn, big with rich increase,
Bearing the wanton burden of the prime
Like widow'd wombs after their lords' decease:
Yet this abundant issue seem'd to me
But hope of orphans, and unfather'd fruit;
For summer and his pleasures wait on thee,
And, thou away, the very birds are mute;

Or if they sing, 'tis with so dull a cheer,
That leaves look pale, dreading the winter's near.

127   NINETY-EIGHTH SONNET

FROM you have I been absent in the spring,
When proud-pied April, dress'd in all his trim,
Hath put a spirit of youth in everything,
That heavy Saturn laugh'd and leap'd with him.
Yet nor the lays of birds, nor the sweet smell
Of different flowers in odour and in hue,
Could make me any summer's story tell,
Or from their proud lap pluck them where they grew;
Nor did I wonder at the Lily's white,
Nor praise the deep vermilion in the Rose;
They were but sweet, but figures of delight,
Drawn after you, you pattern of all those.
    Yet seem'd it Winter still, and you, away,
    As with your shadow I with these did play.

128   ONE HUNDRED AND FOURTH SONNET

To me, fair friend, you never can be old,
For as you were when first your eye I eyed
Such seems your beauty still. Three winters cold
Have from the forests shook three summers' pride;
Three beauteous springs to yellow autumn turn'd
In process of the seasons have I seen,
Three April perfumes in three hot Junes burn'd,
Since first I saw you fresh, which yet are green.
Ah! yet doth beauty, like a dial-hand,
Steal from his figure, and no pace perceived;
So your sweet hue, which methinks still doth stand,
Hath motion, and mine eye may be deceived:
    For fear of which, hear this, thou age unbred,—
    Ere you were born, was beauty's summer dead.

129   ONE HUNDRED AND SIXTH SONNET

WHEN in the chronicle of wasted time
I see descriptions of the fairest wights,
And beauty making beautiful old rhyme

In praise of ladies dead, and lovely knights;
Then in the blazon of sweet beauty's best
Of hand, of foot, of lip, of eye, of brow,
I see their antique pen would have exprest
Ev'n such a beauty as you master now.
So all their praises are but prophecies
Of this our time, all, you prefiguring;
And for they look'd but with divining eyes,
They had not skill enough your worth to sing:
   For we, which now behold these present days,
   Have eyes to wonder, but lack tongues to praise.

130   ONE HUNDRED AND SEVENTH SONNET

NOT mine own fears, nor the prophetic soul
Of the wide world, dreaming on things to come,
Can yet the lease of my true love control,
Suppos'd as forfeit to a confin'd doom.
The mortal moon hath her eclipse endur'd
And the sad augurs mock their own presage;
Incertainties now crown themselves assur'd
And peace proclaims olives of endless age.
Now with the drops of this most balmy time
My love looks fresh, and Death to me subscribes,
Since, spite of him, I'll live in this poor rhyme,
While he insults o'er dull and speechless tribes:
   And thou in this shalt find thy monument,
   When tyrants' crests and tombs of brass are spent.

131   ONE HUNDRED AND NINTH SONNET

O, NEVER say that I was false of heart,
Though absence seem'd my flame to qualify:
As easy might I from myself depart
As from my soul, which in thy breast doth lie;
That is my home of love; if I have ranged,
Like him that travels, I return again,
Just to the time, not with the time exchanged,
So that myself bring water for my stain.
Never believe, though in my nature reign'd
All frailties that besiege all kinds of blood,

That it could so preposterously be stain'd,
To leave for nothing all thy sum of good:
  For nothing this wide universe I call,
  Save thou, my rose; in it thou art my all.

132   ONE HUNDRED AND TENTH SONNET

ALAS, 'tis true I have gone here and there
And made myself a motley to the view,
Gor'd mine own thoughts, sold cheap what is most dear,
Made old offences of affections new;
Most true it is that I have look'd on truth
Askance and strangely: but, by all above,
These blenches gave my heart another youth,
And worse essays prov'd thee my best of love.
Now all is done, have what shall have no end:
Mine appetite I never more will grind
On newer proof, to try an older friend,
A god in love, to whom I am confin'd.
  Then give me welcome, next my heaven the best,
  Even to thy pure and most most loving breast.

133   ONE HUNDRED AND ELEVENTH SONNET

O, FOR my sake do you with Fortune chide,
The guilty goddess of my harmful deeds,
That did not better for my life provide
Than public means, which public manners breeds.
Thence comes it that my name receives a brand,
And almost thence my nature is subdu'd
To what it works in, like the dyer's hand.
Pity me then and wish I were renew'd;
Whilst, like a willing patient, I will drink
Potions of eisel 'gainst my strong infection;
No bitterness that I will bitter think,
Nor double penance, to correct correction.
  Pity me then, dear friend, and I assure ye
  Even that your pity is enough to cure me.

134 ### One Hundred and Sixteenth Sonnet

Let me not to the marriage of true minds
Admit impediments. Love is not love
Which alters when it alteration finds,
Or bends with the remover to remove:
O no! it is an ever-fixèd mark
That looks on tempests, and is never shaken;
It is the star to every wandering bark,
Whose worth's unknown, although his height be taken.
Love's not Time's fool, though rosy lips and cheeks
Within his bending sickle's compass come;
Love alters not with his brief hours and weeks,
But bears it out ev'n to the edge of doom:
    If this be error, and upon me proved,
    I never writ, nor no man ever loved.

135 ### One Hundred and Twenty-ninth Sonnet

Th' expense of Spirit in a waste of shame
Is lust in action; and till action, lust
Is perjured, murderous, bloody, full of blame,
Savage, extreme, rude, cruel, not to trust;
Enjoy'd no sooner but despisèd straight;
Past reason hunted; and, no sooner had,
Past reason hated, as a swallow'd bait
On purpose laid to make the taker mad:
Mad in pursuit, and in possession so;
Had, having, and in quest to have, extreme;
A bliss in proof, and proved, a very woe;
Before, a joy proposed; behind, a dream.
    All this the world well knows; yet none knows well
    To shun the heaven that leads men to this hell.

136 ### One Hundred and Forty-sixth Sonnet

Poor Soul, the centre of my sinful earth,
Fool'd by these rebel powers that thee array,
Why dost thou pine within, and suffer dearth,
Painting thy outward walls so costly gay?
Why so large cost, having so short a lease,

Dost thou upon thy fading mansion spend?
Shall worms, inheritors of this excess,
Eat up thy charge? is this thy body's end?
Then, Soul, live thou upon thy servant's loss,
And let that pine to aggravate thy store;
Buy terms divine in selling hours of dross;
Within be fed, without be rich no more:
    So shalt thou feed on death, that feeds on men,
    And, death once dead, there's no more dying then.

137   ### One Hundred and Forty-eighth Sonnet

O me! what eyes hath love put in my head,
Which have no correspondence with true sight:
Or if they have, where is my judgment fled
That censures falsely what they see aright?
If that be fair whereon my false eyes dote,
What means the world to say it is not so?
If it be not, then love doth well denote
Love's eye is not so true as all men's: No,
How can it? O how can love's eye be true,
That is so vex'd with watching and with tears?
No marvel then though I mistake my view:
The sun itself sees not till heaven clears.
    O cunning Love! with tears thou keep'st me blind,
    Lest eyes well-seeing thy foul faults should find!

ROBERT GREENE
[*1560(?)–1592*]

138   ### Content

Sweet are the thoughts that savour of content,
    The quiet mind is richer than a crown,
Sweet are the nights in careless slumber spent,
    The poor estate scorns Fortune's angry frown:
Such sweet content, such minds, such sleep, such bliss,
Beggars enjoy, when princes oft do miss.

The homely house that harbours quiet rest,
    The cottage that affords no pride nor care,
The mean that 'grees with country music best,

The sweet consort of mirth and modest fare,
Obscurèd life sets down a type of bliss:
A mind content both crown and kingdom is.

RICHARD BARNFIELD

[1574–1627]

139   THE NIGHTINGALE

As it fell upon a day
In the merry month of May,
Sitting in a pleasant shade
Which a grove of myrtles made,
Beasts did leap and birds did sing,
Trees did grow and plants did spring;
Every thing did banish moan
Save the Nightingale alone.
She, poor bird, as all forlorn,
Lean'd her breast up-till a thorn,
And there sung the dolefull'st ditty
That to hear it was great pity.
Fie, fie, fie, now would she cry;
Tereu, tereu, by and by:
That to hear her so complain
Scarce I could from tears refrain;
For her griefs so lively shown
Made me think upon mine own.
—Ah, thought I, thou mourn'st in vain,
None takes pity on thy pain:
Senseless trees, they cannot hear thee,
Ruthless beasts, they will not cheer thee;
King Pandion, he is dead,
All thy friends are lapp'd in lead:
All thy fellow birds do sing
Careless of thy sorrowing:
Even so, poor bird, like thee
None alive will pity me.

THOMAS CAMPION
[1567(?)–1620]

140   CHERRY-RIPE

THERE is a garden in her face
  Where roses and white lilies blow;
A heavenly paradise is that place,
  Wherein all pleasant fruits do flow:
    There cherries grow which none may buy
    Till 'Cherry-ripe' themselves do cry.

Those cherries fairly do enclose
  Of orient pearl a double row,
Which when her lovely laughter shows,
  They look like rose-buds fill'd with snow;
    Yet them nor peer nor prince can buy
    Till 'Cherry-ripe' themselves do cry.

Her eyes like angels watch them still;
  Her brows like bended bows do stand,
Threat'ning with piercing frowns to kill
  All that attempt with eye or hand
    Those sacred cherries to come nigh,
    Till 'Cherry-ripe' themselves do cry.

141   FOLLOW YOUR SAINT

FOLLOW your saint, follow with accents sweet!
Haste you, sad notes, fall at her flying feet!
There, wrapt in cloud of sorrow, pity move,
And tell the ravisher of my soul I perish for her love:
But if she scorns my never-ceasing pain,
Then burst with sighing in her sight, and ne'er return again!

All that I sung still to her praise did tend;
Still she was first, still she my songs did end;
Yet she my love and music both doth fly,
The music that her echo is and beauty's sympathy:
Then let my notes pursue her scornful flight!
It shall suffice that they were breathed and died for her
    delight.

142   WHEN TO HER LUTE CORINNA SINGS

WHEN to her lute Corinna sings,
Her voice revives the leaden strings,
And doth in highest notes appear,
As any challenged echo clear;
But when she doth of mourning speak,
E'en with her sighs, the strings do break,

And as her lute doth live or die,
Led by her passion, so must I:
For when of pleasure she doth sing,
My thoughts enjoy a sudden spring,
But if she doth of sorrow speak,
E'en from my heart the strings do break.

143   FOLLOW THY FAIR SUN

FOLLOW thy fair sun, unhappy shadow,
    Though thou be black as night,
    And she made all of light;
Yet follow thy fair sun, unhappy shadow!

Follow her, whose light thy light depriveth!
    Though here thou livest disgraced,
    And she in heaven is placed;
Yet follow her whose light the world reviveth!

Follow those pure beams, whose beauty burneth!
    That so have scorchèd thee;
    As thou still black must be,
Till her kind beams thy black to brightness turneth!

Follow her, while yet her glory shineth!
    There comes a luckless night
    That will dim all her light;
And this the black unhappy shade divineth.

Follow still, since so thy Fates ordainèd!
    The sun must have his shade,
    Till both at once do fade;
The sun still proved, the shadow still disdainèd!

144 ## Turn All thy Thoughts to Eyes

Turn all thy thoughts to eyes,
Turn all thy hairs to ears,
Change all thy friends to spies
And all thy joys to fears:
    True love will yet be free
    In spite of jealousy.

Turn darkness into day,
Conjectures into truth,
Believe what th' envious say,
Let age interpret youth:
    True love will yet be free
    In spite of jealousy.

Wrest every word and look,
Rack every hidden thought,
Or fish with golden hook;
True love cannot be caught:
    For that will still be free
    In spite of jealousy.

145 ## Integer Vitae

The man of life upright,
    Whose guiltless heart is free
From all dishonest deeds,
    Or thought of vanity;

The man whose silent days
    In harmless joys are spent,
Whom hopes cannot delude,
    Nor sorrow discontent;

That man needs neither towers
    Nor armour for defence,
Nor secret vaults to fly
    From thunder's violence:

He only can behold
    With unaffrighted eyes

The horrors of the deep
And terrors of the skies.

Thus, scorning all the cares
That fate or fortune brings,
He makes the heaven his book,
His wisdom heavenly things;

Good thoughts his only friends,
His wealth a well-spent age,
The earth his sober inn
And quiet pilgrimage.

ROBERT DEVEREUX, EARL OF ESSEX
[1566–1601]

146   A Passion of my Lord of Essex

Happy were he could finish forth his fate
  In some unhaunted desert, where, obscure
From all society, from love and hate
  Of worldly folk; then might he sleep secure;
Then wake again, and ever give God praise,
  Content with hip, with haws, and bramble-berry;
In contemplation passing all his days,
  And change of holy thoughts to make him merry;
Who, when he dies, his tomb might be a bush,
Where harmless Robin dwells with gentle thrush.
  —Happy were he!

SIR HENRY WOTTON
[1568–1639]

147   Elizabeth of Bohemia

You meaner beauties of the night,
  That poorly satisfy our eyes
More by your number than your light,
  You common people of the skies,
What are you, when the Moon shall rise?

Ye violets that first appear,
  By your pure purple mantles known
Like the proud virgins of the year,
  As if the spring were all your own,—
What are you, when the Rose is blown?

Ye curious chanters of the wood
  That warble forth dame Nature's lays,
Thinking your passions understood
  By your weak accents; what's your praise
When Philomel her voice doth raise?

So when my Mistress shall be seen
  In sweetness of her looks and mind,
By virtue first, then choice, a Queen,
  Tell me, if she were not design'd
Th' eclipse and glory of her kind?

148   CHARACTER OF A HAPPY LIFE

How happy is he born and taught
That serveth not another's will;
Whose armour is his honest thought
And simple truth his utmost skill!

Whose passions not his masters are,
Whose soul is still prepared for death,
Not tied unto the world with care
Of public fame, or private breath;

Who envies none that chance doth raise
Or vice; Who never understood
How deepest wounds are given by praise;
Nor rules of state, but rules of good:

Who hath his life from rumours freed,
Whose conscience is his strong retreat;
Whose state can neither flatterers feed
Nor ruin make oppressors great;

Who God doth late and early pray
More of his grace than gifts to lend;
And entertains the harmless day
With a well-chosen book or friend:

—This man is freed from servile bands
Of hope to rise, or fear to fall;
Lord of himself, though not of lands;
And having nothing, yet hath all.

EDWARD DE VERE, EARL OF OXFORD
[1550–1604]

149

A RENUNCIATION

IF women could be fair, and yet not fond,
Or that their love were firm, not fickle still,
I would not marvel that they make men bond
By service long to purchase their good will;
But when I see how frail those creatures are,
I muse that men forget themselves so far.

To mark the choice they make, and how they change,
How oft from Phœbus they do flee to Pan;
Unsettled still, like haggards wild they range,
These gentle birds that fly from man to man;
Who would not scorn and shake them from the fist,
And let them fly, fair fools, which way they list?

Yet for disport we fawn and flatter both,
To pass the time when nothing else can please,
And train them to our lure with subtle oath,
Till, weary of their wiles, ourselves we ease;
And then we say when we their fancy try,
To play with fools, O what a fool was I!

BEN JONSON
[*1573–1637*]

150   Simplex Munditiis

Still to be neat, still to be drest,
As you were going to a feast;
Still to be powdr'd, still perfumed:
Lady, it is to be presumed,
Though art's hid causes are not found,
All is not sweet, all is not sound.

Give me a look, give me a face
That makes simplicity a grace;
Robes loosely flowing, hair as free:
Such sweet neglect more taketh me
Than all th' adulteries of art;
They strike mine eyes, but not my heart.

151   The Triumph

See the Chariot at hand here of Love,
　　Wherein my Lady rideth!
Each that draws is a swan or a dove,
　　And well the car Love guideth.
As she goes, all hearts do duty
　　Unto her beauty;
And enamour'd do wish, so they might
　　But enjoy such a sight,
That they still were to run by her side,
Through swords, through seas, whither she would ride.

Do but look on her eyes, they do light
　　All that Love's world compriseth!
Do but look on her hair, it is bright
　　As Love's star when it riseth!
Do but mark, her forehead's smoother
　　Than words that soothe her;
And from her arch'd brows such a grace
　　Sheds itself through the face,
As alone there triumphs to the life
All the gain, all the good, of the elements' strife.

Have you seen but a bright lily grow
  Before rude hands have touch'd it?
Have you mark'd but the fall of the snow
  Before the soil hath smutch'd it?
Have you felt the wool of beaver,
      Or swan's down ever?
Or have smelt o' the bud o' the brier,
      Or the nard in the fire?
Or have tasted the bag of the bee?
O so white, O so soft, O so sweet is she!

152   THE NOBLE NATURE

IT is not growing like a tree
In bulk, doth make Man better be;
Or standing long an oak, three hundred year,
To fall a log at last, dry, bald, and sere:
      A lily of a day
      Is fairer far in May,
  Although it fall and die that night—
  It was the plant and flower of Light
In small proportions we just beauties see;
And in short measures life may perfect be.

153   TO CELIA

DRINK to me only with thine eyes,
  And I will pledge with mine;
Or leave a kiss but in the cup
  And I'll not look for wine.
The thirst that from the soul doth rise
  Doth ask a drink divine;
But might I of Jove's nectar sup,
  I would not change for thine.

I sent thee late a rosy wreath,
  Not so much honouring thee
As giving it a hope that there
  It could not wither'd be;
But thou thereon didst only breathe
  And sent'st it back to me;

Since when it grows, and smells, I swear,
Not of itself but thee!

154 A Farewell to the World

False world, good night! since thou hast brought
That hour upon my morn of age;
Henceforth I quit thee from my thought,
My part is ended on thy stage.

Yes, threaten, do. Alas! I fear
As little as I hope from thee:
I know thou canst not show nor bear
More hatred than thou hast to me.

My tender, first, and simple years
Thou didst abuse and then betray;
Since stir'd'st up jealousies and fears,
When all the causes were away.

Then in a soil hast planted me
Where breathe the basest of thy fools;
Where envious arts professèd be,
And pride and ignorance the schools;

Where nothing is examined, weigh'd,
But as 'tis rumour'd, so believed;
Where every freedom is betray'd,
And every goodness tax'd or grieved.

But what we're born for, we must bear:
Our frail condition it is such
That what to all may happen here,
If 't chance to me, I must not grutch.

Else I my state should much mistake
To harbour a divided thought
From all my kind—that, for my sake,
There should a miracle be wrought.

No, I do know that I was born
　　To age, misfortune, sickness, grief:
But I will bear these with that scorn
　　As shall not need thy false relief.

Nor for my peace will I go far,
　　As wanderers do, that still do roam;
But make my strengths, such as they are,
　　Here in my bosom, and at home.

155　　A NYMPH'S PASSION

I LOVE, and he loves me again,
　　Yet dare I not tell who;
For if the nymphs should know my swain,
　　I fear they'd love him too;
　　　　Yet if he be not known,
　　　　The pleasure is as good as none,
For that's a narrow joy is but our own.

I'll tell, that if they be not glad,
　　They may not envy me;
But then if I grow jealous mad
　　And of them pitied be,
　　　　It were a plague 'bove scorn;
　　　　And yet it cannot be forborne
Unless my heart would, as my thought, be torn.

He is, if they can find him, fair
　　And fresh, and fragrant too,
As summer's sky or purgèd air,
　　And looks as lilies do
　　　　That are this morning blown:
　　　　Yet, yet I doubt he is not known,
And fear much more that more of him be shown.

But he hath eyes so round and bright,
　　As make away my doubt,
Where Love may all his torches light,
　　Though Hate had put them out;
　　　　But then t' increase my fears
　　　　What nymph soe'er his voice but hears
Will be my rival, though she have but ears.

I'll tell no more, and yet I love,
     And he loves me; yet no
One unbecoming thought doth move
     From either heart I know:
          But so exempt from blame
          As it would be to each a fame,
If love or fear would let me tell his name.

EPODE

Not to know vice at all, and keep true state,
     Is virtue, and not fate:
Next to that virtue is to know vice well,
     And her black spite expel,
Which to effect (since no breast is so sure,
     Or safe, but she'll procure
Some way of entrance) we must plant a guard
     Of thoughts to watch and ward
At th' eye and ear, the ports unto the mind,
     That no strange or unkind
Object arrive there, but the heart, our spy,
     Give knowledge instantly
To wakeful reason, our affections' king:
     Who, in th' examining,
Will quickly taste the treason, and commit
     Close, the close cause of it.
'Tis the securest policy we have,
     To make our sense our slave.
But this true course is not embraced by many:
     By many? scarce by any.
For either our affections do rebel,
     Or else the sentinel,
That should ring larum to the heart, doth sleep:
     Or some great thought doth keep
Back the intelligence, and falsely swears
     They're base and idle fears
Whereof the loyal conscience so complains.
     Thus, by these subtle trains,
Do several passions invade the mind,
     And strike our reason blind:

Of which usurping rank, some have thought love.
　　The first, as prone to move
Most frequent tumults, horrors, and unrests,
　　In our inflamèd breasts:
But this doth from the cloud of error grow,
　　Which thus we over-blow.
The thing they here call Love is blind Desire,
　　Armed with bow, shafts, and fire;
Inconstant, like the sea, of whence 't is born,
　　Rough, swelling, like a storm;
With whom who sails, rides on the surge of fear,
　　And boils as if he were
In a continual tempest. Now, true Love
　　No such effects doth prove;
That is an essence far more gentle, fine,
　　Pure, perfect, nay, divine;
It is a golden chain let down from heaven,
　　Whose links are bright and even,
That falls like sleep on lovers, and combines
　　The soft and sweetest minds
In equal knots: this bears no brands nor darts,
　　To murther different hearts,
But in a calm and godlike unity
　　Preserves community.
O, who is he that in this peace enjoys
　　Th' elixir of all joys?
A form more fresh than are the Eden bowers,
　　And lasting as her flowers:
Richer than Time, and as Time's virtue rare:
　　Sober, as saddest care;
A fixèd thought, an eye untaught to glance:
　　Who, blest with such high chance,
Would, at suggestion of a steep desire,
　　Cast himself from the spire
Of all his happiness? But, soft, I hear
　　Some vicious fool draw near,
That cries we dream, and swears there's no such thing
　　As this chaste love we sing.
Peace, Luxury, thou art like one of those
　　Who, being at sea, suppose,

Because they move, the continent doth so.
  No, Vice, we let thee know,
Though thy wild thoughts with sparrows' wings do fly,
  Turtles can chastely die.
And yet (in this t' express ourselves more clear)
  We do not number here
Such spirits as are only continent
  Because lust's means are spent;
Or those who doubt the common mouth of fame,
  And for their place and name
Cannot so safely sin. Their chastity
  Is mere necessity.
Nor mean we those whom vows and conscience
  Have filled with abstinence:
Though we acknowledge, who can so abstain
  Makes a most blessèd gain;
He that for love of goodness hateth ill
  Is more crown-worthy still
Than he, which for sin's penalty forbears:
  His heart sins, though he fears.
But we propose a person like our Dove,
  Grac'd with a Phœnix' love;
A beauty of that clear and sparkling light,
  Would make a day of night,
And turn the blackest sorrows to bright joys:
  Whose od'rous breath destroys
All taste of bitterness, and makes the air
  As sweet as she is fair.
A body so harmoniously composed,
  As if nature disclosed
All her best symmetry in that one feature!
  O, so divine a creature,
Who could be false to? chiefly when he knows
  How only she bestows
The wealthy treasure of her love on him;
  Making his fortunes swim
In the full flood of her admired perfection?
  What savage, brute affection
Would not be fearful to offend a dame
  Of this excelling frame?

Much more a noble and right generous mind
    To virtuous moods inclined,
That knows the weight of guilt: he will refrain
    From thoughts of such a strain;
And to his sense object this sentence ever,
'Man may securely sin, but safely never.'

157 EPITAPH ON ELIZABETH L. H.

WOULDS'T thou hear what man can say
In a little? Reader, stay.
Underneath this stone doth lie
As much beauty as could die;
Which in life did harbour give
To more virtue than doth live.
If at all she had a fault
Leave it buried in this vault.
One name was *Elizabeth*,
The other, let it sleep with death,
Fitter, where it died, to tell,
Than that it lived at all. Farewell.

158 ON LUCY, COUNTESS OF BEDFORD

THIS morning timely wrapt with holy fire,
I thought to form unto my zealous Muse,
What kind of creature I could most desire
To know, serve, and love, as Poets use.
I meant to make her fair, and free, and wise,
Of greatest blood, and yet more good than great;
I meant the day-star should not brighter rise,
Nor lend like influence from his lucent seat;
I meant she should be courteous, facile, sweet,
Hating that solemn vice of greatness, pride;
I meant each softest virtue there should meet,
Fit in that softer bosom to reside.
Only a learnèd, and a manly soul
I purposed her: that should with even powers,
The rock, the spindle, and the shears control
Of Destiny, and spin her own free hours.
Such when I meant to feign, and wished to see,
My Muse bade BEDFORD write, and that was she!

159

An Ode to Himself

WHERE dost thou careless lie
   Buried in ease and sloth?
Knowledge that sleeps, doth die
And this security,
   It is the common moth
That eats on wits and arts, and that destroys them both.

Are all the Aonian springs
   Dried up? lies Thespia waste?
Doth Clarius' harp want strings,
That not a nymph now sings;
   Or droop they as disgraced,
To see their seats and bowers by chattering pies defaced?

If hence thy silence be,
   As 'tis too just a cause,
Let this thought quicken thee:
Minds that are great and free
   Should not on fortune pause;
'Tis crown enough to virtue still, her own applause.

What though the greedy fry
   Be taken with false baits
Of worded balladry,
And think it poesy?
   They die with their conceits,
And only piteous scorn upon their folly waits.

Then take in hand thy lyre;
   Strike in thy proper strain;
With Japhet's line aspire
Sol's chariot, for new fire
   To give the world again:
Who aided him, will thee, the issue of Jove's brain.

And, since our dainty age
   Cannot endure reproof,
Make not thyself a page

To that strumpet the stage;
  But sing high and aloof,
Safe from the wolf's black jaw, and the dull ass's hoof.

160
Hymn to Diana

Queen and Huntress, chaste and fair,
  Now the sun is laid to sleep,
Seated in thy silver chair
  State in wonted manner keep;
    Hesperus entreats thy light,
    Goddess excellently bright.

Earth, let not thy envious shade
  Dare itself to interpose;
Cynthia's shining orb was made
  Heaven to clear when day did close:
    Bless us then with wishèd sight,
    Goddess excellently bright.

Lay thy bow of pearl apart
  And thy crystal-shining quiver;
Give unto the flying hart
  Space to breathe, how short soever:
    Thou that mak'st a day of night,
    Goddess excellently bright!

161
On Salathiel Pavy
A CHILD OF QUEEN ELIZABETH'S CHAPEL

Weep with me, all you that read
  This little story;
And know, for whom a tear you shed
  Death's self is sorry.
'Twas a child that so did thrive
  In grace and feature,
As Heaven and Nature seem'd to strive
  Which own'd the creature.
Years he number'd scarce thirteen
  When Fates turn'd cruel,
Yet three fill'd zodiacs had he been
  The stage's jewel;

And did act (what now we moan)
   Old men so duly,
As sooth the Parcæ thought him one,
   He play'd so truly.
So, by error, to his fate
   They all consented;
But, viewing him since, alas, too late!
   They have repented;
And have sought, to give new birth,
   In baths to steep him;
But, being so much too good for earth,
   Heaven vows to keep him.

162   HIS SUPPOSED MISTRESS

IF I freely can discover
What would please me in my lover,
   I would have her fair and witty,
   Savouring more of court than city;
   A little proud, but full of pity;
   Light and humourous in her toying;
   Oft building hopes, and soon destroying;
   Long, but sweet in the enjoying,
Neither too easy, nor too hard:
All extremes I would have barred.

She should be allowed her passions,
So they were but used as fashions;
   Sometimes froward, and then frowning,
   Sometimes sickish, and then swowning,
   Every fit with change still crowning.
   Purely jealous I would have her;
   Then only constant when I crave her,
   'Tis a virtue should not save her.
Thus, nor her delicates would cloy me,
Neither her peevishness annoy me.

163
TO THE MEMORY OF MY BELOVED
THE AUTHOR
MR. WILLIAM SHAKESPEARE
AND WHAT HE HATH LEFT US

[Prefixed to the First Folio Edition of Shakespeare's Plays.]

To draw no envy, Shakespeare, on thy name,
Am I thus ample to thy book and fame;
While I confess thy writings to be such
As neither man nor Muse can praise too much.
'Tis true, and all men's suffrage. But these ways
Were not the paths I meant unto thy praise;
For seeliest Ignorance on these may light,
Which, when it sounds at best, but echoes right;
Or blind Affection, which doth ne'er advance
The truth, but gropes and urgeth all by chance;
Or crafty Malice might pretend this praise,
And think to ruin where it seem'd to raise.
These are as some infamous bawd or whore
Should praise a matron. What could hurt her more?
But thou art proof against them, and, indeed,
Above the ill-fortune of them, or the need.
I, therefore, will begin. Soul of the age!
The applause, delight, the wonder of our stage,
My Shakespeare, rise! I will not lodge thee by
Chaucer, or Spenser, or bid Beaumont lie
A little further, to make thee a room:
Thou art a monument without a tomb,
And art alive still, while thy book doth live,
And we have wits to read, and praise to give.
That I not mix thee so, my brain excuses;
I mean, with great but disproportion'd Muses.
For, if I thought my judgment were of years,
I should commit thee, surely, with thy peers.
And tell how far thou didst our Lyly outshine,
Or sporting Kyd, or Marlowe's mighty line.
And though thou hadst small Latin and less Greek,
From thence, to honour thee, I would not seek
For names; but call forth thund'ring Aeschylus,

Euripides, and Sophocles to us,
Paccuvius, Accius, him of Cordova dead
To life again, to hear thy buskin tread
And shake a stage; or when thy socks were on,
Leave thee alone, for the comparison
Of all that insolent Greece or haughty Rome
Sent forth; or since did from their ashes come.
Triumph, my Britain! Thou hast one to show
To whom all scenes of Europe homage owe.
He was not of an age, but for all time!
And all the Muses still were in their prime,
When, like Apollo, he came forth to warm
Our ears, or, like a Mercury, to charm.
Nature herself was proud of his designs,
And joy'd to wear the dressing of his lines,
Which were so richly spun, and woven so fit
As, since, she will vouchsafe no other wit.
The merry Greek, tart Aristophanes,
Neat Terence, witty Plautus, now not please;
But antiquated and deserted lie,
As they were not of Nature's family.
Yet must I not give Nature all! Thy art,
My gentle Shakespeare, must enjoy a part.
For though the Poet's matter Nature be
His art doth give the fashion. And that he
Who casts to write a living line, must sweat
(Such as thine are), and strike the second heat
Upon the Muses' anvil, turn the same
(And himself with it), that he thinks to frame;
Or for the laurel he may gain a scorn!
For a good Poet's made as well as born;
And such wert thou! Look how the father's face
Lives in his issue; even so, the race
Of Shakespeare's mind and manners brightly shines
In his well-turnèd and true-filèd lines;
In each of which he seems to shake a lance
As brandish'd at the eyes of Ignorance.
Sweet Swan of Avon! what a sight it were
To see thee in our water yet appear,
And make those flights upon the banks of Thames

That so did take Eliza, and our James!
But stay, I see thee in the hemisphere
Advanc'd, and made a constellation there!
Shine forth, thou star of poets, and with rage
Or influence, chide, or cheer the drooping stage;
Which since thy flight from hence hath mourn'd like night,
And despairs day, but for thy volume's light.

JOHN DONNE

[1573-1631]

164

THE FUNERAL

WHOEVER comes to shroud me, do not harm
          Nor question much
That subtle wreath of hair about mine arm;
The mystery, the sign you must not touch,
          For 'tis my outward soul,
Viceroy to that which, unto heav'n being gone,
          Will leave this to control
And keep these limbs, her provinces, from dissolution.

For if the sinewy thread my brain lets fall
          Through every part
Can tie those parts, and make me one of all;
Those hairs, which upward grew, and strength and art
          Have from a better brain,
Can better do 't: except she meant that I
          By this should know my pain,
As prisoners then are manacled, when they're condemn'd to die.

Whate'er she meant by't, bury it with me,
          For since I am
Love's martyr, it might breed idolatry
If into other hands these reliques came.
          As 'twas humility
T' afford to it all that a soul can do,
          So 'tis some bravery
That, since you would have none of me, I bury some of you.

165

A Hymn to God the Father

Wilt Thou forgive that sin where I begun,
　　Which was my sin, though it were done before?
Wilt Thou forgive that sin through which I run,
　　And do run still, though still I do deplore?
When Thou hast done, Thou hast not done;
　　　　For I have more.

Wilt Thou forgive that sin which I have won
　　Others to sin, and made my sins their door?
Wilt Thou forgive that sin which I did shun
　　A year or two, but wallow'd in a score?
When Thou hast done, Thou hast not done;
　　　　For I have more.

I have a sin of fear, that when I've spun
　　My last thread, I shall perish on the shore;
But swear by Thyself that at my death Thy Son
　　Shall shine as He shines now and heretofore:
And having done that, Thou hast done;
　　　　I fear no more.

166

Valediction, Forbidding Mourning

As virtuous men pass mildly away,
　　And whisper to their souls to go;
While some of their sad friends do say,
　　Now his breath goes, and some say, No;

So let us melt, and make no noise,
　　No tear-floods, nor sigh-tempests move;
'Twere profanation of our joys
　　To tell the laity our love.

Moving of th' earth brings harms and fears
　　Men reckon what it did and meant;
But trepidations of the spheres,
　　Though greater far, are innocent.

Dull sublunary lovers' love,
   Whose soul is sense, cannot admit
Absence; for that it doth remove
   Those things which elemented it.

But we, by a love so far refined,
   That ourselves know not what it is,
Inter-assurèd of the mind,
   Careless, eyes, lips and hands to miss,

—Our two souls therefore, which are one,
   Though I must go, endure not yet
A breach, but an expansion,
   Like gold to airy thinness beat.

If they be two, they are two so
   As stiff twin compasses are two;
Thy soul, the fixt foot, makes no show
   To move, but doth if th' other do.

And though it in the centre sit,
   Yet when the other far doth roam,
It leans and hearkens after it,
   And grows erect as that comes home.

Such wilt thou be to me, who must,
   Like th' other foot, obliquely run;
Thy firmness makes my circles just,
   And makes me end where I begun.

167   DEATH

DEATH, be not proud, though some have callèd thee
Mighty and dreadful, for thou art not so:
For those whom thou think'st thou dost overthrow
Die not, poor Death; nor yet canst thou kill me.
From Rest and Sleep, which but thy picture be,
Much pleasure, then from thee much more must flow;
And soonest our best men with thee do go—
Rest of their bones and souls' delivery!

Thou'rt slave to fate, chance, kings, and desperate men,
And dost with poison, war, and sickness dwell;
And poppy or charms can make us sleep as well
And better than thy stroke. Why swell'st thou then?
One short sleep past, we wake eternally,
And Death shall be no more: Death, thou shalt die!

168   THE DREAM

DEAR love, for nothing less than thee
Would I have broke this happy dream;
            It was a theme
For reason, much too strong for fantasy.
Therefore thou waked'st me wisely; yet
My dream thou brak'st not, but continued'st it:
Thou art so true that thoughts of thee suffice
To make dreams truths and fables histories.
Enter these arms, for since thou thought'st it best
Not to dream all my dream, let's act the rest.

As lightning, or a taper's light,
Thine eyes, and not thy noise, waked me;
            Yet I thought thee—
For thou lov'st truth—an angel at first sight;
But when I saw thou saw'st my heart,
And knew'st my thoughts beyond an angel's art,
When thou knew'st what I dreamt, when thou knew'st when
Excess of joy would wake me, and cam'st then,
I must confess it could not choose but be
Profane to think thee anything but thee.

Coming and staying show'd thee thee;
But rising makes me doubt that now
            Thou art not thou.
That Love is weak where Fear's as strong as he;
'Tis not all spirit pure and brave,
If mixture it of Fear, Shame, Honour have.
Perchance, as torches, which must ready be,
Men light and put out, so thou dealst with me.
Thou cam'st to kindle, goest to come: then I
Will dream that hope again, but else would die.

169

Song

Go and catch a falling star,
   Get with child a mandrake root,
Tell me where all past hours are,
   Or who cleft the Devil's foot;
Teach me to hear mermaids singing,
Or to keep off envy's stinging,
      Or find
      What wind
Serves to advance an honest mind.

If thou be'st born to strange sights,
   Things invisible go see,
Ride ten thousand days and nights,
   Till age snow white hairs on thee.
Thou at thy return wilt tell me
All strange wonders that befell thee,
      And swear,
      No where
Lives a woman true and fair.

If thou find'st one, let me know,
   Such a pilgrimage were sweet;
Yet do not, I would not go,
   Though at next door we should meet.
Though she were true when you met her,
And last till you write your letter,
      Yet she
      Will be
False, ere I come, to two or three.

170

Sweetest Love, I Do Not Go

Sweetest love, I do not go
   For weariness of thee,
Nor in hope the world can show
   A fitter love for me;
      But since that I
Must die at last, 'tis best
Thus to use myself in jest,
      By feignèd death to die.

Yesternight the sun went hence,
    And yet is here to-day;
He hath no desire nor sense,
    Nor half so short a way.
        Then fear not me,
But believe that I shall make
Hastier journeys, since I take
        More wings and spurs than he.

O how feeble is man's power,
    That, if good fortune fall,
Cannot add another hour,
    Nor a lost hour recall.
        But come bad chance,
And we join to it our strength,
And we teach it art and length,
        Itself o'er us t' advance.

When thou sigh'st, thou sigh'st no wind,
    But sigh'st my soul away;
When thou weep'st, unkindly kind,
    My life's blood doth decay.
        It cannot be
That thou lov'st me as thou say'st,
If in thine my life thou waste,
        That art the best of me.

Let not thy divining heart
    Forethink me any ill.
Destiny may take thy part
    And may thy fears fulfil;
        But think that we
Are but turned aside to sleep:
They who one another keep
        Alive, ne'er parted be.

171   LOVER'S INFINITENESS

IF yet I have not all thy love,
    Dear, I shall never have it all;
I cannot breathe one other sigh to move,

Nor can entreat one other tear to fall;
And all my treasure, which should purchase thee,
Sighs, tears, and oaths, and letters, I have spent;
    Yet no more can be due to me,
    Than at the bargain made was meant:
If, then, thy gift of love was partial,
That some to me, some should to others fall,
    Dear, I shall never have it all.

    Or if then thou gavest me all,
    All was but all which thou hadst then;
But if in thy heart since there be, or shall
New love created be by other men,
Which have their stocks entire, and can in tears,
In sighs, in oaths, in letters outbid me,
    This new love may beget new fears;
    For this love was not vowed by thee,
And yet it was, thy gift being general:
The ground, thy heart, is mine; whatever shall
    Grow there, dear, I should have it all.

    Yet I would not have all yet;
    He that hath all can have no more;
And since my love doth every day admit
New growth, thou shouldst have new rewards in store.
Thou canst not every day give me thy heart;
If thou canst give it, then thou never gav'st it:
Love's riddles are that, though thy heart depart,
It stays at home, and thou with losing sav'st it,
But we will love a way more liberal
Than changing hearts,—to join them; so we shall
    Be one, an one another's All.

172   Love's Deity

I long to talk with some old lover's ghost,
    Who died before the god of love was born:
I cannot think that he, that then loved most,
    Sunk so low as to love one which did scorn.
But since this god produced a destiny,

And that vice-nature, custom, lets it be,
I must love her that loves not me.

Sure they which made him god meant not so much,
   Nor he in his young godhead practised it;
But when an even flame two hearts did touch,
   His office was indulgently to fit
Actives to passives; correspondency
Only his subject was; it cannot be
Love, if I love who loves not me.

But every modern god will now extend
   His vast prerogative as far as Jove;
To rage, to lust, to write too, to commend;
   All is the purlieu of the god of love.
O were we wakened by his tyranny
To ungod this child again, it could not be
I should love her that loves not me.

Rebel and atheist, too, why murmur I,
   As though I felt the worst that love could do?
Love may make me leave loving, or might try
   A deeper plague, to make her love me too,
Which, since she loves before, I am loath to see,
Falsehood is worse than hate; and that must be,
If she whom I love should love me.

173   Stay, O Sweet

Stay, O sweet, and do not rise!
   The light that shines comes from thine eyes;
   The day breaks not: it is my heart,
Because that you and I must part.
   Stay! or else my joys will die,
And perish in their infancy.

 'Tis true, 'tis day: what though it be?
O, wilt thou therefore rise from me?
   Why should we rise because 'tis light?
Did we lie down because 'twas night?
   Love, which in spite of darkness brought us hither,
Should in despite of light keep us together.

Light hath no tongue, but is all eye.
If it could speak as well as spy,
    This were the worst that it could say:—
That, being well, I fain would stay,
    And that I lov'd my heart and honour so,
    That I would not from him, that had them, go.

Must business thee from hence remove?
Oh, that's the worse disease of love!
    The poor, the fool, the false, love can
Admit, but not the busied man.
    He, which hath business, and makes love, doth do
    Such wrong, as when a married man doth woo.

174   THE BLOSSOM

LITTLE think'st thou, poor flower,
Whom I have watched six or seven days,
And seen thy birth, and seen what every hour
Gave to thy growth, thee to this height to raise,
And now dost laugh and triumph on this bough,
            —Little think'st thou
That it will freeze anon, and that I shall
To-morrow find thee fall'n, or not at all.

Little think'st thou, poor heart,
That labourest yet to nestle thee,
And think'st by hovering here to get a part
In a forbidden or forbidding tree,
And hop'st her stiffness by long siege to bow,
            —Little think'st thou
That thou, to-morrow, ere the sun doth wake,
Must with the sun and me a journey take.

But thou, which lov'st to be
Subtle to plague thyself, wilt say—
"Alas! if you must go, what's that to me?
Here lies my business, and here will I stay:
You go to friends, whose love and means present
            Various content

To your eyes, ears, and taste, and every part:
If then your body go, what need your heart?"

Well, then, stay here: but know
When thou hast said and done thy most,
A naked thinking heart, that makes no show,
Is to a woman but a kind of ghost;
How shall she know my heart? Or, having none,
                    Know thee for one?
Practice may make her know some other part,
But take my word, she doth not know a heart.

Meet me in London, then,
Twenty days hence, and thou shalt see
Me fresher and more fat, by being with men,
Than if I had stay'd still with her and thee.
For God's sake, if you can, be you so too:
                    I will give you
There to another friend, whom you shall find
As glad to have my body as my mind.

175   THE GOOD MORROW

I WONDER, by my troth, what thou and I
Did, till we loved? were we not weaned till then?
But sucked on country pleasures, childishly?
Or snored we in the Seven Sleepers' den?
'Twas so; but this, all pleasures fancies be;
If ever any beauty I did see.
Which I desired, and got, 'twas but a dream of thee.

And now good-morrow to our waking souls,
Which watch not one another out of fear;
For love all love of other sights controls,
And makes one little room an everywhere.
Let sea-discoverers to new worlds have gone;
Let maps to other, worlds on worlds have shown,
Let us possess one world; each hath one, and is one.

My face in thine eye, thine in mine appears,
And true plain hearts do in the faces rest;

Where can we find two better hemispheres
Without sharp north, without declining west?
Whatever dies, was not mixed equally;
If our two loves be one, or thou and I
Love so alike that none can slacken, none can die.

176 PRESENT IN ABSENCE

ABSENCE, hear thou my protestation
Against thy strength,
Distance, and length;
Do what thou canst for alteration:
For hearts of truest mettle
Absence doth join, and Time doth settle.

Who loves a mistress of such quality,
His mind hath found
Affection's ground
Beyond time, place, and all mortality.
To hearts that cannot vary
Absence is present, Time doth tarry.

My senses want their outward motion
Which now within
Reason doth win,
Redoubled by her secret notion:
Like rich men that take pleasure
In hiding more than handling treasure.

By absence this good means I gain,
That I can catch her,
Where none can watch her,
In some close corner of my brain:
There I embrace and kiss her;
And so enjoy her and none miss her.

JOSHUA SYLVESTER
[1563–1618]

177   LOVE'S OMNIPRESENCE

WERE I as base as is the lowly plain,
And you, my Love, as high as heaven above,
Yet should the thoughts of me your humble swain
Ascend to heaven, in honour of my Love.

Were I as high as heaven above the plain,
And you, my Love, as humble and as low
As are the deepest bottoms of the main,
Whereso'er you were, with you my love should go.

Were you the earth, dear Love, and I the skies,
My love should shine on you like to the sun,
And look upon you with ten thousand eyes
Till heaven wax'd blind, and till the world were done.

Whereso'er I am, below, or else above you,
Whereso'er you are, my heart shall truly love you.

WILLIAM ALEXANDER, EARL OF STIRLING
[1567(?)–1640]

178   TO AURORA

O IF thou knew'st how thou thyself dost harm,
And dost prejudge thy bliss, and spoil my rest;
Then thou would'st melt the ice out of thy breast
And thy relenting heart would kindly warm.

O if thy pride did not our joys controul,
What world of loving wonders should'st thou see!
For if I saw thee once transform'd in me,
Then in thy bosom I would pour my soul;

Then all my thoughts should in thy visage shine,
And if that aught mischanced thou should'st not moan

Nor bear the burthen of thy griefs alone;
No, I would have my share in what were thine:

And whilst we thus should make our sorrows one,
This happy harmony would make them none.

RICHARD CORBET

[*1582–1635*]

FAREWELL, REWARDS AND FAIRIES

FAREWELL, rewards and fairies,
  Good housewives now may say,
For now foul sluts in dairies
  Do fare as well as they.
And though they sweep their hearths no less
  Than maids were wont to do,
Yet who of late for cleanness
  Finds sixpence in her shoe?

Lament, lament, old Abbeys,
  The Fairies' lost command!
They did but change Priests' babies,
  But some have changed your land.
And all your children, sprung from thence,
  Are now grown Puritans,
Who live as Changelings ever since
  For love of your demains.

At morning and at evening both
  You merry were and glad,
So little care of sleep or sloth
  These pretty ladies had;
When Tom came home from labour,
  Or Cis to milking rose,
Then merrily went their tabor,
  And nimbly went their toes.

Witness those rings and roundelays
  Of theirs, which yet remain,
Were footed in Queen Mary's days
  On many a grassy plain;

But since of late, Elizabeth,
  And later, James came in,
They never danced on any heath
  As when the time hath been.

By which we note the Fairies
  Were of the old Profession.
Their songs were 'Ave Mary's',
  Their dances were Procession.
But now, alas, they all are dead;
  Or gone beyond the seas;
Or farther for Religion fled;
Or else they take their ease.

A tell-tale in their company
  They never could endure!
And whoso kept not secretly
  Their mirth, was punished, sure;
It was a just and Christian deed
  To pinch such black and blue.
Oh how the commonwealth doth want
  Such Justices as you!

THOMAS HEYWOOD
[D. *1650(?)*]

180   PACK, CLOUDS, AWAY

PACK, clouds, away, and welcome day,
  With night we banish sorrow;
Sweet air, blow soft, mount, larks, aloft
  To give my Love good-morrow!
Wings from the wind to please her mind,
  Notes from the lark I'll borrow;
Bird, prune thy wing, nightingale, sing,
  To give my Love good-morrow;
    To give my Love good-morrow
    Notes from them both I'll borrow.

Wake from thy nest, Robin-red-breast,
  Sing, birds, in every furrow;

And from each hill, let music shrill
Give my fair Love good-morrow!
Blackbird and thrush in every bush,
Stare, linnet, and cock-sparrow!
You pretty elves, amongst yourselves
Sing my fair Love good-morrow;
    To give my Love good-morrow
    Sing, birds, in every furrow!

THOMAS DEKKER
[*1570(?)–1614*]

181   COUNTRY GLEE

HAYMAKERS, rakers, reapers, and mowers,
    Wait on your Summer-Queen;
Dress up with musk-rose her eglantine bowers,
    Daffodils strew the green;
        Sing, dance, and play,
        'Tis holiday;
    The sun does bravely shine
    On our ears of corn.
        Rich as a pearl
        Comes every girl,
    This is mine, this is mine, this is mine;
Let us die, ere away they be borne.

Bow to the Sun, to our Queen, and that fair one
    Come to behold our sports;
Each bonny lass here is counted a rare one
    As those in princes' courts.
        These and we
        With country glee,
    Will teach the woods to resound,
    And the hills with echoes hollow:
        Skipping lambs
        Their bleating dams,
    'Mongst kids shall trip it round;
For joy thus our wenches we follow.

Wind, jolly huntsmen, your neat bugles shrilly,
  Hounds make a lusty cry;
Spring up, you falconers, partridges freely,
  Then let your brave hawks fly.
      Horses amain,
      Over ridge, over plain,
  The dogs have the stag in chase:
  'Tis a sport to content a king.
      So ho, ho! through the skies
      How the proud bird flies,
And sousing, kills with a grace!
Now the deer falls; hark! how they ring.

182   COLD'S THE WIND

  COLD's the wind, and wet's the rain,
  Saint Hugh be our good speed!
  Ill is the weather that bringeth no gain,
  Nor helps good hearts in need.

  Troll the bowl, the jolly nut-brown bowl,
  And here's, kind mate, to thee!
  Let's sing a dirge for Saint Hugh's soul,
  And down it merrily.

183   O SWEET CONTENT

ART thou poor, yet hast thou golden slumbers?
      O sweet content!
Art thou rich, yet is thy mind perplex'd?
      O punishment!
Dost thou laugh to see how fools are vex'd
To add to golden numbers, golden numbers?
  O sweet content! O sweet, O sweet content!
Work apace, apace, apace, apace;
Honest labour bears a lovely face;
Then hey nonny nonny, hey nonny nonny!

Canst drink the waters of the crispèd spring?
      O sweet content!
Swimm'st thou in wealth, yet sink'st in thine own tears?
      O punishment!

Then he that patiently want's burden bears
No burden bears, but in a king, a king!
  O sweet content! O sweet, O sweet content!
Work apace, apace, apace, apace;
Honest labour bears a lovely face;
Then hey nonny nonny, hey nonny nonny!

FRANCIS BEAUMONT
[1584–1616]

184   On the Tombs in Westminster Abbey

Mortality, behold and fear
What a change of flesh is here!
Think how many royal bones
Sleep within these heaps of stones;
Here they lie, had realms and lands,
Who now want strength to stir their hands,
Where from their pulpits seal'd with dust
They preach, 'In greatness is no trust.'
Here's an acre sown indeed
With the richest royallest seed
That the earth did e'er suck in
Since the first man died for sin:
Here the bones of birth have cried
'Though gods they were, as men they died!'
Here are sands, ignoble things,
Dropt from the ruin'd sides of kings:
Here's a world of pomp and state
Buried in dust, once dead by fate.

185   Master Francis Beaumont's Letter to
        Ben Jonson

Written before he and Master Fletcher came to London

The sun (which doth the greatest comfort bring
To absent friends, because the self-same thing
They know they see, however absent) is
Here our best haymaker (forgive me this;
It is our country's style): in this warm shine
I lie, and dream of your full *Mermaid* Wine.

O, we have Winter mixed with claret lees,
Drink apt to bring in drier heresies
Than beer, good only for the sonnet's strain,
With fustian metaphors to stuff the brain;
So mixed, that, given to the thirstiest one,
'Twill not prove alms, unless he have the stone:
I think with one draught man's invention fades,
Two cups had quite spoiled Homer's *Iliads!*
'Tis liquor that will find out Sutcliff's wit,
Lie where he will, and make him write worse yet.
Filled with such moisture, in most grievous qualms,
Did Robert Wisdom write his singing *Psalms;*
And so must I do this: and yet I think
It is our potion sent us down to drink,
By special Providence, keeps us from fights,
Makes us not laugh, when we make legs to Knights:
'Tis this that keeps our minds fit for our states;
A medicine to obey our Magistrates;
For we do live more free than you; no hate,
No envy at one another's happy state,
Moves us; we are equal every whit;
Of land that God gives men, here is their wit,
If we consider fully; for our best
And gravest man will with his main-house-jest
Scarce please you: we want subtlety to do
The city-tricks; lie, Hate, and flatter too:
Here are none that can bear a painted show,
Strike, when you wince, and then lament the blow;
Who (like mills set the right way for to grind)
Can make their gains alike with every wind:
Only some fellows with the subtlest pate
Amongst us, may perchance equivocate
At selling of a horse; and that's the most
Methinks the little wit I had is lost
Since I saw you; for wit is like a rest
Held up at tennis, which men do the best
With the best gamesters. What things have we seen
Done at the *Mermaid!* heard words that have been
So nimble, and so full of subtle flame,
As if that every one (from whence they came)
Had meant to put his whole wit in a jest,

And had resolved to live a fool the rest
Of his dull life;—then when there hath been thrown
Wit able enough to justify the town
For three days past; wit that might warrant be
For the whole city to talk foolishly
Till that were cancelled; and, when we were gone,
We left an air behind us; which alone
Was able to make the two next companies
(Right witty; though but downright fools) more wise!
   When I remember this, and see that now
The country gentlemen begin to allow
My wit for dry bobs, then I needs must cry,
'I see my days of ballating grow nigh!'
I can already riddle, and can sing
Catches, sell bargains: and I fear shall bring
Myself to speak the hardest words I find
Over as oft as any, with one wind,
That takes no medicines. But one thought of thee
Makes me remember all these things to be
The wit of our young men, fellows that show
No part of good, yet utter all they know;
Who, like trees of the guard, have growing souls,
Only strong Destiny, which all controls,
I hope hath left a better fate in store
For me, thy friend, than to live ever poor,
Banished unto this home. Fate once again,
Brings me to thee, who canst make smooth and plain
The way of knowledge for me, and then I
(Who have no good, but in thy company,)
Protest it will my greatest comfort be,
To acknowledge all I have, to flow from thee!
Ben, when these Scenes are perfect, we'll taste wine!
I'll drink thy Muse's health! thou shalt quaff mine!

JOHN FLETCHER
[1579-1625]

186   ASPATIA'S SONG

LAY a garland on my hearse
  Of the dismal yew;

Maidens, willow branches bear;
Say, I died true.

My love was false, but I was firm
From my hour of birth.
Upon my buried body lie
Lightly, gentle earth!

187   MELANCHOLY

HENCE, all you vain delights,
As short as are the nights,
Wherein you spend your folly:
There's nought in this life sweet
If man were wise to see't,
    But only melancholy,
    O sweetest melancholy!
Welcome, folded arms, and fixèd eyes,
A sigh that piercing mortifies,
A look that's fasten'd to the ground,
A tongue chain'd up without a sound!
Fountain heads and pathless groves,
Places which pale passion loves!
Moonlight walks, when all the fowls
Are warmly housed save bats and owls!
A midnight bell, a parting groan!
These are the sounds we feed upon;
Then stretch our bones in a still gloomy valley;
Nothing's so dainty sweet as lovely melancholy.

JOHN WEBSTER
[*1580(?)–1625(?)*]

188   CALL FOR THE ROBIN-REDBREAST

CALL for the robin-redbreast and the wren,
Since o'er shady groves they hover
And with leaves and flowers do cover
The friendless bodies of unburied men.
Call unto his funeral dole
The ant, the field-mouse, and the mole

To rear him hillocks that shall keep him warm
And (when gay tombs are robb'd) sustain no harm;
But keep the wolf far thence, that's foe to men,
For with his nails he'll dig them up again.

ANONYMOUS

189 O Waly, Waly

O WALY waly up the bank,
  And waly waly down the brae,
And waly waly yon burn-side
  Where I and my Love wont to gae!
I leant my back unto an aik,
  I thought it was a trusty tree;
But first it bow'd, and syne[1] it brak,
  Sae my true Love did lichtly[2] me.

O waly waly, but love be bonny
  A little time while it is new;
But when 'tis auld, it waxeth cauld
  And fades awa' like morning dew.
O wherefore should I busk[3] my head?
  Or wherefore should I kame[4] my hair?
For my true Love has me forsook,
  And says he'll never loe me mair.

Now Arthur-seat sall be my bed;
  The sheets shall ne'er be prest by me:
Saint Anton's well sall be my drink,
  Since my true Love has forsaken me.
Marti'mas wind, when wilt thou blaw
  And shake the green leaves aff the tree?
O gentle Death, when wilt thou come?
  For of my life I am wearíe.

'Tis not the frost, that freezes fell,
  Now blawing snaw's inclemencie;
'Tis not sic cauld that makes me cry,
  But my Love's heart grown cauld to me.

[1] Then. [2] Slight. [3] Adorn. [4] Comb.

When we came in by Glasgow town
  We were a comely sight to see;
My Love was clad in the black velvét,
  And I mysell in cramasie.[5]

But had I wist, before I kist,
  That love had been sae ill to win;
I had lockt my heart in a case of gowd[6]
  And pinn'd it with a siller[7] pin.
And, O! if my young babe were born,
  And set upon the nurse's knee,
And I mysell were dead and gane,
  And the green grass growing over me!

190   HELEN OF KIRCONNELL

I wish I were where Helen lies;
Night and day on me she cries;
O that I were where Helen lies
  On fair Kirconnell lea!

Curst be the heart that thought the thought,
And curst the hand that fired the shot,
When in my arms burd Helen dropt,
  And died to succour me!

O think na but my heart was sair
When my Love dropt down and spak nae mair!
I laid her down wi' meikle care
  On fair Kirconnell lea.

As I went down the water-side,
None but my foe to be my guide,
None but my foe to be my guide,
  On fair Kirconnell lea;

I lighted down my sword to draw,
I hackèd him in pieces sma',
I hackèd him in pieces sma',
  For her sake that died for me.

[5] Crimson cloth.   [6] Gold.   [7] Silver.

O Helen fair, beyond compare!
I'll make a garland of thy hair
Shall bind my heart for evermair
    Until the day I die.

O that I were where Helen lies!
Night and day on me she cries;
Out of my bed she bids me rise,
    Says, 'Haste and come to me!'

O Helen fair! O Helen chaste!
If I were with thee, I were blest,
Where thou lies low and takes thy rest
    On fair Kirconnell lea.

I wish my grave were growing green,
A winding-sheet drawn ower my een,
And I in Helen's arms lying,
    On fair Kirconnell lea.

I wish I were where Helen lies;
Night and day on me she cries;
And I am weary of the skies,
    Since my Love died for me.

191
          MY LOVE IN HER ATTIRE

My Love in her attire doth shew her wit,
    It doth so well become her:
For every season she hath dressings fit,
    For Winter, Spring, and Summer.
No beauty she doth miss
When all her robes are on:
But Beauty's self she is
When all her robes are gone.

192
            LOVE NOT ME

Love not me for comely grace,
For my pleasing eye or face,
Nor for any outward part,

No, nor for my constant heart,—
  For those may fail, or turn to ill,
  So thou and I shall sever:
Keep therefore a true woman's eye,
And love me still, but know not why—
  So hast thou the same reason still
  To doat upon me ever!

WILLIAM DRUMMOND

[1585-1649]

193   SAINT JOHN BAPTIST

THE last and greatest Herald of Heaven's King
Girt with rough skins, hies to the deserts wild,
Among that savage brood the woods forth bring,
Which he more harmless found than man, and mild.
His food was locusts, and what there doth spring,
With honey that from virgin hives distill'd;
Parch'd body, hollow eyes, some uncouth thing
Made him appear, long since from earth exiled.
There burst he forth: All ye whose hopes rely
On God, with me amidst these deserts mourn,
Repent, repent, and from old errors turn!
—Who listen'd to his voice, obey'd his cry?
  Only the echoes, which he made relent,
  Rung from their flinty caves, Repent! Repent!

194   MADRIGAL

My thoughts hold mortal strife;
I do detest my life,
And with lamenting cries
Peace to my soul to bring
Oft call that prince which here doth monarchize:
—But he, grim grinning King,
Who caitiffs scorns, and doth the blest surprize,
Late having deck'd with beauty's rose his tomb,
Disdains to crop a weed, and will not come.

195   LIFE

THIS Life, which seems so fair,
Is like a bubble blown up in the air
By sporting children's breath,
Who chase it everywhere
And strive who can most motion it bequeath.
And though it sometimes seem of its own might
Like to an eye of gold to be fix'd there,
And firm to hover in that empty height,
That only is because it is so light.
—But in that pomp it doth not long appear;
For when 'tis most admired, in a thought,
Because it erst was nought, it turns to nought.

196   HUMAN FOLLY

OF this fair volume which we World do name
If we the sheets and leaves could turn with care,
Of him who it corrects, and did it frame,
We clear might read the art and wisdom rare:
Find out his power which wildest powers doth tame,
His providence extending everywhere,
His justice which proud rebels doth not spare,
In every page, no period of the same.
But silly we, like foolish children, rest
Well pleased with colour'd vellum, leaves of gold.
Fair dangling ribbands, leaving what is best,
On the great writer's sense ne'er taking hold;
    Or if by chance we stay our minds on aught,
    It is some picture on the margin wrought.

197   THE PROBLEM

DOTH then the world go thus, doth all thus move?
Is this the justice which on Earth we find?
Is this that firm decree which all doth bind?
Are these your influences, Powers above?
Those souls which vice's moody mists most blind,
Blind Fortune, blindly, most their friend doth prove;
And they who thee, poor idol Virtue! love,

Ply like a feather toss'd by storm and wind.
Ah! if a Providence doth sway this all
Why should best minds groan under most distress?
Or why should pride humility make thrall,
And injuries the innocent oppress?
    Heavens! hinder, stop this fate; or grant a time
    When good may have, as well as bad, their prime!

198

To His Lute

My lute, be as thou wert when thou didst grow
With thy green mother in some shady grove,
When immelodious winds but made thee move,
And birds their ramage did on thee bestow.
Since that dear Voice which did thy sounds approve,
Which wont in such harmonious strains to flow,
Is reft from Earth to tune those spheres above,
What art thou but a harbinger of woe?
Thy pleasing notes be pleasing notes no more,
But orphans' wailings to the fainting ear;
Each stroke a sigh, each sound draws forth a tear;
For which be silent as in woods before:
    Or if that any hand to touch thee deign,
    Like widow'd turtle still her loss complain.

199

For the Magdalene

'These eyes, dear Lord, once brandons of desire,
Frail scouts betraying what they had to keep,
Which their own heart, then others set on fire,
Their trait'rous black before thee here out-weep;
These locks, of blushing deeds the gilt attire,
Waves curling, wrackful shelves to shadow deep,
Rings wedding souls to sin's lethargic sleep,
To touch thy sacred feet do now aspire.
In seas of care behold a sinking bark,
By winds of sharp remorse unto thee driven,
O let me not be Ruin's aim'd-at-mark!
My faults confessed, Lord, say they are forgiven.'
    Thus sighed to Jesus the Bethanian fair,
    His tear-wet feet still drying with her hair.

200   CONTENT AND RESOLUTE

As when it happeneth that some lovely town
Unto a barbarous besieger falls,
Who there by sword and flame himself installs,
And, cruel, it in tears and blood doth drown;
Her beauty spoiled, her citizens made thralls,
His spite yet so can not her all throw down
But that some statue, arch, fane of renown
Yet lurks unmaimed within her weeping walls:
So, after all the spoil, disgrace, and wrack,
That time, the world, and death, could bring combined,
Amidst that mass of ruins they did make,
Safe and all scarless yet remains my mind.
    From this so high transcending rapture springs,
    That I, all else defaced, not envy kings.

201   ALEXIS, HERE SHE STAYED; AMONG THESE PINES

ALEXIS, here she stayed; among these pines,
Sweet hermitress, she did alone repair;
Here did she spread the treasure of her hair,
More rich than that brought from the Colchian mines;
She set her by these muskèd eglantines.—
The happy place the print seems yet to bear;—
Her voice did sweeten here thy sugared lines,
To which winds, trees, beasts, birds, did lend their ear:
Me here she first perceived, and here a morn
Of bright carnations did o'erspread her face;
Here did she sigh, here first my hopes were born,
And I first got a pledge of promised grace;
    But ah! what served it to be happy so,
    Sith passèd pleasures double but new woe?

202   SUMMONS TO LOVE

PHŒBUS, arise!
And paint the sable skies
With azure, white, and red:
Rouse Memnon's mother from her Tithon's bed
That she may thy career with roses spread:

The nightingales thy coming eachwhere sing:
Make an eternal Spring!
Give life to this dark world which lieth dead;
Spread forth thy golden hair
In larger locks than thou wast wont before,
And emperor-like decore
With diadem of pearl thy temples fair:
Chase hence the ugly night
Which serves but to make dear thy glorious light

—This is that happy morn,
That day, long-wishèd day
Of all my life so dark,
(If cruel stars have not my ruin sworn
And fates my hopes betray),
Which, purely white, deserves
An everlasting diamond should it mark.
This is the morn should bring unto this grove
My Love, to hear and recompense my love.
Fair King, who all preserves,
But show thy blushing beams,
And thou two sweeter eyes
Shalt see than those which by Penéus' streams
Did once thy heart surprize.
Now, Flora, deck thyself in fairest guise:
If that ye winds would hear
A voice surpassing far Amphion's lyre,
Your furious chiding stay;
Let Zephyr only breathe,
And with her tresses play.
—The winds all silent are,
And Phœbus in his chair
Ensaffroning sea and air
Makes vanish every star:
Night like a drunkard reels
Beyond the hills, to shun his flaming wheels:
The fields with flowers are deck'd in every hue,
The clouds with orient gold spangle their blue;
Here is the pleasant place—
And nothing wanting is, save She, alas!

GEORGE WITHER
[1588–1667]

203 I LOVED A LASS

I LOVED a lass, a fair one,
 As fair as e'er was seen;
She was indeed a rare one,
 Another Sheba Queen;
But, fool as then I was,
 I thought she loved me too:
But now, alas! she's left me,
 Falero, lero, loo!

Her hair like gold did glister,
 Each eye was like a star,
She did surpass her sister,
 Which pass'd all others far;
She would me honey call,
 She'd—O she'd kiss me too!
But now, alas! she's left me,
 Falero, lero, loo!

Many a merry meeting
 My love and I have had;
She was my only sweeting,
 She made my heart full glad;
The tears stood in her eyes
 Like to the morning dew:
But now, alas! she's left me,
 Falero, lero, loo!

Her cheeks were like the cherry,
 Her skin was white as snow;
When she was blithe and merry
 She angel-like did show;
Her waist exceeding small,
 The fives did fit her shoe:
But now, alas! she's left me,
 Falero, lero, loo!

In summer time or winter
    She had her heart's desire;
I still did scorn to stint her
    From sugar, sack, or fire;
The world went round about,
    No cares we ever knew:
But now, alas! she's left me,
    Falero, lero, loo!

To maidens' vows and swearing
    Henceforth no credit give;
You may give them the hearing,
    But never them believe;
They are as false as fair,
    Unconstant, frail, untrue:
For mine, alas! hath left me,
    Falero, lero, loo!

204   THE LOVER'S RESOLUTION

SHALL I, wasting in despair,
Die because a woman's fair?
Or my cheeks make pale with care
'Cause another's rosy are?
Be she fairer than the day
Or the flowery meads in May—
    If she be not so to me
    What care I how fair she be?

Shall my foolish heart be pined
'Cause I see a woman kind;
Or a well disposèd nature
Joinèd with a lovely feature?
Be she meeker, kinder, than
Turtle-dove or pelican,
    If she be not so to me
    What care I how kind she be?

Shall a woman's virtues move
Me to perish for her love?
Or her merits' value known

Make me quite forget mine own?
Be she with that goodness blest
Which may gain her name of Best;
    If she seem not such to me,
    What care I how good she be?.

'Cause her fortune seems too high,
Shall I play the fool and die?
Those that bear a noble mind
Where they want of riches find,
Think what with them they would do
Who without them dare to woo;
    And unless that mind I see,
    What care I how great she be?

Great or good, or kind or fair,
I will ne'er the more despair;
If she love me, this believe,
I will die ere she shall grieve;
If she slight me when I woo,
I can scorn and let her go;
    For if she be not for me,
    What care I for whom she be?

WILLIAM BROWNE (?)

[*1591–1643(?)*]

205   ON THE COUNTESS DOWAGER OF PEMBROKE

UNDERNEATH this sable herse
Lies the subject of all verse:
Sidney's sister, Pembroke's mother:
Death, ere thou hast slain another
Fair and learn'd and good as she,
Time shall throw a dart at thee.

ROBERT HERRICK
[*1591–1674*]

206   CHERRY-RIPE

CHERRY-RIPE, ripe, ripe, I cry,
Full and fair ones; come and buy.
If so be you ask me where
They do grow, I answer: There
Where my Julia's lips do smile;
There's the land, or cherry-isle,
Whose plantations fully show
All the year where cherries grow.

207   A CHILD'S GRACE

HERE a little child I stand
Heaving up my either hand;
Cold as paddocks though they be.
Here I lift them up to Thee,
For a benison to fall
On our meat and on us all. Amen.

208   THE MAD MAID'S SONG

GOOD-MORROW to the day so fair,
    Good-morning, sir, to you;
Good-morrow to mine own torn hair
    Bedabbled with the dew.

Good-morning to this primrose too,
    Good-morrow to each maid
That will with flowers the tomb bestrew
    Wherein my love is laid.

Ah! woe is me, woe, woe is me!
    Alack and well-a-day!
For pity, sir, find out that bee
    Which bore my love away.

I'll seek him in your bonnet brave,
  I'll seek him in your eyes;
Nay, now I think they've made his grave
  I' th' bed of strawberries.

I'll seek him there; I know ere this
  The cold, cold earth doth shake him;
But I will go, or send a kiss
  By you, sir, to awake him.

Pray hurt him not; though he be dead,
  He knows well who do love him,
And who with green turfs rear his head,
  And who do rudely move him.

He's soft and tender (pray take heed);
  With bands of cowslips bind him,
And bring him home—but 'tis decreed
  That I shall never find him!

209   To the Virgins

GATHER ye rose-buds while ye may,
  Old Time is still a-flying:
And this same flower that smiles to-day,
  To-morrow will be dying.

The glorious Lamp of Heaven, the Sun,
  The higher he's a-getting
The sooner will his race be run,
  And nearer he's to setting.

That age is best which is the first,
  When youth and blood are warmer;
But being spent, the worse, and worst
  Times, still succeed the former.

Then be not coy, but use your time;
  And while ye may, go marry:
For having lost but once your prime,
  You may for ever tarry.

210

To Dianeme

SWEET, be not proud of those two eyes
Which starlike sparkle in their skies;
Nor be you proud, that you can see
All hearts your captives; yours yet free:
Be you not proud of that rich hair
Which wantons with the lovesick air;
Whenas that ruby which you wear,
Sunk from the tip of your soft ear,
Will last to be a precious stone
When all your world of beauty's gone.

211

A Sweet Disorder

A SWEET disorder in the dress
Kindles in clothes a wantonness:—
A lawn about the shoulders thrown
Into a fine distractión,—
An erring lace, which here and there
Enthrals the crimson stomacher,—
A cuff neglectful, and thereby
Ribbands to flow confusedly,—
A winning wave, deserving note,
In the tempestuous petticoat,—
A careless shoe-string, in whose tie
I see a wild civility,—
Do more bewitch me, than when art
Is too precise in every part.

212

Whenas in Silks

WHENAS in silks my Julia goes
Then, then (methinks) how sweetly flows
That liquefaction of her clothes.

Next, when I cast mine eyes and see
That brave vibration each way free;
O how that glittering taketh me!

213

To Anthea who may Command Him Any Thing

Bid me to live, and I will live
    Thy Protestant to be:
Or bid me love, and I will give
    A loving heart to thee.

A heart as soft, a heart as kind,
    A heart as sound and free
As in the whole world thou canst find,
    That heart I'll give to thee.

Bid that heart stay, and it will stay,
    To honour thy decree:
Or bid it languish quite away,
    And 't shall do so for thee.

Bid me to weep, and I will weep
    While I have eyes to see:
And having none, yet I will keep
    A heart to weep for thee.

Bid me despair, and I'll despair,
    Under that cypress tree:
Or bid me die, and I will dare
    E'en Death, to die for thee.

Thou art my life, my love, my heart,
    The very eyes of me,
And hast command of every part,
    To live and die for thee.

214

To Daffodils

Fair Daffodils, we weep to see
    You haste away so soon:
As yet the early-rising Sun
    Has not attain'd his noon.
    Stay, stay,

Until the hasting day
Has run
But to the even-song;
And, having pray'd together, we
Will go with you along.

We have short time to stay, as you,
We have as short a Spring!
As quick a growth to meet decay
As you, or any thing.
We die,
As your hours do, and dry
Away
Like to the Summer's rain;
Or as the pearls of morning's dew
Ne'er to be found again.

215   TO BLOSSOMS

FAIR pledges of a fruitful tree,
Why do ye fall so fast?
Your date is not so past,
But you may stay yet here awhile
To blush and gently smile,
And go at last.

What, were ye born to be
An hour or half's delight,
And so to bid good-night?
'Twas pity Nature brought ye forth
Merely to show your worth,
And lose you quite.

But you are lovely leaves, where we
May read how soon things have
Their end, though ne'er so brave:
And after they have shown their pride
Like you, awhile, they glide
Into the grave.

Corinna's Maying

Get up, get up for shame! The blooming morn
Upon her wings presents the god unshorn.
    See how Aurora throws her fair
    Fresh-quilted colours through the air:
    Get up, sweet slug-a-bed, and see
    The dew-bespangling herb and tree!
Each flower has wept and bow'd toward the east,
Above an hour since, yet you not drest;
    Nay! not so much as out of bed?
    When all the birds have matins said,
    And sung their thankful hymns, 'tis sin,
    Nay, profanation, to keep in,
Whenas a thousand virgins on this day
Spring, sooner than the lark, to fetch in May.

Rise, and put on your foliage, and be seen
To come forth, like the spring-time, fresh and green,
    And sweet as Flora. Take no care
    For jewels for your gown or hair:
    Fear not; the leaves will strew
    Gems in abundance upon you:
Besides, the childhood of the day has kept,
Against you come, some orient pearls unwept.
    Come, and receive them while the light
    Hangs on the dew-locks of the night,
    And Titan on the eastern hill
    Retires himself, or else stands still
Till you come forth! Wash, dress, be brief in praying:
Few beads are best when once we go a-Maying.

Come, my Corinna, come; and coming, mark
How each field turns a street, each street a park,
    Made green and trimm'd with trees! see how
    Devotion gives each house a bough
    Or branch! each porch, each door, ere this,
    An ark, a tabernacle is,
Made up of white-thorn neatly interwove,
As if here were those cooler shades of love.

Can such delights be in the street
And open fields, and we not see 't?
    Come, we'll abroad: and let's obey
    The proclamation made for May,
And sin no more, as we have done, by staying
But, my Corinna, come, let's go a-Maying.

There's not a budding boy or girl this day
But is got up and gone to bring in May.
    A deal of youth, ere this, is come
    Back, and with white-thorn laden home.
    Some have dispatch'd their cakes and cream,
    Before that we have left to dream:
And some have wept and woo'd, and plighted troth,
And chose their priest, ere we can cast off sloth:
    Many a green-gown has been given,
    Many a kiss, both odd and even:
    Many a glance, too, has been sent
    From out the eye, love's firmament:
Many a jest told of the keys betraying
This night, and locks pick'd: yet we're not a-Maying.

Come, let us go, while we are in our prime,
And take the harmless folly of the time!
    We shall grow old apace, and die
    Before we know our liberty.
    Our life is short, and our days run
    As fast away as does the sun.
And, as a vapour or a drop of rain,
Once lost, can ne'er be found again,
    So when or you or I are made
    A fable, song, or fleeting shade,
    All love, all liking, all delight
    Lies drowned with us in endless night.
Then, while time serves, and we are but decaying,
Come, my Corinna, come, let's go a-Maying.

FRANCIS QUARLES
[*1592–1644*]

217   AN ECSTASY

E'EN like two little bank-dividing brooks,
    That wash the pebbles with their wanton streams,
And having ranged and search'd a thousand nooks,
    Meet both at length in silver-breasted Thames,
        Where in a greater current they conjoin:
So I my Best-belovèd's am; so He is mine.

E'en so we met; and after long pursuit,
    E'en so we joined; we both became entire;
No need for either to renew a suit,
    For I was flax, and He was flames of fire:
        Our firm-united souls did more than twine;
So I my Best-belovèd's am; so He is mine.

If all those glittering Monarchs, that command
    The servile quarters of this earthly ball,
Should tender in exchange their shares of land,
    I would not change my fortunes for them all:
        Their wealth is but a counter to my coin:
The world's but theirs; but my Belovèd's mine.

GEORGE HERBERT
[*1593–1633*]

218   LOVE

LOVE bade me welcome; yet my soul drew back,
    Guilty of dust and sin.
But quick-eyed Love, observing me grow slack
    From my first entrance in,
Drew nearer to me, sweetly questioning
    If I lacked anything.

'A guest,' I answered, 'worthy to be here:'
    Love said, 'You shall be he.'

'I, the unkind, ungrateful? Ah, my dear,
    I cannot look on Thee.'
Love took my hand and smiling did reply,
    'Who made the eyes but I?'

'Truth, Lord; but I have marred them: let my shame
    Go where it doth deserve.'
'And know you not,' says Love, 'Who bore the blame?'
    'My dear, then I will serve.'
'You must sit down,' says Love, 'and taste my meat.'
    So I did sit and eat.

219   VIRTUE

SWEET day, so cool, so calm, so bright!
The bridal of the earth and sky—
The dew shall weep thy fall to-night;
    For thou must die.

Sweet rose, whose hue angry and brave
Bids the rash gazer wipe his eye,
Thy root is ever in its grave,
    And thou must die.

Sweet spring, full of sweet days and roses,
A box where sweets compacted lie,
My music shows ye have your closes,
    And all must die.

Only a sweet and virtuous soul,
Like season'd timber, never gives;
But though the whole world turn to coal,
    Then chiefly lives.

220   THE ELIXIR

TEACH me, my God and King,
    In all things Thee to see,
And what I do in anything
    To do it as for Thee.

Not rudely, as a beast
    To run into an action;
But still to make Thee prepossest
    And give it his perfection.

A man that looks on glass
    On it may stay his eye,
Or if he pleaseth, through it pass,
    And then the heaven espy.

All may of Thee partake
    Nothing can be so mean
Which with his tincture, 'for Thy sake,'
    Will not grow bright and clean.

A servant with this clause
    Makes drudgery divine;
Who sweeps a room, as for Thy laws,
    Makes that and the action fine.

This is the famous stone
    That turneth all to gold,
For that which God doth touch and own
    Cannot for less be told.

THE COLLAR

221

I STRUCK the board and cried, "No more;
        I will abroad.
What, shall I ever sigh and pine?
My lines and life are free, free as the road,
Loose as the wind, as large as store.
        Shall I be still in suit?
Have I no harvest but a thorn
To let me blood, and not restore
What I have lost with cordial fruit?
        Sure there was wine
Before my sighs did dry it; there was corn
Before my tears did drown it.
Is the year only lost to me?
Have I no bays to crown it?

No flowers, no garlands gay? All blasted?
      All wasted?
Not so, my heart; but there is fruit,
      And thou hast hands.
Recover all thy sigh-blown age
On double pleasure: leave thy cold dispute
Of what is fit and not; forsake thy cage,
      Thy rope of sands
Which petty thoughts have made, and made to thee
Good cable, to enforce and draw
      And be thy law,
While thou didst wink and wouldst not see.
      Away: take heed,
      I will abroad.
Call in thy death's head there: tie up thy fears.
      He that forbears
      To suit and serve his need
      Deserves his load."
But as I raved and grew more fierce and wild
      At every word,
Methought I heard one calling *'Child!'*
And I replied, *'My Lord!'*

222 THE FLOWER

How fresh, O Lord, how sweet and clean
Are thy returns! Ev'n as the flowers in Spring,
   To which, besides their own demean,
The late-past frosts tributes of pleasure bring;
      Grief melts away
      Like snow in May,
  As if there were no such cold thing.

Who would have thought my shrivell'd heart
Could have recover'd greenness? It was gone
   Quite under ground; as flowers depart
To see their mother-root, when they have blown,
      Where they together
      All the hard weather,
  Dead to the world, keep house unknown.

These are Thy wonders, Lord of power,
Killing and quick'ning, bringing down to Hell
And up to Heaven in an hour;
Making a chiming of a passing bell.
We say amiss
This or that is;
Thy word is all, if we could spell.

O that I once past changing were,
Fast in thy Paradise where no flower can wither!
Many a Spring I shoot up fair,
Off'ring at Heaven, growing and groaning thither;
Nor doth my flower
Want a Spring shower,
My sins and I joining together.

223   Easter Song

I got me flowers to strew Thy way,
I got me boughs off many a tree;
But Thou wast up by break of day,
And brought'st Thy sweets along with Thee.

The sun arising in the East,
Though he give light and th' East perfume,
If they should offer to contest
With Thy arising, they presume.

Can there be any day but this,
Though many suns to shine endeavour?
We count three hundred, but we miss:
There is but one, and that one ever.

224   The Pulley

When God at first made Man,
Having a glass of blessings standing by—
Let us (said He) pour on him all we can;
Let the world's riches, which dispersèd lie,
Contract into a span.

So strength first made a way,
Then beauty flow'd, then wisdom, honour, pleasure;
When almost all was out, God made a stay,
Perceiving that, alone of all His treasure,
Rest in the bottom lay.

For if I should (said He)
Bestow this jewel also on My creature,
He would adore My gifts instead of Me,
And rest in Nature, not the God of Nature:
So both should losers be.

Yet let him keep the rest,
But keep them with repining restlessness;
Let him be rich and weary, that at least,
If goodness lead him not, yet weariness
May toss him to My breast.

HENRY VAUGHAN

[1622–1695]

225   BEYOND THE VEIL

THEY are all gone into the world of light!
    And I alone sit lingering here;
Their very memory is fair and bright,
        And my sad thoughts doth clear.

It glows and glitters in my cloudy breast,
    Like stars upon some gloomy grove,
Or those faint beams in which this hill is drest,
        After the sun's remove.

I see them walking in an air of glory,
    Whose light doth trample on my days;
My days, which are at best but dull and hoary,
        Mere glimmerings and decays.

O holy Hope, and high Humility,
    High as the heavens above!
These are your walks, and you have showed them me,
        To kindle my cold love.

Dear, beauteous Death! the jewel of the just,
 Shining nowhere but in the dark,
What mysteries do lie beyond thy dust,
  Could Man outlook that mark!

He that hath found some fledged bird's nest, may know
 At first sight, if the bird be flown;
But what fair well or grove he sings in now,
  That is to him unknown.

And yet, as Angels in some brighter dreams
 Call to the soul when man doth sleep,
So some strange thoughts transcend our wonted themes,
  And into glory peep.

If a star were confined into a tomb,
 Her captive flames must needs burn there;
But when the hand that locked her up, gives room,
  She'll shine through all the sphere.

O Father of eternal life, and all
 Created glories under Thee!
Resume Thy spirit from this world of thrall
  Into true liberty.

Either disperse these mists, which blot and fill
 My perspective still, as they pass;
Or else remove me hence unto that hill
  Where I shall need no glass.

226   THE RETREAT

  HAPPY those early days, when I
  Shined in my Angel-infancy!
  Before I understood this place
  Appointed for my second race,
  Or taught my soul to fancy aught
  But a white, celestial thought;
  When yet I had not walk'd above
  A mile or two from my first Love,
  And looking back, at that short space

Could see a glimpse of his bright face;
When on some gilded cloud or flower
My gazing soul would dwell an hour,
And in those weaker glories spy
Some shadows of eternity;
Before I taught my tongue to wound
My conscience with a sinful sound,
Or had the black art to dispense
A several sin to every sense,
But felt through all this fleshly dress
Bright shoots of everlastingness.

O how I long to travel back,
And tread again that ancient track!
That I might once more reach that plain
Where first I left my glorious train;
From whence th' enlighten'd spirit sees
That shady City of Palm trees!
But ah! my soul with too much stay
Is drunk, and staggers in the way:—
Some men a forward motion love,
But I by backward steps would move;
And when this dust falls to the urn,
In that state I came, return.

FRANCIS BACON, VISCOUNT ST. ALBAN
[1561–1626]

227   ### Life

THE world's a bubble and the life of Man
     Less than a span;
In his conception wretched, from the womb
     So to the tomb;
Curst from his cradle, and brought up to years
     With cares and fears.
Who then to frail mortality shall trust,
But limns on water, or but writes in dust.

Yet whilst with sorrow here we live opprest,
     What life is best?

Courts are but only superficial schools
          To dandle fools:
The rural parts are turn'd into a den
          Of savage men:
And where's a city from foul vice so free,
But may be termed the worst of all the three?

Domestic cares afflict the husband's bed,
          Or pains his head:
Those that live single, take it for a curse
          Or do things worse:
Some would have children: those that have them moan
          Or wish them gone:
What is it, then, to have, or have no wife,
But single thraldom or a double strife?

But our affections still at home to please
          Is a disease:
To cross the seas to any foreign soil,
          Peril and toil:
Wars with their noise affright us: when they cease,
          We are worse in peace;—
What then remains, but that we still should cry
For being born, or being born, to die?

JAMES SHIRLEY

[1596–1666]

228   THE GLORIES OF OUR BLOOD AND STATE

THE glories of our blood and state
          Are shadows, not substantial things;
There is no armour against fate;
          Death lays his icy hand on kings:
                    Sceptre and Crown
                    Must tumble down,
And in the dust be equal made
With the poor crooked scythe and spade.

Some men with swords may reap the field,
  And plant fresh laurels where they kill:
But their strong nerves at last must yield;
  They tame but one another still:
    Early or late
    They stoop to fate,
And must give up their murmuring breath
When they, pale captives, creep to death.

The garlands wither on your brow;
  Then boast no more your mighty deeds;
Upon Death's purple altar now
  See where the victor-victim bleeds:
    Your heads must come
    To the cold tomb;
Only the actions of the just
Smell sweet, and blossom in their dust.

229   THE LAST CONQUEROR

VICTORIOUS men of earth, no more
  Proclaim how wide your empires are;
Though you bind-in every shore
  And your triumphs reach as far
    As night or day,
  Yet you, proud monarchs, must obey
And mingle with forgotten ashes, when
Death calls ye to the crowd of common men.

Devouring Famine, Plague, and War,
  Each able to undo mankind,
Death's servile emissaries are;
  Nor to these alone confined.
    He hath at will
  More quaint and subtle ways to kill;
A smile or kiss, as he will use the art,
Shall have the cunning skill to break a heart.

THOMAS CAREW
[*1595(?)–1639(?)*]

230

THE TRUE BEAUTY

HE that loves a rosy cheek
   Or a coral lip admires,
Or from star-like eyes doth seek
   Fuel to maintain his fires;
As old Time makes these decay,
So his flames must waste away.

But a smooth and steadfast mind,
   Gentle thoughts, and calm desires,
Hearts with equal love combined,
   Kindle never-dying fires:—
Where these are not, I despise
Lovely cheeks or lips or eyes.

231

ASK ME NO MORE

ASK me no more where Jove bestows,
When June is past, the fading rose;
For in your beauty's orient deep
These flowers, as in their causes, sleep.

Ask me no more whither do stray
The golden atoms of the day;
For in pure love did heaven prepare
Those powders to enrich your hair.

Ask me no more whither doth haste
The nightingale when May is past;
For in your sweet dividing throat
She winters and keeps warm her note.

Ask me no more where those stars 'light
That downwards fall in dead of night;
For in your eyes they sit, and there
Fixèd become as in their sphere.

Ask me no more if east or west
The Phœnix builds her spicy nest;
For unto you at last she flies,
And in your fragrant bosom dies.

232   KNOW, CELIA

KNOW, Celia, since thou art so proud,
   'Twas I that gave thee thy renown;
Thou hadst in the forgotten crowd
   Of common beauties lived unknown,
Had not my verse extoll'd thy name,
And with it imp'd the wings of Fame.

That killing power is none of thine:
   I gave it to thy voice and eyes;
Thy sweets, thy graces, all are mine;
   Thou art my star, shin'st in my skies;
Then dart not from thy borrowed sphere
Lightning on him that fixed thee there.

Tempt me with such affrights no more,
   Lest what I made I uncreate;
Let fools thy mystic forms adore,
   I know thee in thy mortal state:
Wise poets, that wrapt Truth in tales,
Knew her themselves through all her veils.

233   GIVE ME MORE LOVE

GIVE me more love, or more disdain;
   The torrid or the frozen zone
Bring equal ease unto my pain;
   The temperate affords me none:
Either extreme, of love or hate,
Is sweeter than a calm estate.

Give me a storm; if it be love—
   Like Danaë in that golden shower,
I'll swim in pleasure; if it prove
   Disdain, that torrent will devour

My vulture hopes; and he's possessed
Of heaven, that's from hell released.
Then crown my joys, or cure my pain;
Give me more love, or more disdain.

SIR JOHN SUCKLING

[*1609–1642*]

234   ### THE CONSTANT LOVER

OUT upon it, I have loved
  Three whole days together!
And am like to love three more,
  If it prove fair weather.

Time shall moult away his wings
  Ere he shall discover
In the whole wide world again
  Such a constant lover.

But the spite on 't is, no praise
  Is due at all to me:
Love with me had made no stays,
  Had it any been but she.

Had it any been but she,
  And that very face,
There had been at least ere this
  A dozen dozen in her place.

235   ### WHY SO PALE AND WAN

WHY so pale and wan, fond lover?
  Prythee, why so pale?
Will, if looking well can't move her,
  Looking ill prevail?
  Prythee, why so pale?

Why so dull and mute, young sinner?
  Prythee, why so mute?

Will, when speaking well can't win her,
   Saying nothing do't?
   Prythee, why so mute?

Quit, quit, for shame! this will not move,
   This cannot take her;
If of herself she will not love,
   Nothing can make her:
   The devil take her!

SIR WILLIAM D'AVENANT
[1606-1668]

236

DAWN SONG

THE lark now leaves his wat'ry nest,
   And climbing shakes his dewy wings.
He takes this window for the East,
   And to implore your light he sings—
Awake, awake! the morn will never rise
Till she can dress her beauty at your eyes.

The merchant bows unto the seaman's star,
   The ploughman from the sun his season takes;
But still the lover wonders what they are
   Who look for day before his mistress wakes.
Awake, awake! break thro' your veils of lawn!
Then draw your curtains, and begin the dawn!

RICHARD LOVELACE
[1618-1658]

237

To LUCASTA, ON GOING TO THE WARS

TELL me not, Sweet, I am unkind
      That from the nunnery
   Of thy chaste breast and quiet mind,
      To war and arms I fly.

True, a new mistress now I chase,
   The first foe in the field;
And with a stronger faith embrace
   A sword, a horse, a shield.

Yet this inconstancy is such
   As you too shall adore;
I could not love thee, Dear, so much,
   Loved I not Honour more.

238

To Althea from Prison

When Love with unconfinèd wings
   Hovers within my gates,
And my divine Althea brings
   To whisper at the grates;
When I lie tangled in her hair
   And fetter'd to her eye,
The birds that wanton in the air
   Know no such liberty.

When flowing cups run swiftly round
   With no allaying Thames,
Our careless heads with roses crown'd,
   Our hearts with loyal flames;
When thirsty grief in wine we steep,
   When healths and draughts go free—
Fishes that tipple in the deep
   Know no such liberty.

When, linnet-like confinèd I
   With shriller throat shall sing
The sweetness, mercy, majesty
   And glories of my King;
When I shall voice aloud how good
   He is, how great should be,
Enlargèd winds, that curl the flood,
   Know no such liberty.

Stone walls do not a prison make,
   Nor iron bars a cage;

Minds innocent and quiet take
That for an hermitage;
If I have freedom in my love
And in my soul am free,
Angels alone, that soar above,
Enjoy such liberty.

239   To Lucasta, Going Beyond the Seas

If to be absent were to be
Away from thee;
Or that when I am gone
You or I were alone;
Then, my Lucasta, might I crave
Pity from blustering wind, or swallowing wave.

But I'll not sigh one blast or gale
To swell my sail,
Or pay a tear to 'suage
The foaming blue god's rage;
For whether he will let me pass
Or no, I'm still as happy as I was.

Though seas and land betwixt us both,
Our faith and troth,
Like separated souls,
All time and space controls:
Above the highest sphere we meet
Unseen, unknown, and greet as Angels greet.

So then we do anticipate
Our after-fate,
And are alive i' the skies,
If thus our lips and eyes
Can speak like spirits unconfined
In Heaven, their earthly bodies left behind.

EDMUND WALLER
[*1606–1687*]

240 ### On a Girdle

THAT which her slender waist confined
Shall now my joyful temples bind;
No monarch but would give his crown
His arms might do what this has done.

It was my Heaven's extremest sphere,
The pale which held that lovely deer:
My joy, my grief, my hope, my love,
Did all within this circle move.

A narrow compass! and yet there
Dwelt all that's good, and all that's fair:
Give me but what this ribband bound,
Take all the rest the Sun goes round.

241 ### Go, Lovely Rose!

Go, lovely Rose!
Tell her, that wastes her time and me,
That now she knows,
When I resemble her to thee,
How sweet and fair she seems to be.

Tell her that's young
And shuns to have her graces spied,
That hadst thou sprung
In deserts, where no men abide,
Thou must have uncommended died.

Small is the worth
Of beauty from the light retired:
Bid her come forth,
Suffer herself to be desired,
And not blush so to be admired.

Then die! that she
The common fate of all things rare
May read in thee:
How small a part of time they share
They are so wondrous sweet and fair!

WILLIAM CARTWRIGHT
[*1611–1643*]

242   ON THE QUEEN'S RETURN FROM THE LOW COUNTRIES

HALLOW the threshold, crown the posts anew!
The day shall have its due.
Twist all our victories into one bright wreath,
On which let honour breathe:
Then throw it round the temples of our Queen!
'Tis she that must preserve those glories green.

When greater tempests than on sea before
Received her on the shore;
When she was shot at 'for the King's own good'
By legions hired to blood;
How bravely did she do, how bravely bear!
And show'd, though they durst rage, she durst not fear.

Courage was cast about her like a dress
Of solemn comeliness:
A gather'd mind and an untroubled face
Did give her dangers grace:
Thus, arm'd with innocence, secure they move
Whose highest 'treason' is but highest love.

JAMES GRAHAM, MARQUIS OF MONTROSE
[*1612–1650*]

243   MY DEAR AND ONLY LOVE

MY dear and only Love, I pray
That little world of thee
Be govern'd by no other sway
Than purest monarchy;

For if confusion have a part
  (Which virtuous souls abhor),
And hold a synod in thine heart,
  I'll never love thee more.

Like Alexander I will reign,
  And I will reign alone;
My thoughts did evermore disdain
  A rival on my throne.
He either fears his fate too much,
  Or his deserts are small,
That dares not put it to the touch,
  To gain or lose it all.

And in the empire of thine heart,
  Where I should solely be,
If others do pretend a part
  Or dare to vie with me,
Or if *Committees* thou erect,
  And go on such a score,
I'll laugh and sing at thy neglect,
  And never love thee more.

But if thou wilt prove faithful then,
  And constant of thy word,
I'll make thee glorious by my pen
  And famous by my sword;
I'll serve thee in such noble ways
  Was never heard before;
I'll crown and deck thee all with bays,
  And love thee more and more.

RICHARD CRASHAW
[*1613(?)–1649*]

244 WISHES FOR THE SUPPOSED MISTRESS

  WHOE'ER she be,
That not impossible She
That shall command my heart and me;

Where'er she lie,
Lock'd up from mortal eye
In shady leaves of destiny:

Till that ripe birth
Of studied Fate stand forth,
And teach her fair steps tread our earth;

Till that divine
Idea take a shrine
Of crystal flesh, through which to shine:

—Meet you her, my Wishes,
Bespeak her to my blisses,
And be ye call'd, my absent kisses.

I wish her Beauty
That owes not all its duty
To gaudy tire, or glist'ring shoe-tie:

Something more than
Taffata or tissue can,
Or rampant feather, or rich fan.

A Face that's best
By its own beauty drest,
And can alone commend the rest:

A Face made up
Out of no other shop
Than what Nature's white hand sets ope.

A Cheek, where youth
And blood, with pen of truth,
Write what the reader sweetly ru'th.

A Cheek, where grows
More than a morning rose,
Which to no box his being owes.

Lips, where all day
A lover's kiss may play,
Yet carry nothing thence away.

Looks, that oppress
Their richest tires, but dress
And clothe their simplest nakedness.

Eyes, that displace
The neighbor diamond, and outface
That sunshine by their own sweet grace.

Tresses, that wear
Jewels but to declare
How much themselves more precious are:

Whose native ray
Can tame the wanton day
Of gems that in their bright shades play.

Each ruby there,
Or pearl that dare appear,
Be its own blush, be its own tear.

A well-tamed Heart,
For whose more noble smart
Love may be long choosing a dart.

Eyes, that bestow
Full quivers on love's bow,
Yet pay less arrows than they owe.

Smiles, that can warm
The blood, yet teach a charm,
That chastity shall take no harm.

Blushes, that bin
The burnish of no sin,
Nor flames of aught too hot within.

Joys, that confess
Virtue their mistress,
And have no other head to dress.

Fears, fond and slight
As the coy bride's, when night
First does the longing lover right.

Days, that need borrow
No part of their good morrow
From a fore-spent night of sorrow:

Days, that in spite
Of darkness, by the light
Of a clear mind are day all night.

Nights, sweet as they
Made short by lovers' play,
Yet long by th' absence of day.

Life, that dares send
A challenge to his end,
And when it comes, say, 'Welcome, friend.'

Sydneian Showers
Of sweet discourse, whose powers
Can crown old Winter's head with flowers.

Soft silken hours,
Open suns, shady bowers;
'Bove all, nothing within that lowers.

Whate'er delight
Can make Day's forehead bright
Or give down to the wings of night.

I wish her store
Of worth may leave her poor
Of wishes; and I wish—no more.

—Now, if Time knows
That Her, whose radiant brows
Weave them a garland of my vows;

Her, whose just bays
My future hopes can raise,
A trophy to her present praise;

Her that dares be
What these lines wish to see:
I seek no further, it is She.

'Tis She, and here
Lo! I unclothe and clear
My Wishes cloudy character.

May she enjoy it
Whose merit dare apply it.
But modesty dares still deny it!

Such worth as this is
Shall fix my flying Wishes,
And determine them to kisses.

Let her full glory,
My fancies, fly before ye;
Be ye my fictions:—but her story.

245   Upon the Book and Picture of the
Seraphical Saint Teresa

Live in these conquering leaves: live all the same;
And walk through all tongues one triumphant flame;
Live here, great heart; and love, and die, and kill:
And bleed, and wound, and yield, and conquer still.
Let this immortal life where'er it comes
Walk in a crowd of loves and martyrdoms.
Let mystic deaths wait on't; and wise souls be
The love-slain witnesses of this life of thee.
O sweet incendiary! show here thy art
Upon this carcase of a hard cold heart;
Let all thy scatter'd shafts of light, that play

Among the leaves of thy large books of day,
Combin'd against this breast at once break in,
And take away from me myself and sin;
This gracious robbery shall thy bounty be
And my best fortunes such fair spoils of me.
O thou undaunted daughter of desires!
By all thy dower of lights and fires;
By all the eagle in thee, all the dove;
By all thy lives and deaths of love;
By thy large draughts of intellectual day,
And by thy thirsts of love more large than they;
By all thy brim-filled bowls of fierce desire,
By thy last morning's draught of liquid fire;
By the full kingdom of that final kiss
That seized thy parting soul, and sealed thee His;
By all the Heav'n thou hast in Him
(Fair sister of the seraphim!);
By all of Him we have in thee;
Leave nothing of myself in me.
Let me so read thy life, that I
Unto all life of mine may die!

THOMAS JORDAN
[1612(?)–1685]

246   LET US DRINK AND BE MERRY

LET us drink and be merry, dance, joke, and rejoice,
With claret and sherry, theorbo and voice!
The changeable world to our joy is unjust,
      All treasure's uncertain,
      Then down with your dust!
In frolics dispose your pounds, shillings, and pence,
For we shall be nothing a hundred years hence.

We'll sport and be free with Moll, Betty, and Dolly,
Have oysters and lobsters to cure melancholy:
Fish-dinners will make a man spring like a flea,
      Dame Venus, love's lady,
      Was born of the sea:
With her and with Bacchus we'll tickle the sense,
For we shall be past it a hundred years hence.

Your most beautiful bride who with garlands is crown'd
And kills with each glance as she treads on the ground.
Whose lightness and brightness doth shine in such splendour
    That one but the stars
    Are thought fit to attend her,
Though now she be pleasant and sweet to the sense,
Will be damnable mouldy a hundred years hence.

Then why should we turmoil in cares and in fears,
Turn all our tranquill'ty to sighs and to tears?
Let's eat, drink, and play till the worms do corrupt us,
    'Tis certain, *Post mortem*
    Nulla voluptas.
For health, wealth and beauty, wit, learning and sense,
Must all come to nothing a hundred years hence.

ABRAHAM COWLEY

[*1618–1667*]

247

A Supplication

    Awake, awake, my Lyre!
And tell thy silent master's humble tale
    In sounds that may prevail;
  Sounds that gentle thoughts inspire:
    Though so exalted she
    And I so lowly be
Tell her, such different notes make all thy harmony.

    Hark, how the strings awake:
And, though the moving hand approach not near,
    Themselves with awful fear
  A kind of numerous trembling make.
    Now all thy forces try;
    Now all thy charms apply;
Revenge upon her ear the conquests of her eye.

    Weak Lyre! thy virtue sure
Is useless here, since thou art only found
    To cure, but not to wound,
  And she to wound, but not to cure.

Too weak too wilt thou prove
My passion to remove;
Physic to other ills, thou'rt nourishment to love.

Sleep, sleep again, my Lyre!
For thou canst never tell my humble tale
In sounds that will prevail,
Nor gentle thoughts in her inspire;
All thy vain mirth lay by,
Bid thy strings silent lie,
Sleep, sleep again, my Lyre, and let thy master die.

248   CHEER UP, MY MATES

(Sitting and drinking in the chair made out of the relics of Sir Francis Drake's ship.)

CHEER up, my mates, the wind does fairly blow;
Clap on more sail, and never spare;
Farewell, all lands, for now we are
In the wide sea of drink, and merrily we go.
Bless me, 'tis hot! another bowl of wine,
And we shall cut the burning Line:
Hey, boys! she scuds away, and by my head I know
We round the world are sailing now.
What dull men are those who tarry at home,
When abroad they might wantonly roam,
And gain such experience, and spy, too,
Such countries and wonders, as I do!
But pr'ythee, good pilot, take heed what you do,
And fail not to touch at Peru!
With gold there the vessel we'll store,
And never, and never be poor,
No, never be poor any more.

249   DRINKING

THE thirsty earth soaks up the rain,
And drinks and gapes for drink again;
The plants suck in the earth, and are
With constant drinking fresh and fair;
The sea itself (which one would think

Should have but little need of drink)
Drinks twice ten thousand rivers up,
So fill'd that they o'erflow the cup.
The busy Sun (and one would guess
By 's drunken fiery face no less)
Drinks up the sea, and when he 's done,
The Moon and Stars drink up the Sun:
They drink and dance by their own light,
They drink and revel all the night:
Nothing in Nature's sober found,
But an eternal health goes round.
Fill up the bowl, then, fill it high,
Fill all the glasses there—for why
Should every creature drink but I?
Why, man of morals, tell me why?

250   ON THE DEATH OF MR. WILLIAM HERVEY

IT was a dismal and a fearful night:
Scarce could the Morn drive on th' unwilling Light,
When Sleep, Death's image, left my troubled breast
    By something liker Death possest.
My eyes with tears did uncommanded flow,
      And on my soul hung the dull weight
      Of some intolerable fate.
What bell was that? Ah me! too much I know!

My sweet companion and my gentle peer,
Why hast thou left me thus unkindly here,
Thy end for ever and my life to moan?
    O, thou hast left me all alone!
Thy soul and body, when death's agony
      Besieged around thy noble heart,
      Did not with more reluctance part
Than I, my dearest Friend, do part from thee.

My dearest Friend, would I had died for thee!
Life and this world henceforth will tedious be:
Nor shall I know hereafter what to do
    If once my griefs prove tedious too.
Silent and sad I walk about all day,

As sullen ghosts stalk speechless by
Where their hid treasures lie;
Alas! my treasure's gone; why do I stay?

Say, for you saw us, ye immortal lights,
How oft unwearied have we spent the nights,
Till the Ledæan stars, so famed for love,
        Wonder'd at us from above!
We spent them not in toys, in lusts, or wine;
        But search of deep Philosophy,
        Wit, Eloquence, and Poetry—
Arts which I loved, for they, my Friend, were thine.

Ye fields of Cambridge, our dear Cambridge, say
Have ye not seen us walking every day?
Was there a tree about which did not know
        The love betwixt us two?
Henceforth, ye gentle trees, for ever fade;
        Or your sad branches thicker join
        And into darksome shades combine,
Dark as the grave wherein my Friend is laid!

Large was his soul: as large a soul as e'er
Submitted to inform a body here;
High as the place 'twas shortly in Heaven to have.
        But low and humble as his grave.
So high that all the virtues there did come,
        As to their chiefest seat
        Conspicuous and great;
So low, that for me too it made a room.

Knowledge he only sought, and so soon caught
As if for him Knowledge had rather sought;
Nor did more learning ever crowded lie
        In such a short mortality.
Whene'er the skilful youth discoursed or writ,
        Still did the notions throng
        About his eloquent tongue;
Nor could his ink flow faster than his wit.

His mirth was the pure spirits of various wit,
Yet never did his God or friends forget;
And when deep talk and wisdom came in view,
    Retired, and gave to them their due.
For the rich help of books he always took,
    Though his own searching mind before
    Was so with notions written o'er,
As if wise Nature had made that her book.

With as much zeal, devotion, piety,
He always lived, as other saints do die.
Still with his soul severe account he kept,
    Weeping all debts out ere he slept.
Then down in peace and innocence he lay,
    Like the Sun's laborious light,
    Which still in water sets at night,
Unsullied with his journey of the day.

But happy Thou, ta'en from this frantic age,
Where ignorance and hypocrisy does rage!
A fitter time for Heaven no soul e'er chose—
    The place now only free from those.
There 'mong the blest thou dost for ever shine;
    And whereso'er thou casts thy view
    Upon that white and radiant crew,
See'st not a soul clothed with more light than thine.

ALEXANDER BROME
[1620–1666]

THE RESOLVE

251

TELL me not of a face that's fair,
    Nor lip and cheek that's red,
Nor of the tresses of her hair,
    Nor curls in order laid,
Nor of a rare seraphic voice
    That like an angel sings;
Though if I were to take my choice
    I would have all these things:
But if that thou wilt have me love,

And it must be a she,
The only argument can move
Is that she will love me.

The glories of your ladies be
But metaphors of things,
And but resemble what we see
Each common object brings.
Roses out-red their lips and cheeks,
Lilies their whiteness stain;
What fool is he that shadows seeks
And may the substance gain?
Then if thou'lt have me love a lass,
Let it be one that's kind:
Else I'm a servant to the glass
That's with Canary lined.

ANDREW MARVELL
[*1621–1678*]

252

A GARDEN

Written after the Civil Wars

SEE how the flowers, as at parade,
Under their colours stand display'd:
Each regiment in order grows,
That of the tulip, pink, and rose.
But when the vigilant patrol
Of stars walks round about the pole,
Their leaves, that to the stalks are curl'd,
Seem to their staves the ensigns furl'd.
Then in some flower's belovèd hut
Each bee, as sentinel, is shut,
And sleeps so too; but if once stirr'd,
She runs you through, nor asks the word.
O thou, that dear and happy Isle,
The garden of the world erewhile,
Thou Paradise of the four seas
Which Heaven planted us to please,

But, to exclude the world, did guard
With wat'ry if not flaming sword;
What luckless apple did we taste
To make us mortal and thee waste!
Unhappy! shall we never more
That sweet militia restore,
When gardens only had their towers,
And all the garrisons were flowers;
When roses only arms might bear,
And men did rosy garlands wear?

253   THE PICTURE OF LITTLE T. C. IN A PROSPECT
                     OF FLOWERS

SEE with what simplicity
This nymph begins her golden days!
In the green grass she loves to lie,
And there with her fair aspect tames
The wilder flowers, and gives them names;
But only with the roses plays,
                    And them does tell
What colour best becomes them, and what smell.

Who can foretell for what high cause
This darling of the gods was born?
Yet this is she whose chaster laws
The wanton Love shall one day fear,
And, under her command severe,
See his bow broke and ensigns torn.
                    Happy who can
Appease this virtuous enemy of man!

O then let me in time compound
And parley with those conquering eyes,
Ere they have tried their force to wound;
Ere with their glancing wheels they drive
In triumph over hearts that strive,
And them that yield but more despise:
                    Let me be laid,
Where I may see the glories from some shade.

Meantime, whilst every verdant thing
Itself does at thy beauty charm,
Reform the errors of the Spring;
Make that the tulips may have share
Of sweetness, seeing they are fair,
And roses of their thorns disarm;
But most procure
That violets may a longer age endure.

But O, young beauty of the woods,
Whom Nature courts with fruits and flowers,
Gather the flowers, but spare the buds;
Lest Flora, angry at thy crime
To kill her infants in their prime,
Do quickly make th' example yours;
And ere we see,
Nip in the blossom all our hopes and thee.

254   HORATIAN ODE UPON CROMWELL'S RETURN
FROM IRELAND

THE forward youth that would appear,
Must now forsake his Muses dear,
Nor in the shadows sing
His numbers languishing.

'Tis time to leave the books in dust,
And oil the unused armour's rust,
Removing from the wall
The corslet of the hall.

So restless Cromwell could not cease
In the inglorious arts of peace,
But through adventurous war
Urgèd his active star:

And like the three-fork'd lightning, first
Breaking the clouds where it was nurst,
Did thorough his own side
His fiery way divide:

For 'tis all one to courage high,
The emulous, or enemy;
 And with such, to enclose
 Is more than to oppose;

Then burning through the air he went
And palaces and temples rent;
 And Cæsar's head at last
 Did through his laurels blast.

'Tis madness to resist or blame
The face of angry heaven's flame:
 And if we would speak true,
 Much to the Man is due

Who, from his private gardens, where
He lived reservèd and austere,
 (As if his highest plot
 To plant the bergamot),

Could by industrious valour climb
To ruin the great work of time,
 And cast the Kingdoms old
 Into another mould.

Though Justice against Fate complain,
And plead the ancient Rights in vain—
 But those do hold or break
 As men are strong or weak,

Nature, that hateth emptiness,
Allows of penetration less,
 And therefore must make room
 Where greater spirits come.

What field of all the civil war
Where his were not the deepest scar?
 And Hampton shows what part
 He had of wiser art,

Where, twining subtle fears with hope,
He wove a net of such a scope
    That Charles himself might chase
    To Carisbrook's narrow case,

That thence the Royal actor borne
The tragic scaffold might adorn:
    While round the armèd bands
    Did clap their bloody hands.

He nothing common did or mean
Upon that memorable scene,
    But with his keener eye
    The axe's edge did try;

Nor call'd the Gods, with vulgar spite,
To vindicate his helpless right
    But bow'd his comely head
    Down, as upon a bed.

—This was that memorable hour
Which first assured the forcèd power:
    So when they did design
    The Capitol's first line,

A Bleeding Head, where they begun,
Did fright the architects to run;
    And yet in that the State
    Foresaw its happy fate!

And now the Irish are ashamed
To see themselves in one year tamed:
    So much one man can do
    That does both act and know.

They can affirm his praises best,
And have, though overcome, confest
    How good he is, how just
    And fit for highest trust;

Nor yet grown stiffer with command,
But still in the Republic's hand—
 How fit he is to sway
 That can so well obey!

He to the Commons' feet presents
A Kingdom for his first year's rents,
 And (what he may) forbears
 His fame, to make it theirs:

And has his sword and spoils ungirt
To lay them at the Public's skirt.
 So when the falcon high
 Falls heavy from the sky,

She, having kill'd, no more does search
But on the next green bough to perch,
 Where, when he first does lure,
 The falconer has her sure.

—What may not then our Isle presume
While victory his crest does plume?
 What may not others fear
 If thus he crowns each year?

As Cæsar he, ere long, to Gaul,
To Italy an Hannibal,
 And to all States not free
 Shall climacteric be.

The Pict no shelter now shall find
Within his parti-colour'd mind,
 But from this valour sad,
 Shrink underneath the plaid—

Happy, if in the tufted brake
The English hunter him mistake,
 Nor lay his hounds in near
 The Caledonian deer.

But Thou, the War's and Fortune's son,
March indefatigably on;
    And for the last effect
    Still keep the sword erect:

Besides the force it has to fright
The spirits of the shady night,
    The same arts that did gain
    A power, must it maintain.

255   Song of the Emigrants in Bermuda

Where the remote Bermudas ride
In the ocean's bosom unespied,
From a small boat that row'd along
The listening winds received this song:

  'What should we do but sing His praise
That led us through the watery maze
Where He the huge sea-monsters wracks,
That lift the deep upon their backs,
Unto an isle so long unknown,
And yet far kinder than our own?
He lands us on a grassy stage,
Safe from the storms, and prelate's rage:
He gave us this eternal spring
Which here enamels everything,
And sends the fowls to us in care
On daily visits through the air.
He hangs in shades the orange bright
Like golden lamps in a green night,
And does in the pomegranates close
Jewels more rich than Ormus shows:
He makes the figs our mouths to meet
And throws the melons at our feet;
But apples plants of such a price,
No tree could ever bear them twice.
With cedars chosen by his hand
From Lebanon he stores the land;
And makes the hollow seas that roar
Proclaim the ambergris on shore.

He cast (of which we rather boast)
The Gospel's pearl upon our coast;
And in these rocks for us did frame
A temple where to sound His name.
Oh! let our voice His praise exalt
Till it arrive at Heaven's vault,
Which then perhaps rebounding may
Echo beyond the Mexique bay!'
—Thus sung they in the English boat
A holy and a cheerful note:
And all the way, to guide their chime,
With falling oars they kept the time.

256   THOUGHTS IN A GARDEN

How vainly men themselves amaze
To win the palm, the oak, or bays,
And their incessant labours see
Crown'd from some single herb or tree,
Whose short and narrow-vergéd shade
Does prudently their toils upbraid;
While all the flowers and trees do close
To weave the garlands of Repose.

Fair Quiet, have I found thee here,
And Innocence thy sister dear?
Mistaken long, I sought you then
In busy companies of men:
Your sacred plants, if here below,
Only among the plants will grow:
Society is all but rude
To this delicious solitude.

No white nor red was ever seen
So amorous as this lovely green.
Fond lovers, cruel as their flame,
Cut in these trees their mistress' name:
Little, alas, they know or heed
How far these beauties her exceed!
Fair trees! where'er your barks I wound,
No name shall but your own be found.

When we have run our passions' heat
Love hither makes his best retreat:
The gods, who mortal beauty chase,
Still in a tree did end their race;
Apollo hunted Daphne so
Only that she might laurel grow;
And Pan did after Syrinx speed
Not as a nymph, but for a reed.

What wondrous life is this I lead!
Ripe apples drop about my head;
The luscious clusters of the vine
Upon my mouth do crush their wine;
The nectarine and curious peach
Into my hands themselves do reach;
Stumbling on melons, as I pass,
Ensnared with flowers, I fall on grass.

Meanwhile the mind from pleasure less
Withdraws into its happiness;
The mind, that ocean where each kind
Does straight its own resemblance find;
Yet it creates, transcending these,
Far other worlds, and other seas;
Annihilating all that's made
To a green thought in a green shade.

Here at the fountain's sliding foot
Or at some fruit-tree's mossy root,
Casting the body's vest aside
My soul into the boughs does glide;
There, like a bird, it sits and sings,
Then whets and claps its silver wings,
And, till prepared for longer flight,
Waves in its plumes the various light.

Such was that happy Garden-state
While man there walk'd without a mate:
After a place so pure and sweet,
What other help could yet be meet!

But 'twas beyond a mortal's share
To wander solitary there:
Two paradises 'twere in one,
To live in Paradise alone.

How well the skilful gardener drew
Of flowers and herbs this dial new!
Where, from above, the milder sun
Does through a fragrant zodiac run:
And, as it works, th' industrious bee
Computes its time as well as we.
How could such sweet and wholesome hours
Be reckon'd, but with herbs and flowers!

ANONYMOUS

Love Will Find Out the Way

257

Over the mountains
And over the waves,
Under the fountains
And under the graves;
Under floods that are deepest,
Which Neptune obey;
Over rocks that are steepest
Love will find out the way.

Where there is no place
For the glow-worm to lie;
Where there is no space
For receipt of a fly;
Where the midge dares not venture
Lest herself fast she lay;
If love come, he will enter
And soon find out his way.

You may esteem him
A child for his might;
Or you may deem him
A coward from his flight;
But if she whom love doth honour

Be conceal'd from the day,
Set a thousand guards upon her,
Love will find out the way.

Some think to lose him
By having him confined;
And some do suppose him,
Poor thing, to be blind;
But if ne'er so close ye wall him,
Do the best that you may,
Blind love, if so ye call him,
Will find out his way.

You may train the eagle
To stoop to your fist;
Or you may inveigle
The phoenix of the east;
The lioness, ye may move her
To give o'er her prey;
But you'll ne'er stop a lover:
He will find out his way.

258   PHILLADA FLOUTS ME

O WHAT a plague is love!
    How shall I bear it?
She will inconstant prove,
    I greatly fear it.
She so torments my mind
    That my strength faileth,
And wavers with the wind
    As a ship saileth.
Please her the best I may,
She loves still to gainsay;
Alack and well-a-day!
    Phillada flouts me.

At the fair yesterday
    She did pass by me;
She look'd another way
    And would not spy me:

I woo'd her for to dine,
　But could not get her;
Will had her to the wine—
　He might entreat her.
With Daniel she did dance,
On me she look'd askance:
O thrice unhappy chance!
　Phillada flouts me.

Fair maid, be not so coy,
　Do not disdain me!
I am my mother's joy:
　Sweet, entertain me!
She'll give me, when she dies,
　All that is fitting:
Her poultry and her bees,
　And her goose sitting,
A pair of mattrass beds,
And a bag full of shreds;
And yet, for all this guedes,
　Phillada flouts me.

She hath a clout of mine
　Wrought with blue coventry,
Which she keeps for a sign
　Of my fidelity:
But i' faith, if she flinch
　She shall not wear it;
To Tib, my t'other wench,
　I mean to bear it.
And yet it grieves my heart
So soon from her to part:
Death strike me with his dart!
　Phillada flouts me.

Thou shalt eat crudded cream
　All the year lasting,
And drink the crystal stream
　Pleasant in tasting;
Whig and whey whilst thou lust,

And bramble-berries,
Pie-lid and pastry-crust,
   Pears, plums, and cherries.
Thy raiment shall be thin,
Made of a weevil's skin—
Yet all's not worth a pin!
   Phillada flouts me.

In the last month of May
   I made her posies;
I heard her often say
   That she loved roses.
Cowslips and gillyflowers
   And the white lily
I brought to deck the bowers
   For my sweet Philly.
But she did all disdain,
And threw them back again;
Therefore 'tis flat and plain
   Phillada flouts me.

Fair maiden, have a care,
   And in time take me;
I can have those as fair
   If you forsake me:
For Doll the dairy-maid
   Laugh'd at me lately,
And wanton Winifred
   Favours me greatly.
One throws milk on my clothes,
T'other plays with my nose;
What wanting signs are those?
   Phillada flouts me.

I cannot work nor sleep
   At all in season:
Love wounds my heart so deep
   Without all reason.
I 'gin to pine away
   In my love's shadow,

Like as a fat beast may,
 Penn'd in a meadow.
I shall be dead, I fear,
Within this thousand year:
And all for that my dear
 Phillada flouts me.

EARL OF ROCHESTER
[1647-1680]

259

EPITAPH ON CHARLES II

HERE lies our Sovereign Lord the King,
 Whose word no man relies on,
Who never said a foolish thing,
 Nor ever did a wise one.

SIR CHARLES SEDLEY
[1639(?)-1701]

260

CHLORIS

AH, Chloris! could I now but sit
 As unconcern'd as when
Your infant beauty could beget
 No happiness or pain!
When I the dawn used to admire,
 And praised the coming day,
I little thought the rising fire
 Would take my rest away.

Your charms in harmless childhood lay
 Like metals in a mine;
Age from no face takes more away
  Than youth conceal'd in thine.
But as your charms insensibly
 To their perfection prest,
So love as unperceived did fly,
 And center'd in my breast.

My passion with your beauty grew,
   While Cupid at my heart
Still as his mother favour'd you
   Threw a new flaming dart:
Each gloried in their wanton part;
   To make a lover, he
Employ'd the utmost of his art—
   To make a beauty, she.

261   CELIA

Not, Celia, that I juster am
   Or better than the rest;
For I would change each hour, like them,
   Were not my heart at rest.

But I am tied to very thee
   By every thought I have;
Thy face I only care to see,
   Thy heart I only crave.

All that in woman is adored
   In thy dear self I find—
For the whole sex can but afford
   The handsome and the kind.

Why then should I seek further store,
   And still make love anew?
When change itself can give no more,
   'Tis easy to be true.

JOHN DRYDEN
[1631–1700]

262   ODE

To the Pious Memory of the accomplished young lady, Mrs. Anne
Killigrew, excellent in the two sister arts of Poesy and Painting

   Thou youngest virgin-daughter of the skies,
   Made in the last promotion of the blest;
   Whose palms, new pluck'd from Paradise,

In spreading branches more sublimely rise,
   Rich with immortal green above the rest:
Whether, adopted to some neighbouring star,
Thou roll'st above us, in thy wandering race,
   Or, in procession fix'd and regular,
   Moved with the heaven's majestic pace;
   Or, call'd to more superior bliss,
Thou tread'st with seraphims the vast abyss:
Whatever happy region be thy place,
Cease thy celestial song a little space;
Thou wilt have time enough for hymns divine,
   Since Heaven's eternal year is thine.
Hear, then, a mortal Muse thy praise rehearse,
     In no ignoble verse;
But such as thy own voice did practise here,
When thy first-fruits of Poesy were given,
To make thyself a welcome inmate there;
   While yet a young probationer,
     And candidate of heaven.

   If by traduction came thy mind,
   Our wonder is the less, to find
A soul so charming from a stock so good;
Thy father was transfused into thy blood:
So wert thou born into a tuneful strain,
An early, rich, and inexhausted vein.
   But if thy pre-existing soul
   Was form'd at first with myriads more,
It did through all the mighty poets roll
   Who Greek or Latin laurels wore,
And was that Sappho last, which once it was before.
   If so, then cease thy flight, O heaven-born mind!
Thou hast no dross to purge from thy rich ore:
   Nor can thy soul a fairer mansion find,
   Than was the beauteous frame she left behind:
Return, to fill or mend the quire of thy celestial kind.

   May we presume to say, that, at thy birth,
New joy was sprung in heaven as well as here on
     earth?

For sure the milder planets did combine
On thy auspicious horoscope to shine,
And even the most malicious were in trine.
Thy brother-angels at thy birth
Strung each his lyre, and tuned it high,
That all the people of the sky
Might know a poetess was born on earth;
And then, if ever, mortal ears
Had heard the music of the spheres.
And if no clustering swarm of bees
On thy sweet mouth distill'd their golden dew,
'Twas that such vulgar miraclès
Heaven had not leisure to renew:
For all the blest fraternity of love
Solemnized there thy birth, and kept thy holiday above.

O gracious God! how far have we
Profaned thy heavenly gift of Poesy!
Made prostitute and profligate the Muse,
Debased to each obscene and impious use,
Whose harmony was first ordain'd above,
For tongues of angels and for hymns of love!
O wretched we! why were we hurried down
This lubrique and adulterate age
(Nay, added fat pollutions of our own),
To increase the streaming ordures of the stage?
What can we say to excuse our second fall?
Let this thy Vestal, Heaven, atone for all!
Her Arethusian stream remains unsoil'd,
Unmix'd with foreign filth, and undefiled;
Her wit was more than man, her innocence a child.

Art she had none, yet wanted none,
For Nature did that want supply:
So rich in treasures of her own,
She might our boasted stores defy:
Such noble vigour did her verse adorn,
That it seem'd borrow'd, where 'twas only born.
Her morals, too, were in her bosom bred,
By great examples daily fed,

What in the best of books, her father's life, she read.
   And to be read herself she need not fear;
   Each test, and every light, her Muse will bear,
   Though Epictetus with his lamp were there.
   Even love (for love sometimes her Muse exprest)
Was but a lambent flame which play'd about her breast,
     Light as the vapours of a morning dream;
   So cold herself, whilst she such warmth exprest,
     'Twas Cupid bathing in Diana's stream. . . .

     Now all those charms, that blooming grace,
   The well-proportion'd shape, and beauteous face,
   Shall never more be seen by mortal eyes;
   In earth the much-lamented virgin lies.
   Not wit, nor piety could fate prevent;
   Nor was the cruel destiny content
   To finish all the murder at a blow,
   To sweep at once her life and beauty too;
   But, like a harden'd felon, took a pride
     To work more mischievously slow,
     And plunder'd first, and then destroy'd.
O double sacrilege on things divine,
     To rob the relic, and deface the shrine!
       But thus Orinda died:
     Heaven, by the same disease did both translate;
   As equal were their souls, so equal was their fate.

     Meantime, her warlike brother on the seas
   His waving streamers to the winds displays,
And vows for his return, with vain devotion, pays.
     Ah, generous youth! that wish forbear,
     The winds too soon will waft thee here!
     Slack all thy sails, and fear to come,
Alas! thou know'st not, thou art wreck'd at home!
   No more shalt thou behold thy sister's face,
   Thou hast already had her last embrace.
   But look aloft, and if thou kenn'st from far,
   Among the Pleiads a new kindled star,
   If any sparkles than the rest more bright,
   'Tis she that shines in that propitious light.

When in mid-air the golden trump shall sound,
  To raise the nations under ground;
When, in the Valley of Jehoshaphat,
The judging God shall close the book of Fate,
  And there the last assizes keep
  For those who wake and those who sleep;
  When rattling bones together fly
  From the four corners of the sky;
When sinews o'er the skeletons are spread,
Those clothed with flesh, and life inspires the dead;
The sacred poets first shall hear the sound,
  And foremost from the tomb shall bound,
For they are cover'd with the lightest ground;
And straight, with inborn vigour, on the wing,
Like mounting larks, to the new morning sing.
There thou, sweet Saint, before the quire shall go,
As harbinger of Heaven, the way to show,
The way which thou so well hast learn'd below.

263   Song to a Fair Young Lady, going out of the
Town in the Spring

  Ask not the cause why sullen Spring
    So long delays her flowers to bear;
  Why warbling birds forget to sing,
    And winter storms invert the year:
  Chloris is gone; and fate provides
  To make it Spring where she resides.

  Chloris is gone, the cruel fair;
    She cast not back a pitying eye:
  But left her lover in despair
    To sigh, to languish, and to die:
  Ah! how can those fair eyes endure
  To give the wounds they will not cure?

  Great God of Love, why hast thou made
    A face that can all hearts command,
  That all religions can invade,
    And change the laws of every land?
  Where thou hadst placed such power before,
    Thou shouldst have made her mercy more.

When Chloris to the temple comes,
   Adoring crowds before her fall;
She can restore the dead from tombs
   And every life but mine recall.
I only am by Love design'd
To be the victim for mankind.

264
       SONG FOR ST. CECILIA'S DAY
            [*1687*]

FROM Harmony, from heavenly Harmony
   This universal frame began:
  When Nature underneath a heap
   Of jarring atoms lay
 And could not heave her head,
The tuneful voice was heard from high,
  'Arise, ye more than dead!'
Then cold, and hot, and moist, and dry
In order to their stations leap,
   And Music's power obey.

From harmony, from heavenly harmony
   This universal frame began:
   From harmony to harmony
Through all the compass of the notes it ran,
The diapason closing full in Man.

What passion cannot Music raise and quell?
   When Jubal struck the chorded shell
  His listening brethren stood around,
   And, wondering, on their faces fell
  To worship that celestial sound.
Less than a god they thought there could not dwell
   Within the hollow of that shell
   That spoke so sweetly and so well.
What passion cannot Music raise and quell?

   The trumpet's loud clangor
     Excites us to arms,
   With shrill notes of anger
     And mortal alarms.

The double double double beat
  Of the thundering drum
  Cries 'Hark! the foes come;
Charge, charge, 'tis too late to retreat!'

The soft complaining flute
  In dying notes discovers
  The woes of hopeless lovers,
Whose dirge is whisper'd by the warbling lute.

Sharp violins proclaim
Their jealous pangs and desperation,
Fury, frantic indignation,
Depth of pains, and height of passion
  For the fair disdainful dame.

But oh! what art can teach,
What human voice can reach
  The sacred organ's praise?
Notes inspiring holy love,
Notes that wing their heavenly ways
  To mend the choirs above.

Orpheus could lead the savage race,
And trees unrooted left their place
  Sequacious of the lyre:
But bright Cecilia raised the wonder higher;
When to her Organ vocal breath was given
An Angel heard, and straight appear'd—
  Mistaking Earth for Heaven.

Grand Chorus

As from the power of sacred lays
  The spheres began to move,
And sung the great Creator's praise
  To all the blest above;
So when the last and dreadful hour
This crumbling pageant shall devour,
The trumpet shall be heard on high,
The dead shall live, the living die,
And Music shall untune the sky.

265   ALEXANDER'S FEAST

OR THE POWER OF MUSIC; AN ODE IN HONOR

OF ST. CECILIA'S DAY

I

'T WAS at the royal feast, for Persia won
  By Philip's warlike son:
  Aloft in awful state
  The godlike hero sate
  On his imperial throne:
  His valiant peers were plac'd around;
  Their brows with roses and with myrtles bound:
  (So should desert in arms be crown'd.)
  The lovely Thais, by his side,
  Sate like a blooming Eastern bride
  In flow'r of youth and beauty's pride.
  Happy, happy, happy pair!
  None but the brave,
  None but the brave,
  None but the brave deserves the fair!

              CHORUS

  Happy, happy, happy pair!
  None but the brave,
  None but the brave,
  None but the brave deserves the fair!

II

    Timotheus, plac'd on high
  Amid the tuneful choir,
  With flying fingers touch'd the lyre:
  The trembling notes ascend the sky,
  And heav'nly joys inspire.
  The song began from Jove,
  Who left his blissful seats above,
  Such is the pow'r of mighty love.
  A dragon's fiery form belied the god:
  Sublime on radiant spires he rode,
  When he to fair Olympia press'd;

And while he sought her snowy breast:
Then, round her slender waist he curl'd,
And stamp'd an image of himself, a sov'reign of the
    world.
The list'ning crowd admire the lofty sound;
"A present deity," they shout around;
"A present deity," the vaulted roofs rebound:
With ravish'd ears
The monarch hears,
Assumes the god,
Affects to nod,
And seems to shake the spheres.

CHORUS

With ravish'd ears
The monarch hears,
Assumes the god,
Affects to nod,
And seems to shake the spheres.

III

The praise of Bacchus then the sweet musician
    sung,
Of Bacchus ever fair and ever young:
The jolly god in triumph comes;
Sound the trumpets; beat the drums;
Flush'd with a purple grace
He shews his honest face:
Now give the hautboys breath; he comes, he comes.
Bacchus, ever fair and young,
Drinking joys did first ordain;
Bacchus' blessings are a treasure,
Drinking is the soldier's pleasure:
Rich the treasure,
Sweet the pleasure,
Sweet is pleasure after pain.

CHORUS

Bacchus' blessings are a treasure,
Drinking is the soldier's pleasure:

Rich the treasure,
Sweet the pleasure,
Sweet is pleasure after pain.

IV

Sooth'd with the sound, the king grew vain;
Fought all his battles o'er again;
And thrice he routed all his foes; and thrice he
    slew the slain.
The master saw the madness rise;
His glowing cheeks, his ardent eyes;
And, while he heav'n and earth defied,
Chang'd his hand, and check'd his pride.
He chose a mournful Muse,
Soft pity to infuse.
He sung Darius great and good,
By too severe a fate,
Fallen, fallen, fallen, fallen,
Fallen from his high estate,
And welt'ring in his blood;
Deserted, at his utmost need,
By those his former bounty fed;
On the bare earth expos'd he lies,
With not a friend to close his eyes.

—With downcast looks the joyless victor sate,
Revolving in his alter'd soul
The various turns of chance below;
And, now and then, a sigh he stole;
And tears began to flow.

Chorus

Revolving in his alter'd soul
The various turns of chance below;
And, now and then, a sigh he stole;
And tears began to flow.

V

The mighty master smil'd, to see
That love was in the next degree:

'T was but a kindred-sound to move,
For pity melts the mind to love.
Softly sweet, in Lydian measures,
Soon he sooth'd his soul to pleasures.
"War," he sung, "is toil and trouble;
Honor, but an empty bubble;
Never ending, still beginning,
Fighting still, and still destroying:
If the world be worth thy winning,
Think, O think it worth enjoying;
Lovely Thais sits beside thee,
Take the good the gods provide thee."

—The many rend the skies with loud applause;
So love was crown'd, but Music won the cause.
The prince, unable to conceal his pain,
Gaz'd on the fair
Who caus'd his care,
And sigh'd and look'd, sigh'd and look'd,
Sigh'd and look'd, and sigh'd again:
At length, with love and wine at once oppress'd,
The vanquish'd victor sunk upon her breast.

Chorus

The prince, unable to conceal his pain,
Gaz'd on the fair
Who caus'd his care,
And sigh'd and look'd, sigh'd and look'd,
Sigh'd and look'd, and sigh'd again:
At length, with love and wine at once oppress'd,
The vanquish'd victor sunk upon her breast.

VI

Now strike the golden lyre again:
A louder yet, and yet a louder strain.
Break his bands of sleep asunder,
And rouse him, like a rattling peal of thunder.
Hark, hark, the horrid sound
Has rais'd up his head:

As awak'd from the dead,
And amaz'd, he stares around.
"Revenge, revenge!" Timotheus cries,
"See the Furies arise!
See the snakes that they rear,
How they hiss in their hair,
And the sparkles that flash from their eyes!
Behold a ghastly band,
Each a torch in his hand!
Those are Grecian ghosts, that in battle were slain,
And unburied remain
Inglorious on the plain:
Give the vengeance due
To the valiant crew.
Behold how they toss their torches on high,
How they point to the Persian abodes,
And glitt'ring temples of their hostile gods!"
—The princes applaud, with a furious joy;
And the king seiz'd a flambeau with zeal to destroy;
Thais led the way,
To light him to his prey,
And, like another Helen, fir'd another Troy.

Chorus

And the king seiz'd a flambeau with zeal to destroy;
Thais led the way,
To light him to his prey,
And, like another Helen, fir'd another Troy.

VII

—Thus, long ago,
Ere heaving bellows learn'd to blow,
While organs yet were mute;
Timotheus, to his breathing flute,
And sounding lyre,
Could swell the soul to rage, or kindle soft desire.
At last, divine Cecilia came,
Inventress of the vocal frame;
The sweet enthusiast, from her sacred store,

Enlarg'd the former narrow bounds,
And added length to solemn sounds,
With nature's mother wit, and arts unknown before.
Let old Timotheus yield the prize,
Or both divide the crown;
He rais'd a mortal to the skies;
She drew an angel down.

Grand Chorus

At last, divine Cecilia came,
Inventress of the vocal frame;
The sweet enthusiast, from her sacred store,
Enlarg'd the former narrow bounds,
And added length to solemn sounds,
With nature's mother wit, and arts unknown before.
Let old Timotheus yield the prize,
Or both divide the crown;
He rais'd a mortal to the skies;
She drew an angel down.

266

On Milton

Three poets, in three distant ages born,
Greece, Italy and England did adorn.
The first in loftiness of thought surpassed;
The next in majesty; in both the last.
The force of nature could no further go;
To make a third, she joined the former two.

MATTHEW PRIOR
[*1664–1721*]

267

To a Child of Quality

Five Years Old, 1704. The Author then Forty

Lords, knights, and squires, the numerous band
　　That wear the fair Miss Mary's fetters,
Were summoned by her high command
　　To show their passions by their letters.

My pen amongst the rest I took,
　　Lest those bright eyes, that cannot read,
Should dart their kindling fires, and look
　　The power they have to be obey'd.

Nor quality, nor reputation,
　　Forbid me yet my flame to tell;
Dear Five-years-old befriends my passion,
　　And I may write till she can spell.

For, while she makes her silkworm beds
　　With all the tender things I swear;
Whilst all the house my passion reads,
　　In papers round her baby's hair;

She may receive and own my flame;
　　For, though the strictest prudes should know it,
She'll pass for a most virtuous dame,
　　And I for an unhappy poet.

Then, too, alas! when she shall tear
　　The rhymes some younger rival sends,
She'll give me leave to write, I fear,
　　And we shall still continue friends.

For, as our different ages move,
　　'Tis so ordain'd (would Fate but mend it!),
That I shall be past making love
　　When she begins to comprehend it.

268　　　　　　　　　CLOE

　　THE merchant, to secure his treasure,
　　　　Conveys it in a borrow'd name:
　　Euphelia serves to grace my measure,
　　　　But Cloe is my real flame.

　　My softest verse, my darling lyre
　　　　Upon Euphelia's toilet lay—
　　When Cloe noted her desire
　　　　That I should sing, that I should play.

My lyre I tune, my voice I raise,
    But with my numbers mix my sighs;
And whilst I sing Euphelia's praise,
    I fix my soul on Cloe's eyes.

Fair Cloe blush'd: Euphelia frown'd:
    I sung, and gazed; I play'd, and trembled:
And Venus to the Loves around
    Remark'd how ill we all dissembled.

269   THE DYING ADRIAN TO HIS SOUL

Poor, little, pretty, fluttering thing,
    Must we no longer live together?
And dost thou prune thy trembling wing,
    To take thy flight thou knowst not whither?
Thy humorous vein, thy pleasing folly,
    Lies all neglected, all forgot:
And pensive, wavering, melancholy,
    Thou dread'st and hop'st thou know'st not what.

270   EPIGRAM

To JOHN I owed great obligation;
    But John unhappily thought fit
To publish it to all the nation,
    Sure John and I are more than quit.

ISAAC WATTS
[1674-1748]

271   TRUE GREATNESS

Were I so tall to reach the pole
Or grasp the ocean with my span,
I must be measured by my soul:
The mind's the standard of the man.

LADY GRISEL BAILLIE
[1665-1746]

272   WERENA MY HEART LICHT I WAD DEE

There ance was a may,[1] and she lo'ed na men;
She biggit[2] her bonnie bow'r doun in yon glen;

    [1] Maid.   [2] Built.

But now she cries, Dool and well-a-day!
Come doun the green gait[3] and come here away!

When bonnie young Johnnie cam owre[4] the sea,
He said he saw naething sae lovely as me;
He hecht[5] me baith rings and mony braw things—
And werena my heart licht, I wad dee.

He had a wee titty[6] that lo'ed na me,
Because I was twice as bonnie as she;
She raised sic a pother 'twixt him and his mother
That werena my heart's licht, I wad dee.

The day it was set, and the bridal to be:
The wife took a dwam[7] and lay doun to dee;
She maned[8] and she graned[9] out o' dolour and pain,
Till he vow'd he never wad see me again.

His kin was for ane of a higher degree,
Said—What had he do wi' the likes of me?
Appose[10] I was bonnie, I wasna for Johnnie—
And werena my heart licht, I wad dee.

They said I had neither cow nor calf,
Nor dribbles o' drink rins thro' the draff,[11]
Nor pickles[12] o' meal rins thro' the mill-e'e—
And werena my heart licht, I wad dee.

His titty she was baith wylie and slee:[13]
She spied me as I cam owre the lea;
And then she ran in and made a loud din—
Believe your ain e'en, an ye trow not me.

His bonnet stood ay fu' round on his brow,
His auld ane look'd ay as well as some's new:
But now he lets 't wear ony gait it will hing,
And casts himsel dowie[14] upon the corn bing.[15]

And now he gaes daund'ring about the dykes,[16]
And a' he dow do is to hund the tykes:[17]
The live-lang nicht he ne'er steeks[18] his e'e—
And werena my heart licht, I wad dee.

---

[3] Path.   [4] Over.   [5] Promised.   [6] Sister.   [7] Sudden illness.   [8] Moaned.   [9] Groaned.
[10] Suppose.   [11] Malt.   [12] Small quantities.   [13] Sly.   [14] Dejected.   [15] Bin.
[16] Stone walls.   [17] Hunt the dogs.   [18] Closes.

Were I but young for thee, as I hae been,
We should hae been gallopin' doun in yon green,
And linkin' [19] it owre the lily-white lea—
And wow, gin I were but young for thee!

JOSEPH ADDISON
[1672–1719]

273 HYMN

THE spacious firmament on high,
With all the blue ethereal sky,
And spangled heavens, a shining frame,
Their great Original proclaim.
Th' unwearied Sun from day to day
Does his Creator's power display;
And publishes to every land
The work of an Almighty hand.

Soon as the evening shades prevail,
The Moon takes up the wondrous tale;
And nightly to the listening Earth
Repeats the story of her birth:
Whilst all the stars that round her burn,
And all the planets in their turn,
Confirm the tidings as they roll,
And spread the truth from pole to pole.

What though in solemn silence all
Move round the dark terrestrial ball;
What though nor real voice nor sound
Amidst their radiant orbs be found?
In Reason's ear they all rejoice,
And utter forth a glorious voice;
For ever singing as they shine,
'The Hand that made us is divine.'

[19] Going arm-in-arm.

ALLAN RAMSAY
[*1686–1758*]

274   PEGGY

My Peggy is a young thing,
　　Just enter'd in her teens,
Fair as the day, and sweet as May,
Fair as the day, and always gay;
　My Peggy is a young thing,
　　And I'm not very auld,
　Yet well I like to meet her at
　　The wawking[1] of the fauld.[2]

My Peggy speaks sae sweetly
　　Whene'er we meet alane,
I wish nae mair to lay my care,
I wish nae mair of a' that's rare;
　My Peggy speaks sae sweetly,
　　To a' the lave[3] I'm cauld,
　But she gars[4] a' my spirits glow
　　At wawking of the fauld.

My Peggy smiles sae kindly
　　Whene'er I whisper love,
That I look down on a' the town,
That I look down upon a crown;
　My Peggy smiles sae kindly,
　　It makes me blyth and bauld,
　And naething gives me sic delight
　　As wawking of the fauld.

My Peggy sings sae saftly
　　When on my pipe I play,
By a' the rest it is confest,
By a' the rest, that she sings best;
　My Peggy sings sae saftly,
　　And in her sangs are tauld
　With innocence the wale[5] of sense,
　　At wawking of the fauld.

[1] Watching.　[2] Sheep-fold.　[3] Rest.　[4] Makes.　[5] Choice.

JOHN GAY
[*1685–1732*]

275   LOVE IN HER EYES SITS PLAYING

LOVE in her eyes sits playing,
    And sheds delicious death;
Love in her lips is straying,
    And warbling in her breath;
Love on her breast sits panting,
    And swells with soft desire:
Nor grace, nor charm, is wanting
    To set the heart on fire.

276   BLACK-EYED SUSAN

ALL in the Downs the fleet was moor'd,
    The streamers waving in the wind,
When black-eyed Susan came aboard;
    'O! where shall I my true-love find?
Tell me, ye jovial sailors, tell me true
If my sweet William sails among the crew.'

William, who high upon the yard
    Rock'd with the billow to and fro,
Soon as her well-known voice he heard
    He sigh'd, and cast his eyes below:
The cord slides swiftly through his glowing hands,
And quick as lightning on the deck he stands.

So the sweet lark, high poised in air,
    Shuts close his pinions to his breast
If chance his mate's shrill call he hear,
    And drops at once into her nest:—
The noblest captain in the British fleet
Might envy William's lip those kisses sweet.

'O Susan, Susan, lovely dear,
    My vows shall ever true remain;
Let me kiss off that falling tear;
    We only part to meet again.

Change as ye list, ye winds; my heart shall be
The faithful compass that still points to thee.

'Believe not what the landmen say
   Who tempt with doubts thy constant mind:
They'll tell thee, sailors, when away,
   In every port a mistress find:
Yes, yes, believe them when they tell thee so,
For Thou art present wheresoe'er I go.

'If to fair India's coast we sail,
   Thy eyes are seen in diamonds bright,
Thy breath is Afric's spicy gale,
   Thy skin is ivory so white.
Thus every beauteous object that I view
Wakes in my soul some charm of lovely Sue.

'Though battle call me from thy arms
   Let not my pretty Susan mourn;
Though cannons roar, yet safe from harms
   William shall to his Dear return.
Love turns aside the balls that round me fly,
Lest precious tears should drop from Susan's eye:

The boatswain gave the dreadful word,
   The sails their swelling bosom spread,
No longer must she stay aboard;
   They kiss'd, she sigh'd, he hung his head.
Her lessening boat unwilling rows to land;
   'Adieu!' she cries; and waved her lily hand.

HENRY CAREY

[d. 1743]

277   SALLY IN OUR ALLEY

Of all the girls that are so smart
   There's none like pretty Sally;
She is the darling of my heart,
   And she lives in our alley.

There is no lady in the land
   Is half so sweet as Sally;
She is the darling of my heart,
   And she lives in our alley.

Her father he makes cabbage-nets
   And through the streets does cry 'em;
Her mother she sells laces long
   To such as please to buy 'em:
But sure such folks could ne'er beget
   So sweet a girl as Sally!
She is the darling of my heart,
   And she lives in our alley.

When she is by, I leave my work,
   I love her so sincerely;
My master comes like any Turk,
   And bangs me most severely—
But let him bang his bellyfull,
   I'll bear it all for Sally;
She is the darling of my heart,
   And she lives in our alley.

Of all the days that's in the week
   I dearly love but one day—
And that's the day that comes betwixt
   A Saturday and Monday;
For then I'm drest all in my best
   To walk abroad with Sally;
She is the darling of my heart,
   And she lives in our alley.

My master carries me to church,
   And often am I blamed
Because I leave him in the lurch
   As soon as text is named;
I leave the church in sermon-time
   And slink away to Sally;
She is the darling of my heart,
   And she lives in our alley.

When Christmas comes about again
  O then I shall have money;
I'll hoard it up, and box it all,
  I'll give it to my honey;
I would it were ten thousand pound,
  I'd give it all to Sally;
She is the darling of my heart,
  And she lives in our alley.

My master and the neighbours all
  Make game of me and Sally,
And, but for her, I'd better be
  A slave and row a galley;
But when my seven long years are out
  O then I'll marry Sally,—
O then we'll wed, and then we'll bed,
  But not in our alley!

ALEXANDER POPE
[1688–1744]

278

SOLITUDE

HAPPY the man, whose wish and care
A few paternal acres bound,
Content to breathe his native air
    In his own ground.

Whose herds with milk, whose fields with bread,
Whose flocks supply him with attire;
Whose trees in summer yield him shade,
    In winter fire.

Blest, who can unconcern'dly find
Hours, days, and years, slide soft away
In health of body, peace of mind,
    Quiet by day.

Sound sleep by night; study and ease
Together mix'd, sweet recreation,
And innocence, which most does please
    With meditation.

Thus let me live, unseen, unknown;
Thus unlamented let me die;
Steal from the world, and not a stone
    Tell where I lie.

279   ON A CERTAIN LADY AT COURT
       [Henrietta Howard, Countess of Suffolk]

I KNOW a thing that's most uncommon
    (Envy, be silent, and attend);
I know a reasonable woman,
    Handsome and witty, yet a friend.

Not warped by passion, awed by rumour,
    Not grave through pride, or gay through folly;
An equal mixture of good humour,
    And sensible soft melancholy.

'Has she no faults then,' Envy says, 'Sir?'
    Yes, she has one, I must aver:
When all the world conspires to praise her
    The woman's deaf, and does not hear!

AN ESSAY ON MAN
TO H. ST. JOHN, L. BOLINGBROKE

THE DESIGN

HAVING proposed to write some pieces on human life and manners, such as (to use my lord Bacon's expression) *came home to men's business and bosoms,* I thought it more satisfactory to begin with considering Man in the abstract, his nature and his state; since, to prove any moral duty, to enforce any moral precept, or to examine the perfection or imperfection of any creature whatsoever, it is necessary first to know what condition and relation it is placed in, and what is the proper end and purpose of its being.

The science of human nature is, like all other sciences, reduced to a few clear points: there are not many certain truths in this world. It is therefore in the anatomy of the mind as in that of the body; more good will accrue to mankind by attending to the large, open, and perceptible parts, than by studying too much such finer nerves and vessels, the conformations and uses of which will for ever escape our observation. The disputes are all upon these last, and I will venture to say, they have less sharpened the wits than the hearts of men against each other, and have diminished the practice, more than advanced the theory of morality. If I could flatter myself that this Essay has any merit, it is in steering betwixt the extremes of doctrines seemingly opposite, in passing over terms utterly unintelligible, and in forming a temperate yet not inconsistent, and a short yet not imperfect, system of ethics.

This I might have done in prose; but I chose verse, and even rhyme, for two reasons. The one will appear obvious; that principles, maxims, or precepts so written, both strike the reader more strongly at first, and are more easily retained by him afterwards: the other may seem odd, but it is true; I found I could express them more shortly this way than in prose itself; and nothing is more certain, than that much of the force as well as grace of arguments or instructions depends on their conciseness. I was unable to treat this part of my subject more in detail, without becoming dry and tedious; or more poetically, without sacrificing perspicuity to ornament, without wandering from the precision, or breaking the chain of reasoning. If any man can unite all these without any diminution of any of them, I freely confess he will compass a thing above my capacity.

What is now published, is only to be considered as a general map of Man, marking out no more than the greater parts, their extent, their limits, and their connection, but leaving the particular to be more fully delineated in the charts which are to follow. Consequently, these Epistles in their progress (if I have health and leisure to make any progress) will be less dry, and more susceptible of poetical ornament. I am here only opening the fountains, and clearing the passage. To deduce the rivers, to follow them in their course, and to observe their effects, may be a task more agreeable.

EPISTLE I—OF THE NATURE AND STATE OF MAN, WITH RESPECT TO THE UNIVERSE

AWAKE, my St. John! leave all meaner things
To low ambition, and the pride of kings.
Let us (since life can little more supply
Than just to look about us, and to die)
Expatiate free o'er all this scene of man;
A mighty maze! but not without a plan;
A wild, where weeds and flow'rs promiscuous shoot;

Or garden, tempting with forbidden fruit.
Together let us beat this ample field,
Try what the open, what the covert yield!
The latent tracts, the giddy heights, explore
Of all who blindly creep, or sightless soar;
Eye nature's walks, shoot folly as it flies,
And catch the manners living as they rise:
Laugh where we must, be candid where we can;
But vindicate the ways of God to man.

    I.   Say first, of God above, or man below,
What can we reason, but from what we know?
Of man, what see we but his station here,
From which to reason, or to which refer?
Thro' worlds unnumber'd tho' the God be known,
'Tis ours to trace him only in our own.
He, who thro' vast immensity can pierce,
See worlds on worlds compose one universe,
Observe how system into system runs,
What other planets circle other suns.
What vary'd being peoples every star,
May tell why heav'n has made us as we are.
But of this frame the bearings and the ties,
The strong connections, nice dependencies,
Gradations just, has thy pervading soul
Look'd thro' or can a part contain the whole?
    Is the great chain, that draws all to agree,
And drawn support, upheld by God, or thee?

    II.   Presumptuous man! the reason wouldst thou find,
Why form'd so weak, so little, and so blind?
First, if thou canst, the harder reason guess,
Why form'd no weaker, blinder, and no less?
Ask of thy mother earth, why oaks are made
Taller or stronger than the weeds they shade?
Or ask of yonder argent fields above,
Why Jove's Satellites are less than Jove?

    Of systems possible, if 'tis confest
That wisdom infinite must form the best,
Where all must full or not coherent be,
And all that rises, rise in due degree;
Then, in the scale of reas'ning life, 'tis plain,

There must be, somewhere, such a rank as man:
And all the question (wrangle e'er so long)
Is only this, if God has plac'd him wrong?
  Respecting man whatever wrong we call,
May, must be right, as relative to all.
In human works, tho' labour'd on with pain,
A thousand movements scarce one purpose gain;
In God's, one single can its end produce;
Yet serves to second too some other use.
So man, who here seems principal alone,
Perhaps acts second to some sphere unknown,
Touches some wheel, or verges to some goal;
'Tis but a part we see, and not a whole.
  When the proud steed shall know why man restrains
His fiery course, or drives him o'er the plains;
When the dull ox, why now he breaks the clod,
Is now a victim, and now Ægypt's god:
Then shall man's pride and dullness comprehend
His actions', passions', being's, use and end;
Why doing, suff'ring, check'd, impell'd; and why
This hour a slave, the next a deity.
  Then say not man's imperfect, heav'n in fault;
Say rather, man's as perfect as he ought:
His knowledge measur'd to his state and place;
His time a moment, and a point his space.
If to be perfect in a certain sphere,
What matter, soon or late, or here or there?
The blest to-day is as completely so,
As who began a thousand years ago.
  III. Heav'n from all creatures hides the book of fate,
All but the page prescrib'd, their present state:
From brutes what men, from men what spirits know:
Or who could suffer being here below?
The lamb thy riot dooms to bleed to-day,
Had he thy reason, would he skip and play?
Pleas'd to the last, he crops the flow'ry food,
And licks the hand just rais'd to shed his blood.
Oh blindness to the future! kindly giv'n,
That each may fill the circle mark'd by heav'n:
Who sees with equal eye, as God of all,

A hero perish, or a sparrow fall,
Atoms or systems into ruin hurl'd,
And now a bubble burst, and now a world.
   Hope humbly then; with trembling pinions soar;
Wait the great teacher death, and God adore.
What future bliss, he gives not thee to know,
But gives that hope to be thy blessing now.
Hope springs eternal in the human breast:
Man never *is*, but always *to be* blest:
The soul, uneasy and confin'd from home,
Rests and expatiates in a life to come.
   Lo, the poor Indian! whose untutor'd mind
Sees God in clouds, or hears him in the wind;
His soul, proud science never taught to stray
Far as the solar walk, or milky way;
Yet simple nature to his hope has giv'n,
Behind the cloud-topt hill, an humbler heav'n;
Some safer world in depth of woods embrac'd,
Some happier island in the wat'ry waste,
Where slaves once more their native land behold,
No fiends torment, no Christians thirst for gold.
To Be, contents his natural desire,
He asks no angel's wing, no seraph's fire;
But thinks admitted to that equal sky,
His faithful dog shall bear him company.
   IV.   Go, wiser thou! and in thy scale of sense,
Weigh thy opinion against providence;
Call imperfection what thou fancy'st such,
Say, here he gives too little, there too much:
Destroy all creatures for thy sport or gust,
Yet cry, If man's unhappy, God's unjust;
If man alone ingross not Heav'n's high care,
Alone made perfect here, immortal there:
Snatch from his hand the balance and the rod,
Re-judge his justice, be the God of God.
In pride, in reas'ning pride, our error lies;
All quit their sphere, and rush into the skies.
Pride still is aiming at the blest abodes,
Men would be angels, angels would be gods.
Aspiring to be gods, if angels fell,

Aspiring to be angels, men rebel:
And who but wishes to invert the laws
Of order, sins against th' eternal cause.
    V. Ask for what end the heav'nly bodies shine,
Earth for whose use? pride answers, ' 'Tis for mine:
For me kind nature wakes her genial pow'r,
Suckles each herb, and spreads out ev'ry flow'r;
Annual for me, the grape, the rose renew
The juice nectareous, and the balmy dew;
For me, the mine a thousand treasures brings;
For me, health gushes from a thousand springs;
Seas roll to waft me, suns to light me rise;
My foot-stool earth, my canopy the skies.'
    But errs not nature from this gracious end,
From burning suns when livid deaths descend,
When earthquakes swallow, or when tempests sweep
Towns to one grave, whole nations to the deep?
'No ('tis reply'd) the first almighty cause
Acts not by partial, but by gen'ral laws;
Th' exceptions few; some change since all began:
And what created perfect?'—Why then man?
If the great end be human happiness,
Then nature deviates; and can man do less?
As much that end a constant course requires
Of show'rs and sunshine, as of man's desires;
As much eternal springs and cloudless skies,
As men for ever temp'rate, calm, and wise.
If plagues or earthquakes break not Heav'n's design,
Why then a Borgia, or a Catiline?
Who knows but he, whose hand the lightning forms,
Who heaves old ocean, and who wings the storms;
Pours fierce ambition in a Cæsar's mind,
Or turns young Ammon loose to scourge mankind?
From pride, from pride, our very reas'ning springs;
Account for moral as for nat'ral things:
Why charge we heav'n in those, in these acquit?
In both, to reason right is to submit.
    Better for us, perhaps, it might appear,
Were there all harmony, all virtue here;
That never air or ocean felt the wind,

That never passion discompos'd the mind.
But all subsists by elemental strife;
And passions are the elements of life.
The gen'ral order, since the whole began,
Is kept in nature, and is kept in man.
   VI. What would this man? Now upward will he soar,
And little less than angel, would be more;
Now looking downwards, just as griev'd appears
To want the strength of bulls, the fur of bears.
Made for his use all creatures if he call,
Say what their use, had he the pow'rs of all;
Nature to these, without profusion, kind,
The proper organs, proper pow'rs assign'd;
Each seeming want compensated of course,
Here with degrees of swiftness, there of force;
All in exact proportion to the state;
Nothing to add, and nothing to abate.
Each beast, each insect, happy in its own:
Is Heav'n unkind to man, and man alone?
Shall he alone, whom rational we call,
Be pleas'd with nothing, if not blest with all?
   The bliss of man (could pride that blessing find)
Is not to act or think beyond mankind;
No pow'rs of body, or of soul to share,
But what his nature and his state can bear.
Why has not man a microscopic eye?
For this plain reason, man is not a fly.
Say what the use, were finer optics giv'n,
T' inspect a mite, not comprehend the heav'n?
Or touch, if tremblingly alive all o'er,
To smart and agonize at ev'ry pore?
Or, quick effluvia darting thro' the brain,
Die of a rose in aromatic pain?
If nature thunder'd in his op'ning ears,
And stunn'd him with the music of the spheres,
How would he wish that Heav'n had left him still
The whisp'ring zephyr, and the purling rill!
Who finds not Providence all good and wise,
Alike in what it gives, and what it denies?
   VII. Far as creation's ample range extends,

The scale of sensual, mental pow'rs ascends:
Mark how it mounts to man's imperial race,
From the green myriads in the peopled grass:
What modes of sight betwixt each wide extreme,
The mole's dim curtain, and the lynx's beam:
Of smell, the headlong lioness between,
And hound sagacious on the tainted green:
Of hearing, from the life that fills the flood,
To that which warbles through the vernal wood?
The spider's touch, how exquisitely fine!
Feels at each thread, and lives along the line:
In the nice bee, what sense so subtly true
From pois'nous herbs extracts the healing dew:
How instinct varies in the grov'ling swine,
Compar'd, half reas'ning elephant, with thine!
'Twixt that, and reason, what a nice barrier?
For ever sep'rate, yet for ever near!
Remembrance and reflection how ally'd;
What thin partitions sense from thought divide?
And middle natures, how they long to join,
Yet never pass th' insuperable line!
Without this just gradation, could they be
Subjected, these to those, or all to thee?
The pow'rs of all subdu'd by thee alone,
Is not thy reason all these pow'rs in one?
    VIII. See, thro' this air, this ocean, and this earth,
All matter quick, and bursting into birth.
Above, how high progressive life may go!
Around, how wide! how deep extend below!
Vast chain of being! which from God began,
Natures æthereal, human, angel, man,
Beast, bird, fish, insect, what no eye can see,
No glass can reach; from infinite to thee,
From thee to nothing. On superior pow'rs
Were we to press, inferior might on ours;
Or in the full creation leave a void,
Where, one step broken, the great scale's destroy'd:
From Nature's chain whatever link you strike,
Tenth, or ten thousandth, breaks the chain alike.
    And, if each system in gradation roll

Alike essential to th' amazing whole,
The least confusion but in one, not all
That system only, but the whole must fall.
Let earth unbalanc'd from her orbit fly,
Planets and suns run lawless thro' the sky;
Let ruling angels from their spheres be hurl'd,
Being on being wreck'd, and world on world;
Heav'n's whole foundations to their centre nod,
And nature tremble to the throne of God.
All this dread order break—for whom? for thee?
Vile worm!—oh madness! pride! impiety!

   IX. What if the foot, ordain'd the dust to tread,
Or hand, to toil, aspir'd to be the head?
What if the head, the eye, or ear repin'd
To serve mere engines to the ruling mind?
Just as absurd for any part to claim
To be another, in this gen'ral frame;
Just as absurd, to mourn the tasks or pains
The great directing mind of all ordains.

   All are but parts of one stupendous whole,
Whose body nature is, and God the soul;
That, chang'd thro' all, and yet in all the same,
Great in the earth, as in th' æthereal frame,
Warms in the sun, refreshes in the breeze,
Glows in the stars, and blossoms in the trees,
Lives thro' all life, extends thro' all extent,
Spreads undivided, operates unspent;
Breathes in our soul, informs our mortal part,
As full, as perfect, in a hair as heart;
As full, as perfect, in vile man that mourns,
As the rapt seraph that adores and burns:
To him no high, no low, no great, no small;
He fills, he bounds, connects, and equals all.

   Cease then, nor order imperfection name:
Our proper bliss depends on what we blame.
Know thy own point: this kind, this due degree
Of blindness, weakness, Heav'n bestows on thee.
Submit. In this, or any other sphere,
Secure to be as blest as thou canst bear:
Safe in the hand of one disposing pow'r,

Or in the natal, or the mortal hour.
All nature is but art, unknown to thee;
All chance, direction, which thou canst not see;
All discord, harmony not understood;
All partial evil, universal good.
And, spite of pride, in erring reason's spite,
One truth is clear, Whatever is, is right.

EPISTLE II—OF THE NATURE AND STATE OF MAN WITH RESPECT TO HIMSELF,
AS AN INDIVIDUAL

    I. Know then thyself, presume not God to scan,
The proper study of mankind is man.
Plac'd on this isthmus of a middle state,
A being darkly wise, and rudely great:
With too much knowledge for the sceptic side,
With too much weakness for the Stoic's pride,
He hangs between; in doubt to act, or rest;
In doubt to deem himself a God, or beast;
In doubt his mind or body to prefer;
Born but to die, and reas'ning but to err;
Alike in ignorance, his reason such,
Whether he thinks too little or too much:
Chaos of thought and passion, all confus'd;
Still by himself abus'd or disabus'd;
Created half to rise, and half to fall;
Great lord of all things, yet a prey to all;
Sole judge of truth, in endless error hurl'd:
The glory, jest, and riddle of the world!

    Go, wondrous creature! mount where science guides,
Go, measure earth, weigh air, and state the tides;
Instruct the planets in what orbs to run,
Correct old time, and regulate the sun:
Go, soar with Plato to th' empyreal sphere,
To the first good, first perfect, and first fair;
Or tread the mazy round his follow'rs trod
And quitting sense call imitating God;
As eastern priests in giddy circles run,
And turn their heads to imitate the sun.
Go, teach eternal wisdom how to rule—
Then drop into thyself, and be a fool!

Superior beings, when of late they saw
A mortal man unfold all nature's law,
Admir'd such wisdom in an earthly shape,
And shew'd a Newton as we shew an ape.

Could he, whose rules the rapid comet bind,
Describe or fix one movement of his mind?
Who saw its fires here rise, and there descend,
Explain his own beginning, or his end?
Alas what wonder! man's superior part
Uncheck'd may rise, and climb from art to art;
But when his own great work is but begun,
What reason weaves, by passion is undone.

Trace science then, with modesty thy guide;
First strip off all her equipage of pride;
Deduct what is but vanity, or dress,
Or learning's luxury, or idleness;
Or tricks to shew the stretch of human brain,
Mere curious pleasure, or ingenious pain;
Expunge the whole, or lop th' excrescent parts
Of all our vices have created arts;
Then see how little the remaining sum,
Which serv'd the past, and must the times to come!

II. Two principles in human nature reign;
Self-love, to urge, and reason, to restrain;
Nor this a good, nor that a bad we call,
Each works its end, to move or govern all:
And to their proper operation still
Ascribe all good, to their improper, ill.

Self-love, the spring of motion, acts the soul;
Reason's comparing balance rules the whole.
Man, but for that, no action could attend,
And, but for this, were active to no end:
Fix'd like a plant on his peculiar spot,
To draw nutrition, propagate, and rot:
Or, meteor-like, flame lawless thro' the void,
Destroying others, by himself destroy'd.

Most strength the moving principle requires;
Active its task, it prompts, impels, inspires.
Sedate and quiet the comparing lies,
Form'd but to check, delib'rate, and advise.

Self-love, still stronger, as its object's nigh;
Reason's at distance, and in prospect lie:
That sees immediate good by present sense;
Reason, the future and the consequence.
Thicker than arguments, temptations throng,
At best more watchful this, but that more strong.
The action of the stronger to suspend
Reason still use, to reason still attend.
Attention habit and experience gains;
Each strengthens reason, and self-love restrains.

Let subtle schoolmen teach these friends to fight,
More studious to divide than to unite;
And grace and virtue, sense and reason split,
With all the rash dexterity of wit.
Wits, just like fools, at war about a name,
Have full as oft no meaning, or the same.
Self-love and reason to one end aspire,
Pain their aversion, pleasure their desire;
But greedy that, its object would devour,
This taste the honey, and not wound the flow'r:
Pleasure, or wrong or rightly understood,
Our greatest evil, or our greatest good.

III. Modes of self-love the passions we may call:
'Tis real good, or seeming, moves them all:
But since not ev'ry good we can divide,
And reason bids us for our own provide:
Passions, tho' selfish, if their means be fair,
List under Reason, and deserve her care;
Those, that imparted, court a nobler aim,
Exalt their kind, and take some virtue's name.

In lazy apathy let stoics boast
Their virtue fix'd; 'tis fix'd as in a frost;
Contracted all, retiring to the breast;
But strength of mind is exercise, not rest:
The rising tempest puts in act the soul,
Parts it may ravage, but preserves the whole.
On life's vast ocean diversely we sail,
Reason the card, but passion is the gale;
Nor God alone in the still calm we find,
He mounts the storm, and walks upon the wind.

Passions, like elements, tho' born to fight,
Yet, mix'd and soften'd, in his work unite:
These 'tis enough to temper and employ;
But what composes man, can man destroy?
Suffice that reason keep to nature's road,
Subject, compound them, follow her and God.
Love, hope, and joy, fair pleasure's smiling train,
Hate, fear, and grief, the family of pain,
These mixt with art, and to due bounds confin'd,
Make and maintain the balance of the mind:
The lights and shades, whose well-accorded strife
Gives all the strength and colour of our life.

Pleasures are ever in our hands or eyes;
And, when in act they cease, in prospect rise:
Present to grasp, and future still to find,
The whole employ of body and of mind.
All spread their charms, but charm not all alike;
On diff'rent senses diff'rent objects strike;
Hence diff'rent passions more or less inflame,
As strong or weak, the organs of the frame;
And hence one master passion in the breast,
Like Aaron's serpent, swallows up the rest.

As man, perhaps, the moment of his breath,
Receives the lurking principle of death;
The young disease, that must subdue at length,
Grows with his growth, and strengthens with his
    strength:
So, cast and mingled with his very frame,
The mind's disease, its ruling passion came;
Each vital humour which should feed the whole,
Soon flows to this, in body and in soul:
Whatever warms the heart, or fills the head,
As the mind opens, and its functions spread,
Imagination plies her dang'rous art,
And pours it all upon the peccant part.

Nature its mother, habit is its nurse;
Wit, spirit, faculties, but make it worse;
Reason itself but gives it edge and pow'r,
As heav'n's blest beam turns vinegar more sour.
We, wretched subjects tho' to lawful sway,

In this weak queen some fav'rite still obey:
Ah! if she lend not arms, as well as rules,
What can she more than tell us we are fools?
Teach us to mourn our nature, not to mend,
A sharp accuser, but a helpless friend!
Or from a judge turn pleader, to persuade
The choice we make, or justify it made;
Proud of an easy conquest all along,
She but removes weak passions for the strong:
So, when small humours gather to a gout,
The doctor fancies he has driv'n them out.

    Yes, nature's road must ever be preferr'd;
Reason is here no guide, but still a guard;
'Tis hers to rectify, not overthrow,
And treat this passion more as friend than foe;
A mightier pow'r the strong direction sends,
And sev'ral men impels to sev'ral ends:
Like varying winds by other passions tost,
This drives them constant to a certain coast.
Let pow'r or knowledge, gold or glory, please,
Or (oft more strong than all) the love of ease;
Thro' life 'tis followed, ev'n at life's expense;
The merchant's toil, the sage's indolence,
The monk's humility, the hero's pride,
All, all alike, find reason on their side.

    Th' eternal art educing good from ill,
Grafts on this passion our best principle:
'Tis thus the mercury of man is fix'd,
Strong grows the virtue with his nature mix'd;
The dross cements what else were too refin'd,
And in one int'rest body acts with mind.

    As fruits, ungrateful to the planter's care,
On savage stocks inserted, learn to bear;
The surest virtues thus from passions shoot,
Wild nature's vigor working at the root.
What crops of wit and honesty appear
From spleen, from obstinacy, hate or fear!
See anger, zeal and fortitude supply;
Ev'n av'rice, prudence; sloth, philosophy;
Lust, thro' some certain strainers well refin'd,

Is gentle love, and charms all womankind;
Envy, to which th' ignoble mind's a slave,
Is emulation in the learn'd or brave;
Nor virtue, male or female, can we name,
But what will grow on pride, or grow on shame.

    Thus nature gives us (let it check our pride)
The virtue nearest to our vice ally'd:
Reason the byas turns to good from ill,
And Nero reigns a Titus, if he will,
The fiery soul abhorr'd in Catiline,
In Decius charms, in Curtius is divine:
The same ambition can destroy or save,
And makes a patriot as it makes a knave.

    This light and darkness in our chaos join'd,
What shall divide? The God within the mind.

    Extremes in nature equal ends produce,
In man they join to some mysterious use;
Tho' each by turns the other's bound invade,
As, in some well-wrought picture, light and shade,
And oft so mix, the diff'rence is too nice
Where ends the virtue or begins the vice.

    Fools! who from hence into the notion fall,
That vice or virtue there is none at all.
If white and black blend, soften, and unite
A thousand ways, is there no black or white?
Ask your own heart, and nothing is so plain;
'Tis to mistake them, costs the time and pain.

    Vice is a monster of so frightful mien,
As, to be hated, needs but to be seen;
Yet seen too oft, familiar with her face,
We first endure, then pity, then embrace.
But where th' extreme of vice, was ne'er agreed:
Ask where's the north? at York, 'tis on the Tweed;
In Scotland, at the Orcades; and there,
At Greenland, Zembla, or the Lord knows where.
No creature owns it in the first degree,
But thinks his neighbour farther gone than he:
Ev'n those who dwell beneath its very zone,
Or never feel the rage, or never own;
What happier natures shrink at with affright,

The hard inhabitant contends is right.
   Virtuous and vicious ev'ry man must be,
Few in th' extreme, but all in the degree;
The rogue and fool by fits is fair and wise;
And ev'n the best, by fits, what they despise.
'Tis but by parts we follow good or ill;
For, vice or virtue, self directs it still;
Each individual seeks a sev'ral goal;
But heav'n's great view is one, and that the whole,
That counter-works each folly and caprice;
That disappoints th' effect of ev'ry vice;
That, happy frailties to all ranks apply'd,
Shame to the virgin, to the matron pride,
Fear to the statesman, rashness to the chief,
To kings presumption, and to crowds belief:
That, virtue's ends from vanity can raise,
Which seeks no int'rest, no reward but praise;
And build on wants, and on defects of mind,
The joy, the peace, the glory of mankind.
   Heav'n forming each on other to depend,
A master, or a servant, or a friend,
Bids each on other for assistance call,
'Till one man's weakness grows the strength of all.
Wants, frailties, passions, closer still ally
The common int'rest, or endear the tie.
To these we owe true friendship, love sincere,
Each home-felt joy that life inherits here;
Yet from the same we learn, in its decline,
Those joys, those loves, those int'rests to resign;
Taught half by reason, half by mere decay,
To welcome death, and calmly pass away.
   Whate'er the passion—knowledge, fame, or pelf,
Not one will change his neighbour with himself.
The learn'd is happy nature to explore,
The fool is happy that he knows no more;
The rich is happy in the plenty giv'n,
The poor contents him with the care of heav'n.
See the blind beggar dance, the cripple sing,
The sot a hero, lunatic a king;
The starving chemist in his golden views

Supremely blest, the poet in his muse.
　　See some strange comfort ev'ry state attend,
And pride bestow'd on all, a common friend;
See some fit passion ev'ry age supply,
Hope travels thro', nor quits us when we die.
　　Behold the child, by nature's kindly law,
Pleas'd with a rattle, tickled with a straw:
Some livelier plaything gives his youth delight,
A little louder, but as empty quite:
Scarfs, garters, gold, amuse his riper stage,
And beads and pray'r-books are the toys of age:
Pleas'd with this bauble still, as that before;
'Till tir'd he sleeps, and life's poor play is o'er.
　　Meanwhile opinion gilds with varying rays
Those painted clouds that beautify our days;
Each want of happiness by hope supply'd,
And each vacuity of sense by pride:
These build as fast as knowledge can destroy;
In folly's cup still laughs the bubble, joy;
One prospect lost, another still we gain;
And not a vanity is giv'n in vain;
Ev'n mean self-love becomes, by force divine,
The scale to measure others' wants by thine.
See! and confess one comfort still must rise;
'Tis this, Tho' man's a fool, yet God is wise.

EPISTLE III—OF THE NATURE AND STATE OF MAN WITH RESPECT TO SOCIETY

　　HERE then we rest; 'The universal cause
Acts to one end, but acts by various laws.'
In all the madness of superfluous health,
The trim of pride, the impudence of wealth,
Let this great truth be present night and day;
But most be present, if we preach or pray.
　　Look round our world; behold the chain of love
Combining all below and all above.
See plastic nature working to this end,
The single atoms each to other tend,
Attract, attracted to, the next in place
Form'd and impell'd its neighbour to embrace.
See matter next, with various life endu'd,

Press to one centre still, the gen'ral good.
See dying vegetables life sustain,
See life dissolving vegetate again:
All forms that perish other forms supply,
(By turns we catch the vital breath, and die),
Like bubbles on the sea of matter born,
They rise, they break, and to that sea return.
Nothing is foreign; parts relate to whole;
One all-extending, all-preserving soul
Connects each being, greatest with the least;
Made beast in aid of man, and man of beast;
All serv'd, all serving: nothing stands alone;
The chain holds on, and where it ends, unknown.

Has God, thou fool! work'd solely for thy good,
Thy joy, thy pastime, thy attire, thy food?
Who for thy table feeds the wanton fawn,
For him as kindly spread the flow'ry lawn:
Is it for thee the lark ascends and sings?
Joy tunes his voice, joy elevates his wings.
Is it for thee the linnet pours his throat?
Loves of his own and raptures swell the note.
The bounding steed you pompously bestride,
Shares with his lord the pleasure and the pride.
Is thine alone the seed that strews the plain?
The birds of heav'n shall vindicate their grain.
Thine the full harvest of the golden year?
Part pays, and justly, the deserving steer:
The hog, that plows not, nor obeys thy call,
Lives on the labours of this lord of all.

Know, nature's children all divide her care;
The fur that warms a monarch, warm'd a bear.
While man exclaims, 'See all things for my use!'
'See man for mine!' replies a pamper'd goose:
And just as short of reason he must fall,
Who thinks all made for one, not one for all.

Grant that the pow'rful still the weak control;
Be man the wit and tyrant of the whole:
Nature that tyrant checks; he only knows,
And helps, another creature's wants and woes.
Say, will the falcon, stooping from above,

Smit with her varying plumage, spare the dove?
Admires the jay the insect's gilded wings?
Or hears the hawk when Philomela sings?
Man cares for all: to birds he gives his woods,
To beasts his pastures, and to fish his floods;
For some his int'rest prompts him to provide,
For more his pleasure, yet for more his pride:
All feed on one vain patron, and enjoy
Th' extensive blessing of his luxury,
That very life his learned hunger craves,
He saves from famine, from the savage saves;
Nay, feasts the animal he dooms his feast,
And, till he ends the being, makes it blest:
Which sees no more the stroke, or feels the pain,
Than favour'd man by touch ether'al slain.
The creature had his feast of life before;
Thou too must perish, when thy feast is o'er!
    To each unthinking being, heav'n, a friend,
Gives not the useless knowledge of its end:
To man imparts it; but with such a view
As, while he dreads it, makes him hope it too:
The hour conceal'd, and so remote the fear,
Death still draws nearer, never seeming near.
Great standing miracle! that heav'n assign'd
Its only thinking thing this turn of mind.
    II. Whether with reason, or with instinct blest,
Know, all enjoy that pow'r which suits them best;
To bliss alike by that direction tend,
And find the means proportion'd to their end.
Say, where full instinct is th' unerring guide,
What Pope or council can they need beside?
Reason, however able, cool at best,
Cares not for service, or but serves when prest,
Stays 'till we call, and then not often near;
But honest instinct comes a volunteer,
Sure never to o'er-shoot, but just to hit;
While still too wide or short is human wit;
Sure by quick nature happiness to gain,
Which heavier reason labours at in vain.
This too serves always, reason never long;

One must go right, the other may go wrong.
See then the acting and comparing pow'rs
One in their nature, which are two in ours;
And reason raise o'er instinct as you can,
In this 'tis God directs, in that 'tis man.

Who taught the nations of the field and flood
To shun their poison, and to chuse their food?
Prescient, the tides or tempests to withstand,
Build on the wave, or arch beneath the sand?
Who made the spider parallels design,
Sure as De Moivre, without rule or line?
Who bid the stork, Columbus-like, explore
Heav'ns not his own, and worlds unknown before?
Who calls the council, states the certain day,
Who forms the phalanx, and who points the way?

III. God, in the nature of each being, founds
Its proper bliss, and sets its proper bounds:
But as he fram'd a whole, the whole to bless,
On mutual wants built mutual happiness:
So from the first, eternal order ran,
And creature link'd to creature, man to man.
Whate'er of life all-quick'ning ether keeps,
Or breathes thro' air, or shoots beneath the deeps,
Or pours profuse on earth, one nature feeds
The vital flame, and swells the genial seeds.
Not man alone, but all that roam the wood,
Or wing the sky, or roll along the flood,
Each loves itself, but not itself alone,
Each sex desires alike, 'till two are one.
Nor ends the pleasure with the fierce embrace;
They love themselves, a third time, in their race.
Thus beast and bird their common charge attend
The mothers nurse it, and the sires defend;
The young dismiss'd to wander earth or air,
There stops the instinct, and there ends the care;
The link dissolves, each seeks a fresh embrace,
Another love succeeds, another race.
A longer care man's helpless kind demands;
That longer care contracts more lasting bands:
Reflection, reason, still the ties improve,

At once extend the int'rest, and the love:
With choice we fix, with sympathy we burn;
Each virtue in each passion takes its turn;
And still new needs, new helps, new habits rise,
That graft benevolence on charities.
Still as one brood, and as another rose,
These nat'ral love maintain'd, habitual those:
The last, scarce ripen'd into perfect man,
Saw helpless him from whom their life began:
Mem'ry and fore-cast just returns engage,
That pointed back to youth, this on to age;
While pleasure, gratitude, and hope, combin'd,
Still spread the int'rest and preserv'd the kind.
    IV. Nor think, in nature's state they blindly trod;
The state of nature was the reign of God:
Self-love and social at her birth began,
Union the bond of all things, and of man.
Pride then was not; nor arts, that pride to aid;
Man walk'd with beast, joint tenant of the shade,
The same his table, and the same his bed;
No murder cloth'd him, and no murder fed.
In the same temple, the resounding wood,
All vocal beings hymn'd their equal God:
The shrine with gore unstain'd, with gold undrest,
Unbrib'd, unbloody, stood the blameless priest:
Heav'n's attribute was universal care,
And man's prerogative, to rule, but spare.
Ah! how unlike the man of times to come!
Of half that live the butcher and the tomb;
Who, foe to nature, hears the gen'ral groan,
Murders their species, and betrays his own.
But just disease to luxury succeeds,
And ev'ry death its own avenger breeds;
The fury-passions from that blood began,
And turn'd on man, a fiercer savage, man.
    See him from nature rising slow to art!
To copy instinct then was reason's part;
Thus then to man the voice of nature spake,
'Go, from the creatures thy instructions take:
Learn from the birds what food the thickets yield;

Learn from the beasts the physic of the field;
Thy arts of building from the bee receive;
Learn of the mole to plow, the worm to weave;
Learn of the little nautilus to sail,
Spread the thin oar, and catch the driving gale.
Here too all forms of social union find,
And hence let reason, late, instruct mankind:
Here subterranean works and cities see;
There towns aërial on the waving tree.
Learn each small people's genius, policies,
The ant's republic, and the realm of bees;
How those in common all their wealth bestow,
And anarchy without confusion know;
And these forever, tho' a monarch reign,
Their separate cells and properties maintain.
Mark what unvary'd laws preserve each state,
Laws wise as nature, and as fix'd as fate.
In vain thy reason finer webs shall draw,
Entangle justice in her net of law,
And right, too rigid, harden into wrong;
Still for the strong too weak, the weak too strong.
Yet go! and thus o'er all the creatures sway,
Thus let the wiser make the rest obey;
And for those arts mere instinct could afford,
Be crown'd as monarchs, or as gods ador'd.'
  V. Great nature spoke; observant man obey'd;
Cities were built, societies were made:
Here rose one little state; another near
Grew by like means, and join'd, thro' love or fear.
Did here the trees with ruddier burdens bend,
And there the streams in purer rills descend?
What war could ravish, commerce could bestow,
And he return'd a friend, who came a foe.
Converse and love mankind might strongly draw,
When love was liberty, and nature law.
Thus states were form'd; the name of king unknown,
'Till common int'rest plac'd the sway in one.
'Twas virtue only (or in arts or arms,
Diffusing blessings, or averting harms)
The same which in a sire the sons obey'd,

A prince the father of a people made.

    VI.   'Till then, by nature crown'd, each patriarch sate,
King, priest and parent of his growing state;
On him, their second providence, they hung,
Their law his eye, their oracle his tongue.
He from the wand'ring furrow call'd the food,
Taught to command the fire, control the flood,
Draw forth the monsters of th' abyss profound,
Or fetch th' aërial eagle to the ground,
'Till drooping, sick'ning, dying, they began
Whom they rever'd as God to mourn as man:
Then, looking up from sire to sire, explor'd
One great first father, and that first ador'd.
Or plain tradition that this All begun,
Convey'd unbroken faith from sire to son;
The worker from the work distinct was known,
And simple reason never sought but one:
Ere wit oblique had broke that steady light,
Man, like his maker, saw that all was right;
To virtue, in the paths of pleasure trod,
And own'd a father when he own'd a God.
Love all the faith, and all th' allegiance then;
For nature knew no right divine in men,
No ill could fear in God; and understood
A sov'reign being, but a sov'reign good.
True faith, true policy, united ran,
That was but love of God, and this of man.

    Who first taught souls enslav'd, and realms undone,
Th' enormous faith of many made for one;
That proud exception to all nature's laws,
T' invert the world, and counter-work its cause?
Force first made conquest, and that conquest, law;
'Till superstition taught the tyrant awe,
Then shar'd the tyranny, then lent it aid,
And gods of conqu'rors, slaves of subjects made:
She, 'midst the lightning's blaze, and thunder's sound,
When rock'd the mountains, and when groan'd the
      ground,
She taught the weak to bend, the proud to pray,
To pow'r unseen, and mightier far than they:

She, from the rending earth, and bursting skies,
Saw gods descend, and fiends infernal rise:
Here fix'd the dreadful, there the blest abodes;
Fear made her devils, and weak hope her gods;
Gods partial, changeful, passionate, unjust,
Whose attributes were rage, revenge, or lust;
Such as the souls of cowards might conceive,
And, form'd like tyrants, tyrants would believe.
Zeal then, not charity, became the guide;
And hell was built on spite, and heav'n on pride.
Then sacred seem'd th' ether'al vault no more;
Altars grew marble then, and reek'd with gore:
Then first the flamen tasted living food;
Next his grim idol smear'd with human blood;
With heav'n's own thunders shook the world below,
And play'd the god an engine on his foe.
    So drives self-love, thro' just, and thro' unjust,
To one man's pow'r, ambition, lucre, lust.
The same self-love, in all, becomes the cause
Of what restrains him, government and laws.
For, what one likes, if others like as well,
What serves one will, when many wills rebel?
How shall he keep, what, sleeping or awake,
A weaker may surprise, a stronger take?
His safety must his liberty restrain:
All join to guard what each desires to gain.
Forc'd into virtue thus, by self-defence,
Ev'n kings learn'd justice and benevolence:
Self-love forsook the path it first pursu'd,
And found the private in the public good.
    'Twas then the studious head or gen'rous mind,
Follow'r of God, or friend of human-kind,
Poet or patriot, rose but to restore
The faith and moral nature gave before;
Relum'd her ancient light, not kindled new,
If not God's image, yet his shadow drew:
Taught pow'r's due use to people and to kings,
Taught nor to slack, nor strain its tender strings,
The less, or greater, set so justly true,
That touching one must strike the other too;

'Till jarring int'rests, of themselves create
Th' according music of a well-mix'd state.
Such is the world's great harmony, that springs
From order, union, full consent of things:
Where small and great, where weak and mighty, made
To serve, not suffer, strengthen, not invade;
More pow'rful each as needful to the rest,
And in proportion as it blesses, blest;
Draw to one point, and to one centre bring
Beast, man, or angel, servant, lord, or king.

　For forms of government let fools contest;
Whate'er is best administer'd is best:
For modes of faith, let graceless zealots fight;
His can't be wrong whose life is in the right:
In faith and hope the world will disagree,
But all mankind's concern is Charity:
All must be false that thwart this one great end;
And all of God, that bless mankind, or mend.

　Man, like the gen'rous vine, supported lives;
The strength he gains is from th' embrace he gives.
On their own axis as the planets run,
Yet make at once their circle round the sun;
So two consistent motions act the soul;
And one regards itself, and one the whole.
Thus God and nature link'd the gen'ral frame,
And bade self-love and social be the same.

Epistle IV—Of the nature and state of man with respect to happiness

Oh Happiness! our being's end and aim!
Good, pleasure, ease, content! whate'er thy name:
That something still which prompts th' eternal sigh,
For which we bear to live, or dare to die,
Which still so near us, yet beyond us lies,
O'er-look'd, seen double, by the fool, and wise.
Plant of celestial seed! if dropt below,
Say, in what mortal soil thou deign'st to grow?
Fair op'ning to some court's propitious shine,
Or deep with di'monds in the flaming mine?
Twin'd with the wreaths Parnassian laurels yield,

Or reap'd in iron harvests of the field?
Where grows?—where grows it not? If vain our
    toil,
We ought to blame the culture, not the soil:
Fix'd to no spot is happiness sincere,
'Tis nowhere to be found, or ev'rywhere:
'Tis never to be bought, but always free,
And fled from monarchs, St. John! dwells with thee.
    Ask of the learn'd the way? The learn'd are blind;
This bids to serve, and that to shun mankind;
Some place the bliss in action, some in ease,
Those call it pleasure, and contentment these;
Some sunk to beasts, find pleasure end in pain;
Some swell'd to gods, confess e'en virtue vain;
Or indolent, to each extreme they fall,
To trust in ev'ry thing, or doubt of all.
    Who thus define it, say they more or less
Than this, that happiness is happiness?
    Take nature's path, and mad opinion's leave;
All states can reach it, and all heads conceive;
Obvious her goods, in no extreme they dwell;
There needs but thinking right, and meaning well;
And mourn our various portions as we please,
Equal is common sense, and common ease.
    Remember, man, 'The universal cause
Acts not by partial, but by gen'ral laws';
And makes what happiness we justly call
Subsist not in the good of one, but all.
There's not a blessing individuals find,
But some way leans and hearkens to the kind:
No bandit fierce, no tyrant mad with pride,
No cavern'd hermit, rests self-satisfy'd:
Who most to shun or hate mankind pretend,
Seek an admirer, or who would fix a friend:
Abstract what others feel, what others think,
All pleasures sicken, and all glories sink:
Each has his share; and who would more obtain,
Shall find the pleasure pays not half the pain.
    Order is heav'n's first law; and this confest,
Some are, and must be, greater than the rest,

More rich, more wise; but who infers from hence
That such are happier, shocks all common sense.
Heav'n to mankind impartial we confess,
If all are equal in their happiness:
But mutual wants this happiness increase;
All nature's diff'rence keeps all nature's peace.
Condition, circumstance is not the thing;
Bliss is the same in subject or in king,
In who obtain defence, or who defend,
In him who is, or him who finds a friend:
Heav'n breathes thro' ev'ry member of the whole
One common blessing, as one common soul.
But fortune's gifts if each alike possest,
And each were equal, must not all contest?
If then to all men happiness was meant,
God in externals could not place content.

 Fortune her gifts may variously dispose,
And these be happy call'd, unhappy those;
But heav'n's just balance equal will appear,
While those are plac'd in hope, and these in fear:
Not present good or ill, the joy or curse,
But future views of better, or of worse.
Oh sons of earth! attempt ye still to rise,
By mountains pil'd on mountains, to the skies?
Heav'n still with laughter the vain toil surveys,
And buries madmen in the heaps they raise.

 Know, all the good that individuals find,
Or God and nature meant to mere mankind,
Reason's whole pleasure, all the joys of sense,
Lie in three words, health, peace, and competence
But health consists with temperance alone;
And peace, oh virtue! peace is all thy own.
The good or bad the gifts of fortune gain;
But these less taste them, as they worse obtain.
Say, in pursuit of profit or delight,
Who risk the most, that take wrong means, or right?
Of vice or virtue, whether blest or curst,
Which meets contempt, or which compassion first?
Count all th' advantage prosp'rous vice attains,
'Tis but what virtue flies from and disdains:

And grant the bad what happiness they would,
One they must want, which is, to pass for good.
    Oh blind to truth, and God's whole scheme below,
Who fancy bliss to vice, to virtue woe!
Who sees and follows that great scheme the best,
Best knows the blessing, and will most be blest.
But fools the good alone unhappy call,
For ills or accidents that chance to all.
See Falkland dies, the virtuous and the just!
See god-like Turenne prostrate on the dust!
See Sidney bleeds amid the martial strife!
Was this their virtue, or contempt of life?
Say, was it virtue, more tho' heav'n ne'er gave,
Lamented Digby! sunk thee to the grave?
Tell me, if virtue made the son expire,
Why, full of days and honour, lives the sire?
Why drew Marseilles' good bishop purer breath,
When nature sicken'd and each gale was death!
Or why so long (in life if long can be)
Lent heav'n a parent to the poor and me?
    What makes all physical or moral ill?
There deviates nature, and here wanders will.
God sends not ill; if rightly understood,
Or partial ill is universal good,
Or change admits, or nature lets it fall,
Short, and but rare, 'till man improv'd it all.
We just as wisely might of heav'n complain
That righteous Abel was destroy'd by Cain,
As that the virtuous son is ill at ease,
When his lewd father gave the dire disease.
Think we, like some weak prince, th' eternal cause
Prone for his fav'rites to reverse his laws?
    Shall burning Ætna, if a sage requires,
Forget to thunder, and recall her fires?
On air or sea new motions be imprest,
Oh blameless Bethel! to relieve thy breast?
When the loose mountain trembles from on high
Shall gravitation cease, if you go by?
Or some old temple, nodding to its fall,
For Chartres' head reserve the hanging wall?

But still this world (so fitted for the knave)
Contents us not. A better shall we have?
A kingdom of the just then let it be:
But first consider how those just agree.
The good must merit God's peculiar care;
But who, but God, can tell us who they are?
One thinks on Calvin heav'n's own spirit fell;
Another deems him instrument of hell;
If Calvin feel heav'n's blessing, or its rod,
This cries there is, and that, there is no God.
What shocks one part will edify the rest,
Nor with one system can they all be blest.
The very best will variously incline,
And what rewards your virtue, punish mine.
Whatever is, is right.—This world, 'tis true,
Was made for Cæsar—but for Titus too;
And which more blest, who chain'd his country, say,
Or he whose virtue sigh'd to lose a day?
    'But sometimes virtue starves, while vice is fed.'
What then? is the reward of virtue bread?
That vice may merit, 'tis the price of toil;
The knave deserves it, when he tills the soil,
The knave deserves it, when he tempts the main,
Where folly fights for kings, or dives for gain.
The good man may be weak, be indolent;
Nor is his claim to plenty, but content.
But grant him riches, your demand is o'er?
'No, shall the good want health, the good want pow'r?'
Add health and pow'r, and ev'ry earthly thing,
'Why bounded pow'r? why private? why no king?
Nay, why external for internal giv'n?
Why is not man a God, and earth a heav'n?'
Who ask and reason thus, will scarce conceive
God gives enough, while he has more to give:
Immense the pow'r, immense were the demand;
Say, at what part of nature will they stand?
    What nothing earthly gives, or can destroy,
The soul's calm sunshine, and the heart-felt joy,
Is virtue's prize: a better would you fix?
Then give humility a coach and six,

Justice a conq'ror's sword, or truth a gown,
Or public spirit its great cure, a crown.
Weak, foolish man! will heav'n reward us there
With the same trash mad mortals wish for here?
The boy and man an individual makes,
Yet sigh'st thou now for apples and for cakes?
Go, like the Indian, in another life
Expect thy dog, thy bottle, and thy wife,
As well as dream such trifles are assign'd,
As toys and empires, for a god-like mind.
Rewards, that either would to virtue bring
No joy, or be destructive of the thing:
How oft by these at sixty are undone
The virtues of a saint at twenty-one!

   To whom can riches give repute, or trust,
Content, or pleasure, but the good and just?
Judges and senates have been bought for gold,
Esteem and love were never to be sold.
Oh fool! to think God hates the worthy mind,
The lover and the love of human-kind,
Whose life is healthful, and whose conscience clear,
Because he wants a thousand pounds a year.

   Honour and shame from no condition rise;
Act well your part, there all the honour lies.
Fortune in men has some small diff'rence mad'
One flaunts in rags, one flutters in brocade;
The cobler apron'd, and the parson gown'd,
The frier hooded, and the monarch crown'd.
'What differ more (you cry) than crown and cowl?'
I'll tell you, friend! a wise man and a fool.
You'll find, if once the monarch acts the monk,
Or, cobler-like, the parson will be drunk,
Worth makes the man, and want of it, the fellow;
The rest is all but leather or prunella.

   Stuck o'er with titles and hung round with strings,
That thou may'st be by kings, or whores of kings.
Boast the pure blood of an illustrious race,
In quiet flow from Lucrece to Lucrece:
But by your fathers' worth if your's you rate,
Count me those only who were good and great.

Go! if your ancient, but ignoble blood
Has crept thro' scoundrels ever since the flood,
Go! and pretend your family is young;
Nor own your fathers have been fools so long.
What can ennoble sots, or slaves, or cowards?
Alas! not all the blood of all the Howards,
   Look next on greatness; say where greatness lies.
'Where, but among the heroes and the wise?'
Heroes are much the same, the point's agreed,
From Macedonia's madman to the Swede;
The whole strange purpose of their lives, to find
Or make, an enemy of all mankind!
Not one looks backward, onward still he goes,
Yet ne'er looks forward farther than his nose.
No less alike the politic and wise;
All sly slow things, with circumspective eyes:
Men in their loose unguarded hours they take,
Not that themselves are wise, but others weak.
But grant that those can conquer, these can cheat;
'Tis phrase absurd to call a villain great:
Who wickedly is wise, or madly brave,
Is but the more a fool, the more a knave.
Who noble ends by noble means obtains,
Or failing, smiles in exile or in chains,
Like good Aurelius let him reign, or bleed
Like Socrates, that man is great indeed.
   What's fame? a fancy'd life in others' breath,
A thing beyond us, ev'n before our death.
Just what you hear, you have, and what's unknown
The same (my lord) if Tully's, or your own.
All that we feel of it begins and ends
In the small circle of our foes or friends;
To all beside as much an empty shade
An Eugene living, as a Cæsar dead;
Alike or when, or where they shone, or shine,
Or on the Rubicon, or on the Rhine.
A wit's a feather, and a chief a rod;
An honest man's the noblest work of God.
Fame but from death a villain's name can save,
As justice tears his body from the grave;

When what t' oblivion better were resign'd,
Is hung on high, to poison half mankind.
All fame is foreign, but of true desert;
Plays round the head, but comes not to the heart:
One self approving hour whole years out-weighs
Of stupid starers, and of loud huzzas;
And more true joy Marcellus exil'd feels,
Than Cæsar with a senate at his heels.
   In parts superior what advantage lies?
Tell (for you can) what is it to be wise?
'Tis but to know how little can be known;
To see all others' faults, and feel your own:
Condemn'd in bus'ness or in arts to drudge,
Without a second, or without a judge:
Truths would you teach, or save a sinking land?
All fear, none aid you, and few understand.
Painful preëminence! yourself to view
Above life's weakness, and its comforts too.
   Bring then these blessings to a strict account;
Make fair deductions; see to what they 'mount:
How much of other each is sure to cost;
How each for other oft is wholly lost;
How inconsistent greater goods with these;
How sometimes life is risqu'd, and always ease:
Think, and if still the things thy envy call,
Say, would'st thou be the man to whom they fall?
To sigh for ribbands if thou art so silly,
Mark how they grace Lord Umbra, or Sir Billy.
Is yellow dirt the passion of thy life;
Look but on Gripus, or on Gripus' wife.
If parts allure thee, think how Bacon shin'd,
The wisest, brightest, meanest of mankind:
Or ravish'd with the whistling of a name,
See Cromwell, damn'd to everlasting fame!
If all, united, thy ambition call,
From ancient story learn to scorn them all.
There, in the rich, the honour'd, fam'd and great,
See the false scale of happiness complete!
In hearts of kings, or arms of queens who lay,
How happy those to ruin, these betray.

Mark by what wretched steps their glory grows,
From dirt and sea-weed as proud Venice rose;
In each how guilt and greatness equal ran,
And all that rais'd the hero, sunk the man:
Now Europe's laurels on their brows behold,
But stain'd with blood, or ill-exchang'd for gold:
Then see them broke with toils, or sunk in ease,
Or infamous for plunder'd provinces.
Oh, wealth ill-fated! which no act of fame
E'er taught to shine, or sanctify'd from shame!
What greater bliss attends their close of life?
Some greedy minion, or imperious wife,
The trophy'd arches, story'd halls invade,
And haunt their slumbers in the pompous shade.
Alas! not dazzled with their noon-tide ray,
Compute the morn and ev'ning to the day;
The whole amount of that enormous fame,
A tale, that blends their glory with their shame!
    Know then this truth, enough for man to know.
'Virtue alone is happiness below.'
The only point where human bliss stands still,
And tastes the good without the fall to ill;
Where only merit constant pay receives,
Is blest in what it takes, and what it gives;
The joy unequal'd, if its end it gain,
And if it lose, attended with no pain:
Without satiety, tho' e'er so bless'd,
And but more relish'd as the more distress'd:
The broadest mirth unfeeling folly wears,
Less pleasing far than virtue's very tears;
Good, from each object, from each place acquir'd,
For ever exercis'd, yet never tir'd;
Never elated, while one man's oppress'd;
Never dejected, while another's bless'd;
And where no wants, no wishes can remain,
Since but to wish more virtue, is to gain.
    See the sole bliss heav'n could on all bestow!
Which who but feels can taste, but thinks can know:
Yet poor with fortune, and with learning blind,
The bad must miss, the good, untaught, will find;

Slave to no sect, who takes no private road,
But looks through nature up to nature's God:
Pursues that chain which links th' immense design,
Joins heav'n and earth, and mortal and divine;
Sees, that no being any bliss can know,
But touches some above, and some below;
Learns, from this union of the rising whole,
The first, last purpose of the human soul;
And knows where faith, law, morals, all began,
All end, in love of God, and love of man.

    For him alone, hope leads from goal to goal,
And opens still, and opens on his soul;
'Till lengthen'd on to faith, and unconfin'd,
It pours the bliss that fills up all the mind.
He sees, why nature plants in man alone
Hope of known bliss, and faith in bliss unknown:
(Nature, whose dictates to no other kind
Are giv'n in vain, but what they seek they find)
Wise is her present; she connects in this
His greatest virtue with his greatest bliss;
At once his own bright prospect to be blest,
And strongest motive to assist the rest.

    Self-love thus push'd to social, to divine,
Gives thee to make thy neighbour's blessing thine.
Is this too little for the boundless heart?
Extend it, let thy enemies have part:
Grasp the whole worlds of reason, life, and sense,
In one close system of benevolence:
Happier as kinder, in whate'er degree,
And height of bliss but height of charity.

    God loves from whole to parts: but human soul
Must rise from individual to the whole.
Self-love but serves the virtuous mind to wake
As the small pebble stirs the peaceful lake;
The centre mov'd, a circle strait succeeds,
Another still, and still another spreads;
Friend, parent, neighbour, first it will embrace;
His country next; and next all human race;
Wide and more wide, th' o'erflowings of the mind
Take ev'ry creature in, of ev'ry kind;

Earth smiles around, with boundless bounty blest,
And heav'n beholds its image in his breast.
  Come then, my friend, my genius, come along;
Oh master of the poet, and the song!
And while the muse now stoops, or now ascends,
To man's low passions, or their glorious ends,
Teach me, like thee, in various nature wise,
To fall with dignity, with temper rise;
Form'd by thy converse, happily to steer
From grave to gay, from lively to severe;
Correct with spirit, eloquent with ease,
Intent to reason, or polite to please.
Oh! while along the stream of time thy name
Expanded flies, and gathers all its fame;
Say, shall my little bark attendant sail,
Pursue the triumph, and partake the gale?
When statesmen, heroes, kings, in dust repose,
Whose sons shall blush their fathers were thy foes,
Shall then this verse to future age pretend
Thou wert my guide, philosopher, and friend?
That, urg'd by thee, I turn'd the tuneful art
From sounds to things, from fancy to the heart;
For wit's false mirror held up nature's light;
Shew'd erring pride, *whatever is, is right;*
That reason, passion, answer one great aim;
That true self-love and social are the same;
That virtue only makes our bliss below;
And all our knowledge is, ourselves to know.

AMBROSE PHILIPS
[*1675(?)–1749*]

281

To Charlotte Pulteney

Timely blossom, Infant fair,
Fondling of a happy pair,
Every morn and every night
Their solicitous delight,
Sleeping, waking, still at ease,
Pleasing, without skill to please;

Little gossip, blithe and hale,
Tattling many a broken tale,
Singing many a tuneless song,
Lavish of a heedless tongue;
Simple maiden, void of art,
Babbling out the very heart,
Yet abandon'd to thy will,
Yet imagining no ill,
Yet too innocent to blush;
Like the linnet in the bush
To the mother-linnet's note
Moduling her slender throat;
Chirping forth thy pretty joys,
Wanton in the change of toys,
Like the linnet green, in May
Flitting to each bloomy spray;
Wearied then and glad of rest,
Like the linnet in the nest:—
This thy present happy lot
This, in time will be forgot:
Other pleasures, other cares,
Ever-busy Time prepares;
And thou shalt in thy daughter see,
This picture, once, resembled thee.

COLLEY CIBBER

[*1671–1757*]

282

THE BLIND BOY

O SAY what is that thing call'd Light,
    Which I must ne'er enjoy;
What are the blessings of the sight,
    O tell your poor blind boy!

You talk of wondrous things you see,
    You say the sun shines bright;
I feel him warm, but how can he
    Or make it day or night?

My day or night myself I make
　　Whene'er I sleep or play;
And could I ever keep awake
　　With me 'twere always day.

With heavy sighs I often hear
　　You mourn my hapless woe;
But sure with patience I can bear
　　A loss I ne'er can know.

Then let not what I cannot have
　　My cheer of mind destroy:
Whilst thus I sing, I am a king,
　　Although a poor blind boy.

JAMES THOMSON
[*1700–1748*]

283　　　　RULE, BRITANNIA

WHEN Britain first at Heaven's command
　　Arose from out the azure main,
This was the charter of her land,
　　And guardian angels sung the strain:
Rule, Britannia! Britannia rules the waves!
　　Britons never shall be slaves.

The nations not so blest as thee
　　Must in their turn to tyrants fall,
Whilst thou shalt flourish great and free
　　The dread and envy of them all.

Still more majestic shalt thou rise,
　　More dreadful from each foreign stroke:
As the loud blast that tears the skies
　　Serves but to root thy native oak.

Thee haughty tyrants ne'er shall tame;
　　All their attempts to bend thee down
Will but arouse thy generous flame,
　　And work their woe and thy renown.

To thee belongs the rural reign;
    Thy cities shall with commerce shine;
All thine shall be the subject main,
    And every shore it circles thine!

The Muses, still with Freedom found,
    Shall to thy happy coast repair;
Blest Isle, with matchless beauty crown'd
    And manly hearts to guard the fair:—
Rule, Britannia! Britannia rules the waves!
    Britons never shall be slaves!

284

To Fortune

For ever, Fortune, wilt thou prove
An unrelenting foe to Love,
And when we meet a mutual heart
Come in between, and bid us part?

Bid us sigh on from day to day,
And wish and wish the soul away;
Till youth and genial years are flown,
And all the life of life is gone?

But busy, busy, still art thou,
To bind the loveless, joyless vow,
The heart from pleasure to delude,
To join the gentle to the rude.

For once, O Fortune, hear my prayer,
And I absolve thy future care;
All other blessings I resign,
Make but the dear Amanda mine.

THOMAS GRAY
[1716–1771]

285

Elegy
(Written in a Country Churchyard)

The curfew tolls the knell of parting day,
    The lowing herd winds slowly o'er the lea,

The ploughman homeward plods his weary way,
　And leaves the world to darkness and to me.

Now fades the glimmering landscape on the sight,
　And all the air a solemn stillness holds,
Save where the beetle wheels his droning flight,
　And drowsy tinklings lull the distant folds:

Save that from yonder ivy-mantled tower
　The moping owl does to the moon complain
Of such as, wandering near her secret bower,
　Molest her ancient solitary reign.

Beneath those rugged elms, that yew-tree's shade
　Where heaves the turf in many a mouldering heap,
Each in his narrow cell for ever laid,
　The rude Forefathers of the hamlet sleep.

The breezy call of incense-breathing morn,
　The swallow twittering from the straw-built shed,
The cock's shrill clarion, or the echoing horn,
　No more shall rouse them from their lowly bed.

For them no more the blazing hearth shall burn
　Or busy housewife ply her evening care:
No children run to lisp their sire's return,
　Or climb his knees the envied kiss to share.

Oft did the harvest to their sickle yield,
　Their furrow oft the stubborn glebe has broke;
How jocund did they drive their team afield!
　How bow'd the woods beneath their sturdy stroke!

Let not Ambition mock their useful toil,
　Their homely joys, and destiny obscure;
Nor Grandeur hear with a disdainful smile
　The short and simple annals of the Poor.

The boast of heraldry, the pomp of power,
　And all that beauty, all that wealth e'er gave
Awaits alike th' inevitable hour:—
　The paths of glory lead but to the grave.

Nor you, ye Proud, impute to these the fault
  If Memory o'er their tomb no trophies raise,
Where through the long-drawn aisle and fretted vault
  The pealing anthem swells the note of praise.

Can storied urn or animated bust
  Back to its mansion call the fleeting breath,
Can Honour's voice provoke the silent dust,
  Or Flattery soothe the dull cold ear of Death?

Perhaps in this neglected spot is laid
  Some heart once pregnant with celestial fire;
Hands, that the rod of empire might have sway'd,
  Or waked to ecstasy the living lyre:

But Knowledge to their eyes her ample page,
  Rich with the spoils of time, did ne'er unroll;
Chill Penury repress'd their noble rage,
  And froze the genial current of the soul.

Full many a gem of purest ray serene
  The dark unfathom'd caves of ocean bear:
Full many a flower is born to blush unseen,
  And waste its sweetness on the desert air.

Some village-Hampden, that with dauntless breast
  The little tyrant of his fields withstood,
Some mute inglorious Milton here may rest,
  Some Cromwell, guiltless of his country's blood.

Th' applause of listening senates to command,
  The threats of pain and ruin to despise,
To scatter plenty o'er a smiling land,
  And read their history in a nation's eyes

Their lot forbad: nor circumscribed alone
  Their growing virtues, but their crimes confined;
Forbad to wade through slaughter to a throne,
  And shut the gates of mercy on mankind;

The struggling pangs of conscious truth to hide,
   To quench the blushes of ingenuous shame,
Or heap the shrine of Luxury and Pride
   With incense kindled at the Muse's flame.

Far from the madding crowd's ignoble strife
   Their sober wishes never learn'd to stray;
Along the cool sequester'd vale of life
   They kept the noiseless tenour of their way.

Yet e'en these bones from insult to protect
   Some frail memorial still erected nigh,
With uncouth rhymes and shapeless sculpture deck'd,
   Implores the passing tribute of a sigh.

Their name, their years, spelt by th' unletter'd Muse,
   The place of fame and elegy supply:
And many a holy text around she strews,
   That teach the rustic moralist to die.

For who, to dumb forgetfulness a prey,
   This pleasing anxious being e'er resign'd,
Left the warm precincts of the cheerful day,
   Nor cast one longing lingering look behind?

On some fond breast the parting soul relies,
   Some pious drops the closing eye requires;
E'en from the tomb the voice of Nature cries,
   E'en in our ashes live their wonted fires.

For thee, who, mindful of th' unhonour'd dead,
   Dost in these lines their artless tale relate;
If chance, by lonely Contemplation led,
   Some kindred spirit shall enquire thy fate,—

Haply some hoary-headed swain may say,
   'Oft have we seen him at the peep of dawn
Brushing with hasty steps the dews away,
   To meet the sun upon the upland lawn;

'There at the foot of yonder nodding beech
 That wreathes its old fantastic roots so high,
His listless length at noon-tide would he stretch,
 And pore upon the brook that babbles by.

'Hard by yon wood, now smiling as in scorn,
 Muttering his wayward fancies he would rove;
Now drooping, woeful-wan, like one forlorn,
 Or crazed with care, or cross'd in hopeless love.

'One morn I miss'd him on the custom'd hill,
 Along the heath, and near his favourite tree;
Another came; nor yet beside the rill,
 Nor up the lawn, nor at the wood was he;

'The next with dirges due in sad array   [borne,—
 Slow through the church-way path we saw him
Approach and read (for thou canst read) the lay
 Graved on the stone beneath yon agèd thorn:'

The Epitaph

Here rests his head upon the lap of Earth
 A youth, to Fortune and to Fame unknown;
Fair Science frown'd not on his humble birth
 And Melancholy mark'd him for her own.

Large was his bounty, and his soul sincere;
 Heaven did a recompense as largely send:
He gave to Mis'ry all he had, a tear,
 He gain'd from Heaven, 'twas all he wish'd, a friend.

No farther seek his merits to disclose,
 Or draw his frailties from their dread abode,
(There they alike in trembling hope repose,)
 The bosom of his Father and his God.

286   ODE ON A DISTANT PROSPECT OF ETON COLLEGE

Ye distant spires, ye antique towers,
 That crown the watery glade,
Where grateful Science still adores

Her Henry's holy shade;
And ye, that from the stately brow
Of Windsor's heights th' expanse below
Of grove, of lawn, of mead survey,
Whose turf, whose shade, whose flowers among
Wanders the hoary Thames along
    His silver-winding way:

Ah happy hills! ah pleasing shade!
    Ah fields beloved in vain!
When once my careless childhood stray'd,
    A stranger yet to pain!
I feel the gales that from ye blow
A momentary bliss bestow,
As waving fresh their gladsome wing
My weary soul they seem to soothe
And, redolent of joy and youth,
    To breathe a second spring.

Say, Father Thames, for thou hast seen
    Full many a sprightly race
Disporting on thy margent green
    The paths of pleasure trace;
Who foremost now delight to cleave
With pliant arm, thy glassy wave?
The captive linnet which enthral?
What idle progeny succeed
To chase the rolling circle's speed
    Or urge the flying ball?

While some on earnest business bent
    Their murmuring labours ply
'Gainst graver hours, that bring constraint
    To sweeten liberty:
Some bold adventurers disdain
The limits of their little reign
And unknown regions dare descry:
Still as they run they look behind,
They hear a voice in every wind,
    And snatch a fearful joy.

Gay Hope is theirs by fancy fed,
  Less pleasing when possest;
The tear forgot as soon as shed,
  The sunshine of the breast:
Theirs buxom Health, of rosy hue,
Wild Wit, Invention ever new,
And lively Cheer, of Vigour born;
The thoughtless day, the easy night,
The spirits pure, the slumbers light
  That fly th' approach of morn.

Alas! regardless of their doom
  The little victims play!
No sense have they of ills to come
  Nor care beyond to-day:
Yet see how all around 'em wait
The ministers of human fate
And black Misfortune's baleful train!
Ah shew them where in ambush stand
To seize their prey, the murderous band!
  Ah, tell them they are men!

These shall the fury Passions tear,
  The vultures of the mind,
Disdainful Anger, pallid Fear,
  And shame that sculks behind;
Or pining Love shall waste their youth,
Or Jealousy with rankling tooth
That inly gnaws the secret heart,
And Envy wan, and faded Care,
Grim-visaged comfortless Despair,
  And Sorrow's piercing dart.

Ambition this shall tempt to rise,
  Then whirl the wretch from high
To bitter Scorn a sacrifice
  And grinning Infamy.
The stings of Falsehood those shall try
And hard Unkindness' alter'd eye,
That mocks the tear it forced to flow;

And keen Remorse with blood defiled,
And moody Madness laughing wild
    Amid severest woe.

Lo, in the Vale of Years beneath
    A griesly troop are seen,
The painful family of Death,
    More hideous than their Queen:
This racks the joints, this fires the veins,
That every labouring sinew strains,
Those in the deeper vitals rage:
Lo! Poverty, to fill the band,
That numbs the soul with icy hand,
    And slow-consuming Age.

To each his sufferings: all are men,
    Condemn'd alike to groan;
The tender for another's pain,
    Th' unfeeling for his own.
Yet, ah! why should they know their fate,
Since sorrow never comes too late,
And happiness too swiftly flies?
Thought would destroy their paradise!
No more;—where ignorance is bliss,
    'Tis folly to be wise.

287   HYMN TO ADVERSITY

DAUGHTER of Jove, relentless power,
    Thou tamer of the human breast,
Whose iron scourge and torturing hour
    The bad affright, afflict the best!
Bound in thy adamantine chain
The proud are taught to taste of pain,
And purple tyrants vainly groan
With pangs unfelt before, unpitied and alone.

When first thy Sire to send on earth
    Virtue, his darling child, design'd,
To thee he gave the heavenly birth
    And bade to form her infant mind.

Stern, rugged Nurse! thy rigid lore
With patience many a year she bore;
What sorrow was, thou bad'st her know,
And from her own she learn'd to melt at others' woe.

Scared at thy frown terrific, fly
    Self-pleasing Folly's idle brood,
Wild Laughter, Noise, and thoughtless Joy,
    And leave us leisure to be good.
Light they disperse, and with them go
The summer Friend, the flattering Foe;
By vain Prosperity received,
To her they vow their truth, and are again believed.

Wisdom in sable garb array'd
    Immersed in rapturous thought profound,
And Melancholy, silent maid,
    With leaden eye, that loves the ground,
Still on thy solemn steps attend:
Warm Charity, the general friend,
With Justice, to herself severe,
And Pity dropping soft the sadly-pleasing tear.

O! gently on thy suppliant's head
    Dread Goddess, lay thy chastening hand!
Not in thy Gorgon terrors clad,
    Nor circled with the vengeful band
(As by the impious thou art seen)
With thundering voice, and threatening mien,
With screaming Horror's funeral cry,
Despair, and fell Disease, and ghastly Poverty;—

Thy form benign, O Goddess, wear,
    Thy milder influence impart,
Thy philosophic train be there
    To soften, not to wound my heart.
The generous spark extinct revive,
Teach me to love and to forgive
Exact my own defects to scan,
What others are to feel, and know myself a Man.

288 Ode on the Spring

Lo! where the rosy-bosom'd Hours,
  Fair Venus' train, appear,
Disclose the long-expecting flowers
  And wake the purple year!
The Attic warbler pours her throat
Responsive to the cuckoo's note,
The untaught harmony of Spring:
While, whispering pleasure as they fly,
Cool Zephyrs thro' the clear blue sky
  Their gather'd fragrance fling.

Where'er the oak's thick branches stretch
  A broader, browner shade,
Where'er the rude and moss-grown beech
  O'er-canopies the glade,
Beside some water's rushy brink
With me the Muse shall sit, and think
(At ease reclined in rustic state)
How vain the ardour of the Crowd,
How low, how little are the Proud,
  How indigent the Great!

Still is the toiling hand of Care;
  The panting herds repose:
Yet hark, how thro' the peopled air
  The busy murmur glows!
The insect youth are on the wing,
Eager to taste the honied spring
And float amid the liquid noon:
Some lightly o'er the current skim,
Some show their gaily-gilded trim
  Quick-glancing to the sun.

To Contemplation's sober eye
  Such is the race of Man:
And they that creep, and they that fly
  Shall end where they began.
Alike the busy and the gay

But flutter thro' life's little day,
In Fortune's varying colours drest:
Brush'd by the hand of rough Mischance,
Or chill'd by Age, their airy dance
   They leave, in dust to rest.

Methinks I hear in accents low
   The sportive kind reply:
Poor moralist! and what art thou?
   A solitary fly!
Thy joys no glittering female meets,
No hive hast thou of hoarded sweets,
No painted plumage to display:
On hasty wings thy youth is flown;
Thy sun is set, thy spring is gone—
   We frolic while 'tis May.

289
       THE PROGRESS OF POESY

A Pindaric Ode

AWAKE, Aeolian lyre, awake,
And give to rapture all thy trembling strings.
From Helicon's harmonious springs
   A thousand rills their mazy progress take:
The laughing flowers that round them blow
Drink life and fragrance as they flow.
Now the rich stream of Music winds along
Deep, majestic, smooth, and strong,
Through verdant vales, and Ceres' golden reign;
Now rolling down the steep amain
Headlong, impetuous, see it pour:
The rocks and nodding groves re-bellow to the roar.

   O Sovereign of the willing soul,
Parent of sweet and solemn-breathing airs,
Enchanting shell! the sullen Cares
   And frantic Passions hear thy soft control.
On Thracia's hills the Lord of War
Has curb'd the fury of his car
And dropt his thirsty lance at thy command.

Perching on the sceptred hand
Of Jove, thy magic lulls the feather'd king
With ruffled plumes, and flagging wing:
Quench'd in dark clouds of slumber lie
The terror of his beak, and lightnings of his eye.

Thee the voice, the dance, obey
Temper'd to thy warbled lay.
O'er Idalia's velvet-green
The rosy-crownéd Loves are seen
On Cytherea's day,
With antic Sport, and blue-eyed Pleasures,
Frisking light in frolic measures;
Now pursuing, now retreating,
    Now in circling troops they meet:
To brisk notes in cadence beating
    Glance their many-twinkling feet.
Slow melting strains their Queen's approach declare:
    Where'er she turns, the Graces homage pay:
With arms sublime that float upon the air
    In gliding state she wins her easy way:
O'er her warm cheek and rising bosom move
The bloom of young Desire and purple light of Love.

    Man's feeble race what ills await!
Labour, and Penury, the racks of Pain,
Disease, and Sorrow's weeping train,
    And Death, sad refuge from the storms of Fate!
The fond complaint, my song, disprove,
And justify the laws of Jove.
Say, has he given in vain the heavenly Muse
Night, and all her sickly dews,
Her spectres wan, and birds of boding cry
He gives to range the dreary sky:
Till down the eastern cliffs afar
Hyperion's march they spy, and glittering shafts of war.

    In climes beyond the solar road
Where shaggy forms o'er ice-built mountains roam,
The Muse has broke the twilight gloom

To cheer the shivering native's dull abode.
And oft, beneath the odorous shade
Of Chili's boundless forests laid,
She deigns to hear the savage youth repeat
In loose numbers wildly sweet
Their feather-cinctured chiefs, and dusky loves.
Her track, where'er the Goddess roves,
Glory pursue, and generous Shame,
Th' unconquerable Mind, and Freedom's holy flame.

Woods, that wave o'er Delphi's steep,
Isles, that crown th' Aegean deep,
Fields that cool Ilissus laves,
Or where Maeander's amber waves
In lingering lab'rinths creep,
How do your tuneful echoes languish,
Mute, but to the voice of anguish!
Where each old poetic mountain
    Inspiration breathed around;
Every shade and hallow'd fountain
    Murmur'd deep a solemn sound:
Till the sad Nine, in Greece's evil hour
    Left their Parnassus for the Latian plains.
Alike they scorn the pomp of tyrant Power,
    And coward Vice, that revels in her chains.
When Latium had her lofty spirit lost,
They sought, O Albion! next, thy sea-encircled coast.

    Far from the sun and summer-gale
In thy green lap was Nature's Darling laid,
What time, where lucid Avon stray'd,
    To him the mighty Mother did unveil
Her awful face: the dauntless Child
Stretch'd forth his little arms, and smiled.
This pencil take (she said), whose colours clear
Richly paint the vernal year:
Thine, too, these golden keys, immortal Boy!
This can unlock the gates of Joy;
Of Horror that, and thrilling Fears,
Or ope the sacred source of sympathetic Tears.

Nor second He, that rode sublime
Upon the seraph-wings of Ecstasy
The secrets of the Abyss to spy:
   He pass'd the flaming bounds of Place and Time:
The living Throne, the sapphire-blaze
Where Angels tremble while they gaze,
He saw; but blasted with excess of light,
Closed his eyes in endless night.
Behold where Dryden's less presumptuous car
Wide o'er the fields of Glory bear
Two coursers of ethereal race,
With necks in thunder clothed, and long-resounding pace.

Hark, his hands the lyre explore!
Bright-eyed Fancy, hovering o'er,
Scatters from her pictured urn
Thoughts that breathe, and words that burn.
But ah! 'tis heard no more—
Oh! Lyre divine, what daring Spirit
Wakes thee now! Tho' he inherit
Nor the pride, nor ample pinion,
   That the Theban Eagle bear,
Sailing with supreme dominion
   Thro' the azure deep of air:
Yet oft before his infant eyes would run
   Such forms as glitter in the Muse's ray
With orient hues, unborrow'd of the sun:
   Yet shall he mount, and keep his distant way
Beyond the limits of a vulgar fate:
Beneath the Good how far—but far above the Great.

290   THE BARD

Pindaric Ode

'RUIN seize thee, ruthless King!
  Confusion on thy banners wait!
Tho' fann'd by Conquest's crimson wing
  They mock the air with idle state.
Helm, nor hauberk's twisted mail
Nor e'en thy virtues, tyrant, shall avail

To save thy secret soul from nightly fears,
From Cambria's curse, from Cambria's tears!'
—Such were the sounds that o'er the crested pride
 Of the first Edward scatter'd wild dismay,
As down the steep of Snowdon's shaggy side
 He wound with toilsome march his long array:—
Stout Glo'ster stood aghast in speechless trance;
'To arms!' cried Mortimer, and couch'd his quivering
  lance.

 On a rock, whose haughty brow
Frowns o'er old Conway's foaming flood,
 Robed in the sable garb of woe
With haggard eyes the Poet stood;
(Loose his beard and hoary hair
Stream'd like a meteor to the troubled air)
And with a master's hand and prophet's fire
Struck the deep sorrows of his lyre:
 'Hark, how each giant-oak and desert-cave
Sighs to the torrent's awful voice beneath!
O'er thee, O King! their hundred arms they wave
 Revenge on thee in hoarser murmurs breathe;
Vocal no more, since Cambria's fatal day,
To high-born Hoel's harp, or soft Llewellyn's lay.

 'Cold is Cadwallo's tongue,
 That hush'd the stormy main:
Brave Urien sleeps upon his craggy bed:
 Mountains, ye mourn in vain
 Modred, whose magic song
Made huge Plinlimmon bow his cloud-topt head.
 On dreary Arvon's shore they lie
Smear'd with gore and ghastly pale:
Far, far aloof the affrighted ravens sail;
 The famish'd eagle screams, and passes by.
Dear lost companions of my tuneful art,
 Dear as the light that visits these sad eyes,
Dear as the ruddy drops that warm my heart,
 Ye died amidst your dying country's cries—
No more I weep; They do not sleep;

On yonder cliffs, a griesly band,
I see them sit; They linger yet,
　Avengers of their native land:
With me in dreadful harmony they join,
And weave with bloody hands the tissue of thy line.'

Weave the warp and weave the woof
　The winding sheet of Edward's race:
Give ample room and verge enough
　The characters of hell to trace.
Mark the year, and mark the night,
When Severn shall re-echo with affright
The shrieks of death thro' Berkley's roof that ring,
Shrieks of an agonizing king!
　She-wolf of France, with unrelenting fangs
That tear'st the bowels of thy mangled mate,
　From thee be born, who o'er thy country hangs
The scourge of Heaven! What terrors round him wait
Amazement in his van, with Flight combined,
And Sorrow's faded form, and Solitude behind.

'Mighty victor, mighty lord,
　Low on his funeral couch he lies!
No pitying heart, no eye, afford
　A tear to grace his obsequies.
Is the sable warrior fled?
Thy son is gone. He rests among the dead.
The swarm that in thy noon-tide beam were born?
—Gone to salute the rising morn.
Fair laughs the Morn, and soft the zephyr blows,
　While proudly riding o'er the azure realm
In gallant trim the gilded Vessel goes:
　Youth on the prow, and Pleasure at the helm:
Regardless of the sweeping Whirlwind's sway,
That hush'd in grim repose expects his evening prey.

'Fill high the sparkling bowl,
The rich repast prepare;
　Reft of a crown, he yet may share the feast:
Close by the regal chair

Fell Thirst and Famine scowl
  A baleful smile upon their baffled guest.
Heard ye the din of battle bray,
  Lance to lance, and horse to horse?
  Long years of havock urge their destined course,
And thro' the kindred squadrons mow their way.
  Ye towers of Julius, London's lasting shame,
With many a foul and midnight murder fed,
  Revere his Consort's faith, his Father's fame,
And spare the meek usurper's holy head!
Above, below, the rose of snow,
  Twined with her blushing foe, we spread:
The bristled boar in infant-gore
  Wallows beneath the thorny shade.
Now, brothers, bending o'er the accursèd loom,
Stamp we our vengeance deep, and ratify his doom.

'Edward, lo! to sudden fate
  (Weave we the woof; The thread is spun;)
Half of thy heart we consecrate.
  (The web is wove; The work is done.)
—Stay, oh stay! nor thus forlorn
Leave me unbless'd, unpitied, here to mourn:
In yon bright track that fires the western skies
They melt, they vanish from my eyes.
But O! what solemn scenes on Snowdon's height
  Descending slow their glittering skirts unroll?
Visions of glory, spare my aching sight,
Ye unborn ages, crowd not on my soul!
No more our long-lost Arthur we bewail:—
All hail, ye genuine kings! Britannia's issue, hail!

  'Girt with many a baron bold
Sublime their starry fronts they rear;
And gorgeous dames, and statesmen old
In bearded majesty, appear.
In the midst a form divine!
Her eye proclaims her of the Briton-Line:
Her lion-port, her awe-commanding face
Attemper'd sweet to virgin-grace.

What strings symphonious tremble in the air,
    What strains of vocal transport round her play?
Hear from the grave, great Taliessin, hear;
    They breathe a soul to animate thy clay.
Bright Rapture calls, and soaring as she sings,
Waves in the eye of Heaven her many-coloured wings.

'The verse adorn again
    Fierce War, and faithful Love,
And Truth severe, by fairy Fiction drest.
    In buskin'd measures move
Pale Grief, and pleasing Pain,
With Horror, tyrant of the throbbing breast.
A voice as of the cherub-choir
    Gales from blooming Eden bear,
    And distant warblings lessen on my ear
That lost in long futurity expire.
Fond impious man, think'st thou yon sanguine cloud
    Raised by thy breath, has quench'd the orb of day?
To-morrow he repairs the golden flood
    And warms the nations with redoubled ray.
Enough for me: with joy I see
    The different doom our fates assign:
Be thine Despair and sceptred Care,
    To triumph and to die are mine.'
—He spoke, and headlong from the mountain's height
Deep in the roaring tide he plunged to endless night.

291   ODE ON THE PLEASURE ARISING FROM VICISSITUDE

Now the golden Morn aloft
    Waves her dew-bespangled wing,
With vermeil cheek and whisper soft
    She woos the tardy Spring:
Till April starts, and calls around
The sleeping fragrance from the ground,
And lightly o'er the living scene
Scatters his freshest, tenderest green.

New-born flocks, in rustic dance,
    Frisking ply their feeble feet;

Forgetful of their wintry trance
  The birds his presence greet:
But chief, the sky-lark warbles high
His trembling thrilling ecstasy;
And lessening from the dazzled sight,
Melts into air and liquid light.

Yesterday the sullen year
  Saw the snowy whirlwind fly;
Mute was the music of the air,
  The herd stood drooping by;
Their raptures now that wildly flow
No yesterday nor morrow know;
'Tis Man alone that joy descries
With forward and reverted eyes.

Smiles on past Misfortune's brow
  Soft Reflection's hand can trace,
And o'er the cheek of Sorrow throw
  A melancholy grace;
While Hope prolongs our happier hour,
Or deepest shades, that dimly lour
And blacken round our weary way,
Gilds with a gleam of distant day.

Still, where rosy Pleasure leads,
  See a kindred Grief pursue;
Behind the steps that Misery treads
  Approaching Comfort view:
The hues of bliss more brightly glow
Chastised by sabler tints of woe,
And blended form, with artful strife,
The strength and harmony of life.

See the wretch that long has tost
  On the thorny bed of pain,
At length repair his vigour lost
  And breathe and walk again:
The meanest floweret of the vale,
The simplest note that swells the gale,

The common sun, the air, the skies,
To him are opening Paradise.

292   ON A FAVOURITE CAT, DROWNED IN A TUB OF
GOLD FISHES

'TWAS on a lofty vase's side,
Where China's gayest art had dyed
The azure flowers that blow,
Demurest of the tabby kind
The pensive Selima, reclined,
Gazed on the lake below.

Her conscious tail her joy declared:
The fair round face, the snowy beard,
The velvet of her paws,
Her coat that with the tortoise vies,
Her ears of jet, and emerald eyes—
She saw, and purr'd applause.

Still had she gazed, but 'midst the tide
Two angel forms were seen to glide,
The Genii of the stream:
Their scaly armour's Tyrian hue
Through richest purple, to the view
Betray'd a golden gleam.

The hapless Nymph with wonder saw:
A whisker first, and then a claw
With many an ardent wish
She stretch'd, in vain, to reach the prize—
What female heart can gold despise?
What Cat's averse to fish?

Presumptuous maid! with looks intent
Again she stretch'd, again she bent,
Nor knew the gulf between—
Malignant Fate sat by and smiled—
The slippery verge her feet beguiled;
She tumbled headlong in!

Eight times emerging from the flood
She mew'd to every watery God
Some speedy aid to send:—
No Dolphin came, no Nereid stirr'd.
Nor cruel Tom nor Susan heard—
A favourite has no friend!

From hence, ye Beauties! undeceived
Know one false step is ne'er retrieved,
And be with caution bold:
Not all that tempts your wandering eyes
And heedless hearts, is lawful prize,
Nor all that glisters, gold!

GEORGE BUBB DODINGTON, LORD MELCOMBE
[*1691(?)–1762*]

293 ### SHORTEN SAIL

LOVE thy country, wish it well,
    Not with too intense a care;
'Tis enough that, when it fell,
    Thou its ruin didst not share.

Envy's censure, Flattery's praise,
    With unmoved indifference view:
Learn to tread Life's dangerous maze
    With unerring Virtue's clue.

Void of strong desire and fear,
    Life's wide ocean trust no more;
Strive thy little bark to steer
    With the tide, but near the shore.

Thus prepared, thy shorten'd sail
    Shall, when'er the winds increase,
Seizing each propitious gale,
    Waft thee to the port of Peace.

Keep thy conscience from offence
   And tempestuous passions free,
So, when thou art call'd from hence,
   Easy shall thy passage be.

—Easy shall thy passage be,
   Cheerful thy allotted stay,
Short the account 'twixt God and thee.
   Hope shall meet thee on thy way.

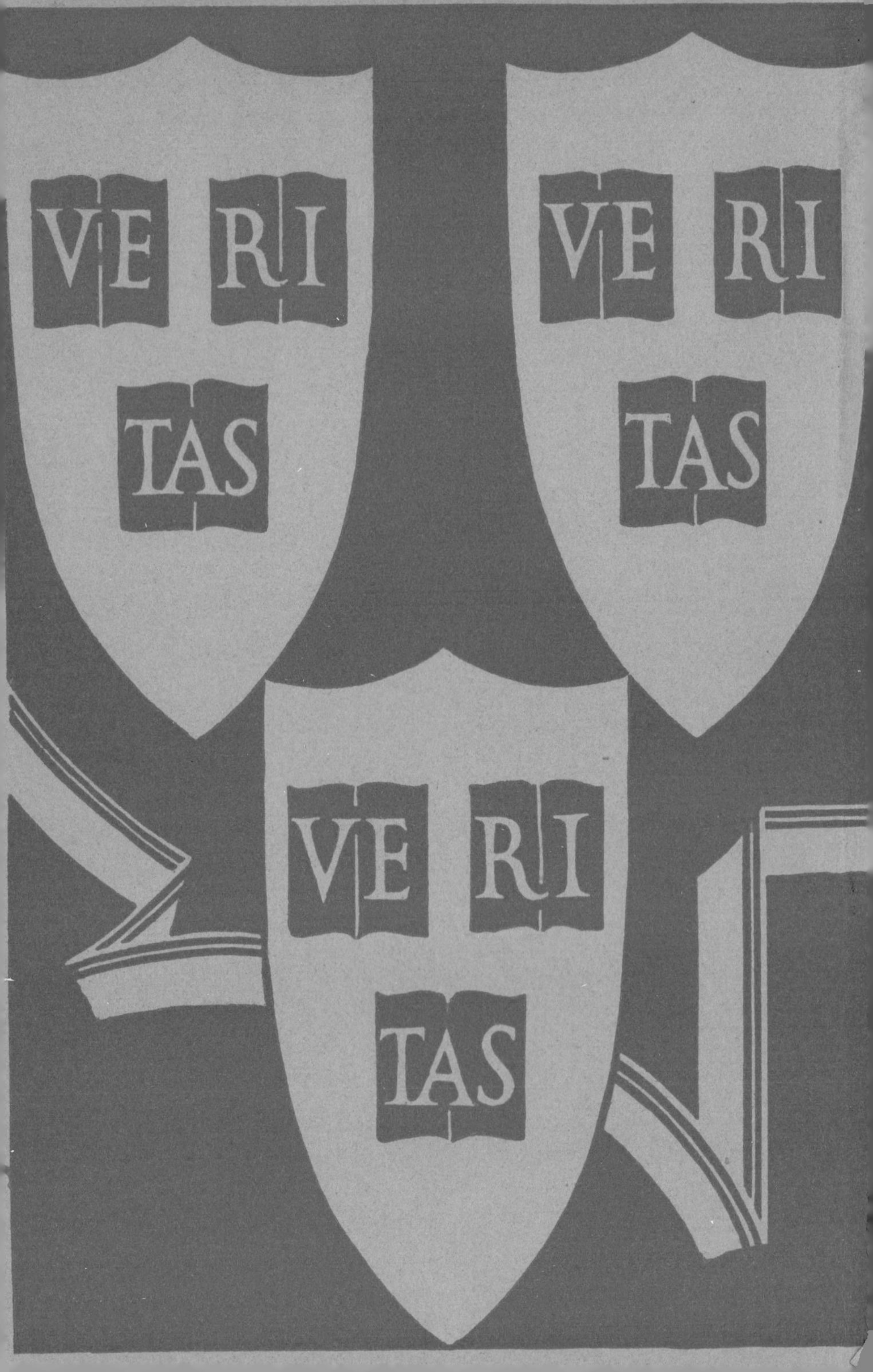
VE RI
TAS
VE RI
TAS
VE RI
TAS